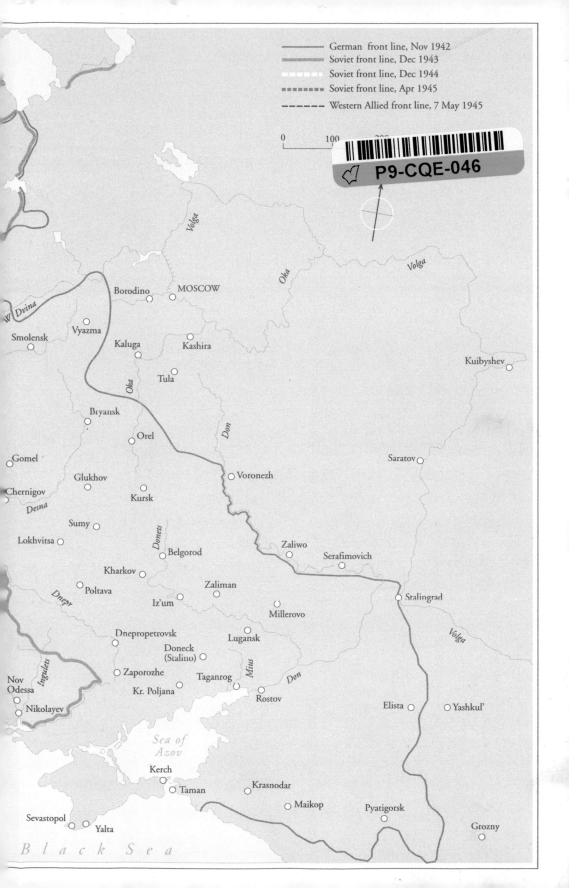

German front line, Nov 1942
Soviet front line, Dec 1943
Soviet front line, Dec 1944
Soviet front line, Apr 1945
Western Allied front line, 7 May 1945

0   100   200

Volga

W Dvina

Smolensk

Borodino   MOSCOW

Vyazma

Kaluga   Kashira

Oka   Kuibyshev

Tula

Oka

Bryansk

Orel   *Don*

Gomel   Saratov

Glukhov   Voronezh

Chernigov   Kursk

Desna

Sumy

Lokhvitsa   *Donets*   Zaliwo
                Belgorod   Serafimovich

Kharkov

Poltava   Zaliman

Dnepr   Iz'um   Millerovo   Stalingrad

Dnepropetrovsk   Lugansk   *Volga*

Doneck
(Stalino)

Ingulets   Zaporozhe   *Mius*
                Taganrog   *Don*
Nov   Kr. Poljana
Odessa   Rostov   Elista   Yashkul'

Nikolayev

*Sea of
Azov*

Kerch

Taman   Krasnodar

Sevastopol   Maikop   Pyatigorsk

Yalta   Grozny

B l a c k   S e a

A Writer at War

Also by Vasily Grossman in English

LIFE AND FATE
FOREVER FLOWING

A Writer at War

Vasily Grossman with the Red Army
1941–1945

EDITED AND TRANSLATED BY
Antony Beevor & Luba Vinogradova

PANTHEON BOOKS
NEW YORK

Library of Congress Cataloging-in-Publication Data
Grossman, Vasilii Semenovich.
A writer at war: Vasily Grossman with the Red Army, 1941–1945 /
Vasily Grossman ; edited and translated by Antony Beevor and Luba
Vinogradova.
          p.   cm.
Includes bibliographical references and index.
ISBN 0-375-42407-5
1. World War, 1939–1945—Soviet Union. 2. World War, 1939–1945—
Personal narratives, Soviet.   3. Grossman, Vasiliæ Semenovich.
4. World War, 1939–1945—Destruction and pillage—Soviet Union.
I. Title: Vasily Grossman with the Red Army, 1941–1945. II. Beevor,
Antony, [date]   III. Vinogradova, Luba. IV. Title.
   D764.G772 2006   940.54'217'092—dc22   [B]   2005051033

www.pantheonbooks.com
Printed in the United States of America
First American Edition
4 6 8 7 5 3

Contents

Introduction

Vasily Grossman's place in the history of world literature is assured by his masterpiece *Life and Fate*, one of the greatest Russian novels of the twentieth century. Some critics even rate it more highly than Pasternak's *Doctor Zhivago* or the novels of Solzhenitsyn.

This volume is based on his wartime notebooks, but also some essays which are all in the Russian State Archive for Literature and the Arts (RGALI). We have also included some letters in the possession of his daughter and step-son. The notebooks reveal a good deal of the raw material which he accumulated for his novels as well as his articles. Grossman, a special correspondent for the Red Army newspaper, *Krasnaya Zvezda*, or *Red Star*, proved to be the most perceptive and honest eyewitness of the Soviet frontlines between 1941 and 1945. He spent more than a thousand days at the front – nearly three out of the four years of war. The sharpness of his observation and the humanity of his understanding offer an invaluable lesson for any writer and historian.

Vasily Grossman was born in the Ukrainian town of Berdichev on 12 December 1905. Berdichev had one of the largest Jewish populations in central Europe and the Grossmans were part of its educated elite. Vasily had been given the name of Iosif, but like many assimilated families, the Grossmans russified their names. His father, born Solomon Iosifovich, had changed his to Semyon Osipovich.

Grossman's parents separated and, as a young boy, he lived in Switzerland for two years with his mother before the First World War. In 1918, just after the revolution, he was back in Berdichev. The Ukraine and its rich agriculture was destroyed first by Field Marshal von Eichhorn's German occupation, which stripped the countryside.[1] Then, as the German armies withdrew in November as revolution broke out at home, the Russian civil war began in earnest with fighting between White and Red Armies, while Ukrainian nationalists and anarchists resisted both

1 Field Marshal Hermann von Eichhorn (1848–1918). Following the harsh terms exacted by the Germans in the Treaty of Brest-Litovsk, Eichhorn's task in 1918 was to supervise the stripping of the Ukraine to feed German cities starving from the British blockade. This policy was naturally hated by the Ukrainians and Eichhorn was assassinated in July.

sides. Whites and nationalists, and in some cases Red Guards, vented their blind hatred with pogroms across the Ukraine. Some say that around 150,000 Jews, roughly a third of the Jewish population, were murdered during the civil war. Famine followed between 1920 and 1922, with hundreds of thousands of deaths in the Ukraine alone.

Grossman went to Moscow University in 1923 where he studied chemistry. Even at that early stage, the unmilitary Grossman demonstrated a fascination for the army. 'At first glance, Father was a completely civilian person', said his only child, Ekaterina Korotkova-Grossman. 'One could see this immediately from the way he stooped and the way he wore his glasses. And his hands were so clumsy. [Yet] he first showed an interest in the army when he was still a student. He wrote in one letter that if he was not called up he would volunteer.'

In 1928, when only twenty-three and still a student, he married his girlfriend in Kiev, Anna Petrovna Matsuk, known as Galya. This relationship produced a daughter in January 1930. They called her Ekaterina, or Katya, after Grossman's mother. In 1932, ten years after the civil war, an even worse man-made famine, provoked by Stalin's campaign against the kulaks and the forced collectivisation of agriculture, killed over seven million people.[2] Parents crazed by hunger ate their own children. It was the epitome of what Osip Mandelstam described in a memorable poem as 'the wolfhound century'. If Grossman did not witness the worst horrors of the famine, he certainly heard of them or saw the results, as skeletal figures begged beside railway tracks in the hope of a generous traveller throwing them a crust. He described this Ukrainian famine in his last novel, *Forever Flowing*, including the execution of a woman accused of eating her two children.

The consequence of Stalin's cruel treatment of the region, as Grossman himself was to discover, would be the widespread Ukrainian welcome to invading German forces a decade later. Stalinist agents are said to have spread the rumour that the Jews were responsible for the famine. This may well have been a factor later in the Ukrainians' enthusiastic aid to the Germans in their massacres of the Jews.

Grossman's marriage, frequently interrupted by his absence in Moscow, did not last long. Galya had left their daughter with his mother, because

2   The latest estimates for famine victims between 1930 and 1933 range from 7.2 million up to 10.8 million.

Kiev was the epicentre of the famine and the child stood a far better chance of survival in Berdichev. Over the following years, Katya often returned to stay with Grossman's mother.

Writing started to interest Grossman rather more than his scientific studies, but he needed a job. On his eventual graduation, he went in 1930 to work at Stalino (now Donetsk) in the eastern Ukraine as an engineer in a mine. The Donbass, the area enclosed by the sharp curve of the lower Don and Donets, was a region he came to know again during the war, as the notebooks show. In 1932, Grossman, exploiting a misdiagnosis which listed him as chronically tubercular, managed to leave Stalino and move back to Moscow. There, he published his first novel, *Glück auf!* (*Good luck!*) set in a coal mine. It was followed by *Stepan Kolchugin*. Although both novels followed the Stalinist dictates of the time, the characters were entirely convincing. A short story, 'In the Town of Berdichev', published in April 1934, brought praise from Mikhail Bulgakov.[3] Maxim Gorky, the grand old man of Soviet letters, although suspicious of Grossman's failure to embrace socialist realism, supported the young writer's work.[4] Grossman, whose literary heroes were Chekhov and Tolstoy, was never likely to be a Stalinist hack, even though he was initially convinced that only Soviet communism could stand up to the threat of fascism and anti-Semitism.

In March 1933, Grossman's cousin and loyal supporter, Nadezhda Almaz, was arrested for Trotskyism. Grossman was interrogated by the OGPU secret police (which became the NKVD in the following year). Both Almaz and Grossman had been in touch with the writer Victor Serge,[5] who was soon to be exiled, in 1936, and became in Paris one of the most

---

3   Bulgakov, Mikhail Afanasievich (1891–1940), the author of the novel *The White Guard* (1924) which he adapted for the Moscow Art Theatre as *The Day of the Turbins* (1926). Most improbably, this humane depiction of tsarist officers and intellectuals turned out to be Stalin's favourite play. His masterpiece, *The Master and Margarita*, was edited but unpublished when he died.
4   Gorky, Maksim, pen name of Aleksei Maksimovich Peshkov (1868–1936), playwright and novelist. Gorky had supported the revolution and been a friend of Lenin, but the dictatorial stance of the Bolsheviks horrified him and he left for Western Europe in 1921. Stalin, using flattery and underhand methods, persuaded him to return to the Soviet Union in 1928, where he was fêted. The city of Nizhni Novgorod was renamed Gorky in his honour. In return Gorky became a tool of the regime, supporting the doctrine of socialist realism in October 1932. He was the grand old man of Soviet literature until his death.
5   Victor Serge (1890–1947), pen name of Viktor Kibalchich. Born in Belgium, he was the son of an Imperial Guards officer turned revolutionary and a Belgian mother. Serge, an anarchist in France, was a libertarian socialist, who went to Russia in 1918 to join the revolution, but was horrified by Bolshevik authoritarianism. He is best known for his outstanding autobiography, *Memoirs of a Revolutionary* (1945), and the novels *Men in Prison, Birth of our Power* and *The Case of Comrade Tulayev*.

outspoken critics of Stalin on the left. The cousins were extremely fortunate. Nadya Almaz was exiled, then given a short labour camp sentence
which kept her out of the way during the Great Terror towards the end
of the decade. Grossman was not touched. Their fate would have been
very different if the interrogations had taken place three or four years
later.

Life for a writer, especially one as truthful and politically naive as
Grossman, was not easy over the next few years. It was a miracle that he
survived the purges, which Ilya Ehrenburg later described as a lottery.[6]
Ehrenburg was well aware of Grossman's gauche and ingenuous nature.
'He was an extremely kind and devoted friend,' he wrote, 'but could
sometimes say giggling to a fifty-year-old woman: "You have aged a lot
in the last month." I knew about this trait in him and did not get
offended when he would remark suddenly: "You've started to write so
badly for some reason".'

In 1935, when his marriage to Galya had been over for several years,
Grossman began a relationship with Olga Mikhailovna Guber, a large
woman five years his senior. Like Galya, Lyusya, as he called her, was
Ukrainian. Boris Guber, her husband and a fellow writer, realised that
his wife adored Grossman and did not try to fight events. A Russian of
German ancestry and from a distinguished family, Guber was arrested
and executed in 1937 during the madness of the 'yezhovshchina', as the
purges were called.[7]

That year, Grossman became a member of the Writers' Union, an official seal of approval which provided many perks. But in February 1938,
Olga Mikhailovna was arrested, simply for having been Guber's wife.
Grossman moved quickly to persuade the authorities that she was now his
wife, even though she had retained the name of Guber. He also adopted
the two Guber sons to save them from being sent to a camp for the orphans
of 'enemies of the people'. Grossman himself was interrogated in the
Lubyanka on 25 February 1938. Although a political innocent, he proved
extremely adept in distancing himself from Guber without betraying

6   Ehrenburg, Iliya Grigorievich (1891–1967), writer, poet and public figure, wrote for *Krasnaya
Zvezda* during the war. Later, he worked with Grossman on the Jewish Anti-Fascist Committee
and the Black Book on atrocities against Jews, which the Stalinist authorities suppressed soon after
the war. Ehrenburg had a much better nose for surviving the dangers of Stalinist politics.
7   This name came from the chief of the NKVD at the time, Nikolai Ivanovich Yezhov (1895–1939),
known as the 'Dwarf' because he was so short and suffered from a crippled leg. Yezhov took over
the NKVD on Stalin's order from Genrikh Yagoda (1891–1938) in September 1936. He was replaced
by Lavrenty Beria in December 1938, and thus took the blame for the excesses away from Stalin.
Like his predecessor, Yagoda, he was accused of treason and executed.

anybody. He also took a great risk in writing to Nikolai Yezhov, the chief of the NKVD, bravely quoting Stalin out of context as the reason that his wife should not share any guilt attributed to her former husband. Olga Mikhailovna was also saved by the bravery of Guber himself, who did not implicate her even though he was almost certainly urged to do so during brutal interrogation sessions.

It was a time of profound moral humiliation. Grossman was as helpless as the rest of the population. He had little alternative but to sign when presented with a declaration of support for the show trials of old Bolsheviks and others accused of 'Trotskyist-fascist' treason. But he never forgot the horrors of that time, and recreated them with powerful effect in a number of important passages in *Life and Fate*.

The worst of the terror seemed to have passed once Stalin made his pact with Hitler in 1939. Grossman had been able to spend that summer on the Black Sea with his wife and adopted stepsons at the Writers' Union resort. They spent a similar holiday in May 1941, but he returned to Moscow a month later and was there when the Wehrmacht invaded the Soviet Union on 22 June 1941. Like most writers he immediately volunteered for the Red Army, yet Grossman, although only thirty-five, was completely unfit for war.

The next few weeks became traumatic for Grossman, not just because of the crushing German victories, but for personal reasons. He was living in Moscow with his second wife in a small apartment and, for reasons of space, she discouraged him from asking his mother to leave Berdichev and seek refuge with them in Moscow. A week later, by the time he realised the extent of the danger, it was becoming too late for his mother to escape. In any case, she was refusing to leave behind an incapacitated niece. Grossman, who failed to get on a train to bring her back, would reproach himself for the rest of his life. In *Life and Fate*, the morally tortured physicist Viktor Shtrum is made guilty of exactly this.

The notebooks begin on 5 August 1941, when Grossman was sent to the front by General David Ortenberg, the editor of *Krasnaya Zvezda*. Although it was the official Red Army newspaper, civilians read it even more avidly during the war than *Izvestia*. Stalin insisted on checking every page before it was printed, which prompted Grossman's colleague Ehrenburg to joke in private that the Soviet dictator was his most devoted reader.

Ortenberg, concerned that Grossman would not survive the rigours of the front, found younger and militarily experienced companions to

Vasily Grossman's mother in her passport photograph

go with him. Grossman joked about his unfit state and lack of military training, but it was not long before, to their utter astonishment, the bespectacled novelist dramatically lost weight, toughened up and beat his companions at pistol shooting.

'I'll tell you about myself,' he wrote to his father in February of 1942. 'I have been almost constantly on the move for the last two months. There are days when one sees more than in ten years of peace. I've become thin now. I weighed myself in the *banya*, and it turned out I am only seventy-four kilos, and do you remember my terrible weight a year ago – ninety-one? My heart is much better . . . I've become an experienced *frontovik:* I can tell immediately by the sound what is happening and where.'

Grossman studied everything military: tactics, equipment, weaponry – and army slang which fascinated him especially. He worked so hard on his notes and articles that he had little time for anything else. 'During the whole war,' he wrote later, 'the only book that I read was *War and Peace* which I read twice.' Above all, he demonstrated extraordinary bravery right at the front, when most war correpondents hung around head-quarters. Grossman, who was so obviously a Jewish member of the Moscow intelligentsia, managed to win the trust and admiration of ordinary Red Army soldiers. It was a remarkable feat. In Stalingrad, he got to know Chekhov, the top-scoring sniper in the 62nd Army, and was allowed to accompany him to his killing lair and watch as he shot one German after another.

Unlike most Soviet journalists, eager to quote politically correct clichés, Grossman was exceptionally patient in his interviewing technique. He relied, as he explained later, on 'talks with soldiers withdrawn for a short break. The soldier tells you everything he has on his mind. One does not even need to ask questions.' Soldiers more than almost anyone else, can quickly spot the self-serving, the devious and the false. Grossman was honest to a fault, often too honest for his own good, and soldiers respected that. 'I like people,' he wrote. 'I like to study life. Sometimes a soldier makes me toe the line. I know army life as a whole now. It was very difficult at first.'

Grossman was not a dispassionate observer. The power of his writing came from his own emotional responses to the disasters of 1941. He later wrote of 'the penetrating, sharp foreboding of imminent losses, and the tragical realisation that the destiny of a mother, a wife and a child had become inseparable from the destiny of the encircled regiments and retreating armies. How can one forget the front in those days – Gomel and Chernigov dying in flames, doomed Kiev, carts of retreat, and poisonous-green rockets over silent forests and rivers?' Grossman, along with his companions, was present at the destruction of Gomel, then they had to flee south as General Guderian's 2nd Panzer Group swung round in the vast encirclement operation to cut off Kiev. The German armies captured more than 600,000 prisoners in the most crushing victory ever known.

Early that October, Grossman was attached to the headquarters of General Petrov's 50th Army. His descriptions of this general, who punched underlings and turned aside from his tea and raspberry jam to sign death sentences, read like a terrible satire of the Red Army, but they are devas-tatingly accurate. Grossman's uncomfortable honesty was dangerous. If the NKVD secret police had read these notebooks he would have disappeared into the Gulag. Grossman was not a member of the Communist Party, and this made his position even less secure.

Grossman was once again nearly encircled by Guderian's panzers as they raced for the city of Orel and then enveloped the Bryansk Front. His description of their flight is the most gripping account of those events to have survived. Grossman and his companions returned to Moscow exhausted, their shot-up 'Emka' car proof of the danger that they had been in, but Ortenberg ordered them straight back to the front. That night, searching for an army headquarters, they almost drove right into the arms of the Germans. As a Jew, Grossman's fate would have been certain.

That winter of 1941, after the Germans were halted outside Moscow, Grossman covered the fighting further south on the eastern edge of the Ukraine and close to the Donbass which he knew from pre-war years. He began to prepare his great novel of the first year of the war which was published during the early summer of 1942 in instalments in *Krasnaya Zvezda*. It was hailed as the only true account by the *frontoviki*, as the front-line soldiers of the Red Army were known, and Grossman's fame extended across the Soviet Union, far beyond the respect he earned in literary circles.

In August, as the German Sixth Army advanced on Stalingrad, Grossman was ordered down to the threatened city. He would be the longest serving journalist in the embattled city. Ortenberg, with whom he had a difficult relationship, recognised Grossman's extraordinary talents. 'All the correspondents on the Stalingrad Front were amazed at how Grossman had made the divisional commander General Gurtiev, a silent and reserved Siberian, talk to him for six hours without a break, telling him all that he wanted to know, at one of the hardest moments [of the battle]. I know that the fact that he never wrote anything down during the interview helped Grossman to win people's confidence. He would write it all down later, after he returned to a command post or to the correspondents' *izba*. Everyone would go to bed, but the tired Grossman wrote everything meticulously in his notebook. I knew about it and had seen his notebooks when I came to Stalingrad. I even had to remind him about the strict ban on keeping diaries and told him never to write any so-called secret information there. But it was not until [after his] death that I had a chance to read their contents. These notes are extremely pithy. Characteristic features of life at war are seen in just one phrase, as if on photographic paper when the photo is developed. In his notebooks one finds the pure, unretouched truth.' It was at Stalingrad that Grossman honed his power of description: 'the usual smell of the front line – a cross between a morgue and a blacksmith's'.

For Grossman, the battle of Stalingrad was undoubtedly one of the most important experiences of his life. In *Life and Fate*, the Volga is more than a symbolic thread for the book, it is the main artery of Russia pumping its lifeblood to the sacrifice in Stalingrad. Grossman, like many fellow idealists, believed passionately that the heroism of the Red Army at Stalingrad would not just win the war, it would change Soviet society for ever. Once victory over the Nazis had been won by a strongly unified people, they believed that the NKVD, the purges, the show trials and the Gulag could be consigned to history. Officers and soldiers at the front, with the freedom of the condemned man to say whatever they wanted, openly criticised the disastrous collectivisation of farms, the arrogance of the *nomenklatura* and the flagrant dishonesty of Soviet propaganda. Grossman later described this in *Life and Fate* through the reaction of Krymov, a commissar. 'Ever since he had arrived in Stalingrad, Krymov had had a strange feeling. Sometimes it was as though he were in a kingdom where the Party no longer existed; sometimes he felt he was breathing the air of the first days of the Revolution.' Some of these optimistic ideas and aspirations appear to have been encouraged in a whispering campaign instigated by the Soviet authorities, but as soon as the end of the war came in sight, Stalin began to tighten the screws again.

The Soviet dictator, who took a close interest in literature, appears to have disliked Grossman. Ilya Ehrenburg thought that he suspected Grossman of admiring Lenin's internationalism too much (a fault close to the crime of Trotskyism). But it is far more likely that the Soviet leader's resentment was based on the fact that Grossman never bowed to the personality cult of the tyrant. Stalin was conspicuously absent from Grossman's journalism, and his sole appearance in Grossman's fiction, written after the tyrant's death, consists of a late-night telephone call to Viktor Shtrum in *Life and Fate*. This constitutes one of the most sinister and memorable passages in any novel. It is a scene which may well have been inspired by a similar night-time call from the master of the Kremlin to Ehrenburg, in April 1941.

In January 1943, Grossman was ordered to leave Stalingrad. Ortenberg had called on Konstantin Simonov to cover the dramatic end of the battle in his place. The young, good-looking Simonov, was a great hero in the eyes of the Red Army and almost worshipped as the author of the poem 'Wait for Me'.[8] This poem had been written in 1941, just after the outbreak of war, when he had to leave his great love, the actress Valentina Serova. The song and poem became sacred to many soldiers of the Red Army, with its central idea that only the love of a faithful fiancée or wife could keep a soldier alive. Many of them kept a hand-written copy of it folded in their breast-pocket like a talisman.

Grossman, who had been in Stalingrad far longer than any other correspondent, felt betrayed by this decision. Ortenberg sent him nearly three hundred kilometres south of Stalingrad down into Kalmykia, which had just been liberated from German occupation. This in fact gave Grossman the opportunity to study the region before Lavrenty Beria's battalions of NKVD security police moved in to take revenge by massive deportations of the less than loyal population. His notes on the German occupation and on the degrees of collaboration with the enemy are poignant and brilliantly revealing of the compromises and temptations which faced civilians caught up in an international civil war.

Later that year he was present at the battle of Kursk, the largest tank engagement in history, which ended the Wehrmacht's ability to launch another major offensive until the Ardennes in December 1944. In January 1944, when attached to the Red Army advancing westwards through the Ukraine, Grossman finally reached Berdichev. There, all his fears about his mother and other relations were confirmed. They had been slaughtered in one of the first big massacres of the Jews, the main one just before the mass executions at the ravine of Babi Yar, outside Kiev. The slaughter of the Jews in the town in which he grew up made him reproach himself even more for the failure to save his mother in 1941. An additional shock was to discover the role played by their Ukrainian neighbours in the persecution. Grossman was determined to discover as much as he could about the Holocaust, a subject which the Soviet authorities tried to suppress. The Stalinist line was that the Jews should never be seen as special victims. The crimes committed against them should be seen entirely as crimes committed against the Soviet Union.

Just after the Red Army reached Polish territory, Grossman was one of the first correspondents to enter the death camp of Majdanek near Lublin. He then visited the extermination camp of Treblinka, north-east

---

8   Simonov, Konstantin (Kyrill Mikhailovich), (1915–1979), poet, playwright, novelist and correspondent of *Krasnaya Zvezda*. Simonov later wrote his own Hemingway-style novel about the Battle of Stalingrad entitled *Days and Nights*, published in 1944. Although physically brave, Simonov, as Grossman reflected later, lacked moral courage in his relationship with the Soviet regime.

of Warsaw. His essay, 'The Hell Called Treblinka', is one of the most important in Holocaust literature and was quoted at the Nuremberg tribunal.

For the advance on Berlin in 1945, Grossman arranged another attachment to the 8th Guards Army, the former 62nd Army of Stalingrad fame, and he again spent time in the company of its commander, General Chuikov. Grossman's painful honesty ensured that he recorded the crimes of the Red Army as much as its heroism, above all the mass rape of German women. His descriptions of the sack of Schwerin are some of the most powerful and moving of all eyewitness accounts. Similarly, his Berlin notebooks, when he was there to cover the fighting in the city and the final victory, deserve the widest possible audience. The fact that Grossman had seen more of the war in the East than almost anybody is of inestimable value. 'I think that those who never experienced all the bitterness of the summer of 1941,' he wrote, 'will never be able fully to appreciate the joy of our victory.' This was not boasting. It was the simple truth.

These pages from his notebooks, together with some articles and extracts from letters, show not just a great writer's raw materials. They represent by far the best eyewitness account of the terrible Eastern Front, perhaps the finest descriptions ever of what Grossman himself called 'the ruthless truth of war'.

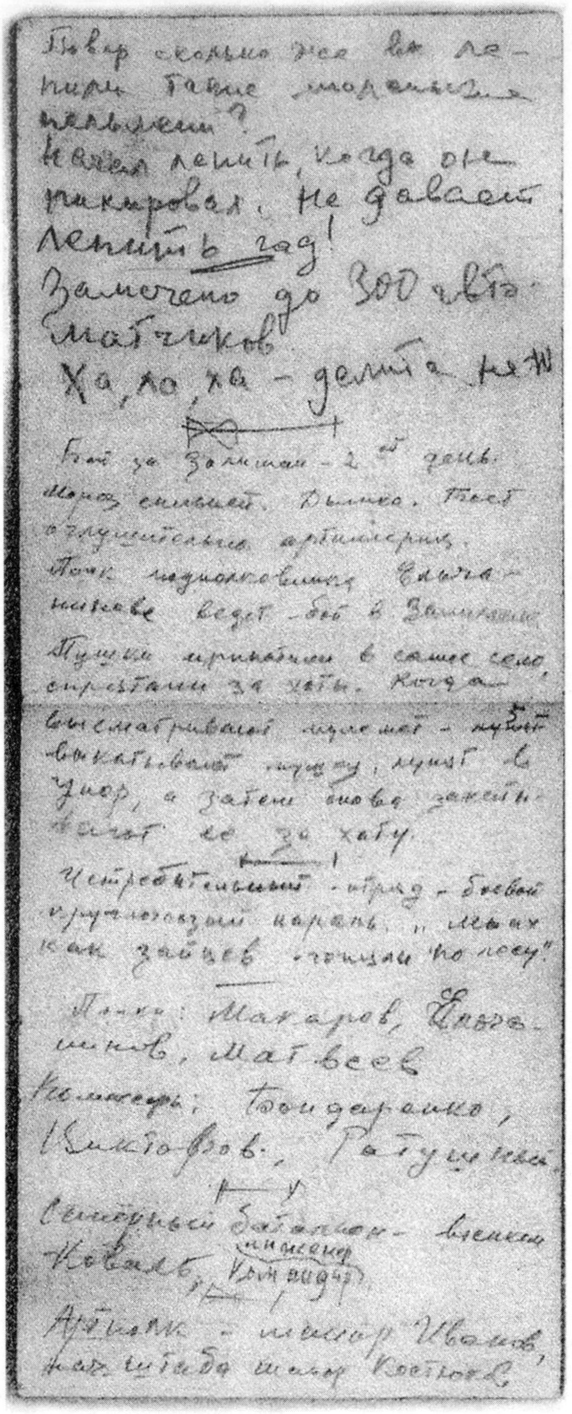

A page from one of Grossman's many notebooks.

Translators' Note

Any translation from the Russian which hopes to be readable in English requires a slight compression of the original, through the deletion of superfluous words and repetitions. This is especially true of the bureaucratic solemnities of military Russian, but we have, in the cases where Grossman himself was clearly amused by the original formulation, rendered a virtually literal translation to convey the flavour. Certain Red Army terms, like 'tankists' and 'artillerists' have also been left in their original form. The Russian words, acronyms and initials which we have left untranslated are listed in the glossary.

The Red Army, when talking of the enemy, used to say 'he', not 'they'. As this can be highly confusing in places, we have avoided a literal translation and substituted 'they' or 'the Germans'.

We have provided details on most of the characters mentioned in the text, but it has not been possible to obtain information on Grossman's colleagues at *Krasnaya Zvezda* whose personnel files remain closed as the newspaper is still a military unit.

It is extremely hard, especially when dealing with some of the fragmentary notes, to achieve the right balance between intervention in the interests of general understanding and respect for the original jottings. We have strived to keep all explanations to the linking passages and to footnotes, but occasionally words have been added in square brackets to aid comprehension.

Glossary

Front, when written with a capital letter refers to the Soviet equivalent of an army group, for example, Central Front, Western Front or Stalingrad Front. A Front was commanded by a colonel general or marshal later in the war and usually consisted of between four and eight armies.

Frontoviki, is the Red Army term for soldiers with real experience of fighting at the front.

GLAVPUR (*Glavnoye politicheskoye upravleniye*), was the main political department of the Red Army, headed for most of the Great Patriotic War by Aleksandr Shcherbakov. It was a Communist Party organisation, controlling the political officers and political departments – the commissar system first instituted during the Russian civil war to watch commanders, of whom many had been tsarist officers, and ensure that they were not secretly in league with the Whites. Commissars, or political officers and instructors, were not part of the NKVD, but worked with them on cases of suspected disaffection.

Gold Star, a popular term for the medal of Hero of the Soviet Union.

Hero of the Soviet Union, the Soviet Union's highest award for valour and distinguished service, consisted of a small gold bar with red ribbon from which hung a gold star.

Izba, was a peasant house, or log cabin, consisting usually of one or two rooms. The window frames were often decorated with ornamental carving.

Komsomol, acronym for the Communist Youth movement. Membership could extend until around the age of twenty, so there were many active Komsomol cells within the Red Army. Children joined the Young Pioneers.

Muzhik, archetypal Russian peasant.

NKVD (*Narodnyi Komissariat Vnutrennikh Del* – People's Commissariat of Internal Affairs), a direct descendant of the Cheka and the OGPU secret police.

NKVD Special Departments were attached to Red Army formations in a counter-intelligence role, which in Stalinist terms meant looking for treason within as much as espionage without. Their role was also to investigate cases of cowardice as well as 'extraordinary events' – anything deemed to be anti-Soviet – and provide execution squads when necessary. The Special Departments were replaced in the spring of 1943 by SMERSh, Stalin's acronym for *smert shpionam*, or death to spies.

OBKOM, acronym for the Oblast (or Regional) Party Committee.

Political officers, *politruks*, or political instructors – see GLAVPUR.

RAIKOM, acronym for local Party Committee.

Stavka, the general staff, a name which Stalin resuscitated from the tsarist command in the First World War. He, of course, was commander-in-chief.

Ushanka, a typical Russian fur hat with flaps tied up over the crown.

Valenki, large felt snowboots.

The Writer at War

PART ONE

The Shock of Invasion
1941

ONE

Baptism of Fire

Hitler's invasion of the Soviet Union began in the early hours of 22 June 1941. Stalin, refusing to believe that he could be tricked, had rejected more than eighty warnings. Although the Soviet dictator did not collapse until later, he was so disorientated on discovering the truth that the announcement on the wireless at midday was made by his foreign minister, Vyacheslav Molotov, in a wooden voice. The people of the Soviet Union proved rather more robust than their leaders. They queued to volunteer for the front.

Vasily Grossman, bespectacled, overweight and leaning on a walking stick, was dejected when the recruiting station turned him down. He should not have been surprised, considering his unimpressive physical state. Grossman was only in his mid-thirties, yet the girls in the next-door apartment called him 'uncle'.

Over the next few weeks he tried to get any form of employment he could which was connected with the war. The Soviet authorities, meanwhile, gave little accurate information on what was happening at the front. Nothing was said of the German forces, more than three million strong, dividing the Red Army with armoured thrusts, then capturing hundreds of thousands of prisoners in encirclements. Only the names of towns mentioned in official bulletins revealed how rapidly the enemy was advancing.

Grossman had put off urging his mother to abandon the town of Berdichev in the Ukraine. His second wife, Olga Mikhailovna Guber, convinced him that they had no room for her. Then, before Grossman realised fully what was happening, the German Sixth Army seized Berdichev on 7 July. The enemy had advanced over 350 kilometres in just over two weeks. Grossman's failure to save his mother burdened him for the rest of his life, even after he discovered that she had refused to leave because there was nobody else to look after a niece. Grossman was also extremely concerned about the fate of Ekaterina, or Katya, his daughter by his first wife. He did not know that she had been sent away from Berdichev for the summer.

Soviet citizens listen to Molotov's announcement of the
German invasion, 22 June 1941

Desperate to be of some help to the war effort, Grossman badgered
the Main Political Department of the Red Army, known by the acronym
GLAVPUR, even though he was not a member of the Communist Party.
His future editor, David Ortenberg, a commissar with the rank of general,
recounted later how he came to work for *Krasnaya Zvezda*, the newspaper of the Soviet armed forces which was far more attentively read
during the war than any other paper.[1]

1 Ortenberg, David I. (took the non-Jewish name of Vadimov in *Krasnaya Zvezda*).

I remember how Grossman turned up for the first time at the editorial office. This was in late July. I had dropped in at the Main Political Department and heard that Vasily Grossman had been asking them to send him to the front. All that I knew about this writer was that he had written the novel *Stepan Kolchugin* about the Donbass.

'Vasily Grossman?' I said. 'I've never met him, but I know *Stepan Kolchugin*. Please send him to *Krasnaya Zvezda*.'

'Yes, but he has never served in the army. He knows nothing about it. Would he fit in at *Krasnaya Zvezda*?'

'That's all right,' I said, trying to persuade them. 'He knows about people's souls.'

I did not leave them in peace until the People's Commissar signed the order to conscript Vasily Grossman into the Red Army and appoint him to our newspaper. There was one problem. He was given the rank of private, or, as Ilya Ehrenburg liked to joke about both himself and Grossman, 'untrained private'. It was impossible to give him an officer's rank or that of a commissar because he was not a Party member. It was equally impossible to make him wear a private's uniform, as he would have had to spend half his time saluting his seniors. All that we could do was to give him the rank of quartermaster. Some of our writers, such as Lev Slavin, Boris Lapin and even, for some time, Konstantin Simonov, were in the same situation. Their green tabs used to cause them a lot of trouble, as the same tabs were worn by medics, and they were always being mistaken for them. Anyway, on 28 July 1941 I signed the order: 'Quartermaster of the second rank Vasily Grossman is appointed a special correspondent of *Krasnaya Zvezda* with a salary of 1,200 roubles per month.'

The next day Grossman reported at the editorial office. He told me that although this appointment was unexpected, he was happy about it. He returned a few days later fully equipped and in an officer's uniform. [His tunic was all wrinkled, his spectacles kept sliding down his nose, and his pistol hung on his unfastened belt like an axe.]

'I am ready to depart for the front today,' he said.

'Today?' I asked. 'But can you fire that thing?' I pointed to the pistol hanging at his side.

'No.'

'And a rifle?'

'No, I can't, either.'

'So how can I allow you to go to the front? Anything can happen there. No, you will have to live at the editorial office for a couple of weeks.'

Colonel Ivan Khitrov, our tactical expert and a former army officer, became Grossman's coach. He would take him to one of the shooting ranges of the Moscow garrison and teach him how to shoot.

On 5 August, Ortenberg allowed Grossman to set off for the front. He arranged for him to be accompanied by Pavel Troyanovsky, a correspondent of great experience, and Oleg Knorring, a photographer. Grossman described their departure in some detail.

We are leaving for the Central Front. Political Officer Troyanovsky, camera reporter Knorring, and I are going to Gomel. Troyanovsky, with his thin dark face and big nose, has received the medal 'For Achievements in Battle'. He has seen a lot although he isn't old, in fact he is some ten years younger than me. I had at first thought that Troyanovsky was a real soldier, a born fighter, but it turned out that he had started his career in journalism not long ago as a correspondent of *Pionerskaya Pravda* [the Communist Youth Movement newspaper]. I was told that Knorring is a good photo-journalist. He is tall, a year younger than me. I am older than the other two, but alongside them I am a mere baby in matters of war. They take a perfectly justified pleasure in regaling me with the forthcoming horrors.

We leave tomorrow by train. We will travel in a 'soft' railway carriage all the way to Bryansk, and from there by whatever transport God sends our way. We were briefed before our departure by Brigade Commissar Ortenberg. He told us that an advance was about to take place. Our first meeting was at GLAVPUR. Ortenberg had a conversation with me and finally told me that he thought I was an author of children's books. This was a big surprise for me, I had no idea that I had written any books for children. When we were saying goodbye I said to him: 'Goodbye, Comrade Boev.' He burst out laughing. 'I am not Boev, I am Ortenberg.' Well, I paid him back. I had mistaken him for the chief of the publications department of GLAVPUR.

I have been drinking all day, just as a recruit should. Papa turned up, as well as Kugel, Vadya, Zhenya and Veronichka. Veronichka was looking at me with very sad eyes, as if I were Gastello.[2] I was very touched. The whole family sang songs and had sad conversations. The atmosphere was melancholy and concentrated. I lay alone that night, thinking. I had a lot of things, as well as people, to think about.

The day of our departure is a lovely one, it's hot and rainy. Sunshine and rain alternate suddenly. Pavements and sidewalks are wet. Sometimes they shine and sometimes are slate grey. The air is filled with hot, stifling moisture. A beautiful girl, Marusya, has come to see Troyanovsky off. She works at the editorial offices [of *Krasnaya Zvezda*], but apparently she is seeing him off on her own initiative, not at the editor's request. Knorring and I are tactful. We avoid looking in their direction.

Then the three of us [go to the platform]. I have so many memories of the Bryansky railway station. It's the station I arrived at when I first came to Moscow. Perhaps my departure from it today is my last. We drink lemonade and eat disgusting cakes in the cafeteria.

Our train pulls out of the station. All the names of stations along the line are familiar. I passed them so many times as a student, going back to Mama, to Berdichev, for my holidays. For the first time in a long while I can catch up on sleep in this 'soft' compartment, after all the air raids on Moscow.

[After reaching Bryansk] we spend a night at the railway station. Every corner is filled with Red Army soldiers. Many of them are badly dressed, in rags. They have already been 'there'. Abkhazians look the worst. Many of them are barefoot.

We have to sit up all night. German aircraft appear above the station, the sky is humming, there are searchlights everywhere. We all rush to some wasteland as far as possible from the station. Fortunately, the Germans don't bomb us here, they only frighten us. In the morning we listen to a broadcast from Moscow. It is a

2   Captain Gastello, a famous hero who had fought as a pilot in the Spanish Civil War, was a squadron commander with the the 207th Regiment of the 42nd Aviation Division. A German anti-aircraft gun damaged the fuel tank of his aircraft on 26 June 1941 in the area of Molodechno. The aircraft began to burn, and Gastello drove the burning aircraft at a column of German vehicles on the road. The explosion and fire that followed was said to have destroyed dozens of vehicles, enemy soldiers and tanks. Gastello was made a Hero of the Soviet Union, posthumously.

press conference given by Lozovsky [the head of the Soviet Information Bureau]. Sound was bad, we were listening hungrily. He used a lot of proverbs as usual, but they didn't make our hearts feel any lighter.

We go to the freight station to look for a train. They put us on a hospital train going to Unecha [midway between Bryansk and Gomel]. We board the train, but then suddenly there is panic. Everyone starts running, and firing. It turns out that a German aircraft is machine-gunning the railway station. I myself was caught up in this considerable commotion.

After Unecha, we travelled in a freight car. The weather was wonderful, but my travel companions said this was bad, and I realised this myself. There were black holes and craters from bombs everywhere along the railway. One could see trees broken by explosions. In the fields there were thousands of peasants, men and women, digging anti-tank ditches.

We watch the sky nervously and decided to jump off the train if the worst came to the worst. It was moving quite slowly. The moment we arrived in Novozybkov there was an air raid. A bomb fell by the station forecourt. This train wasn't going any further. We lay on the green grass, waiting and enjoying the warmth and grass around us, but we still kept glancing up at the sky. What if a German [aircraft] turned up all of a sudden?

We jump to our feet in the middle of the night. There is a hospital train going to Gomel. We take hold of the handrails when the train is already moving. We hang on the steps, knock at the door, pleading with them to let us at least on to the platform of the freight car. Suddenly a woman looks out and shouts: 'Jump off this second! It is forbidden to travel on hospital trains!' The woman is a doctor whose calling is to relieve people's suffering. 'Excuse us, but the train is moving at full speed, how are we to jump off?' There are five of us holding on to the handrails, we are all officers and all we are asking for is to be allowed to stand on the covered platform. She starts kicking us with her great boot, silently and with extraordinary force. She punches us on the hands with her fist, trying to make us let go of the handrails. Things are looking bad: if one lets go, that would be the end. Fortunately, it dawns on us that we aren't on a Moscow tram, and switch from the defensive to the attack. A few seconds later, the covered platform is ours, and the bitch with the rank of doctor is screaming in a frightened way and disappears very quickly. This is our first taste of fighting.

We arrive in Gomel. The train stops very far from the railway station, so we have a painful walk along the track in the dark. One has to crawl under the carriages to cross railways. I bang my forehead on them and stumble; my damned suitcase turns out to be extremely heavy.

Finally we reach the station building. It is completely destroyed. We utter 'Ahs' and 'Ohs' looking at the ruins. A railway worker who is passing reassures us by saying that the station had been demolished just before the invasion in order to build a bigger and better one.

Gomel! What sadness there is in this quiet green town, in these sweet public gardens, in its old people sitting on the benches, in sweet girls walking along the streets. Children are playing in the piles of sand brought here to extinguish incendiary bombs . . . Any minute a huge cloud may cover the sun, a storm may whip up sand and dust, and whirl them about. The Germans are less than fifty kilometres away.

Gomel welcomes us with an air-raid warning. Locals say that the custom here is to sound the alarm when there are no German aircraft around and, on the contrary, to sound the all-clear as soon as bombing starts.

Bombing of Gomel. A cow, howling bombs, fire, women . . . The strong smell of perfume – from a pharmacy hit in the bombardment – blocked out the stench of burning, just for a moment.

The picture of burning Gomel in the eyes of a wounded cow.

The colours of smoke. Typesetters had to set their newspaper by the light of burning buildings.

We stay the night with a tyro journalist. His articles aren't going to join a Golden Treasury of Literature. I've seen them in the Front newspaper. They are complete rubbish, with stories such as 'Ivan Pupkin has killed five Germans with a spoon'.

We went to meet the editor, regimental commissar Nosov, who kept us waiting for a good two hours. We had to sit in a dark corridor, and when finally we saw this tsar-like person and spoke with him for a couple minutes, I realised that this comrade was, to put it mildly, not particularly bright and that his conversation wasn't worth even a two-minute wait.

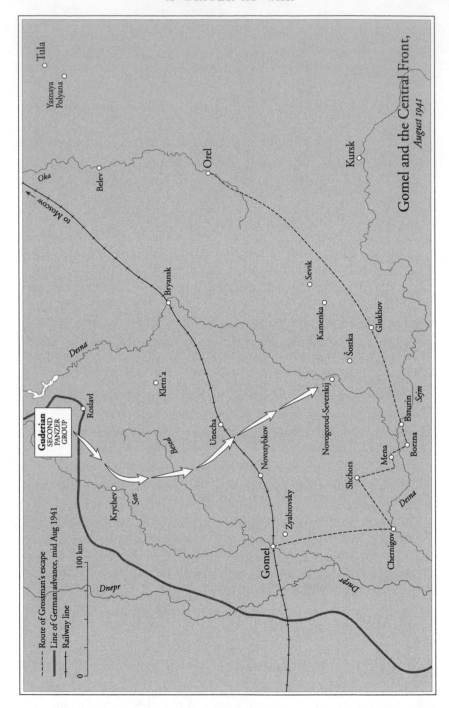

Gomel and the Central Front, August 1941

The headquarters of the Central Front was the first port of call for Grossman, Troyanovsky and Knorring. The Central Front, commanded by General Andrei Yeremenko, had been set up hurriedly following the collapse of the Western Front at the end of June.[3] The Western Front's unfortunate commander, General D.G. Pavlov, was made the chief scapegoat for Stalin's refusal to prepare for war. In characteristic Stalinist fashion, Pavlov, the commander of Soviet tank forces during the Spanish Civil War, was accused of treason and executed.

> The headquarters has been set up in the Paskevich Palace. There is a wonderful park, and a lake with swans. Lots of slit trenches have been dug everywhere. Chief of the political department of the front, Brigade Commissar Kozlov, receives us. He tells us that the Military Council is very alarmed by the news that arrived yesterday. The Germans have taken Roslavl and assembled a great tank force there.[4] Their commander is Guderian, author of the book *Achtung! Panzer!*[5]
>
> We leafed through a series of the Front newspaper. I came across the following phrase in a leading article: 'The much-battered enemy continued his cowardly advance.'
>
> We sleep on the floor in the library of the 'Komintern' club, keeping our boots on, and using gas masks and field pouches as pillows. We have dinner at the canteen of the headquarters. It is situated in the park, in an amusing multicoloured pavilion. They feed us well, as if we were in a *dom otdykha* [Soviet house of rest] before the war. There's sour cream, curds, and even ice-cream as a dessert.

Grossman became increasingly horrified and disillusioned the more he discovered about the Red Army's lack of preparation. He began to suspect, despite the official silence on the subject, that the person most responsible for the catastrophe was Stalin himself.

---

3 General A.I. Yeremenko (1892–1970) took part in the partition of Poland in 1939. After the fighting round Gomel in August 1941, he took command of the Bryansk Front, and that autumn he was badly wounded in the leg and nearly captured when Guderian's panzers outflanked his forces. He was later the commander-in-chief of the Stalingrad Front, where Grossman interviewed him.

4 Roslavl was some two hundred kilometres to their north-west, so the area around Gomel was left dangerously exposed. It soon became known as the Gomel salient.

5 General Heinz Guderian (1888–1953) was the commander of the Second Panzer Group (later the Second Panzer Army). Grossman was almost captured by his forces on two occasions.

On the outbreak of war, a lot of senior commanders and generals were on holiday in Sochi. Many armoured units were having new engines installed in their tanks, many artillery units had no shells, many aviation regiments had no fuel. When telephone calls began to come in from the frontier to the higher headquarters with reports that war had begun, some of them received the following answer: 'Don't give in to provocation.' This produced surprise in the most frightful and most severe sense of the word.

The disaster right along the front from the Black Sea to the Baltic was of great personal importance to Grossman, as a letter to his father on 8 August reveals.

My dear [Father], I arrived at my destination on 7 [August] . . . I so regret that I haven't got a blanket with me, it's no good sleeping under a raincoat. I am constantly worried about Mama's fate. Where is she, what's happened to her? Please let me know immediately if you have some news of her.

Grossman made visits to the front lines and jotted down these observations.

I was told how, after Minsk began to burn, blind men from the invalid home there walked along the motorway in a long file, tied to one another with towels.

A photographer remarks: 'I saw some very good refugees yesterday.'

A Red Army soldier is lying on the grass after the battle, talking to himself: 'Animals and plants fight for existence. Human beings fight for supremacy.'

The dialectics of war – the skill of hiding, of saving one's life, and the skill of fighting, of giving one's life.

Stories about being cut off. Everyone who has escaped back can't stop telling stories about being encircled, and all the stories are terrifying.

A pilot escaped back through enemy lines wearing only his underwear, but he had held on to his revolver.

Specially trained dogs with Molotov cocktails strapped to them are sent in to attack tanks and burst into flames.[6]

Bombs are exploding. The battalion commander is lying on the grass and doesn't want to go to the shelter. A comrade shouts to him: 'You've become a complete sloth. Why don't you at least go and take cover in those little bushes?'

A headquarters in a forest. Aircraft are swanning about overhead above the canopy. [Officers] remove their caps because the peaks shine, and they cover up papers. In the morning typewriters chatter everywhere. When aircraft appear, soldiers put greatcoats on the typists because they wear coloured dresses. Hidden in the bushes, clerks continue their quarrels about files.

A chicken belonging to the headquarters staff is taking a walk between earth dugouts, with ink on its wings.

There are many boletus mushrooms in the forest – it's sad to look at them.[7]

[Political] instructors have been ordered to the front. Those who want to go, and those who do not can be spotted easily. Some simply obey the order, others dodge. Everyone is sitting around and everyone can see all this, and those who dodge know that everyone can see through their tricks.

A long road. Wagons, pedestrians, strings of carts. A yellow dust cloud above the road. Faces of old people and women. Driver Ivan Kuptsov was sitting on the back of his horse a hundred metres away from the position. When a retreat started and there was one cannon left, German batteries rained shells on them, but instead of galloping

---

6 These dogs were trained on Pavlovian principles. Their food was always given to them under a tank so that they would run under armoured vehicles as soon as they saw one. The explosive was strapped to their backs with a long trigger arm, which would detonate the charge as soon as it touched the underside of the target vehicle.

7 This entry presumably inspired the passage in his novel *The People Immortal*: 'Bogaryov saw a family of boletus mushrooms in the grass. They were standing there on their fat white stems, and he remembered with what passion he and his wife had been picking mushrooms the year before. They would have been mad with joy had they found so many boletus. But he was never so lucky in peacetime.'

to the rear he rode to the field gun and rescued it from a swamp. When the political officer asked how he had found the courage to commit this feat of bravery in the face of death, he answered: 'I've got a simple soul, as simple as a balalaika. It isn't afraid of death. It's those with precious souls who fear death.'

A tractor driver loaded all the wounded men on to his vehicle and took them to the rear. Even the heavily wounded men kept their weapons.

[According to] Lieutenant Yakovlev, a battalion commander, the Germans attacking him were completely drunk. Those they captured stank of alcohol, and their eyes were bloodshot. All the attacks were fought off. Soldiers wanted to carry Yakovlev, who was heavily wounded, to the rear, on a groundsheet. He shouted: 'I've still got my voice and I am able to give orders. I am a communist and I can't leave the battlefield.'

Sultry morning. Calm air. The village is full of peace – nice, calm village life – with children playing, and old people and women sitting on benches. We hardly had arrived when three Junkers appeared. Bombs exploded. Screams. Red flames with white and black smoke. We pass the same village again in the evening. The people are wild-eyed, worn out. Women are carrying belongings. Chimneys have grown very tall, they are standing tall amid the ruins. And flowers – corn-flowers and peonies – are flaunting themselves so peacefully.

We came under fire near a cemetery. We hid beneath a tree. A truck was standing there, and in it was a dead rifleman-signaller, covered with a tarpaulin. Red Army soldiers were digging a grave for him nearby. When there's a raid of Messers, the soldiers try to hide in ditches. The lieutenant shouts: 'Carry on digging, otherwise we won't finish until the evening.' Korol hides in the new grave, while everyone runs in different directions. Only the dead signaller is lying full length, and machine guns are chattering above him.

Grossman and Knorring visited the 103rd Red Army Aviation Fighter Regiment stationed near Gomel. Grossman soon discovered that the Red Army on the ground had mixed feelings about their own air force, which rapidly acquired a reputation for attacking anything which moved, whether friend or foe. 'Ours, ours?' ran the universal joke. 'Then where's my helmet?'

I went with Knorring to the Zyabrovsky airfield near Gomel. Commissar Chikurin of Red Army Aviation, a big, slow fellow, had lent us his ZIS staff car. He was cursing German [fighter pilots]: 'They chase vehicles, individual trucks, cars. It's hooliganism, an outrage!'

At the same regiment, there are two comrades, who had both been decorated. Once they shot down one of our planes and were punished. After receiving their sentences, they started to work better. It was proposed to have them acquitted.

Notes from an interview with a pilot:
'Comrade Lieutenant Colonel, I've shot down a Junkers-88 for the Soviet motherland.'
About Germans:
   'There are pilots who aren't bad, but the majority are crap. They avoid fighting. They don't fight till the bitter end.'

Grossman takes his first flight at Zyabrovsky airfield, near Gomel, August 1941.

'There's no anxiety – anger, fury. And when you see he's on fire, light comes into your soul.'

'Who is going to turn away? Him or me? I am not going to. I have become a single whole with the plane and don't feel anything any longer.'

A young Red Army soldier set off a rocket at the [airfield] command post and hit the Chief of Staff in the behind.

The headquarters are in a building which had been a Young Pioneers' palace. A huge pilot festooned with pouches, a pistol, and so on, emerges from a door on which is written 'For young girls'.

Buildings at the airfield have been destroyed by bombing, the field ploughed up by explosions. Ilyushin and MiG aircraft are concealed under camouflage nets. Vehicles go round the airfield delivering fuel to the aeroplanes. There is also a truck with cakes and a truck carrying vacuum flasks of food. Girls in white overalls fuel the pilots with dinner. The pilots eat capriciously, reluctantly. The girls are coaxing them to eat. Some aircraft are hidden in the forest.

It was remarkably interesting when Nemtsevich [commander of the aviation regiment] told us about the first night of the war, about the terrible, swift retreat. He drove around day and night in a truck picking up officers' wives and children. In one house he found officers who had been stabbed to death. Apparently, they had been killed in their sleep by saboteurs. This was close to the frontier. He said that on that night of the German invasion he had to make a telephone call on some unimportant business and it turned out that communications weren't working . . . He was annoyed, but didn't pay much attention to this.

Nemtsevich said to me that German aircraft haven't appeared over his airfield for ten days. He was categorical about his conclusion: the Germans have no fuel, the Germans have no aircraft, they have all been shot down. I've never heard such a speech – what optimism! This trait of character is both good and harmful at the same time, but at any rate he'll never make a strategist.

We had lunch in a cosy little canteen. There was a pretty waitress and Nemtsevich moaned with desire when he looked at her. He spoke to her in a fawning, shy, pleading voice. She was ironically indulgent. This was that brief triumph of a woman over a man in the days, or maybe even hours, preceding the 'surrender' of her heart. It is strange to see in this handsome and masculine commander of a fighter regiment this timid submissiveness to the power of a woman. Evidently, he is a great skirt-chaser.

We spent the night in a huge, multi-storeyed building. It was deserted, dark, frightening, and sad. Hundreds of women and children were living here a short time ago, families of pilots. At night we were woken by a frightening low humming and went out into the street. Squadrons of German bombers were flying eastwards over our heads, evidently, those very ones Nemtsevich spoke about during the day, the ones he said had no fuel and were destroyed.

There was the roar of engines starting up, dust, and wind – that very special aircraft wind, flattened against the ground. Aircraft went up into the sky one after another, circled and flew away. And immediately the airfield became empty and silent, like a classroom when the pupils have skipped away. It's like poker: the regimental commander threw his whole fortune into the air. The playing field is empty. He is standing there alone looking into the sky, and the skies above him are empty. He'll either be left a pauper, or will get everything back with interest. That's a game, where stakes are life and death, victory or defeat. I am forever feeling as if I am on a cinema screen, not just watching it. Major events are coming thick and fast.

Finally, after a successful attack on a German column, the fighters returned and landed. The lead aircraft had human flesh stuck in the radiator. That's because the supporting aircraft had hit a truck with ammunition that blew up right at the moment when the leader was flying over it. Poppe, the leader, is picking the meat out with a file. They summon a doctor who examines the bloody mass attentively and pronounces [it] 'Aryan meat!' Everyone laughs. Yes, a pitiless time – a time of iron – has come!

TWO

The Terrible Retreat

A general impression of the first few months of the Nazi-Soviet war is one of constant movement, of rapid advances and sweeping panzer encirclements. But on the Soviet side there were also many brief periods of inaction, to say nothing of confusion, rumours and waiting as orders failed to get through or were countermanded. Grossman, Troyanovsky and Knorring were taken back to the front. Grossman once again jotted everything down which caught his eye or his imagination, using one of his tiny notepads, with squared pages similar to a schoolboy's maths exercise book.

Reaching the front. The humming of artillery is becoming increasingly loud. Anxiety and tension are growing. Artillery, ammunition and horse-drawn carts are moving on a wide, white, sandy road, in the golden dust of sunset, among the red pines. Infantry is on the march. A young officer covered in dust and sweat, with a huge yellow dahlia lit by the setting sun. They are heading towards the west.

At the front, when there's trench warfare, Germans shout every morning: 'Zhuchkov, surrender.' Zhuchkov answers sullenly: 'Fuck you.'

A Red Army soldier with a beard. Officer: 'Why don't you shave?' Soldier: 'I haven't a razor.' Officer: 'Very well, you'll go on a reconnaissance mission, with your beard.' Soldier: 'I'll shave today, comrade commander.'

Ganakovich – a wonderful man – puffing on his pipe, radiating waves of calmness and common sense. He is sad sometimes, and likes to sit alone. He sits thinking for a long, long time. He uses colourful language. 'Well, I remember the cavalry from 1914. They

steal chickens and fuck women even as far as two hundred kilometres behind the front.'

Battle at night. Cannonade. Field guns bang, shells howl, first in a
shrill tone, then humming like wind. Barking of mines. A lot of
rapid, white fire. The tap dance of machine guns and rifles is the
most disturbing. Green and white German rockets. Their light is
mean, dishonest, not like daylight. A ripple of shots. People are
neither seen nor heard. It is like a riot of machines.

Morning. A battlefield. Shell craters, flat like saucers, with earth
spilt around them. Gas masks. Flasks. Little holes dug by soldiers
during the attack for machine-gun and mortar nests. They did
themselves no good when they dug the holes so close to one
another. One can see how they huddled together, two holes – two
friends, five holes – soldier comrades from the same region. Blood.
A man killed behind a haystack, his fist clenched, leaning back
like a frightening sculpture – *Death on the Field of Battle*. There
is a little pouch with *makhorka* [black tobacco] and a box of
matches.
    The bottom of a German trench is covered with straw. The straw
has kept the shapes of human bodies. By the trenches there are
empty cans, lemon peel, wine and brandy bottles, newspapers,
magazines. There are no traces of food by the machine-gun nests,
only a lot of cigarette butts and multicoloured cigarette boxes. One
wants to wash one's hands carefully after touching anything German
– newspapers, photographs, letters.

The divisional commander, the tall, embittered Colonel Meleshko,
wore a soldier's padded jacket. To a correspondent's sugary remark
about how happy and excited are the faces of wounded soldiers
when they return from the battle, he remarked, with a sardonic
grin: 'Especially the faces of those wounded in the left hand.'

Soldiers frequently shot themselves through the left hand in a naive attempt
to escape battle. In fact, such a wound, whatever the circumstances, was
automatically deemed to have been self-inflicted and thus an attempt to
evade battle. The soldier faced summary execution at the hands of the
NKVD Special Departments (later SMERSh counter-intelligence). A few
Red Army surgeons dared to save a boy's life by amputating the hand

entirely before the Special Department checked the wounds of every new patient.

A German PoW on the edge of a forest – a miserable dark-haired boy. He is wearing a white-and-red neckerchief. He is being searched. The main feeling of soldiers towards him is surprise, as he is a stranger, a total stranger to these aspens, pines and the sad harvested fields.

The shifting sense of danger. A place seems frightening at first, but afterwards you will remember it being as safe as your Moscow apartment.

A cemetery. Fighting is going on below in the valley, the village is burned out. Twelve German bombers are diving over to the left. The cemetery is quiet, [but] chickens are cackling in the smoking village. They are laying, and our driver Petlyura says with an arch smile: 'I'm going to fetch some eggs for you in a second.' At this very moment, a Messerschmitt attacks with a howling roar and Petlyura scurries into a gap between graves, forgetting the eggs.

Grossman then heard that Utkin, a famous poet, had been wounded nearby.[1]

Morning. We went to the field hospital to see Utkin, whose fingers had been torn off by shrapnel. It was overcast, raining. There were about nine hundred wounded men in a little clearing among young aspens. There were bloodstained rags, scraps of flesh, moans, subdued howling, hundreds of dismal, suffering eyes. The young red-haired 'doctoress' had lost her voice – she had been operating all night. Her face was white – as if she might faint at any minute. Utkin had already been taken away in a staff car. She smiled. 'While I was making incisions, he recited poetry for me.' One could barely hear her voice, she was helping herself speak with gestures. Wounded men kept arriving, they were all wet with blood and rain.

1　The poet Iosif Pavlovich Utkin (1903–1944) volunteered for the Red Army in June 1941, and was wounded. After these wounds healed, he returned to the front as a military correspondent. Many of his wartime poems were used in songs. He died in a plane crash in 1944 when returning to Moscow from the front.

Like all Russians, Grossman was touched by stories of the war orphans, the countless innocents whose lives had been destroyed.

> When this lieutenant colonel was walking from Volkovysk, he found a three-year-old boy in a forest. He carried the boy in his arms for hundreds of kilometres though marshes and forests. I saw them at the headquarters. The blond boy was asleep hugging the lieutenant colonel's neck. The lieutenant colonel was red-haired and his clothes were all rags.[2]

> A joke about how to catch a German. One simply needs to tie a goose by the leg and a German would come out for it. Real life: Red Army soldiers have tied chickens by the leg and let them out into a clearing in the woods, and hid in the bushes. And Germans really did appear when they heard the chickens clucking. They fell right into the trap.

In the third week of August, part of General Heinz Guderian's Second Panzer Group swung southwards to outflank the Soviet forces in the Gomel salient. The German advance forced the Red Army to abandon the city, and soon the last part of Belorussian territory fell to the enemy. Grossman encountered the leaders of the Belorussian Communist Party at an outdoor meeting of its Central Committee with senior military officers.[3] Grossman developed the scene in his novel the following year.

> Who can describe the austerity of this session held on the last free patch of the Belorussian forest? The wind coming from Belorussia sounded melancholy and solemn, and it seemed as if millions of voices were whispering in the leaves of oaks. People's Commissars [government ministers] and members of the Central Committee, men in military tunics with tanned and tired faces, were brief in what they said . . . It became dark. The artillery opened fire. Long flashes lit the dark skies in the west.

2 Grossman used this episode in his novel *The People Immortal*, when the commissar's son is rescued in a similar manner.
3 Ortenberg wrote later: 'The next day [21 September] we were able to offer more to the readers: Vasily Grossman and Pavel Troyanovsky had sent a selection of various materials from Gomel. It contained an interview with the Secretary of the Communist Party of Belorussia about the feats of partisans.'

In the original notebook, he wrote:

> Session of the Central Committee of Belorussian Communist Party
> – on the last piece of Belorussian soil . . . Severe matters are being
> resolved, not a single unnecessary word is spoken . . . Ponomarenko
> – speaking to a Red Army commander: 'You can't use foul language
> about a member of the Central Committee.' The General was
> frightened: 'I didn't curse him, I was cursing in general.'[4]

> The order was received during the night to bombard Novo-Belitsa
> and Gomel. The sky was burning. A subdued conversation in the
> commander's hut. Voice of the commander: 'If you remember, in
> *Travel to Arzrum.*' Another voice: 'Karaims aren't Jews, they descend
> from Khazars.'[5]

> Dogs rush over the bridge from the burning city of Gomel along-
> side cars.

> During the bombing, an old man climbed out of the trench to
> retrieve his hat, and his head was chopped off together with all of
> the neck.

News of the growing military disaster spread among the civilian population. Grossman, Troyanovsky and Knorring were a part of the flight
south to avoid Guderian's panzer columns. This took them into the
north-eastern tip of the Ukraine. The companions escaped south along
the main road to Kiev as far as Chernigov, then eastwards to Mena. In
both places, Red Army staff officers did not take the danger seriously, as
Grossman discovered.

Stalin in the Kremlin also refused to face the reality of the threat.
Guderian's panzers, striking south from Gomel, could cut off the
Ukrainian capital Kiev from the north, but by the time the Soviet leader

4 Ponomarenko, Panteleimon Kondratyevich (1902–1984), First Secretary of the Belorussian
Communist Party, 1938–1947, in exile in Moscow during German occupation 1941–44 where he
supervised the organisation of partisan resistance. Ponomarenko, a Stalinist stalwart, was an improb-
able jazz fan who set up the Belorussian National Jazz Orchestra in Minsk in 1940. After the war
he served as Soviet ambassador in a number of posts and was closely connected with the KGB.
5 'Two military journalists and a photojournalist were sitting on the trunk of a fallen tree near
the shack made of branches where the Military Council was accommodated . . . They heard the
commander's voice from the shack: 'If you remember, in *Travel to Arzrum* . . .' *Travel to Arzrum*
was a travelogue parody written by Pushkin in 1836, the year before his death in a duel.

recognised the danger, it was too late. This was to be the biggest single military defeat in Soviet history. In the 'Kiev concentration', the Red Army lost more than half a million men captured and killed. Grossman and his companions only just escaped the trap as the 3rd, 4th and 17th Panzer Divisions drove south from Gomel into eastern Ukraine. The 3rd Panzer Division captured the crucial bridge over the River Desna near Novgorod-Seversky on 25 August.

Troyanovsky described their route. 'We were driving and driving past smouldering ruins. The ruins of Chernigov, Borzna, Baturin were smouldering . . . Whenever there was an air raid, P.I. Kolomeitsev would organise small arms fire at the fascist aircraft. Even such utterly civilian men as Oleg Knorring and Vasily Grossman would fire at the aircraft with their rifles.' Grossman, however, was equally concerned with the human tragedy about them.

Civilians. They are crying. Whether they are riding somewhere, or standing by their fences, they begin to cry as soon as they begin to speak, and one feels an involuntary desire to cry too. There's so much grief!

An empty house. The family moved out the day before, the owner is leaving too. The neighbour, an old man, has come to see him off: 'And the doggy will stay?'

'He didn't want to go.'

And the house remains where it has always stood. Green tomatoes are ripening on the roof, flowers amuse themselves in the garden. In the room there are little cups and jars, fig trees in flowerpots, a lemon tree, a palm tree. Everywhere, in everything, one can feel the owner's hands.

Dust. White, yellow, red dust. It is stirred up by the feet of sheep, pigs, horses, cows, and by the carts of refugees, Red Army soldiers, trucks, staff cars, tanks, guns and artillery tractors. Dust is hanging, swirling, whirling over the Ukraine.

Heinkels and Junkers are flying at night. They spread among the stars like lice. The blackness of air is filled with their humming. Bombs are crashing down. Villages are burning all around. The dark August sky becomes lighter. When a star falls down, or when there is thunder during the day, everyone gets scared, but then they laugh: 'That's from the sky, from the real sky.'

*In the terrible retreats of 1941, Red Army soldiers
walked for hundreds of kilometres.*

An old woman thought she might see her son in the column that
was trudging through the dust. She stood there until evening and
then came up to us. 'Soldiers, take some cucumbers, eat, you are
welcome.' 'Soldiers, drink this milk.' 'Soldiers, apples.' 'Soldiers,
curds.' 'Soldiers, please take this.' And they cry, [these women],
they cry, looking at the men walking past them.

The girl Orinka in the village Dugovaya – the grief itself, the very
black-eyed poetry of the people. Black legs, torn dress. We offered
her apples from the garden of her collective farm. Well, this garden
is hers. The old guardian of the orchard watches in silence as we
pick the apples.

A massive gun is moving along the road in the black-yellow cloud
of dust. Two Red Army soldiers are sitting on its barrel, their faces
black with dust. They are drinking water from a helmet.

Grossman, leaving Ukraine only a step ahead of Guderian's panzers, was no doubt thinking of his mother, trapped in Berdichev, nearly five hundred kilometres behind him to the south-west. From Shchors (named after a Bolshevik hero of the civil war), Grossman, Troyanovsky and Knorring travelled to Glukhov and then took the main road north eastwards to Orel.

To think of the towns now occupied which one had visited before is like remembering friends who have died. It is infinitely sad. They seem terribly remote and close at the same time, and life in them seems like the 'other world'.

Talk in villages. All sorts: angry, sincere. Today a loud-voiced young woman shouted: 'How can we possibly take orders from the Germans? How can we allow such a disgrace to happen?'

Cucumbers. Four men from the fruit and vegetable store load cucumbers at the station, during a bombing raid. They are crying with fear, get drunk, and in the evenings they recount, with Ukrainian humour, how scared they were and laugh at one another, eating honey, *salo* [pork lard], garlic and tomatoes. One of them imitates wonderfully the howling and explosion of a bomb.

B. Korol is teaching them how to use a hand grenade. He thinks they'll become partisans under German occupation, while I sense from their conversation that they are ready to work for the Germans. One of them, who wants to be an agronomist for this area, looks at Korol as if he were an imbecile.

Face and soul of the people. In three days we went through Belorussia, Ukraine, and arrived in the Orel area. Hard times reveal the best side of people. They are kind and noble. There are similar traits in the three nations, and also some deeply different aspects. Russians are the strongest and most enduring. The face of a Ukrainian is sad and gentle, they are sly and a little disloyal. The grief of Belorussians is quiet and black.

Orel. Driving in the dark. The brakes of our vehicle are not working. We stop hard in front of a group of refugees. A woman screams. Jewish refugees.

Arrival in Orel. The city is blacked out. Before the war one could see the murky shine of the city even from the remote countryside. Now, it's dark. Hotel. Bed! We sleep without our boots or clothes on for the first time on this journey. A telephone conversation with Moscow. This ability to communicate freely with the city of my friends, my family and my work leaves a melancholy aftertaste.

THREE

On the Bryansk Front

Ortenberg allowed Grossman and Troyanovsky no time to rest in Orel after their escape. They were ordered back to work on the Bryansk Front, which would soon suffer the full force of Operation Typhoon when General von Bock's Army Group Centre launched its offensive against Moscow.

Drive to the front. Two Red Army soldiers in a lush empty garden. A quiet clear morning. They are alone, they're signallers. 'Comrade officers, I am going to shake some apples off the tree for you, right now.' Heavy soft thuds of apples falling. On the ground in the silent abandoned garden. The mournful white house of the landlord, it's abandoned once again and its second master is gone, too. A new master will be here soon. Yet the soldier's face is happy and dirty. He is holding a heap of apples in his hands.

A old woman says: 'Who knows whether God exists or not. I pray to Him. It's not a difficult job. You give Him two or three nods, and who knows, perhaps He'll accept you.'

In empty *izbas*. Everything has been taken away, except for icons. It's so unlike Nekrasov's peasants, who would first of all save icons when there is a fire, leaving other pieces of property to burn.[1]
   A boy keeps crying all night. He has an abscess on his leg. His mother keeps whispering to him quietly, calming him: 'Darling, darling.' And a night battle is thundering outside their window.

---

1   Nekrasov, Nikolai Alekseevich (1821–1878), poet. His Polish mother taught him about the plight of the Russian peasantry, the main subject of his work, especially 'On the Road', 'Homeland' and *Red-Nose Frost*.

Bad weather – gloom, rain, fog – everyone is wet and cold, yet everyone is happy. There is no German aviation. Everybody says in a pleased way: 'It's a nice day.'

The approach of the Germans prompted the more foresighted peasants to turn livestock into hams and sausage which were easier to conceal.

Slaughter of pigs. Terrible screams making one's hair stand on end.

The interrogation of a traitor in a little meadow on a quiet, clear autumn day with a gentle, pleasant sun. He has an overgrown beard and is wearing a torn brown russet coat, a big peasant hat. His feet are dirty and bare, his legs naked to the calf. He is a young peasant with bright blue eyes. One hand is swollen, the other one is small – it looks like a woman's hand, with clean fingernails. He speaks, stretching words softly in Ukrainian. He is from Chernigov. He deserted several days ago and was captured last night on the front line when he was trying to get back to our rear wearing this almost opera-like peasant costume. By chance he was captured by his comrades, soldiers from his own company, who recognised him, and there he is in front of them now. The Germans had bought him for a hundred marks. He was going back to look for head-quarters and airfields. 'But it was only a hundred marks,' he says dragging out the words. He thinks that the modesty of this sum might make them more forgiving. 'But that makes me uncomfortable too, I see, I see.' He isn't a human being any more, all his movements, his grin, his glances, his noisy, greedy breathing – all that belongs to a creature that senses a close and imminent death. He has trouble with his memory.
   'And what's your wife's name?'
   'Wife's name, I remember. Gorpyna.'
   'And your son's?'
   'I remember his name, too. Pyotr.' He reflects for a while and adds: 'Dmitrievich. Five years old.' 'I'd like to have a shave,' he continues. 'The men are looking at me, and I feel embarrassed.' He strokes his beard with his hand. He picks at grass, earth and chips of wood, in quick, frenzied movements, as if doing some work that will save him. When he looks at the soldiers and their rifles, there's an animal fear in his eyes.
   Then the colonel slaps his face, shouting and crying at the same

time: 'Do you realise what you've done?' The guard, a Red Army soldier, then shouts at him, too: 'You've disgraced your son! He won't be able to live with this shame!'

'Don't you think I don't know what I've done, comrades?' the traitor says, addressing both the colonel and the sentry as if they might sympathise with him in his trouble. He was shot in front of the company where he had been a soldier only a short time before.

Major Garan received a letter from his wife. As he was busy with work at that moment, he sternly put the letter aside unopened. He read it later and then said with a smile: 'I didn't know whether my wife and son were alive or dead; I had left them in Dvinsk. And now my son has written to me: "I climbed on the roof during an air raid and fired at aircraft with a revolver." He's got a wooden revolver.'

Grossman wrote to his father still desperately concerned about his mother and his daughter Katya. He did not know that Katya had in fact been sent to a Young Pioneers' camp well to the east.

I am in good health, feeling well and my spirits are high. Only I am worried day and night about Mama and Katyusha, and I so want to see all my dear ones. I'll probably be allowed to spend a few days in Moscow in about three weeks. I'll have a good wash then and a proper sleep with no boots on – that's now my idea of supreme comfort.

Grossman also wrote to his wife shortly afterwards. This letter, dated 16 September, like those of any front-line soldier, provides very little information except the reassurance that the sender was still alive on the date when it was sent.

Dear Lyusenka,
I am seeing a lot of interesting things. I keep moving from one place to another all the time, that's what life at the front is like. Are you writing to me? A drop of pitch fell on the card from the beam in the bunker while I was writing.
Look through *Krasnaya Zvezda*. Two or three of my articles are published there every month. They would be an additional hello to you from me.
Your Vasya

Soviet citizens were desperate for news of the war,
but newspapers gave little reliable news in 1941.

Two days earlier, *Krasnaya Zvezda* had just published his latest article. It was entitled 'In the Enemy's Bunker – On the Western Axis'.

German trenches, strongpoints, officers' and soldiers' bunkers. The enemy has been here. There are French wines and brandy; Greek olives; yellow, carelessly squeezed lemons from their 'ally', slavishly-obedient Italy; a jar of jam with a Polish label; a big oval tin of fish preserve – Norway's tribute; a bucket of honey from Czechoslovakia. And fragments of a Soviet shell are lying amid this fascist feast.

Soldiers' bunkers are a different sight: here one won't see empty chocolate boxes and unfinished sardines. There are only tins of pressed peas and chunks of bread as heavy as cast iron. Weighing in their palms these loaves that are similar to asphalt in both colour and density, Red Army soldiers grin and say: 'Well, brother, that's real bread!'

FOUR

With the 50th Army

During that September on the Bryansk Front, Grossman visited the headquarters of the 50th Army. It consisted of seven rifle divisions, and was
commanded by Major-General Mikhail Petrov.[1] The headquarters were
housed in an *izba*.

> In the *izba* are Member of the Military Council [i.e. Commissar]
> Shlyapin, and Commander-in-Chief Petrov. Petrov is short and large-
> nosed, wearing a soiled general's tunic with the Gold Star [of Hero
> of the Soviet Union] which he received for service in the Spanish
> campaign [Civil War]. He is explaining at great length to the cook
> how to make sponge cake, how to make pastry rise, and all about
> the difference between wheat and rye bread. Petrov is very cruel
> and very brave. He told us how he escaped the encirclement on
> foot in his uniform and medals and the Gold Star [because] he
> didn't want to put on civilian clothes. He marched alone, in full
> parade gear, with a club to keep away village dogs. He said to me:
> 'I've always dreamed of getting to Africa, chop my way through the
> tropical forest, alone, with an axe and a rifle.' He loves cats, espe-
> cially kittens, and plays with them.

> Commander of the 50th Army Petrov spoke to a woman in a
> village seized back from the Germans. 'So, what do you think of
> Germans?'
> 'They aren't bad people,' [she replied]. The general swore at
> her.

> There was one officer who ate very little. A woman said of him:
> 'He is so spoilt.'

---

1 Major-General Mikhail P. Petrov (1898–1941).

The general's cook who had worked in a restaurant before the war stays in the *izba*. He is critical of the food in the village. The village women are angry with him. They call [the cook] Timka instead of Timofei. His appearance is awe-inspiring.

Timka: 'When I was working in the front line, I would drive there, gulp down a glass of "denaturate" [industrial alcohol], and I didn't give a damn any longer. Shells and bullets were whistling all around me, and I was singing and pouring food for soldiers. Oh, they loved me, how the soldiers loved me.' Timka demonstrates with ballet movements how he poured portions, and sings. It looks as if he's had his glass today, too.

The adjutants: Shlyapin's adjutant is the tall, handsome [Lieutenant] Klenovkin. Petrov's adjutant is short like a teenager, with monstrously broad shoulders and chest. This 'teenager' could bring down an *izba* with one heave of his shoulder. He is loaded down with all kinds of pistols, a sub-machine gun and grenades. In his pockets are sweets stolen from the general's table and hundreds of cartridges to protect the general's life.

Petrov watched his adjutant eat rapidly, using his fingers instead of a fork. 'If you don't learn some culture,' the general shouted at him, 'I'll send you to the front line. You should eat with a fork, not fingers!'

The general's and the commissar's adjutants are sorting out their chiefs' underwear, trying to borrow an extra pair – the commissar's adjutant from the general's, and vice versa. Crossing a small stream, the general jumps over it, the commissar steps in and washes his boots. The general's adjutant then jumps over, but the commissar's steps in and washes his boots.

Evening by candlelight. Petrov's speech is brusque. He responds to the request of a divisional commander to postpone the attack because of the loss of men: 'Tell him I'll postpone it when he's the only one left.' Then we played dominoes for a long time – Petrov, Shlyapin, a fat-cheeked pretty nurse called Valya, and I. The army commander puts his dominoes on the table with a bang and puts his palm over them, like a real player. From time to time a major arrives from the operations department bringing reports.

Morning. Breakfast. Petrov isn't hungry. He has a glass [of vodka]. 'It's been allowed by the Minister,' he says with a grin. [A ration of one hundred grams of vodka a day had been authorised.]

Before going to the forward division, the general plays with the cats. We go to the divisional headquarters first, and then to one of the regiments. We leave the car and walk in a field of wet clay. Our feet get stuck in the mud. Petrov shouts Spanish words which sound out of place here, under these autumn skies, on this wet ground.[2] The regiment is in combat. It fails to seize the village. There is the noise of sub-machine- and machine-gun fire, the whistling of bullets. The army commander severely reprimands the regimental commander: 'If you fail to capture this village within an hour, you will have to give up your regiment and take part in the attack as a private.' The regimental commander answers: 'Yes, Comrade Army Commander.' His hands are shaking. There isn't a single man walking upright. Men are running stooping low or crawling on all fours from one hole to another. They are afraid of bullets, and there aren't any bullets. They are all covered in mud and wet. Shlyapin is walking around as if on a country stroll and shouts to the soldiers: 'Bend lower, cowards, bend lower!'

When we arrive at the second regiment, its headquarters are empty. There are three clean cats in the empty house and lots of weapons and icons.

After dinner, the military prosecutor arrives from 50th Army [rear] headquarters. We are all drinking tea with raspberry jam while the prosecutor reports on pending cases: cowards, deserters – among them Pochepa, an old major – [also] cases of peasants accused of [circulating] German propaganda. Petrov pushes his glass aside. In the corner of the document, he approves the death sentence in red capitals written in a small childish hand.

The prosecutor reports on another case: a woman who urged peasants to greet Germans with bread and salt.

'And who is she?' Petrov asks.

'An old maid,' the prosecutor laughs.

Petrov laughs, too. 'Well, since she's an old maid, I'll replace it with ten years.' And he writes in the new sentence. Then they drink

2 General Petrov had been one of the Soviet 'advisers' attached under 'Operatsii X' to the Republican Army during the Spanish Civil War.

more tea. The prosecutor says goodbye. 'Remind them to send my samovar from headquarters,' Petrov tells him. 'I am used to having it around.'

Grossman clearly had far more respect for Brigade Commissar Nikolai Alekseevich Shlyapin than for Petrov.

Shlyapin is intelligent, strong, calm, big and slow. People sense his inner power over them.

This visit to 50th Army headquarters later proved important to Grossman's work. During their long conversations, Shlyapin told Grossman the story of his experiences in the 94th Rifle Division during the terrible summer of the Nazi invasion. A month after the outbreak of war, his division had been part of the smashed Western Front, commanded by General Pavlov. The remains of the division had been attempting to escape encirclement in Belorussia and retreat eastwards to Vitebsk, when they were attacked by the 20th Panzer Division in late July. They had to retreat into the forest, then fight their way out. Shlyapin's account was inevitably coloured by the Soviet formulae of the time and by exaggerated figures of enemy strengths and losses, yet the basic facts and the heroism of Shlyapin's leadership were almost certainly accurate. Grossman used the notes from these conversations the following year in *The People Immortal*. Shlyapin's death a month after the visit made him yet more determined to honour his memory.

Shlyapin told me all this when we were lying on some hay in a shed. There was thundering all around. Afterwards in the same shed the girl Valya[3] wound up the gramophone and we listened to 'The Little Blue Shawl'.[4] Slim aspens were trembling from explosions, and tracer bullets soared into the sky.

At the end of the month, Grossman heard from his father that at least his daughter Katya was safe.

3 Valya was probably the 'campaign wife' of General Petrov. Grossman later fulminates on the practice, widespread among senior officers, of selecting mistresses from their headquarters and medical staff in this way.
4 'The Little Blue Shawl' was a famous song about the promise of a soldier's girlfriend never to forget him when he departs for the front. She is wearing a modest blue shawl as she waves goodbye. The music was by G. Peterburgsky, the words by Yakov Galitsky. It is interesting, considering Stalin's subsequent attack on Jews as 'cosmopolitans', that most of the Soviet Union's popular patriotic songs during the war were written by Jews.

My dear [Father], I've received several postcards at once, and two of them were from you. It was the first news that I have had for two months. I am very happy that Katyusha is well, but my sorrow about Mama is now doubled . . . I am longing to see you, but it is out of the question until the chiefs summon me back.

FIVE

Back into the Ukraine

On 20 September, Grossman and Troyanovsky set off southwards again, to Glukhov in the extreme north-eastern Ukraine, which they had passed through on their escape from Gomel.

Stalin's refusal to face up to the danger of encirclement round Kiev meant that Guderian's Second Panzer Group had linked up with Kleist's First Panzer Group near Lokhvitsa. General Kirponos's South-Western Front, consisting of the 5th, 21st, 26th and 37th Armies was cut off. Stalin's old crony, Marshal Budenny escaped, as did Nikita Khrushchev and General Timoshenko. Some 15,000 troops managed to slip through the German cordon, but the remaining half-million were condemned to a terrible fate of starvation, disease and exposure in Wehrmacht prison camps.

Despite the military situation, most Ukrainian civilians were reluctant to be evacuated eastwards to the Volga region. Grossman himself, although born and brought up in the Ukrainian town of Berdichev, saw these Ukrainian peasants almost as foreigners since he had never had any contact at all with rural life.

Ukrainians had suffered in the civil war which had raged back and forth across their lands, and above all in the terrible famines triggered by Stalin's policy to suppress the rich peasants or kulaks, and enforce the collectivisation of farms. Accordingly, many Ukrainians were prepared to welcome German troops as liberators. Grossman would later discover that Ukrainian volunteer police had even played a significant role in rounding up Jews in Berdichev, including his mother and their friends, and assisted in their massacre.

> Out in the fields. Wind, wind, wind. Cold. Nature is waiting for snow. Women, cold, in sackcloths. They are rebelling. They don't want to leave this place and go to the Volga German Republic with their little children. Some have five or six children.
>
> They raise their sickles. The sickles shine dully in the grey autumn light. Their eyes are crying. The next moment, the women laugh

and swear, but then their anger and grief returns. They shout: 'An old man, he's got two sons, lieutenants. He hung himself yesterday. He didn't want to go to the Volga German Republic. Germans will get us there, too. They'll get us anywhere. We won't leave, we'd rather die here. If any lousy snake comes to force us out of our homes, we'll meet him with sickles.'

The next moment one says: 'When you haven't got a man, you can take a cat and purr with it all night long.'

'Look at the sky. Cranes are flying south. And we, where shall we go? Comrades, please help us.'

Oh, women! These eyes of women in danger – alive, excited, angry, childish, and you can see murder in them. Women had carried rusks to their men in Kursk, which is two hundred kilometres away.

The secretary of the local Raikom [the district Party Committee]: 'Come and visit me, my friends. I've got spirits and women who aren't too old.'

Second night. A telephone rang. For a moment I thought it was for me. The Germans were thudding away. We lit a fire in the stove. The poignant heartache of somebody else's stove. A sweet little girl with intelligent, dark eyes says softly: 'You're sitting in Daddy's place.' Girls. They are cursing Hitler, who's taken away their boyfriends, their music, their dancing and singing.

Troops are moving in the darkness. A girl runs to look at them: 'To search for my brother.' She looks like a doll, with a round face, blue eyes and a doll's lips. These lips say the following about a one-year-old girl who is crying: 'It will be just as well if she dies. One mouth less.'

A wounded soldier was brought here last night. He was gasping for breath, and cried. Two women wept together with him all night long, they were cutting his bandages which were swollen with blood. He began to feel better. The men were afraid to take him to the hospital at night. He lay there until dawn came.

Edinolochniks [individual peasant farmers] are whitewashing their *khatas* [simple Ukrainian houses]. They look at us with a challenge in their eyes: 'It's Easter.'

37

The implication behind this strange remark in autumn was the hint that they were celebrating the arrival of the most joyful moment of the year. Some historians have suggested that the Germans, with black crosses on their vehicles, were seen as bringing Christian liberation to a population oppressed by Soviet atheism. Many Ukrainians did welcome the Germans with bread and salt, and many Ukrainian girls consorted cheerfully with German soldiers. It is hard to gauge the scale of this phenomenon in statistical terms, but it is significant that the *Abwehr*, the Germany Army intelligence department, recommended that an army of a million Ukrainians should be raised to fight the Red Army. This was firmly rejected by Hitler who was horrified at the suggestion of Slavs fighting in Wehrmacht uniform.

> The village of Kamenka. A house owned by three women. They speak in a mixture of Ukrainian and Russian. They went to look at the captured Germans. One of them, wearing spectacles, is a painter. Another one is a student. He would get up, entertain a baby for a while and lie down again. An old woman was constantly asking: 'Is it true that Germans believe in God?' Apparently, there are many rumours about German [occupation] circulating in the village. 'Starostas are cutting strips of land,' and so forth.[1]
>
> We spent the whole evening explaining to them what Germans really are. They listened, sighed, exchanged glances, but clearly did not express their secret thoughts. The old woman said quietly: 'We've seen what's been, we'll see what comes.'

> The head of the driver of a heavy tank had been torn off by a shell, and the tank came back driving itself because the dead driver was pressing the accelerator. The tank drove through the forest breaking trees and reached our village. The headless driver was still sitting in it.

During his time near Glukhov, Grossman learned about the 395th Rifle Regiment commanded by Major Babadzhanyan fighting desperately on a tiny piece of land on the west bank of the Kleven River. 'Grossman decided to write about this heroic regiment,' wrote Ortenberg, 'and wanted

---

1 In tsarist times there were church starostas and village starostas, usually the richest and thus the most influential peasants. The Germans reintroduced the system to use them as local mayors. 'Cutting strips of land' meant dividing up the hated collective farms and putting fields back into private cultivation by individual families.

Ukrainian women taking home the bodies of their menfolk.

to get across the river to join Babadzhanyan. The political department did not allow this, despite Grossman's protests. When Grossman later enquired about the fate of the 395th Regiment, he was told that the regiment had fulfilled its task with valour, but suffered great losses, and its commander, Major Babadzhanyan, was among those killed. Grossman described this in *The People Immortal* leaving the commander's name unchanged.'

Grossman also wrote of these events just after the war because Major Babadzhanyan became a symbol for him of the Red Army's ability to surmount such a terrible disaster.

The first time that we, military correspondents, heard the name Babadzhanyan was in the Ukraine, during the hard days of September of 1941, near the town of Glukhov. Overripe, heavy wheat was standing in the fields. Fruit was falling from the trees, tomatoes were rotting in the vegetable gardens, cucumbers and juicy cabbage were wilting, unpicked corn ears were drying out on the tall stems. Clearings in the forest were covered by a patterned carpet, boletus mushrooms showed under the trees and in the grass.

Life for the people was terrible in that generous Ukrainian autumn. At night, the sky became red from dozens of distant fires, and a grey screen of smoke hung all along the horizon during the day. Women with children in their arms, old men, herds of sheep, cows and collective farm horses sinking in the dust were moving east on the country roads, by cart and on foot. Tractor drivers drove their machines which rattled deafeningly. Trains with factory equipment, engines and boilers went east day and night.

Thousands of German aircraft droned in the sky continually. The earth moaned under the steel caterpillars of German tracked vehicles. These steel caterpillars crawled through marshes and rivers, tortured the earth and crushed human bodies. German officers who had studied in academies led their fascist battalions and regiments eastwards, through smoke and dust.

Babadzhanyan first saw German infantry in the summer of 1941, when our troops surrendered Smolensk. One red-cheeked [German] officer, a dandy, who wanted to escape from the dust raised by thousands of boots and wheels, turned off the road. No one heard the muffled shot because of the noise of wheels, neighing of horses, heavy sniffing of vehicle engines. The officer fell into some bushes. A few minutes later, Babadzhanyan was holding in his hands the documents of the dead man. Among them was a new leather-bound notepad. On its first page, German phrases and their Russian translations were written: 'You are a prisoner'; 'Hands up'; 'What is the name of this village?'; 'How many kilometres to Moscow?'

Babadzhanyan looked at the grey, tired faces of his reconnaissance men, looked at the grey houses of the village, so defenceless and small, looked at the incessant flow of German troops, and suddenly, seized by pain, anger and anxiety, took a stump of red pencil from his pocket and wrote in big letters across a notepad page: 'You'll never see Moscow! The day will come when we will ask you: "How many kilometres to Berlin?"'

The situation in those days was so desperate then that everyone, Grossman included, was happy to believe almost any rumour about German problems and low morale. Most of these stories, particularly anything involving the SS and Gestapo forcing German soldiers to fight, were optimistic, to say the least.

Germans captured by the reserve 159th Battalion say that the mood affecting everyone is to surrender. Almost all the corpses of [German] soldiers and many junior officers were found to have our leaflets and newspapers on them. Five Soviet newspapers were found on an *unteroffizier*, the first one dated 27 July. Newspapers were found with a summary of results of the two-month period, German newspapers and ours. The figures were underlined with red pencil, for comparison.

An ersatz battalion was brought up to full strength with Gestapo and SS troops. They are distributed in reserve units.

During some mortar bursts in Novaya, Germans were throwing themselves into the pond. Dozens of men drowned, including an officer. Reconnaissance men report that terrible screams were heard.

Up to 1,500 [German] fatal casualties registered, all others were taken away by Germans. Reports about big field hospitals in the area of Kletnya, hospitals in which there are up to 4,000 wounded Germans. Germans do not take them away, there's an influx of them.

Reconnaissance mission on the 11th. Six men led by Sergeant Nikolaev, and Red Army soldier Dedyulya – to get a 'tongue'.[2] Nikolaev learned from locals about vehicle movement. They organised an ambush in the forest by the road. They threw grenades at the last three motocyclists. Dedyulya killed two motocyclists and captured [a German soldier named] Alvin Gunt.

Grossman heard a joke about a German armoured vehicle abandoned by the roadside. A boy 'with one cube' [i.e. a second lieutenant] was sitting in it.

'You will be fired at,' [the lieutenant is warned].

'But by whom?' [he replies]. 'The Germans will think it's their vehicle, and our men will see it and run away.' Sad humour.

The sky has become German. We've seen none of our aircraft for weeks.

This note was inside the improvised locket of Lieutenant Miroshnikov who was killed: 'If someone is brave enough to remove the contents of this locket, could they send this to the following

---

2 A 'tongue' was Red Army slang for an enemy soldier, usually a sentry or rations carrier, who was seized by a patrol for interrogation.

address . . . "My sons, I am in another world now. Join me here, but first you must take revenge on the enemy for my blood. Forward to victory, and you, friends, too, for our Motherland, for glorious Stalin's deeds.'"

The brigade commissar's story:

A supply officer of the second rank, who had recently escaped having been cut off behind enemy lines, all of a sudden shot the commissar and commander of his rifle regiment whom he had suspected of espionage. He took their belongings and money, and buried the bodies in a shed. This supply officer was shot in front of officers from the division. He was shot by the man who was the most senior in age, a colonel.

Grossman could not resist local details of human interest, even if they had nothing to do with the war.

An old woman. She has three mute sons. All three are hairdressers. 'The oldest one is half a century old,' [she said]. 'They fight like hell and squabble like horses, they grab knives and fly at one another all the time.'

House painters or stonemasons, when they are angry with an employer, brick up into a wall an egg or a box with cockroaches (with some bran for them to eat). The egg stinks and the cockroaches rustle. This torments the owners.

During the last week of September, Grossman was present at the almost farcically inept interrogation of a captured Austrian motorcyclist. The intelligence officer failed to act upon their prisoner's boast of hundreds of German tanks in the area. It was only later that Grossman realised that these must have been part of Guderian's Second Panzer Group, redeploying after the Kiev encirclement for their next attack. Purely by luck, Grossman and Troyanovsky managed to keep ahead of Guderian's tanks over the next couple of weeks, only just avoiding capture on several occasions. Grossman's status as a war correspondent would not have saved him. He would almost certainly have been treated as a 'Jewish commissar' and shot.

In Ermakov's group. Village of Pustogorod.[3] Political department.
A girl – a Jewish beauty who has managed to escape from the
Germans – has bright, absolutely insane eyes.

A [Wehrmacht] motorcyclist is being interrogated at night in the
house where the political department is stationed. He is Austrian,
tall, good-looking. Everyone admires his long, soft, steel-coloured
leather coat. Everyone is touching it, shaking their heads. This means:
how on earth can one fight people who wear such a coat? Their
aircraft must be as good as their leather coats. The interpreter is a
Jew, barely literate. He is speaking in Yiddish. The Austrian is
muttering in his language. They are both sweating from their desire
to understand each other, but sweating seems to be the only result.
The interrogation proceeds with difficulty. The Austrian, turning
now and then to look at the door, is thumping his chest and
recounting that he has seen a vast accumulation of Guderian's tanks
in this area, a huge number – 'five hundred! Here, here, right near
you.' He shows how close they are with his hand.

'What did he say?' the intelligence officer asks impatiently. The
interpreter shrugs his shoulders in an embarrassed way. 'He saw
some tanks, up to five hundred of them.'

'Oh, to hell with him. He must tell us names of settlements
through which his unit has driven from Germany to the front,' says
this big intelligence officer, studying his questionnaire. Oh, these
highly qualified people![4]

Night in a house of female teachers. An apartment of intellectuals:
there are books that I used to read which evoke a lot of memories.
The books of my childhood. And there are objects from my childhood, too: ashtrays made from seashells, candlelights, albums, wall
clocks. A palm tree in a tub . . . During the night, Kolomeitsev
and I were suddenly seized by an insane anxiety. We woke up as if
we had been ordered to, dressed and went out into the yard. We
listened in silence for a long time. The west was silent. The Germans
are fifteen kilometres away from here.

3 Pustogorod in the Oblast of Sumy is about fifty kilometres north-north-east of Glukhov.
4 Establishing the exact path of German units from the Soviet frontier was one of the highest
priorities of Soviet prisoner interrogations. This was to establish which Wehrmacht units to connect
to which massacres. The information obtained played a large part in the post-war trials of German
generals.

Grossman then returned via Sevsk (120 kilometres south of Bryansk) on his way back to Orel.

> Sevsk. We were told that a German armoured vehicle was here yesterday. Two officers got out, looked around and then drove off. And this place is supposed to be far behind the front line.

Grossman and Troyanovsky were still not fully aware of the danger. They drove on north towards Orel. Whenever they stopped, even just for a moment, civilians asked for news.

> An old man asks: 'Where are you retreating from?'

The German Capture of Orel

By the time Grossman and Troyanovsky returned to Orel, it too was in danger. Operation Typhoon, the Wehrmacht drive on Moscow, began on 30 September with Guderian's assault against the Bryansk Front commanded by General Yeremenko. General Petrov's 50th Army, which Grossman had so recently visited, was cut off by the German 2nd Army. Orel itself was threatened by Guderian's XXIV Panzer Corps.

Grossman's account, beginning on 2 October, partly contradicts the usual version of the capture of Orel. This claims that the German tanks raced with total surprise into the city in the late afternoon of 3 October, overtaking trams in the street. Even though the military authorities were astonishingly complacent, his descriptions indicate that large numbers of civilians were well aware of the danger and were attempting to flee before the German panzer troops arrived.

Orel, Orel once again. There are aircraft over it. Trucks. People carry children in their arms. Children sitting on bundles. [There is a constant] rattling noise during the night: the city is on the move. We are in a hotel once again. It is a normal provincial hotel, but now it seems an extremely nice one after all the travelling, because it is such an ordinary, such a peaceful one.

There is a school map of Europe. We go to look at it. We are terrified at how far we have retreated. I am approached in the corridor by a photo-journalist called Redkin whom I'd met at front head-quarters. He looks alarmed. 'The Germans are rushing straight for Orel. There are hundreds of tanks. I had a narrow escape under fire. We must leave immediately, otherwise they'll catch us here.' And he tells us how he was sitting in a very quiet rear headquarters having dinner, when suddenly they heard a noice. They looked out the window and saw an NKVD man running past. He was covered in flour. It turned out that he had been driving along a few kilometres away, completely unaware of how close the Germans were, when suddenly a tank turned its turret and fired, hitting the truck in which he was carrying sacks of flour. 'Tanks are everywhere!' Redkin got into a car and rushed to Orel. German tanks were advancing along the same road, and there was no resistance. Redkin tells us this news in a frightened, hissing whisper.

I go to the room where two officers I know are staying: a bearded major and a captain from the operations department. I ask whether they know anything about the German breakthrough. They look at me, their eyes filled with a pig-headed, self-confident stupidity. 'That's nonsense,' they say and continue drinking.

The city is rumbling all night long, vehicles and carts move without stopping. In the morning the city is gripped by horror and agony, almost like typhus. There's weeping and commotion in our hotel. I try to pay for my room. No one wants to take the money, but I force the woman on duty to take seven roubles, I don't know why. People with sacks and suitcases are running past in the street, some carrying children. The major, 'the great strategist', and the captain scurry past me, their faces sheepish. We go to the headquarters of the military district, but they won't let us in without passes. Clerks and lower-ranking officials are completely calm. We are told that passes can be issued only after 10 a.m. We have to wait for an hour, and the chiefs will not turn up before 11. Oh, how I know this unshakeable calmness that originates from ignorance and which can in no time turn into a hysterical fear and panic. I have seen all this before – in Gomel, Bezhitsk, Shchors, Mena, Chernigov, Glukhov.

We come across a colonel we know. 'Is it possible to get to Front headquarters by the Bryansk highway?'

'Maybe,' he says, 'but most likely German tanks have already reached that sector.'

After that we visit the *banya* [for a steam bath] and then set off on the Bryansk highway. Never say die! A female military doctor of Georgian origin comes with us. She also needs to reach the rear echelon of Front headquarters. She sings love songs all the way in an extremely artificial voice. She recently arrived from the rear areas and hasn't the slightest idea of the danger we are in. All of us, her audience, are all the time looking over to the left, as if twisted. The road is empty, there isn't a single vehicle, not a single pedestrian, no peasant carts, everything is dead! There is a dreadful air about these deserted roads along which our last units have just passed and the first enemy ones may appear at any minute. The empty road is like an abandoned no man's land between our lines and the Germans.

We make it safely [to] Bryansk forest, which seems to us almost like the family home. German tanks were following us on the very same highway just two hours behind. The Germans entered Orel at six in the evening by the Kromy road [from the south]. Perhaps they washed in the same *banya* which had been heated for us that morning.

In our *izba* that night, I suddenly remember the interrogation, by the light of a wick lamp, of the Austrian in the luxurious leather coat. It was these very tanks that he had been talking about!

Grossman, on this evening of 3 October 1941, still did not know that one of Guderian's panzer columns was cutting off General Yeremenko's Bryansk Front from the rear and that they were far from safe where they were in the forest. Within two days the Bryansk Front was virtually demolished. Yeremenko spent most of the night of 5 October waiting for a telephone call from Stalin authorising a more 'mobile defence' – a euphemism for withdrawal. And in the early hours of 6 October, his own headquarters realised that it too was under threat. The Germans had nearly sealed the last escape route.

The staff commissar summoned us and said: 'At 4 a.m., not a minute later, you must set off on the following route.' He didn't bother to give us any explanation, but it wasn't necessary anyway. It was all clear, particularly after we looked at the map. Our headquarters was caught in a sack. Germans were advancing on the right to Sukhinichi and on the left to Bolkhov from Orel, and we were sitting in a forest near Bryansk. We went back to our lodge and started packing: mattresses, chairs, lamp, sacks. Thrifty Petlyura even fetched a supply of cranberries from the attic. We loaded everything on to the truck given to us by General Yeremenko and set off precisely at 4 a.m. under a clear cold sky by the light of autumn stars. We were in a race. Either we had to get out of the sack first, or the Germans would tie it up while we were still inside.

The 50th Army, with whom Grossman had been earlier, tried to fight its way out of the Bryansk forest. Brigade Commissar Shlyapin, like General Petrov, was caught in the encirclement. Petrov died from gangrene in a woodcutter's hut deep in the forest near Belev. The manner of Shlyapin's death remains unclear, which is no doubt why Grossman wanted to include him in *The People Immortal*. On 4 October, Grossman and his companions found themselves far from alone in their determination to escape.

I thought I'd seen retreat, but I've never seen anything like what I am seeing now, and could never even imagine anything of the kind. Exodus! Biblical exodus! Vehicles are moving in eight lanes, there's the violent roaring of dozens of trucks trying simultaneously to tear their wheels out of the mud. Huge herds of sheep and cows are driven through the fields. They are followed by trains of horse-driven carts, there are thousands of wagons covered with coloured sackcloth, veneer, tin. In them are refugees from Ukraine. There are also crowds of pedestrians with sacks, bundles, suitcases.

This isn't a flood, this isn't a river, it's the slow movement of a flowing ocean, this flow is hundreds of metres wide. Children's heads, fair and dark, are looking out from under the improvised tents covering the carts, as well as the biblical beards of Jewish elders, shawls of peasant women, hats of Ukrainian uncles, and the black-haired heads of Jewish girls and women. What silence is in their eyes, what wise sorrow, what sensation of fate, of a universal catastrophe!

In the evening, the sun comes out from the multilayered blue, black and grey clouds. Its rays are wide, stretching from the sky down to the ground, as in Doré's paintings depicting those frightening biblical scenes when celestial forces strike the Earth. This movement of elders, of women carrying babies in their arms, of herds of sheep and of warriors seems in these broad yellow sunrays so majestic and so tragic. There are moments when I feel with complete vividness as if we have been transported back in time to the era of biblical catastrophes.

Everyone keeps looking up into the sky, but not because they are waiting for the Messiah. They are watching out for German bombers. Suddenly there are shouts: 'Here they are! They're coming, they are coming straight for us!'

Dozens of aerial boats are gliding in the sky, slowly and smoothly, in triangular ranks. They are moving towards us. Dozens, hundreds of people climb over the sides of trucks, jump out of cabins, run towards the forest. Everyone is infected with panic, the running crowd is growing bigger every minute. And then everyone hears the shrill voice of a woman: 'Cowards, cowards, they are just cranes flying over!' Confusion.

Staying the night in Komarichi. Some of the staff have arrived. The colonel advises us not to go to sleep and to visit him every hour. He himself knows absolutely nothing, he has no means of communication, and with whom, anyway, would he communicate? Troyanovsky had said he would keep visiting the colonel, but suddenly he disappears, we are furious, then alarmed: the lad has disappeared, and there's no sign of him. Lysov and I take turns to go and see the colonel, and in the pauses we keep looking out of the window and develop dozens of theories for Troyanovsky's disappearance. I go out into the yard and suddenly hear some muffled noises coming from our Emka automobile. I open the door. Our missing youth is there enjoying the company of our landlady's niece. I embarrassed them and they embarrassed me. I removed Troyanovsky from the car and he received a severe reprimand from us in the house. 'Do you realise what sort of situation we are all in, you young fool, how dare you!'

Yes, he understands everything and agrees with everything. He is very sorry. There's a sweet, pacified expression in his face. He is yawning, stretching. This is probably what makes us so angry. We haven't had even half as good a time as he has. The niece comes back to the *izba*. Oh, there's calmness and peace in her face. One could paint [pictures entitled] 'Innocence', 'Purity', 'Morning'. This makes us furious. We have to move on again at dawn.

The race is continuing: who is faster, the Germans or us? We give a lift in our truck to the medical personnel from a regional hospital. The doctors aren't used to walking. They are utterly exhausted. We give them a lift to Belev. The elderly doctor thanks us touchingly with lofty phrases like: 'You've saved our lives.' The old *noblesse oblige*.[1] The 'doctoresses' don't even say goodbye to us. They pick up their bundles and hurry to the platform of the railway station.

Belev, with a steep drive into the town, horrendous mud, narrow and not so narrow streets, is unable to receive the whole mass pouring in from village roads. Lots of mad rumours are circulating, ridiculous and absolutely panic-stricken. Suddenly, there is a mad storm

---

1 In the original, *blagorodnaya kost*, literally 'noble bone'.

of firing. It turns out that someone has switched on the street lights, and soldiers and officers opened rifle and pistol fire at the lamps in order to put them out. If only they had fired like this at the Germans. Those who don't know the reason for this shooting flee in all directions. They think that the Germans have broken through. What else could it be?

We sleep in a monstrously poor room. Such terrible, black poverty is only possible in a town, in a slum. The landlady, a real mastodon with a husky voice, rattles, swears, hisses at children and objects. I thought – we all thought – her a fury, a spawn of hell, but then we see that she is kind, generous, caring. With what anxiety she makes us rag beds on the floor, and how she treats us to the food!

At night, in the darkness I hear someone sobbing. 'Who's that?' The landlady replies in a husky whisper: 'It's me. I've got seven children, I am lamenting them.' This poverty, this urban poverty is somehow worse than the village sort. It's deeper and blacker, an all-embracing poverty, deprived even of air and light.

In an *izba*, there are peacetime newpapers pasted on the walls instead of wallpaper. We look at them and say: 'Look, it's all about peacetime.' Yesterday we saw a house with wartime newpapers instead of wallpaper. If that house survives, people will one day remark: 'Look at these wartime newspapers!'

We spend the night near Belev, in the house of a young teacher. She is very pretty and very silly, an absolute lamb. A girlfriend of hers is staying there for the night, too. She is also very young but not so pretty. They talk throughout the night in a whisper, arguing passionately. In the morning we learn that our teacher is going to abandon the house and move east, while her friend has decided to go west to join her relatives who are living on the other side of Belev. That means to return to [enemy] occupied territory.

Our teacher asks us to give her a lift. We agree. I call our one-and-a-half-ton truck the Noah's Ark. It has already saved so many dozens of people from the flood that came from the west. The two friends' eyes are red in the morning from weeping all night. These days everyone cries at night and is calm, indifferent and patient in the daytime. We pack our things, and our young landlady comes out to the truck with a tiny bundle. She does not want to take her mirror, her curtains, her perfume bottles, not even her dresses. 'I don't need anything,' she says. I think I've underestimated the spiritual wisdom in this eighteen-year-old girl.

We try to persuade her friend to go with us. Her face is dead, the lips are pressed together tightly, she says nothing and does not look at us. The two friends say goodbye coldly, they don't even shake hands.

'Start the engine, let's go!' Yes, the problems these eighteen-year-old girls now have to resolve are no trifle. At the last minute, we go into the sweet little room of the girl who is already sitting in the truck. It is nobody's room now. We polish our boots using face cream and white collars. I think we do that to emphasise to ourselves that life has been ruined.

SEVEN

The Withdrawal before Moscow

Stalin did not react to the growing disaster on the Bryansk Front until 5 October. That was the day when a fighter patrol of Red Army aviation spotted a German armoured column, some twelve miles long, advancing on Yukhno. The *Stavka*, the Red Army general staff headquarters in Moscow, refused to accept this report and a subsequent confirmation. Beria even wanted to arrest the air force officer concerned and accuse him of spreading defeatism, but Stalin finally woke up to the threat to the capital.

There was only one thing which could slow the German advance on Moscow at this stage, and that was the *rasputitsa*, the season of mud before winter set in for the duration. After a short freeze and snowfall on 6 October, a thaw rapidly followed the next morning. Grossman described the effect.

I don't think anyone has ever seen such terrible mud. There's rain, snow, hailstones, a liquid, bottomless swamp, black pastry mixed by thousands and thousands of boots, wheels, caterpillars. And everyone is happy once again. The Germans must get stuck in our hellish autumn, both in the sky and on the ground. At any rate, we have managed to escape from the sack. Tomorrow we will get on to the Tula highway.

A village near Tula. Brick houses. Night. Snow and rain. Everyone is frozen, especially those sitting in the Noah's Ark: Regimental Commissar Konstantinov, a teacher, and Baru, correspondent of *Stalinsky sokol*.[1] Lysov, Troyanovsky and I are warmer: we are travelling in the Emka. The vehicles stop in the middle of a dark village street. Petlyura, who is a real magician at procuring milk and apples and digging slit trenches, disappears into the night. But just for

1 *Stalin's Falcon*, a Red Army Aviation newspaper.

once he fails. We enter an *izba*, which is cold and dark, like a grave. In the *izba*, a seventy-year-old woman is sitting amid the cold and darkness. She is singing songs. She welcomes us merrily and eagerly, like a young person, without grunting or whining, although, apparently, she has all the reasons to complain about her fate.

Her daughter, a factory worker, brought her to this village to stay with her son and went back to Moscow. The son, who is the chairman of the collective farm here, couldn't allow her to stay in his house because his wife wouldn't let him. This wife has also forbidden her husband to help his mother, and the old woman is living off what kind people give her. Sometimes the son secretly brings her a little millet or potatoes. The younger son, Vanya, had been working at a plant in Tula. He volunteered. He was fighting near Smolensk, [but] she hasn't had any letters from him for a month. Vanya is her favourite.

She tells us the whole story in a kindly, calm voice, without any bitterness, resentment, pain or reproach. With a tsarina-like generosity, she gives all that she has to our frozen horde: a dozen logs which would have lasted her for a week, a handful of salt, leaving not a single grain for herself, half a bucket of potatoes. She keeps only a dozen, along with her pillow, a sack stuffed with straw, and her torn blanket. She brings a kerosene lamp. When our drivers want to pour some petrol into it, she does not allow this. 'You will need this petrol yourselves.' And she brings a tiny bottle in which she keeps her sacred reserve of kerosene and pours it into the lamp.

Having graced us with warmth, food, light and soft beds, she retires to the cold part of the *izba*. She sits down there and begins singing.

I went to her and said: 'Babushka, are you going to sleep here in the darkness, in the cold, on bare wood?' She just waved me off with her hand. 'How do you live here alone? Do you have to sleep in the cold and dark here every night?'

'Ah well, I sit in the dark, sing songs, or tell stories to myself.' She boiled a cast-iron pot of potatoes, we ate and went to sleep, and she started singing to us in a hoarse voice, like an old man's.

'Oh, I used to be so healthy, like a stallion,' she told me. 'The Devil came to me last night and gripped my palm with his fingernails. I began to pray: "May God rise again and may His enemies be scattered." And the Devil paid no attention. Then I began to swear and curse at him and he went away immediately. My Vanya came to me last night. He sat down on a chair and looked at the window. I said to him: "Vanya, Vanya!," but he didn't reply.'

If we do win in this terrible, cruel war, it will be because there are such noble hearts in our nation, such righteous people, souls of immense generosity, such old women, mothers of sons who, from their noble simplicity, are now losing their lives for the sake of their nation with the same generosity with which this old woman from Tula has given us all that she had. There is only a handful of them in our land, but they will win.

The regal generosity of this pauper has shaken all of us. In the morning we leave her all our supplies, and our drivers, in a frenzy of kindness, loot the whole area and bring her so much firewood and potatoes that she will be able to last till spring on them. 'What an old woman,' Petlyura says when we set off, and shakes his head.

Soon after reaching the Orel–Tula road, Grossman spotted a sign to Yasnaya Polyana, the Tolstoy estate, some twenty kilometres south of Tula. He persuaded his companions that they should visit it. As things turned out, the next visitor after them would be General Guderian, who decided to turn the writer's home into his headquarters for the assault on Moscow.

Yasnaya Polyana. I suggested we take a look at it. The Emka turned off the panic-stricken highway, and the Noah's Ark followed. One could see the green roofs and white walls of the houses amid the curly gold of the autumnal park. The gate. Chekhov, when he first came here, only managed to walk up to this gate and then turned away, intimidated by the thought that he would meet Tolstoy in a few minutes. He walked back to the station and returned to Moscow. The road leading to the house is paved by countless red, orange and yellow leaves. This is so beautiful. The more lovely the surroundings, the sadder one feels in times like these.

There's an angry, pre-departure confusion in the house. Piles of boxes. Bare walls. Suddenly I feel with a terrible intensity that this place has turned into Lysye Gory, which the old and sick Prince is about to leave.[2] Everything has combined to produce an entirely new image, the events that occurred a century ago and those happening

2 Prince Bolkonsky in *War and Peace* had to leave his house of Lysye Gory on the approach of Napoleon's Grande Armée.

today, and what the book tells with such strength and truthfulness about the old Prince Bolkonsky now seems to refer to the old Count Tolstoy himself and has become inseparable from reality.

Meeting with Sofya Andreevna.[3] She is calm and depressed. [She] says that the secretary of the local Party Committee has promised to provide her with railway carriages to evacuate the museum, but she isn't sure that it is still possible, now that the Germans are so close and are advancing so fast. We talk about Moscow and friends who have passed away, and then we remain silent for a while thinking of their unfortunate fate. Then we discuss the theme that everyone is now talking about with pain, bewilderment and sorrow: the retreat.

Tolstoy's grave. Roar of fighters over it, humming of explosions and the majestic calm autumn. It is so hard. I have seldom felt such pain.

Tula, seized with that deadly fever, the tormenting, terrible fever we've seen in Gomel, Chernigov, Glukhov, Orel and Bolkhov. Is this really happening to Tula? Complete confusion. An officer finds me in the Voentorg military canteen. He asks me to come to the OBKOM. A representative of the *Stavka* who is there at the moment would like to find out from me where the headquarters of the Bryansk Front is at the moment, as he needs to send units there. Fragments of divisions are arriving. They say that only part of the 50th Army has managed to escape the encirclement. Where is Petrov, and Shlyapin? Where is Valya, the girl nurse who played dominoes with us and wound up the gramophone to play 'The Little Blue Shawl'?

The streets are filled with people, they are walking on pavements and in the road and still there isn't enough room. Everyone is dragging bundles, baskets and suitcases. At the hotel where we are given a room we run into all the other correspondents. Krylov with whom we had bolted from the Central Front is here too. The correspondents have already made themselves at home in the hotel. Some have embarked on blitz affairs.

We say goodbye to our travelling companion, the teacher whose face cream and collars we used to clean our boots. This night our

3   Leo Tolstoy's granddaughter.

truck performs the function of Noah's Ark for the last time: we give
a lift to the railway station to the families of people from the Tula
office of the newspaper,[4] with their belongings. Petlyura is angry:
'We should have made them pay.' But Seryozha Vasiliev, who drives
the Noah's Ark, is against it. He is a wonderfully kind, sweet and
modest fellow.

Suddenly during the night, a conversation with Moscow on a direct
line. Order to go to Moscow. Violent, irrational joy. Sleepless night.

In the battered Emka, the two-hundred-kilometre journey due north
from Tula to the Soviet Capital may well have taken them most of the
day.

Moscow. Barricades at the outer approaches, and also closer in,
particularly around the suburbs, as well as in the city itself.

We all had a luxurious shave [at a barber's] on Serpukhovskaya
Square. The public was kind and gentle, asking us to go first, asking
about the war. Without going home we went straight to the editorial office [of *Krasnaya Zvezda*].

The editor [Ortenberg] came to meet us. He was up in arms.
'Why have you left the headquarters of the Bryansk Front?'

'We were ordered to leave, and we left, after all the other correspondents did.'

'Why didn't you write anything about the heroic defence of
Orel?'

'Because there was no defence.'

'That's all. You may go. At six o'clock tomorrow morning you
– Grossman, Troyanovsky, Lysov – will return straight to the
front.'

People say that [Ortenberg] is a good editor. Perhaps he is. But how
come this small-town man who hasn't even completed his secondary
school education is as ambitious and arrogant towards his juniors
as a Roman patrician? After all the months we've spent at the front
he hasn't even asked his subordinates, if only out of politeness, how
they feel and whether their health is all right.

4   Presumably *Krasnaya Zvezda*.

Ortenberg later felt uneasy at the way he had behaved. This is how he recorded the events of 7 October.

The morning and evening reports from the Sovinformburo recounted the same things as at the beginning of the month: hard battles with the enemy everywhere. Nothing on the situation at the Western and Bryansk fronts. And Orel has already fallen. I learned this at the *Stavka*.

Our correspondents at the Bryansk Front, Pavel Troyanovsky and Vasily Grossman, who had arrived back from the area of Orel, confirmed this, too. I saw their Emka – dented all over by shell fragments. Staff from the editorial office had gathered round the car. They were examining it, shaking their heads, as if saying: 'Look at what these fellows have just been through! They are lucky to have got out alive.'

After they had spent enough time with their friends by the Emka, Grossman and Troyanovsky came to talk to me and told me about the disaster at the front. I listened attentively to what they had to say, but couldn't refrain from harsh words. Of course, the newspaper couldn't publish their report about the breakthrough at the Bryansk Front and the capture of Orel before the official confirmation came. We thought, however, that any battle, even a disastrous one for us, reveals the true heroes and feats, about which one should and must write!

I told Grossman and Troyanovsky point-blank: 'We don't need your shot-up Emka. We need material for the newspaper. Go back to the front!' This was probably unfair. I want to make no excuses even now when I know for sure that the special correspondents had achieved a miraculous escape from the enemy's encirclement. I had to, when looking into the lost and worried faces of these men, who were in fact brave, even courageous, to find some other words for them, to be nicer. But let us remember that time! One could not indulge in sentiment.

Grossman and Troyanovsky left at once for the I Guards Rifle Corps of Major-General D.D. Lelyushenko, which had succeeded on that very day in stopping the enemy near Mtsensk. And my remark about the shot-up Emka started circulating around the lobbies at the editorial office and even our correspondents' offices at the front.

Despite Ortenberg's order to return to the front early the next morning, Grossman managed a fleeting visit to his father that night.

> I spent some time at home [with] Papa and Zhenni Genrikhovna.[5] I spoke to Papa about my biggest worry, but I don't need to write about it. It is in my heart day and night. Is she alive? No, she isn't! I know, I feel this.

Part of Lelyushenko's I Guards Rifle Corps of two rifle divisions and two tank brigades had been airlifted to the area of Orel on Stalin's personal order to halt the German breakthrough.[6] Mtsensk, where the T-34s of the 4th Tank Brigade under Colonel Katukov counter-attacked, is fifty kilometres north-east of Orel on the road to Tula and Moscow. Both Lelyushenko and Katukov would become famous commanders of Guards Tank Armies in the assault on Berlin four years later.

> We set off in the morning along the same highway by which we had returned to Moscow yesterday. Everyone at the editorial office was indignant, complaining (in a whisper of course) that the editor hadn't allowed us even one day's rest. And the main thing is that [this hasty mission] is foolish.
>
> We rushed without respite through Serpukhov and Tula. Terrible weather. We were lying in the back of the truck, huddled against each other. Night came, but we went racing on. In Moscow we had been given the name of the settlement where the headquarters of the tank corps is situated: Starukhino. We drove and drove without rest. The radiator began to boil over, so we stopped the vehicle. The road was completely empty, we had driven dozens of kilometres without seeing a single vehicle.
>
> Suddenly a Red Army soldier steps out from behind a birch tree and asks in a husky voice: 'Where are you going?'
>
> 'To Starukhino,' we reply.
>
> 'Are you off your heads?' It turns out that the Germans have been there since yesterday. 'I am the sentry and this is the front

5 Zhenni Genrikhovna, the family's Volga German nanny, appeared in her own guise and under her own name in *Life and Fate*. She was fortunate not to have been arrested as a spy in Moscow during the panic of October 1941 as she still spoke a broken Russian with a heavy German accent.
6 LXI Guards Rifle Corps was formed on 27 September as part of the *Stavka* Reserve. It consisted of 5th Guards Rifle Division, 6th Guards Rifle Division, 4th Tank Brigade and 11th Tank Brigade. The Corps headquarters then became the basis for 5th Army.

line here. Go back quickly, before the Germans see you. They're just over there.' Naturally, we turn back. Had the radiator not boiled over, it would have been the end of our careers as journalists.

We look for the headquarters in the terrible darkness and terrible mud. Eventually we find it. It is hot and stuffy in a small *izba* filled with blue smoke. After the fourteen-hour drive we immediately feel sleepy in the warm room. We are dropping off, but there's no time. We start asking officers different questions, reading political reports, doing all this as if in a daze.

At dawn, having had no rest, we boarded the truck and returned to Moscow. Deadlines remained unrelenting. We arrived at the editorial office in the evening . . . We chain-smoked all the time to keep awake, and drank tea. We got the story down, as journalists say, and submitted our copy. The editor didn't publish a single line.

Whatever the frustrations of journalistic life, Grossman was not deterred from his persistent note-taking, whether for novels or articles.

In some villages – for example, the village of Krasnoye – the Germans built concrete pillboxes concealed inside houses. They destroyed one of the walls of a house, pushed a field gun in and built a concrete wall.

When they approach a wood, Germans start firing like madmen and then rush through it at full speed.

Germans opening fire. In the evenings they would go to the edge of a wood and open fire with sub-machine guns. Captain Baklan approached to a distance of fifty metres. He lay there watching. They spotted him. Their behaviour reminded him of madmen. They started running about with terrible shouting. Dozens of rockets soared into the air, artillery started firing without aim, machine guns started rattling away, sub-machine guns too. They were firing all over the place, and Baklan lay there watching the Germans in astonishment.

Grossman, perhaps tiring slightly of journalism, seems to have longed to convey his thoughts and feelings about the war in fictional form. At this stage, when the Soviet Union was fighting for its life, his ideas were very close to that of the Party line. It was only at Stalingrad, a year later, that his view of the Stalinist regime began to change. This outline, may well have formed part of the idea for *The People Immortal*, his novel written and published the following year:

> Sketch for a short story: 'Notes of signals officer Egorov.' Idea of the story: a young, jovial Soviet man is full of interest and curiosity when he goes to the war. In the flames of war, seeing the suffering of people, having himself suffered some personal, severe losses, he turns into a hardened, stern warrior, full of hatred for the oppressor of his people. The main theme of the story is hatred, irreconcilability. In this story, we want broadly to show the army and the fighting people, our generals, officers, soldiers, collective farmers, workers, our towns and villages, conducting the great defence. Its inner idea: the iron characters of the Soviet people, whose only fate can be victory, having become hardened in the flames of burning towns, in villages destroyed by Germans.

Egorov was probably the prototype for Ignatiev in the novel, a happy-go-lucky character turned avenger.

> 'It's a fact, Comrade Commissar,' he said, 'it's as if I've become a different person in this war: only now have I seen Russia as she really is. Honestly, I mean it. You walk along and you get to feel so sorry for every river and every bit of woodland that your heart aches . . . I thought can it really be true that this little tree will go to the Germans?'

It is very hard to track Grossman's exact movements during this period. The Soviet defenders were fortunate with the weather. Frosts and then sudden thaws turning earth roads into churned-up swamps delayed the German Army's advance. On 14 October, the 10th Panzer Division and the SS Das Reich reached the old battlefield of Borodino, 120 kilometres west of Moscow. Meanwhile, the 1st Panzer Division had seized Kalinin on the Volga north-west of the capital, and to the south Guderian's tanks had advanced round Tula. On 15 October, foreign embassies were told to prepare to abandon Moscow and leave for Kuibyshev. Panic gripped the capital. Grossman, like other war correspondents, was desperate for any examples of German demoralisation which could bring hope to readers rather than despair.

His notebooks – at least one and probably two are missing – contain little about his experiences in November, when General Georgi Zhukov ground

down the German attacks, while preparing a great counter-offensive with
fresh troops brought in from Siberia and the Far East. Stalin was finally
convinced, partly by Richard Sorge, the Soviet spy in Tokyo, but mainly
by signals intercepts, that Japan was going to attack the United States Navy
in the Pacific at Pearl Harbor, and not the Soviet Union.

In mid-November, Grossman was allowed back to Moscow, but he
was distraught to find that he had missed his father by a day. His wife,
along with the families of many members of the Writers' Union, had
been evacuated to Chistopol.

> My dear and good [Father], I was mortally upset when I arrived in
> Moscow and didn't find you there. I arrived the day after you left
> for Kuibyshev. My dear one, we shall see each other again, remember
> this. I hope for it and believe it . . . Lyusya is working hard at the
> collective farm [in Chistopol]. She's become as thin as a rail. It is
> likely that I will leave for the front soon, perhaps for the Southern
> Front.

In the end Grossman may have met up with his father in Kuibyshev,
because, according to Ilya Ehrenburg, Grossman stayed with him there
for a short time. 'We were given an apartment at that moment, and
we put up Grossman and Gabrilovich. Endless conversations went on
into the night, and during the day we sat there writing. Vasily
Semyonovich [Grossman] had been in Kuibyshev for two weeks, when
an order came from the editor of *Krasnaya Zvezda* for him to fly to
the Southern Front. He had told me a lot about confusion and about
resistance, that some units were standing firm, that grain was not being
harvested. He told me about Yasnaya Polyana. It was then that he
started his novel *The People Immortal*, and when I read it later, many
of its pages seemed to me very familiar. He found himself as a writer
during the war. His pre-war books were nothing more than searching
for his theme and language. He was a true internationalist and
reproached me frequently for saying "Germans" instead of "Hitler's
men" when describing the atrocities of the occupiers.' Ehrenburg was
persuaded that it was Grossman's all-embracing world view which made
the xenophobic Stalin hate him.

It appears that Grossman went not to the Southern Front itself, but just
north of it, to the 21st Army with the South-Western Front. The situation
in the south was as volatile as round Moscow. On 19 November, Field
Marshal von Kleist's First Panzer Group broke through to Rostov-on-Don,

the entrance to the Caucasus. But his armoured divisions were soon forced to pull back as a result of Marshal Timoshenko's counter-attacks, harsh frosts for which the German troops were not prepared and overextended supply lines. Hitler was furious, because it was the first German retreat of the war. The Soviet press reported surprisingly little. Perhaps Stalin did not want to admit that the Germans had got as far as Rostov.

On the South-Western Front, Grossman was attached to the head-quarters of the 1st Guards Rifle Division commanded by General Russiyanov.[7] None of his notebooks covering this journey remain. In any case, he missed one of the most dramatic moments in Moscow's history. The Kalinin Front to the north of the city launched its counter-attack on 5 December through snow more than a metre deep. The ground really was as hard as iron, and the Germans had to light fires under their armoured vehicles before they could start the engines. The Western Front attacked just afterwards. The rapid German retreat saved the Wehrmacht from disaster, but the Soviet capital was saved.

Although it was hard to distinguish at the time, this was the turning point of the war in the sense that the Wehrmacht stood no further chance of winning. And the United States, which was to supply the Red Army with the trucks and jeeps it needed for rapid advances in 1943 and 1944, had just entered the war. In the euphoria of the counter-attack round Moscow, Grossman sensed a new mood in Soviet ranks.

Grossman returned to Moscow on 17 December, and three days later Ortenberg remarked on his method of working. 'Vasily Grossman has returned . . . He did not manage to submit the article for the next issue of the newspaper, and we didn't ask him to hurry up. We knew how he worked. Although he had taught himself to write in any conditions, however bad, in a bunker by a wick lamp, in a field, lying in bed or in an *izba* stuffed with people, he always wrote slowly, persistently giving all of his strength to this process.' That same day, 20 December, Grossman took the chance to catch up on his own correspondence. He wrote to a friend, M.M. Shkapskaya.

'It is still too early to be looking at your son's fate in such a dark light, he is probably alive and healthy. And the post is so bad now.

---

7   The 1st Guards Rifle Division had been formed on 18 September from the 100th Rifle Division, which had been badly mauled in the retreat from Minsk and Smolensk, and then the counter-attack at Elyna, where it won its Guards designation. Lt. Gen. I.N. Russiyanov later commanded I Guards Mechanised Corps in Operation Little Saturn in December 1942 during the latter stages of the Stalingrad campaign.

There are lots of people here who cannot get in touch with their families. I am living well here, and it is interesting. I am in good spirits, the situation at the front is good, very good even . . . By the way, I very nearly lost the chance to contact my relatives ever again: I found myself under attack from five Junkers and had a narrow escape climbing out of the house which they destroyed with a bomb and machine-gun fire. Of course, you shouldn't write to Chistopol about this.

Chistopol was where his wife, Olga Mikhailovna Guber, was staying. He wrote to her too, but naturally omitted to recount his narrow escape from the air attack.

There are very nice people around me. By the way, Tvardovsky[8] is here too. He is a good chap. Could you tell his wife that he looks extremely well and everything is absolutely fine with him? I came back from the front three days ago and now I am writing. I have seen a lot. Everything is very different to how it was in the summer. There are lots of broken German vehicles on the roads and in the steppe, lots of abandoned guns, hundreds of German corpses, helmets and weapons are lying everywhere. We are advancing!

Grossman, like many Russians at this time, was convinced by the sudden turnaround in December, that the Germans, suffering so badly in their thin uniforms from the vicious winter, were collapsing under the weight of the Soviet general offensive launched by Stalin after the counter-attacks either side of Moscow. His last article for *Krasnaya Zvezda* to be published that year bore the title 'Accursed and Derided'.

When marching into European capitals, they tried to look impressive, these fascist *frontoviki*. And it was the same men who entered this Russian village one morning. There were shawls over these soldiers' heads. Some were wearing women's bonnets under their black helmets

---

8 Tvardovsky, Aleksandr Trifonich (1910–1971), poet and later editor of the literary journal *Novy Mir*, 1950–4 and 1958–70, in which he published Solzhenitsyn's *One Day in the Life of Ivan Denisovich* and *Cancer Ward*. Tvardovsky came originally from a village near Smolensk. His father, a kulak, suffered deportation under Stalin. Tvardovsky, however, had just won a Stalin Prize for his long poem *Strana Muraviya* (*The Land of Muraviya*), about a kulak who sets off on a quixotic journey to find somewhere in Russia where there were no collective farms, but finally returns home to a collective farm and happiness.

A soldier with an old woman in a newly liberated village near Moscow. The village had been occupied for about two months.

and women's knitted pantaloons. Many soldiers were dragging sledges loaded with quilts, pillows, bags with food, or old buckets.

Germans were camping in this *izba* just six hours ago. Their papers, bags, helmets are still on the table. The *izbas* that they had set on fire are still smouldering. Their bodies smashed by Soviet steel are lying around in the snow. And women, feeling that the nightmare of the last days is over at last, suddenly exclaim through sobs: 'You are our dear ones, you are back at last!'

'Well, this is how it was [one of the women recounted]. The Germans came. They knocked at the door, crowded into the house, and stood by the stove like sick dogs, their teeth chattering, shaking, putting their hands right into the stove, and their hands were red like raw meat. "Light the stove, light it!" they shouted as their teeth chattered. Well, as soon as they got warmer, they began to scratch themselves. It was awful to watch, and funny. Like dogs, scratching themselves with their paws. Lice had started moving again on their bodies because of the warmth.'

PART TWO

The Year of Stalingrad
1942

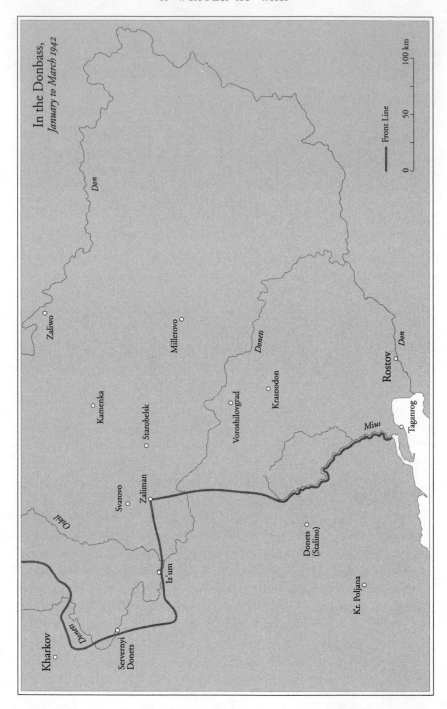

In the Donbass, January to March 1942

Kharkov · Servernyi Donets · Iz'um · Svatovo · Zaliman · Kamenka · Starobelsk · Zaliwo · Millerovo · Voroshilovgrad · Krasnodon · Donets (Stalino) · Kr. Poljana · Rostov · Taganrog · Mius

Don · Donets · Oskil · Serrvernyi Donets

In the Donbass, January to March 1942

Front Line

100 km

EIGHT

In the South

In January 1942, Grossman was sent to cover operations to the south-east of Kharkov. This appears to have been at his own request. 'Vasily Grossman persuaded me to send him to the South-Western Front,' Ortenberg wrote soon afterwards. 'This is the part of the country that he comes from.' Grossman, although not born or brought up there, knew the region from his days as a mining engineer in the Donbass. In any case, it was Grossman's articles during this period which opened Ortenberg's eyes to his talents. 'The ruthless truth of war!' he wrote. 'Vasily Grossman, whose talent as a writer was developing right in front of our eyes, remained true to it.'

Ortenberg may well have been surprised by Grossman's request. The other correspondents were keen to stay close to Moscow since everyone expected the key battles to take place on the central axis. Yet it was almost as if Grossman was drawn to the region and the enemy – the German Sixth Army – which would create the defining period of his life: in Stalingrad.

When Field Marshal von Rundstedt demanded permission from OKH, the Army High Command, to pull back to the line of the River Mius, Hitler was outraged at the idea of withdrawal. Rundstedt insisted that it was essential and offered his resignation. Hitler dismissed him and appointed Field Marshal von Reichenau, the commander of the Sixth Army and a convinced Nazi, in his place. Yet Reichenau too insisted on withdrawal to the Mius. Hitler, who flew down to see for himself, discovered to his amazement that even Sepp Dietrich, the commander of the SS Division *Leibstandarte Adolf Hitler*, was of the same mind.

Reichenau's Sixth Army had captured the Ukrainian capital of Kiev. At the end of September 1941, his troops were used to help transport 33,771 Jews to the ravine of Babi Yar outside the city, where they were systematically slaughtered by SS Sonderkommando 4a. The Sixth Army also took Kharkov, and the 38th Army, to which Grossman was attached in that January of 1942, faced them.

Division commander Lazko and his wife Sofya Efimovna.[1] Night. The *izba* is hot. Bukovsky and I enter the house after having spent the long night in the cold, travelling.

They are both extremely hospitable. There is a large assortment of home-made foods: dumplings, pastries, pickles. While we wash the cold away with water, Lazko is holding for us a white canvas towel with Ukrainian embroidery. Polyak is the chief of staff of the division. Before the war he was a high official at the Foreign Ministry. He is a rude and morose man.

Grossman went to watch the attack being prepared on the enemy-occupied village of Zaliman some twenty kilometres south of Svatovo. An earlier reconnaissance mission found that the Germans had pegged out live geese along the sector to act as a warning device. The geese made a great deal of noise.

Night. Snowstorm. Vehicles. Artillery. They are moving in silence. Suddenly a hoarse voice is heard at a road junction: 'Hey, which is the road to Berlin?' A roar of laughter.

We are able to watch a German counter-attack from a small hill. They run a few steps and then lie down. A little figure is running about, waving its arms. It's an officer. A few more steps forward, then they rush back and the figure appears again. Again, several steps forward and more rushing about. The counter-attack failed.

Dreams do come true. As soon as the Germans form up in a group: Bang! Here's a shell for them. It's Morozov, the gun-layer. As soon as there's an accumulation of Germans and one begins to think it would be wonderful to scatter them, then: Bang! A shell! Even we jump up in amazement.

The Red Army loved to vaunt any soldier who demonstrated a particular skill with his weapon, whether a sniper, a champion grenade thrower or a gun-layer like Morozov. They were exalted like Stakhanovite workers and their achievements were often wildly exaggerated in the retelling.

Battle for Zaliman, the second day. It's very cold. Haze. Artillery is firing, an ear-splitting racket. The regiment of Lieutenant Colonel

1 Major-General Grigorii Semenovich Lazko (1903–).

Elchaninov is fighting for Zaliman. They have brought field guns right into the village and hidden them behind the houses. When they spot a machine gun, they wheel the gun out, fire point-blank and then push it back behind the house.

Problems for the artillery: battle in a village. Everything has got mixed up. One house is ours, another one is theirs.

Talking to a woman: 'There were forty Germans walking – I even shut my eyes, ah, my God – straight into the village, and when I opened my eyes, some of them were lying on the ground, and some were running back.' (That was gun-layer Morozov.)

How Zaliman was taken. We leaped in when the Germans were regrouping. Some units had already left and others hadn't replaced them. We lost only three men wounded. Had we chosen a different way we would have lost thousands. The Germans had wire fences, log bunkers, concrete pillboxes, trenches and dugouts. There were even fireplaces in the bunkers tiled like those in houses. Company reconnaissance had provided detailed reports about the pillboxes. When our troops took Zaliman, these reports proved totally accurate, almost as if we had built the pillboxes ourselves.

Grossman picked up on the 'fireplaces in the bunkers tiled like those in houses', because Red Army soldiers were frequently amazed at how German troops often tried to make their defensive positions so homely. It seemed so sedentary and civilian in an army which believed in martial qualities and Blitzkrieg. Grossman joined the commander and staff of the regiment which had carried out the attack.

At the regimental command post. The *izba* has been stripped bare. The Germans had taken everything away. Chairs, beds, brooms, stools. Colonel Pesochin is fat and big. He looks like a member of the intelligentsia, but people say that he punches his subordinates in the face with his fist. He has hit the editor of the divisional newspaper.

Divisional Commissar Snitser is fat, big. They are making fun of one another all the time and constantly muffle each other up, button up each other's collars. There are jokes the whole time. German heavy artillery is firing. 'Why don't you destroy it?'

'It's hard to grasp it,' comes the jovial answer.

'Of course it's easier to grasp women.'

Grossman took down a number of these bantering exchanges of heavy military humour.

'You are growing fatter all the time, Major Kostyukov.'
'I am competing with my chief, Comrade Divisional Commander.'
'I am sure you are going to win this competition.'
'No. My weight stabilised in 1936.'
'Everyone is fat in your regiment.'
'It would be too great an honour to the Germans to lose weight because of them.'

Dinner at regimental headquarters. 'Cook, how long has it taken you to make such tiny *pelmeni*?'
'I began making them when he [a German aircraft] was diving down at us. The serpent wouldn't let me finish my *pelmeni*.'
A captain runs in while we are having dinner. 'May I report, up to three hundred [enemy] sub-machine-gunners have been sighted.'
Snitser, pouring the vodka: 'Ha-ha-ha! Divide that by ten.'

Pesochin punches commissars and divisional commissar Serafim Snitser punches his own *politruks* [political officers]. Each of them has his own chain of command of punching. They are both huge, massive men, with fat, meaty fists. Actions have been brought against both of them in the Army Party Commission, but they aren't deterred. They give promises, but are unable to keep them, like drunkards. They blow their top every time. Spitser punched a tankist yesterday in an argument about 'trophies' [i.e. loot].

Grossman, despite such depressing relics of the Red Army at its most unenlightened, was optimistic about the new mood developing.

The spirit of the army – a great, subtle force. It is a reality.

He compared this change with the stiff new measures introduced for the Wehrmacht (even though these were no more ruthless than the sanctions meted out by the NKVD's Special Departments attached to Soviet formations).

Hitler's address to the troops: 'Not a step back from the captured territory.' The order had been read out and people were forced to sign. 'A death sentence was read out to us, and we signed it,' the [German] prisoners say.

Grossman was evidently allowed by Lieutenant Colonel Elchaninov to see the regiment's records over the previous months. As well as examples of Soviet heroism, Grossman noted down 'extraordinary events', which was the official euphemism for cowardice, desertion, treason, anti-Soviet activities and all other crimes which carried the death penalty. Grossman was clearly fascinated by military phraseology and the bizarre juxtaposition of observations. His own notes, however, were far more dangerous, for they recorded many incidents of desertion and insubordination. If any of his notebooks had been discovered by the 'Special Detachments', the NKVD military agents of counter-intelligence which were reformed as SMERSh in the spring of 1943, he would have been in very serious trouble.

8 October [1941]. Kravtsov in the 3rd Mortar Company constantly tried to stop for rest on the march without his superior's permission, thus putting his company in danger.

13 October. Red Army soldier Matrosov distinguished himself on a mounted reconnaissance mission. He got killed. One of our squads surrendered to the enemy, under the slogan 'Down with Soviet government'.

19 October. Red Army soldier shot in the 8th Company for collaborating in a desertion to the enemy.[2]

24 October. Squad Commander Marchenko isn't certain of the Red Army winning. He says: 'Hitler is going to push us back to Siberia.'

15 November. Machine-gunner declared: 'Comrade Stalin's report gave me more strength.' Red Army soldier Oska declared: 'I give you my word, Comrade Stalin, I'll go on fighting the enemy as long as my heart beats.'

---

2 Any soldier who failed to denounce and to shoot down comrades who attempted to desert was treated as an accomplice.

At the meetings conducted by commissars or '*politruks*', soldiers were told of heroic acts and encouraged to come up with slogans and suitable declarations themselves.

> *Politruk* Glyanko broke into the village Kupchinovka, shouting '*Ura!*'

> Horse driver Klochko was captured by Germans. They led him to a house where [Soviet] soldiers were stationed. When he approached the entrance, Klochko shouted: 'Corporal! Germans!'

> 'I request the execution of the two Germans who have personally killed a soldier from the 9th Rifle Company, Comrade Gorelov.'
> Red Army soldier Pilyugin said: 'General Frost is happy to help us. Boys are dying in the [German] army, too.'
> Red Army soldier Ryaboshtan declared: 'I am going to dig a trench right now and no enemy fire will force me to retreat from here.'
> Red Army soldier from the 9th Company Kozyrev said: 'It is hard to surrender one's own land. If only we could advance soon.'
> Red Army soldier Zhurba: 'Death is better than fascist captivity.'

Some soldiers, on the other hand, were dangerously naive in their complaints. They risked being handed over to the Special Department as defeatists and enemy agitators.

> Red Army soldier Manyuk stated: 'We won't get any rest at all if we are on duty every day.'
> Red Army soldier Burak refused to accept a sub-machine gun: he says he's got bad eyes. Company Commander Kovalenko swore at him with obscene language.

Grossman noted many examples of soldiers and even officers expressing their religious belief. It is not clear, however, whether soldiers had been told of Stalin's recognition of the Orthodox Church in the hour of the Motherland's crisis.

> Red Army soldier Golyaperov declared: 'I will only take the oath if there is a cross [to swear on].'

> The Special Department arrested an ex-deserter, soldier Manzhulya, who has come back of his own accord.

Manzhulya, even though he had returned voluntarily, and may simply have been a straggler, rather than a deserter, probably faced a firing squad or service in a *shtrafbat*, or punishment battalion, which virtually guaranteed death, since they were forced to undertake the most hazardous tasks, including, on some occasions, marching across minefields ahead of attacking troops.[3]

'The political-moral state of the troops is good. Deserter Toropov was shot in front of [his company].'

Dr Dolenko. Her husband went off with the partisans, and she went away with the Germans.

Such a stark contrast between the heroic and the despicable begs many questions. Dr Dolenko, a Ukrainian to judge by the name, may have simply wanted to rejoin her family behind German lines, but that was treason in Soviet eyes.

As in all armies, the delivery of letters from home was an important factor in morale.

There is a widespread opinion among soldiers that the field post isn't functioning well.

In the Red Army, even more than in any other, the consumption of alcohol presented the greatest threat to discipline, as it loosened tongues dangerously.

Red Army soldier Kazakov said to his platoon commander: 'My rifle has been loaded for a long time waiting to shoot you.'

Red Army soldier Evsteev refused to go to his post claiming that he was wet. On 20 October he left his post without permission, abandoning the machine-gun crew. He went to the 7th Company, where he said to the soldiers: 'Commanders taunt us, drink the last drop of our blood, and stuff their faces with food.' During a conversation with the *politruk*, he started arguing, declared that 'the time will soon come when we'll raise you too on our bayonets'. The *politruk* shot him with his pistol.

---

3 According to Russian military sources, 422,700 men died in punishment units during the war.

Throughout the war, the chief obsession of many members of the Red Army was to obtain alcohol or anything which even looked like alcohol.

> Deputy platoon commander Anokhin and Corporal Matyukhin drank the contents of bottles with anti-yperite liquid [an antidote for chemical warfare attacks]. The deputy platoon commander died immediately. The corporal died on the way [to hospital].

Grossman noted examples of the tortured language of official military reports.

> Podus, chief of pharmacy, performs plunder of spirits from the pharmacy, diluting the remaining spirits with water.

Alcohol also played a large part in matters of lust and love, perhaps partly because it released minds from the deep sexual repression of the Stalinist era, when the slightest hint of eroticism was deemed 'anti-Party'.

> Lieutenant Boginava abandoned his platoon during the night, went to a girl called Marusya, who refused to have anything to do with him. Boginava told her that she should marry him, and threatened to shoot her.

There was in some quarters a genuinely high-minded attitude to culture, even if it was generally directed by political officers at hatred of the enemy and love of the Soviet Union.

> A string orchestra is functioning in the 1st Machine-Gun Company . . . Red Army soldiers organise concerts and performances in their battalions. The play *In the Farmstead Fyodorovka* has been staged . . . A lecture on philosophy was organised for officers.

> A musical ensemble of Red Army soldiers . . . 'A concert given by the ensemble is a well-aimed shot at fascism.' The ensemble has been going for about two months. They learn songs with the soldiers, [such as] 'Oi, there was a man shouting at the side of the road'. Kalisty, who works at the tribunal, sings: 'Oh, Dnepr, Dnepr, you flow far away, and your water is as clear as tears.' When it is being sung, not only do their listeners cry, but so do the singers themselves. Soldier members of the ensemble – infantrymen, artillerists, tankists – are

An informal troop concert.

badly dressed, and one of them suffers from frostbite. They come under fire, as they usually give concerts just before battles. In one village, Dubrova, participants ran in dashes, one by one, to the place where the concert was going to take place in the forest. An old woman came out, Vasilisa Nechivoloda, and danced with Kotlyarov to the accordeon music. She is seventy-five. After the concert she said: 'Thank you, sons, live many, many years, beat the fascists.'

Villagers were not always so welcoming.

The owner of the accommodation where the 6th Company is billeted is hostile towards the soldiers – she pours ash into their tea, and fills the house with smoke.

Artillery regiment commanded by Major Ivanov. When the cold weather began in earnest, artillery guns were cleaned of grease and the working parts smeared with spindle oil. Groups of tank destroyers were organised and training is being carried out. In *Politruk* Malyshev's battery there's a wonderful choir. They built and organised a *banya* entirely through their own efforts.

From the latest political report: 'In the battle for the village of Zaliman, a wounded Red Army soldier entered the backyard of citizen Yakimenko. Galya Yakimenko was going to give him medical aid. A German fascist broke into the yard and shot both the soldier and Galya and tried to shoot Yakimenko's fourteen-year-old son. A neighbour, old man Semyon Belyavtsev, grabbed a stick and hit the fascist on the head. Soldier Petrov rushed up and shot the German.'

In almost all Soviet units, there was a very high casualty rate through firearm accidents.

Junior Lieutenant Evdokimov (born 1922, education ten classes, member of Komsomol) wounded Junior Lieutenant Zorin in the stomach. This was an accident, yet Junior Lieutenant Evdokimov committed suicide afterwards.

Soviet hyperbole grossly inflated enemy casualties.

'Comrade Myshkovsky fought like a hero and killed up to a platoon of fascists with his machine-gun fire. He himself died from wounds.'

'Malomed, Naum Moiseevich, fought bravely together with his platoon and captured enemy weapons. Malomed was killed. Mortar-gunner Sivokon smashed the enemy without mercy. Regimental Commander Comrade Avakov was buried at 1500 hours. He died like a hero. All the unit said goodbye to their commander. There were also local people at the funeral.'

'*Politruk* Usachev pelted Germans with grenades and started a bayonet attack. Usachev died like a hero.'

Listening to the reports from the battlefield, Pesochin [the divisional commander] says in a melodious voice: 'Oh, my God.'

The retaking of Zaliman and other villages made Grossman think even more about life for those under German occupation. Rumours from the other sides of the lines concerned everyone.

Girls in the occupied villages put on rags and rub ash on their faces.

This was to avoid the attention of German soldiers.

German women took the same precautions in 1945 in the hope of escaping rape at the hands of the Red Army. Yet Grossman, like many, was sometimes misled into ascribing the worst of motives to those under enemy occupation.

> Six beautiful girls from Zaliman went away together with Germans.

This could well have been malicious gossip. The most attractive girls were often seized for service in Wehrmacht brothels, a fate far worse even than gang rape, since it was on a permanent basis and the young women had to pretend to enjoy it or face severe punishment.

For most civilians caught up in the fighting, survival was all that mattered. But sometimes a young peasant could be too clever for his own good.

> A boy had tracked down the Germans. Late at night, he recounted everything to the commander, who was in his *izba*. 'Give me some vodka, I am cold,' he said in a husky voice. The regimental commander, who was having supper, started fussing about the boy: 'Vanya, Vanya, have some chicken.' The boy had some vodka and chicken. Then his mother turned up and gave him a good whipping. It transpired that he had made everything up.

Grossman was fed snippets by the political officers to help him with his articles. Many came from interrogations of German prisoners and captured letters and documents, but not all were reliable.

> From a German soldier's letter: 'Don't worry and don't be sad. Because the sooner I'll be under the earth the more suffering I will spare myself.'

It is possible that the latter sentence became common among depressed German soldiers, yet these very words turn up in a suspiciously large number of letters which the Soviet authorities claim to have intercepted, but never in collections of letters from the front assembled back in Germany. Political officers, having heard the phrase, may well have claimed to have found it in other letters. Grossman then quotes another frequently repeated example which needs also to be treated with caution.

'Often we think: "Well, now Russia is bound to capitulate," but of course these illiterate people are too stupid to understand this.'

From a letter: 'Situation with food isn't bad. Yesterday we killed a pig, 150kg for seven men. We melted 30kg of fat.'

From a letter: 'We boil dumplings. At first we had too much flour in them, then too much potato. In all, we made 47 dumplings. Enough for the three of us. Now I am boiling cabbage and apples. I don't know what they'll taste like, but at least we don't have food coupons. We get everything from the population. There's no time to write, we cook all the time. It is so nice in the army. The four of us have slaughtered a piggy for ourselves. I found lots of honey here, just what I need.'

A letter from a German girl: 'I am going insane gradually, come back, my love. I hope you will survive, because the war would be lost for me if you don't. Goodbye, my treasure, goodbye. Mizzi.'

Hitler's address to his troops, (recorded from the words of a captured German). 'My soldiers! I demand that you don't take a single step back from the conquered territory for which you have paid with your blood. Let the fires in Russian villages light the roads for our reserves coming up and inspire cheerfulness. My soldiers, I have done everything for you. It is your turn now to do what you can for me.'

NINE

The Air War in the South

On New Year's Day 1942, Grossman wrote to his wife again, amid the euphoria that the Germans were retreating on all fronts.

> Dearest Lyusenka, well, we've celebrated the new year: you in Chistopol, I at the front . . . The horizon is clearing for us. There is a feeling of confidence and strength in the army, and each day brings the victory closer . . .

Ten days later, he wrote again.

> My articles are published quite often now, and the editor has become kinder to me. I learned of Gaidar's death yesterday.[1] He died in battle . . . Lyusenka, do you remember Gaidar? Where are our friends? I am still unable to realise that Vasya Bobryshev is dead. I read his last letter the other day, and my heart contracted. I often remember Roskin with a great pain in my soul. I think of Mama, I still don't believe she is dead. I still cannot accept it. The real pain for her will grip me later . . .

Towards the end of January, Grossman set off to visit an airfield at Svatovo, but it was not an easy journey in that winter.

> There was a snowstorm when we left Zaliman for Svatovo. The road disappeared under snow. Soon we were hopelessly stuck. Fortunately, a tank which was passing spotted us. We climbed on to it and it took us back to Zaliman and towed our car.

He mentioned this adventure in his next letter to his father.

1 Arkady Gaidar, famous and much-loved children's writer, commanded a regiment at the age of eighteen during the Russian Civil War. In 1941, after the Germans invaded, he went to the front as a correspondent.

It is still stinging cold here. The other day a snowstorm caught me in the steppe, and a tank took me back to the village, otherwise I would have frozen to death out there. There is a lot of work, and the work is interesting. My spirits are high. Only I am worried about all my dear ones, all of you who are scattered in different places. I often dream of Mama. What's happened to her, is she alive?

Throughout the war, Grossman was always intrigued by specialist arms. During the first part of the war, fighter pilots appear to have attracted him the most; then at Stalingrad, snipers caught his imagination; and during the last six months of the war, tank troops.

At the beginning of February, he visited a Red Army aviation fighter regiment supporting the South-Western Front from its airfield at Svatovo, north of the Donets. They were equipped with Yak fighters. In the early part of the war especially, Soviet aircraft, although far more numerous, could not match the technological superiority of their Luftwaffe opponents, so some fighter pilots resorted to ramming German aircraft. Only a few managed to bail out.

Salomatin: 'Ramming – that's Russian character. It's the Soviet upbringing.'

Sedov, Mikhail Stepanovich, born 1917: 'Ramming isn't heroism. Heroism is to shoot down as many of them as possible.'

Skotnoi: 'What sort of a hero is a man who has a full load [of ammunition] and doesn't manage to shoot [an enemy plane] down and has to ram [it]?' Skotnoi does not talk much. He is melancholy. 'I would have been embarrassed to go to a good club. I would be too shy to talk to a girl.'

Some of the pilots he interviewed, especially unit commanders, stuck rigidly to the Party line, even if that meant claiming, against all evidence to the contrary, that their aircraft and engines never let them down. During some parts of the war, Red Army aviation was losing almost as many aircraft through accidents as from enemy action.

Major Fatyanov, Ivan Sidorovich: 'Our men work in pairs. They will even give up their prey in order to stick with their companion.

What is most important is to believe in one another. We help others when they are in trouble. This tradition existed before us, but we always follow it. We have faith in our equipment. Neither an engine nor an aircraft would let one down.'

On the subject of the Germans: 'They cover their Junkers when they go in and come out of an attack. But they can't stand rapid changes. There isn't much comradeship among them. Pairs are easily broken up. They escape using their speed. They flee from an active enemy, but never let go of a damaged one. I wouldn't say I am very experienced.' (He is modesty itself.)

An aviation general is speaking on the field telephone about bombs, the take-off of bomber aircraft, the beginning of the attack, and so forth. Suddenly, he says: 'A baby is crying somewhere at the other end of the line. Must be in the *izba*.'

Grossman appears to have been intrigued by the minor contradictions in their accounts.

Martynov, Al[eksandr] Vas[ilievich], born 1919: 'One can spot the whole character of a pilot in the movement of his machine. I can see if the enemy is strong and persistent. Fritzes look for simpletons. They pick them off from behind. You see what your partner is like from his character as a pilot, and his whole nature is shown by the way he flies his machine. Yet in an air battle, it is very difficult to distinguish between pilots . . . I must protect my comrade, rather than shoot down that bloody Fritz . . . You see a Fritz, how he wags his head, and you give him a couple of hot ones! Close-quarter battle in the air is a bit hard for Fritz. Close-quarter battle is a struggle to the last drop of blood. The enemy does not like fighting on a horizontal plane, or when banking. They try to fight on a vertical axis. The enemy do everything smoothly, and evade sharp bankings. It's therefore possible to break away on the horizontal by side-slipping. Their firing is not carefully aimed.

'Good coordination in the pair secures success. You follow your leader and he gives the signal when to break off . . . I was on fire in the air, having been hit by anti-aircraft artillery. (I had burns and was wounded.) Yet I felt no fear when I was burning. There was no time for fear. The characteristics [of a good pilot are]:

1) to know your machine and equipment in order to be able to use it

2) to have confidence and to love your machine

3) to have courage, a cool mind and a burning heart

4) to feel true comradeship

5) to display selflessness in battle, devotion to the Motherland, and hatred [of the enemy].

'My first meeting with a Heinkel. I attacked him twelve times, he became a bit [covered with soot]. The first time is a bit scary. I've returned with lot of holes. Once I was completely covered with bullet-holes, like an old quail.'

Salomatin, [explaining why] he does not wait for the slower ones: 'I want the main one, that's why I start a fight. It's not decorations I am after. I want to beat the Germans, even if it costs me my life.'

Salomatin then spoke of Demidov, a fellow pilot who had recently been killed in an air battle. They had remembered him in the toasts drunk after receiving a medal. It was the custom in the Red Army to place the new medal in a mug of vodka, drain the alcohol in one go and finish with the decoration clenched between the teeth.

'Demidov [a comrade who had been killed] used to infect everyone with his courage. Baranov burst into tears when we were being awarded decorations. The first toast was to Stalin, the second one was to the dead Demidov.'

Captain Zapryagalov: '[On] the first day of the war in Chernovitsy, the alarm was sounded soon after four o'clock. We ran to the airfield. I took off while it was being bombed. [I later had to do] another take-off from an airfield destroyed by bombs.

'The main thing is that we believe. We haven't any doubts and we will help those in trouble. We weren't the ones who started this tradition, but we follow it reverently. [The Germans] are a very strong nation in technological matters.'

Eryomin, Boris Nik[olayevich], twenty-nine years old: 'The main principle is the coordination in pairs, and comradeship. There's coordination and they know each other's peculiarities. Martynov (the second in command) flies with Korol and trained him. The second pair [consists of] Balashov and Sedov. I fly with Skotnoi.

'One sees how the tracer ends in his black planes. The Me[sser-schmitt] is long, like a pike. I looked, and saw a yellow spinner, and banked, but a bit late. I saw them firing at me, and a blue flash, and at that moment Martynov rushed at him, and he fell off me. It's interesting, of course, one really gets carried away with it.

'We should protect the little seagulls, they are all good people in them.'[2]

'I took off with Salomatin when the alarm sounded, and shot down [a plane]. A very nice feeling. You fly there planning all the time: 'Ah, it would be better this way, it would be better that way.'

'The commander explained things to me, and I understood what he wanted from me. We had agreed on the ground – if you waggle your wings – that means, prepare to attack.'

Lieutenant Salomatin (Sedov's wingman), born 1921: 'Their leader was coming straight at me, but I didn't turn my plane away. He broke off and turned away. Ramming him would have been more convenient. It is nothing, when there is one against one. One is afraid to be attacked by a horde of them, but when there is a group, you forget everything, you get really agitated: "They are flying to bomb our troops!"'

About ramming: 'It is very good and expedient to exchange a fighter for a Junker. But I wouldn't give out the title [Hero of the Soviet Union] for such an action. Anyone can do it. I have long been thinking about ramming, about striking [the enemy aircraft] with my propeller. It can do a lot of damage.

'I went for them and drove into the middle of them, nearly touched one of them with my wing. I was coming out of the sun, and they didn't shoot. I almost collided with another one and shot him down from a distance of twenty-five metres. Then I turned back and started shooting at anything.

'The second flight – the leader was about two metres under my belly, and a blast of slipstream hit me. I dived and escaped from nine Messers. I started to hurry, in order to knock out a Messer tailing one of our 'Yaks' (Lieutenant Skotnoi was flying it), but I couldn't make it in time. [Skotnoi] went into a glide, but I managed

2   The plane affectionately known as the *chaechka*, or 'little seagull', was in fact the Polikarpov I–15, a very small fighter with gull-shaped wings which never stood a chance against a Messerschmitt 109.

to send two Messers away. He landed. I made two circuits so that they wouldn't kill him. I saw that he was alive and waved my hand at him.'

[Skotnoi:] 'We went at one another head to head. He pierced my radiator, and I set him on fire. I went to help Eryomin. One Me[sserschmitt] set my oil tank and fuel pipes on fire. My plane was burning on the inside, and there was a lot of smoke. I dropped in altitude. Sedov covered me. I didn't get any burns myself, only my boots were burned. I climbed out, and waved at Sedov [telling him that he could go]. My plane was completely burned out.'

TEN

On the Donets with
the Black Division

Grossman was with the 37th Army, near Servernyi Donets, forty kilo-metres south-east of Kharkov. They faced the German Sixth Army, which was now commanded by General Friedrich Paulus and which Grossman would encounter at Stalingrad.

Visit the division commanded by Colonel Zinoviev, a Hero of the Soviet Union, born 1905, and a peasant. 'I am a *muzhik*,' he says of himself. He joined the Red Army in 1927 and served with the frontier guards troops in Central Asia. He commanded a company during the Finnish Campaign. He spent fifty-seven days surrounded by the Germans (a feat for which he received the medal Hero of the Soviet Union).

'The most frightening thing of all,' Zinoviev told us, 'is when they are crawling. You shoot at them with machine guns, fire mortars and artillery. You crush them, but they crawl, they crawl. And now I try to persuade my soldiers: "Crawl!" He has studied at the [Frunze] Academy, but it is hard for him to speak fluently. He is shy and stumbles over his words. He is ashamed of being such a simple man.

The division consists entirely of miners. All the men come from the Donbass. Germans call it the 'Black Division'. The miners didn't want to retreat. 'We won't let a single German cross the Donets.' They call their commander 'our Chapaev'.[1]

In the first battle the division was attacked by one hundred German tanks. The miners stopped the attack. When the Germans

---

1 Chapaev, Vassili Ivanovich (1887–1919), was a Red hero of the Russian civil war, famous for having defended the line of the River Ural, but he drowned in it when swimming for the shore with a bullet in his shoulder.

breached a flank of the division, the divisional commander galloped on a horse along the front line shouting: 'Miners, forward!'

'Miners don't retreat!' the soldiers shouted in reply.

'They sleep in the forest when it's minus 35° centigrade. They aren't afraid of tanks. "A mine is more frightening," they say.'

The divisional commander's creed is: 'The key character here is the Red Army soldier. He sleeps in the snow and is prepared to sacrifice his life. And it isn't easy to sacrifice one's life. Everyone wants to live, including heroes. Authority is gained through daily conversations. A soldier must know his task and understand it. One has to speak to soldiers, and sing and dance for them. But authority shouldn't be cheap, it is hard won. I learned this in the frontier units. And knowing that soldiers trust me, I know they will fulfil all my orders and risk their lives. When it is necessary to take a little town or block a road, I know that they will do it.'

Severe frost. The snow is creaking. Icy air makes one catch one's breath. The insides of one's nostrils stick together, teeth ache from the cold. Germans, frozen to death, lie on the roads of our advance. Their bodies are absolutely intact. We didn't kill them, it was the cold. Practical jokers put the frozen Germans on their feet, or on their hands and knees, making intricate, fanciful sculpture groups. Frozen Germans stand with their fists raised, or with their fingers spread wide. Some of them look as if they are running, their heads pulled into the shoulders. They are wearing torn boots, thin *shinel-ishki* [greatcoats], paper undershirts that don't hold the warmth. At night the fields of snow seem blue under the bright moon, and the dark bodies of frozen German soldiers stand in the blue snow, placed there by the jokers.

Again, [frozen] Germans standing up. One of them is in his underwear, in a paper jersey.

In a village which has just been liberated, there are five dead Germans and one dead Red Army soldier lying in the square. The square is empty, there is no one to ask what's happened, but one does not need this to be able to reconstruct the whole drama. One of the Germans was killed with a bayonet, another one with a rifle butt, third one with a bayonet, two were shot. And the soldier who killed them all was shot in the back.

Grossman, who preferred working with just a couple of colleagues or on his own, had to join a much larger group of war correspondents.

The *izba* is crowded with dozens of people. There's confusion, the headquarters is in the process of setting itself up. A beautiful girl is there in an overcoat which is too big for her, a big *ushanka* [fur hat] which keeps falling over her eyes, and huge *valenki* [felt boots], but one can tell there is a sweet, slim girl underneath all this ugly grey stuff. She is standing there looking lost, not knowing where she can sit down. She is holding a red handbag in her hands. This lady's handbag, which has seen better days, looks stunningly sad in these grey military surroundings. A soldier slaps her on the back jokingly, but with full force. Suddenly she begins to cry. 'Forgive me, Lidochka,' the soldier says to her. 'I'm a miner, I've got heavy hands.'

Back in peacetime, we always used to put on the wrong galoshes in the hall. Now, about fifteen photographers and reporters sleep in one *izba*, and there's a terrible confusion all the time – 'Whose *valenki* are these? Whose foot bandages, mittens, hats?'[2] Everything looks the same to people who were civilians the day before. This does not happen with soldiers.

The owners of the *izba* told us how the Germans fled from the village under the fire of our artillery. They were carrying their belongings which they hadn't had time to pack; they were panic-stricken, some fell into the snow and sobbed.

'We had a German here who brought with him a cat from Poltava [Sixth Army headquarters]. The cat knew him. When he walked into the house, the cat would run to him and rub against his boots. He fed it with fat, pure fat. And when they fled, he took the cat with him, he was so fond of it.'

'The divisional doctor was quartered here. He used to work all night. He worked like an ox. He wrote and wrote and then shouted into the telephone like a raven: "Kamyshevakha! Kamyshevakha!" and carried on writing, regardless of the light. He worked like an ox. And he would shout at his orderly: "Why is the Russian so quiet?" He liked it when I chopped wood in the mornings. They would wake me up specially.'

---

2   The Red Army, like the Tsarist Army, did not believe in socks. Soldiers wore foot bandages a little like puttees, inside their boots. There was a strong belief that foot bandages were far more effective in preventing frostbite.

A woman told us: 'She was a good cow, and young. [The Germans] caught her because they wanted to eat something fatty.'

The artillery commander gave the order: 'At the retreating whores, fire!'

Gun-layers and mortarmen, such as this one wearing a pilotka *fore-and-aft cap, would sometimes receive flamboyant fire orders from their commanders at moments of triumph. When they reached Berlin, it would be: 'At the lair of the Fascist beast, fire!'*

Colonel Zinoviev allowed Grossman to go through the divisional war diary over the previous months.

[October]
Komsomol Secretary Eretik had wanted, when dying from a serious wound, to throw a grenade, but he didn't have enough strength. The grenade exploded in his hand, killing him and some Germans.

A damaged plane was drawn away by oxen. Soldiers carried their wounded commander Muratov for twelve kilometres.

Red Army soldier Petrov says: 'At the front we have bad leadership.'

A reconnaissance party of six men headed by Junior Lieutenant Drozd didn't return from their mission. Drozd was found afterwards with two bayonet wounds. He was dead and his revolver was missing, but documents and money were on him. The soldiers weren't found.[3]

Turilin and Likhatov tore up their [Communist] Party membership cards.[4] Gulyaev declared: 'Why dig trenches, they are useless.'

Red Army soldier Tikhy[5] tried to rape the owner of the house where he stayed for the night. Fearing retribution, Tikhy darted out of the house, took a rifle, jumped on a horse and left in an unknown direction. The search for Tikhy has still brought no positive results.

Mass complaints from soldiers about the complete absence of letters.

A handwritten leaflet was dropped from a plane on the town of Yampol: 'During a morning service in the city of Jerusalem, the Saviour's voice was heard. Those who pray, even just once, will be saved.'

3   Evidently, the soldiers were suspected either of killing the officer themselves, or of having abandoned him.
4   The most frequent reason for tearing up a Communist Party membership card was a fear of execution if it was found by the Germans.
5   Tikhy means 'quiet' in Russian.

Junior Lieutenant Churelko shouted at his soldiers: 'You swine! You don't like me because I'm a Gypsy!' After that, he jumped on his horse and wanted to go to the front line. They stopped him, and he wanted to shoot himself.

Red Army soldier Duvansky was driving his ox and was hitting the ox with a rifle butt. The butt broke when he hit the ox, and the rifle went off wounding Duvansky. He was sent to hospital and brought to trial.

Communist Evseev lost his notepad. Some Red Army soldiers found this notepad. In it he kept a hand-copied prayer.

Reconnaissance men Kapitonov and Deiga [presumably on a scouting mission behind enemy lines] changed into civilian clothes and visited a meeting where Germans were holding the election of a starosta [village leader in German-occupied territory].[6] Germans shouted: 'Those who aren't locals, stand up!' They stood up and were arrested.

Menu of a German field kitchen. In the morning – breakfast: coffee, usually without sugar, and bread spread with dripping (pig fat). Dinner consists of one course: borscht or soup (meat soup). Supper: coffee and bread. Second course with meat is given to them once a week.

In response to Comrade Stalin's report, Nurse Rud donated 250 cubic centimetres of her blood, and Nurse Tarabrina 350 cubic centimetres.

During breakfast at the headquarters battery, a frog was found in the soup.

Soldier Nazarenko carried two heavily wounded men out of the line of fire and after that he killed ten fascist soldiers, one corporal and one officer. When someone said to him: 'You're a hero,' he answered: 'Is this heroism? To reach Berlin – that's heroism!' He

6 The term 'reconnaissance' in the Red Army covered both the usual sense of the word and military intelligence on a local level. It would appear that these spies were untrained and unimaginative.

added: 'One would be all right with *Politruk* Chernyshev in combat! He crawled up to me in the heat of the battle, laughed and cheered me up.'

Three German sub-machine-gunners were surrounded in a field by some haystacks. This was at night. 'Surrender!' [the Soviet soldiers shouted]. There was no reply. It turned out that they were standing there dead, leant against a haystack, frozen solid. Apparently, practical jokers had placed them there during the day.

Grossman, as well as gleaning what he could from official reports, carried on noting down vignettes and snippets of conversation from military life.

Divisional commanders: 'I am at . . .' 'I am on the line.' The inevitable phrase: 'My neighbour on the left is letting me down.' 'Oh, neighbour, neighbour.' 'This booty is mine.' 'It was my anti-aircraft men who shot down that German, but he came down in the neighbour's sector, and the neighbours claimed that they had shot him down.' 'One is always having trouble with one's neighbours.'

If a division has managed to break through, its commander says: 'My neighbour is holding me back.' And the commander who is left behind, says: 'It's easy for them to say that. While I received the main brunt of the battle, of course it was easy for them to push on.'

On a clear frosty morning, *izbas* produce smoke like battleships in harbour. There is no wind. Not a breeze, and several dozen smoke pillars stand like props between the snowy white of the ground and the sky of cruel blue.

Immediately after the battle ended, a crowd of women rushed out into the field, to German trenches, to get back their quilts and pillows.

In a Ukrainian village, the *khata* houses are being whitewashed after the departure of the Germans, as if after a dangerous, infectious disease which devastated the village.

When Germans entered a house, the cat left and stayed away for three months. (Stories like this circulate in all the villages.) Presumably the cats sense strangers, or know the smell of Germans.

Reading between the lines of Grossman's account, villagers who had been under German occupation were nervous about how they might be treated by the Soviet authorities. Many of them had destroyed their identity documents and needed to be reassured that they would not be punished.

In the morning, Kuzma Ogloblin came back to the village which had just been liberated. He was the chairman of the village soviet and had been with the partisans. He is dark and solid like cast iron, wearing a black sheepskin coat and armed with a rifle. The *izba* became crowded with people. Ogloblin said: 'Don't be afraid of anything. Just get on with life. You should hand in any German boots. I myself, for example, hit a vehicle with a grenade. It had three hundred pairs of boots in it, and although I needed boots, I didn't even take a single pair. What do you want documents for? We all know each other. Don't be afraid, live! The Germans are done for. They won't be back.'

Return to Voronezh. Night in a field hospital. We meet a woman doctor. It is dark. There is only a weak light from the coals in the stove. The doctor becomes talkative, she recites poetry and philosophises. 'Excuse me, are you, er, blonde?' Rozenfeld asks. 'No, my hair is completely white,' she replies. An embarrassed silence.

A wounded man: 'Comrade Major, we are having a furious argument here. May I speak to you?'
   'What, what?' The major is alarmed.
   'Well, we were discussing whether Germany will exist after the war?'

The wounded men demand newpapers and snatch them from medical orderlies: they want to smoke.

A hospital train is standing on the track. There are military trains all around. Whenever Ulyana, Galya or Lena want to climb into a heated freight [*teplushka*] wagon, soldiers appear at once out of nowhere 'helping' nurses into the wagon. Screams and laughter are heard all over the station.

We said goodbye to the field hospital. I remembered again how on my way to the front I had dropped in to see the commandant. I was hungry and they put a plate of wonderful home-made Ukrainian borscht in front of me. Just when I was raising the first spoonful to my mouth Bukovsky stormed in shouting: 'Hurry up! Let's run. The train is moving already.' I rushed out after him. That borscht haunted me for weeks.

We change on to an ordinary [civilian] train. It is very crowded. The inspector says to a man in a black coat: 'Give these soldiers your seat, they are here on the train today, and tomorrow they will perhaps be dead.' A soldier, an Uzbek, is singing loudly in Uzbekian. The whole carriage can hear him. The sounds seem absurd to our ears, and the words are unfamiliar. Red Army soldiers are listening to him attentively, with a caring and embarrassed expression. There isn't a single grin or smile.

Grossman once again heard stories from the enemy-occupied territories.

An old man was waiting for the Germans to arrive. He put a table-cloth on the table, and laid it with different delicacies. The Germans came and robbed and looted the house. The old man hanged himself.

Regimental commander Kramer. He beats Germans devilishly. When he became ill during a battle and had a forty-degree temperature, they poured some boiling water into a barrel, this fat man climbed into the barrel and recovered.

The January general offensive, launched on Stalin's insistence and against Zhukov's advice, had proved unsustainable, as the realists had feared. The German Army was not on the point of collapse, as Stalin had claimed after the successful counter-attacks near Moscow in December. Grossman came across some reports from the fighting in the First World War which had an uncomfortably familiar tone. Such implicit criticisms of the handling of the offensive in his notebook was almost as dangerous as copying down negative comments and 'extraordinary events'.

From the order by General of Artillery Ivanov to the commanders of the 7th, 8th, 9th, and 11th Armies: '26 January 1916. Almost all our attacks in the recent battles possessed the same characteristic pattern: the troops broke through a sector of the enemy's line, forced the remains of the enemy's front-line troops to abandon trenches and fortifications, followed them uncontrollably and then, attacked in their turn by enemy neighbouring units or reserves, retreated not only back to the captured line, but, having found no support in them as they had just been taken, often back to the positions before the attack, usually having suffered great losses . . . A tactical victory without strategic results is an expensive and beautiful but useless toy.' These observations made by generals then and those made in the Zaliman area this winter are stunningly similar.

More about poverty. The sad but beautiful poverty of our people. Wounded men are treated to a piece of herring and fifty grams of vodka if seriously wounded. Sheets. Fighter pilots who are now performing great deeds – their drinking glasses are made from bottles with the necks crudely broken off. Their [*unty*] sheepskin boots have no heels. A political officer [tells a quartermaster corporal]: '[This pilot] should be given another pair, his feet get cold.'

The corporal shakes his head. 'We haven't got any.'

'That's all right,' says the pilot. 'I'm warm enough.'

The shortage of equipment was largely a consequence of the disastrous retreats of 1941 when so much kit and so many stores had been abandoned in the retreat. The only way to obtain replacements was to bribe a quartermaster with vodka, a solution which angered many soldiers.

ELEVEN

With the Khasin Tank Brigade

After the Soviet general offensive of January 1942 had petered out disastrously, Grossman began to reflect on the Russian roller coaster of emotions. They had gone from despairing disbelief in the terrible summer of 1941, to panic in the autumn as the Germans approached Moscow, then wild optimism in the great counter-attack around the capital, and now depression again.

A Russian man has to work very hard, and his life is hard too, but in his soul he does not realise the inevitability of this hard work and hard life. At war, I have seen only two kinds of reaction to the things happening around one: either extreme optimism, or complete gloom. Transition from one to the other is quick and sudden, and easy. There is nothing in between. No one lives with the thought that the war is going to be long, that only hard work, month after month, could lead to victory. Even those who say so don't believe it. There are only two feelings: the first one – the enemy is defeated; the other one – the enemy cannot be defeated.

Grossman was so deeply affected by the genuine spirit of sacrifice among ordinary soldiers and front-line officers that he became quite emotional on the subject.

At war, a Russian man puts on a white shirt. He may live in sin, but he dies like a saint. At the front [there is] a purity of thought and soul, a kind of monastic austerity.
 The rear [the civilian part of the country] lives by different laws and it would never be able to merge morally with the front. Its law is life, and the struggle for survival. We Russians don't know how to live like saints, we only know how to die like saints. The front [represents] the holiness of Russian death, the rear is the sin of Russian life.
 At the front, there is patience and resignation, submission to

unthinkable hardships. This is the patience of a strong people. This is the patience of a great army. The greatness of the Russian soul is incredible.

On the other hand, Grossman was extremely impatient with much of the propaganda that tried to conceal the incompetence of Soviet military leadership during the previous six months.

The Kutuzov myth about the strategy of 1812. The blood-soaked body of war is being dressed in snow-white robes of ideological, strategic and artistic convention. There are those who saw the retreat and those who dressed it. The myth of the First and the Second Great Patriotic War.

Still on the Southern Front, with the 37th Army, Grossman visited a tank brigade commanded by Colonel Khasin. There he spent quite some time with Captain Kozlov, a Jewish officer.

At Khasin's tank brigade, Captain Kozlov, the commander of the motorised rifle battalion, was philosophising about life and death while talking to me at night. He is a young man with a small beard. Before the war he was studying music at the Moscow Conservatoire. 'I have told myself that I will be killed whatever happens, today or tomorrow. And once I realised this, it became so easy for me to live, so simple, and even somehow so clear and pure. My soul is very calm. I go into battle without any fear, because I have no expectations. I am absolutely convinced that a man commanding a motorised rifle batallion will be killed, that he cannot survive. If I didn't have this belief in the inevitability of death, I would be feeling bad and, probably, I wouldn't be able to be so happy, calm and brave in the fighting.'
    Kozlov told me how in 1941 he used to sing arias from operas at night in a forest near Bryansk in front of German trenches. Usually the Germans would listen to him for a little while and then start firing at the voice with machine guns. Probably they didn't like his singing.
    Kozlov told me that, in his opinion, Jews aren't fighting well enough. He says that they fight like ordinary people, while in a war like this Jews should be fighting like fanatics.

The spike of racial hatred is directed against the Orthodox Jews, who in essence are racists and fanatics of racial purity. There are two poles now: on one side are racists who suppress the world; on the other, Jewish racists, the most suppressed in the world.

One is afraid of things one isn't used to. One can get used to anything but not death, probably because one only dies once.

War is an art. Within it elements of calculation, cool knowledge and experience are combined with inspiration, chance and something completely irrational (battle for Zaliman, Pesochin). These elements are compatible with one another, but sometimes they come into conflict. It's like a musical improvisation which is unthinkable without a brilliant technique.

Moon over the snow-covered battlefield.

Grossman continued to collect character sketches together with his other vignettes.

The driver of a heavy tank: Krivorotov, Mikhail Pavlovich, twenty-two. (He is a huge, blue-eyed fellow.) Worked as a combine-harvester driver in a sovkhoz[1] in Bashkiria, from the age of twenty. Joined the army in December 1940. 'I had never seen tanks before that, and I liked them incredibly at first sight. Tanks are very beautiful. I was a mechanic-driver. This machine, with its firepower, is a golden machine, very strong.

'They had guns and mortars, we crossed a gully and broke into the village. I shouted: "Gun on the left flank!" We destroyed this gun and some machine guns. Then, a shell hit the left side. The tank caught fire. The crew jumped out, and I stayed in the burning tank and knocked out the enemy battery. My back was feeling a little hot, everything was on fire. Such a fast machine it was. I was sorry to give it up. Very sorry. I clambered back into the hull and jumped out through the top hatch, just like a pike. The tank's oil and paint were already on fire.'

Marusya, the telephone operator. Everyone praises her, everyone knows her. She addresses everyone by their first name and

---

1 A sovkhoz was a *sovetskoe khozyaistvo* (Soviet farm), a large collection of buildings, usually with two-storey houses, while a kolkhoz was a collective farm based on a small village or settlement.

patronymic. Everyone is calling her: 'Marusya, Marusya!' No one has ever seen her face.

Abashidze, a convivial fellow, member of Komsomol, battalion commander and vulgar person. His sickening, insolent, rude dialogue with the old landlady. When he asks for a light [from one's cigarette, he says]: 'May I touch the tip of your delight?'

One does not say now of somebody that they have been 'killed', but 'he has covered himself'. 'My friend has covered himself, he was such a great chap!'[2]

A beautiful, bright day. Air battles are going on above the village houses. Terrible sights – birds with black crosses, birds with stars. All the terror, all thoughts, all the fear of a human mind and heart are in these last moments of a machine's life, when its wings seem to express all that is in a pilot's eyes, hands, forehead. They were fighting low, just above the tops of the roofs. One of them hit the ground. Five minutes later – another one. A man died in front of their eyes, a very young man, very strong, he so wanted to live. How he was flying, how he trembled, how frightening were the misfirings [of the engine]. They are the misfirings of a heart above the field of snow. The fox's and wolf's nature of yellow-tipped Messers.

Pilots say: 'Our life is like a child's shirt – it's short and covered with shit all over.'[3]

Strange paradox – the Messers are almost helpless against our seagulls, because the seagulls are so slow.

Joy of a cameraman who has managed to film a tragic air battle: 'I'll just need to retouch the crosses, that's all!'

A dead pilot lay all night on a beautiful hill covered with snow: it was very cold and the stars were very bright. At dawn the hill became completely pink, and the pilot lay on a pink hill.

2 This euphemism refers to the cover being placed on a coffin and sealed.
3 This became a common saying, and was used by Germans as well as Red Army soldiers.

Grossman, not surprisingly, was fascinated by the unusual story of a commissar prepared to stick his neck out to prevent a terrible miscarriage of justice.

Senior *politruk* Mordukhovich, a small Jew from Mozyr, is the commissar of an artillery battalion. One of the soldiers in his battalion is a huge worker from Tula, called Ignatiev. He is extremely brave, one of the best soldiers in the battalion. The commissar had to go away for some time, and during his absence, Ignatiev lagged behind and joined up with another unit. They fought a defensive action. From there he was sent back to his unit during a lull. On his way he was stopped by an NKVD patrol. He was arrested as a deserter and sent to the military tribunal. He was sentenced to death. Meanwhile, Commissar Mordukhovich had returned to the unit and learned about his fate. Mordukhovich rushed to the divisional commissar and told him what a great soldier Ignatiev was. The commissar took his head ['his ears'] in his hands. 'There is nothing I can do to help now!'

Ignatiev was taken off to be executed by a representative of the Special Department, the commandant from headquarters, two soldiers and the deputy *politruk*. They led him to a little wood. The commandant took out his pistol, and pointed at the back of Ignatiev's head. Misfire. Ignatiev turned to look back, cried out, and ran towards the forest. They fired at him, but missed. He disappeared. The Germans were only three kilometres away. Ignatiev spent three days wandering in the forest. Then he managed to return to the battalion unnoticed and came to Mordukhovich's bunker. Mordukhovich said: 'I will hide you, don't worry.' Mordukhovich gave him some food, but Ignatiev was trembling and crying so much that he couldn't eat. Mordukhovich went to speak to the divisional commissar. By then he had been hiding Ignatiev for five days. 'The man came back of his own accord. He said to me: "I'd rather die at the hands of my own people, than at the hands of the Germans."' The divisional commissar went to see the corps commissar, and the corps commissar went to see the [army] commander. The sentence was cancelled. Ignatiev now follows Mordukhovich around day and night.

'Why are you following me?'

'I am afraid that the Germans may kill you, Comrade Commissar. I am guarding you.'

Some stories, however, may have been little more than the front equivalent of an urban myth.

> A soldier accused of desertion was being escorted to the tribunal
> when the Germans attacked. His guards hid in the bushes. The
> deserter grabbed one of their rifles and killed two Germans, and
> took the third one with him to the tribunal. 'Who are you?' [they
> demanded.]
>   'I've come to be tried.'

Those sentenced to *shtrafroty*, or punishment companies, were known as
'*smertniks*', dead men, because none were expected to survive. They were
being given the chance by the Soviet state to wipe out their shame with
their blood. Many demonstrated exceptional bravery. One *smertnik*,
Vladimir Karpov, even received the highest order, Hero of the Soviet
Union. Evidently, he was not a political offender, because they, on Stalin's
order, could never receive any sort of decoration.

> The company of *smertniks* consists of men whose sentences have been
> replaced with assignment to the front line. Its commander is a lieu-
> tenant with a self-inflicted wound who was sentenced to execution.
>   Men in this doomed company have skewbald, frostbitten faces,
> with pink traces from the cold of minus 40°, torn greatcoats, terrible
> coughs, as if coming from somewhere in the stomach, hoarse,
> barking, husky voices, and they all are overgrown with beards. Using
> the fire of their guns and also their tracks, tankists broke the line
> of fortifications and brought to Volobuevka a squad of tank infantry
> commanded by Senior Sergeant Tomilin. The battle lasted for eight
> hours. Tomilin's tank infantry seized twelve houses. Tomilin himself
> killed ten fascists. The section of Sergeant Galkin killed thirty men,
> set on fire six houses with sub-machine-gunners and pillboxes, and
> destroyed a battalion headquarters with grenades. In the morning
> they joined up with our advancing troops in the southern outskirts
> of Volobuevka. When leading his soldiers into battle, Tomilin
> shouted: 'Come on, bandits, forward!'

From the war diary of the 7th Guards Howitzer Artillery Regiment:

> On 12 January, Junior Sergeant Ivanov and reconnaissance man
> Ofitserov saw seven men on a slope of a hill. They turned out to

be fascists who kept plunging a man into an ice hole. The fascists were frightened by our fire and fled, leaving a half-frozen medical assistant. He was paralysed with fear.

On 13 January, Junior Lieutenant Belousov was sent to establish communication with the infantry. He had to cross a gully over-grown with forest. While skiing through the forest, he noticed a cable connecting two German signals stations. The station closer to him was not guarded. Belousov took his skis off and cut the cable. Then he went into the forest, found an empty reel and wound seventy metres of telephone cable on to it.

Grossman continued to note down strange sayings and terms. Vodka was known as 'Product 61' because that was its place on the list of items issued.

A cook in a guards regiment [continually used the phrase] 'put into shape'. 'I'll just put it into shape on the table.' 'I'll put mutton into shape.' 'I'll put soured cabbage into shape.'

A raid by twenty-eight aircraft. Not a single artillerist retreated. 'They are wedded to their guns.'

A commissar in the 5th Guards went insane after an aviation raid and an attack by enemy tanks.

Large icons were used to make plotters for battery commanders.

A commissar cut bars from red rubber bands.[4]

At night, Lieutenant Colonel Tarasov, the commander of a guards howitzer regiment, reads *Faust* lying on the floor of an *izba*. He wears a pince-nez which he cleans with a piece of suede.

A story told by Lieutenant Colonel Tarasov on how he had 'dusted the Germans' jackets'. The story shows the psyche of an artillerist. Infantry had reported that the Germans went to have lunch once

4 These parallel 'bars' or 'railway sleepers', as they were known, were badges of rank. Junior offi-cers had square insignia, known as 'cubes'.

a bugle was blown. Field kitchens were detected by the smoke. Tarasov gave the order: 'Collect data, load guns and report on readiness!' The Germans were shelled with concentrated fire. The artillerists heard screams.

A captured German in a medical train. He needed a blood transfusion which would save his life. He shouted: *'Nein, nein!'* (He didn't want any Slav blood.) He died three hours later.

Soldiers started running away from the battlefield. A battalion commissar, armed with two revolvers, began shouting: 'Where are you running, you whores, where? Go forward, for our Motherland, for Jesus Christ, motherfuckers! For Stalin, you whores!' They turned round and occupied their defensive position again.

A soldier with curly hair, surname unknown, had been driving a sledge around in the German rear for twelve days. A mortar and bombs were hidden under the straw on the sledge. He would fire and then hide the mortar in the straw again. When he saw Germans, he would burst into song. They never suspected him. He would drive away from them, take out his mortar and fire at them.

Photographer Ryumkin was swearing at guards artillerists, who turned the wrong way (not photogenic) while firing their guns in earnest.

Lieutenant Matyushko commands a destroyer detachment, whose task is to annihilate Germans occupying the houses. The annihilators break into the village and rush into the houses. Matyushko said: 'My men are all bandits. This war in villages is a bandit war.' They sometimes strangle Germans with their hands.

A sergeant's voice is heard coming out of smoke and flames: 'Don't fire in here, I've captured this house.'

A member of the destroyer detachment entered a house and swept the people sitting there with his quick dark glance. Everyone understood that this had become his habit, the habit of a man who breaks into a house and kills. Lieutenant Matyushko, too, interpreted his glance this way and said, laughing: 'He could have done away with all of us on his own!'

We enter Malinovka with the battalion of motorised infantry

[commanded by Captain Kozlov]. The houses are ablaze. Germans are screaming, they are dying. One of them, all black and scorched, is smoking. Our soldiers haven't eaten for two days and are chewing dry millet concentrate while they advance. They look into destroyed cellars and immediately get some potatoes, stuff snow into their kettles and put them on embers found in the burning *izbas*.

How could a dead horse have got into the cellar? It's impossible to understand! In the same cellar there's a broken barrel of [soured] cabbage. Soldiers are gobbling it up greedily. 'It's all right, it isn't poisoned.' In the same cellar someone is bandaging a wounded photo-correspondent leaning against the horse's corpse.

'Then our aircraft raided the place and bombed us [said a member of the motorised battalion]. The battalion commander Kozlov withstood an attack of tanks. He was on great form and completely drunk. The tanks were thrown back in a dashing fashion.'

III Guards Cossack Corps is leaving for the front. Men are putting the headquarters equipment on a truck, reeling in signal wire. The frosty evening is full of inexplicable beauty. It's quiet and clear. Firewood is crackling in the field kitchens. Cavalrymen are leading horses. In the middle of the street, a girl is kissing a Cossack and crying. He has become her family over the last three days. For this girl from the village of Pogorelovo near Kursk, he has become her very own.

A wonderful gun-layer at the battery, who had been fighting from the first day of the war, was killed by a fragment of shell while he was laughing. And there he lay laughing, dead. He lay there for a day, and then another day. No one wanted to bury him. They are all lazy. The earth is as hard as granite from the cold. He had bad comrades. They don't bury the corpses! They leave the killed men behind and go away. There are no burial detachments. No one cares. I informed front headquarters about it with a coded message. What mad Asiatic heartlessness! How often one can see the reserves reaching the front line and reinforcements sent to the sites of recent battles, walking among unburied dead soldiers. Who can read what is going on in the souls of these men advancing to replace those lying around in the snow?

Execution of a traitor. While the sentence was being announced, sappers were digging a grave for him with picks. He said suddenly: 'Step aside, comrades, a stray bullet may get you.'

'Take off your boots,' they told him. He took off one boot very deftly, with the toe of the other foot. The other boot took some time, he was jumping on one leg for a while.

The Kursk magnetic anomaly is a problem for rocket detachments and artillerists – it confuses compasses and other equipment. The magnetic anomaly has played a joke on the Katyusha batteries, and the Katyushas played a trick on our infantry. They hit our front line.

In the morning, they put a table covered with red cloth in the snow-covered village street. Tankists from the Khasin Brigade were lined up, and the distribution of medals began. All the men awarded with medals have been fighting constantly for a long time. The queue of them looks like a line of workers from a hot workshop: they are wearing torn overalls, clothes glossy from oil, they have black working hands, and faces typical of workers. They walk to the table to get the medals in the deep snow, they walk heavily, waddling. 'I congratulate you on receiving this high governmental award!'

'I serve the Soviet Union!' they answer in the hoarse voices of Russians, Ukrainians, Jews, Tatars, Georgians. It's the Workers' International at war.

That night we were talking, not very soberly, with Kozlov, the commander of the motorised rifle battalion. He told me that the hero who received two medals that morning and whom I had eyed with admiration, the reconnaissance chief of the brigade, is no hero at all. This shocked me because I couldn't imagine a truer hero than the one I had seen that morning in the village street.

Kozlov gave me a metal cross which he had taken from a dead [German] officer. The officer had been lying there, Kozlov told me, heavily wounded, drunk, with a hundred sub-machine-gun cartridge cases around him. The soldiers shot him. They found a pornographic postcard in his pocket.

In the morning, Kozlov and Bukovsky decided to have a revolver-shooting competition. They went behind some sheds and fastened a target to an old pear tree. They looked at me with pity and indulgence – a civilian who has no experience at all. Perhaps entirely by accident, all my bullets hit the bull's-eye. The veterans – Kozlov and Bukovsky – didn't hit the target even once. This, I think, was no accident.

In the *izba*, surrounded by his staff, stands Khasin, with his bulging dark eyes, crooked nose and cheeks blue from recent shaving. He looks Persian. His hand moving on the map looks like the claw of a huge carnivorous bird. He is explaining to me about the recent raid carried out by the tank brigade. He likes the word 'roundabout' very much and uses it all the time: 'Tanks were moving in a roundabout way.'

I was told back at the front headquarters that Khasin's family had all been killed in Kerch by Germans carrying out a mass execution of civilians. Purely by chance, Khasin saw photographs of the dead people in a ditch and recognised his wife and children. I was thinking, what does he feel when he leads his tanks into the fighting? It is very hard to have a clear impression of this man, because there is a young woman, a doctor, in the staff *izba*, who is ordering him about in a vulgar and impertinent manner. People say that she not only controls the colonel, but also his tank brigade. She interferes with all orders, and even amends lists of people put forward for decorations.

Interviews with soldiers from a motorised infantry battalion:

Mikhail Vasilievich Steklenkov, thin, blond, born 1913. He ran away from school when he was in the fifth form, and started to work.

'We never feel bored, we sit down and start to sing. There isn't time to feel bored! One forgets oneself when one thinks about home. Germans poisoned my father with gas during the Imperialist War. I was sent to the Military-Political school in Ivanovo on 23 July. The alarm was sounded, the cadets were lined up and we were given what we were supposed to have, and we went.

'They ask me: "Why are you so happy all the time?" And why should I be sad? My landlady asks: "Why do you sing songs? We're at war now!" I answer: "But now is the best time to sing songs."

'I had such a brave crew, they would never leave the gun. I lie and watch out for bombs. I'll manage to crawl away if needed . . . Only

With Khasin's tank brigade. Grossman talks to an old peasant decor-
ated in the First World War with the St. George Cross.

we'd run out of tobacco . . . [I man] a 45mm [anti-tank] gun. It's
interesting to fire point-blank from this gun . . .

'What is there to live for after the war? If I survive, I'll return
home, and if not, well, what's so special about that? I didn't have
time to get married before the war began. I can't live without the
war now. When we're out of the fighting, I begin to feel bored.'
He had frostbite in a hand and a foot, but had not reported sick.

'I am not afraid of a bullet – to hell with it – even if it kills me.
We fire, and I feel good.'

Ivan Semyonovich Kanaev, born 1905 in Ryazan, married with
four children.

'I was drafted on 3 July. I was chopping wood [at the time when
the postman brought my call-up order]. We sang songs, drank wine
and didn't give a damn. I trained in Dashki to be a driver. My
mother and wife came to see me there. Commanders were very
kind and allowed me to go on leave. I had six home leaves.

'When we were brought close to the front, it was frightening. I felt better once the fighting began. I go to fight like one goes to work, to a factory. It was terrifying at first, but now I am not afraid of bullets. It's only mortar bombs that upset me. I've taken part in a bayonet attack, too, but the Germans didn't wait to receive it. We shouted "*Ura!*", and they got up and ran.

'It's good if there's an amusing fellow, who starts to tell or sing something funny.

'The rifle is my personal weapon, it never lets me down. I dropped it in the mud in Bogdukhanovka. I thought it would be wrecked, but no, thank God, it still worked.

'I feel less homesick now, only I want to see the kids, especially the youngest one. I've never seen him yet. And actually, I do miss home. I've got one friend, Selidov, we've been together from the first day.

'We marched fifty kilometres during the day. It isn't so difficult when one's feet are all right.

'My bag for personal kit: first of all, some bread to eat, a notebook, a set of underwear, extra foot bandages. We took "trophies" in Petrishchevo. There was enough stuff even for my grandchildren and great-grandchildren, but I took nothing. What do I need it for? I'll be killed anyway. I could have collected a dozen watches. It may be my nature, but I feel it's disgusting to touch [the enemy and his belongings]. My comrades are prepared to touch them, but I, personally, am afraid to handle them.

'Tanks? Why, of course I've seen them.

'Face to face [fighting]. [A German] wounded me, and I killed him. He sprang out, and I thought I wanted to take him alive. "Halt!" He fired a burst at me and wounded me in the hand. I took aim, he fell. A woman brought out an earthenware pot of milk for me. I used up my bandage on a wounded boy. I bandaged his shoulder.

'Never run back under mortar fire. If you go back, that'll be the end of you! When [the enemy] fires [at you] with a machine gun, he isn't very accurate either. You can lie down and then run to another place. When he stops, run forward! Because if you run back he'll get you!

'Aircraft, well, what can you do? We all scatter. But the mortar, I find it terrible. It's their most effective weapon.

'I used to be scared even of squeaking of gates at home, and now

I fear nothing. In Petrishchevo, I knocked a machine-gunner off a roof. We approached and lay down. I got very cold and jumped up to my feet. Aiiee, aiiee, I was frozen. I took aim with my rifle. He shut up immediately. I checked later, the bullet had hit him in the eyebrow. I killed about fifteen of their men.

'It was really good advancing to the battle in Morozovka. They were retreating, and we were pursuing. Was it I who came to attack them? We are fighting on our land.

'One hears so much from the locals, such meanness, how can one forgive them? A woman pleaded with me, and I gave her my needle. During a battle, I lost the strap on my greatcoat, I got hold of one, but there was nothing to sew it on with. But as for buttons, my pockets are always full of them.

'My conclusion is that we've got to come out the winner. Only I don't know how. Weren't they winning in the summer? They are great fighters, but cowards.

'I was wounded, you know, in an embarrassing place, and I was afraid there would be nothing left to go back to my wife with. The doctor examined me and said: "Lucky bastard! Everything's all right."

'It's good to fight at dawn. It's as if you were going to work. It's a bit dark and one can see all their points well because of tracer bullets, and when we break into a village, it is already light.

'I've lost my desire for women. Ah, I'd love to see the kids, if only for one day, and then I would fight again, till the end.

'In the village, we sometimes had to work harder than here. As for hardships, life is harder in the village. I've become used to noise here. One sleeps through artillery and mortar fire. One snores out in the middle of a field. I've suffered a lot of cold, this winter.'

'There are moral obligations for a soldier: one has to drag out not only the wounded, but also those killed in the fighting. When I was deafened during a battle, a soldier, my comrade, came to help me and led me out of the battle.'

'Bullets don't hit brave men,' says Kanaev. Everyone else is lying down, but he is standing up. 'Soldiers, follow me!' Near Bogodukhov he led the squad into attack. He isn't a coward. 'Don't worry, Comrade *politruk*!' [he shouted.] 'We won't get wounded.'

From the reflections of Captain Kozlov:

'One needs a lot of courage to take an aimed shot during a battle. Sixty per cent of our soldiers haven't fired a single shot during the war at all.[5] We are fighting thanks to heavy machine guns, battalion mortars and the courage of some individuals. I suggest that rifles should be cleaned before a battle and checked afterwards. If any man doesn't fire – then he's a deserter.

'I am not afraid of saying that we haven't carried out a single bayonet attack. Just look, we haven't even got bayonets. Actually, I am afraid of spring. The Germans might start pushing us again when it gets warmer.'

Captain Kozlov's fears were well grounded. Hitler was preparing a major offensive in the south to seize the oilfields of the Caucasus, whereas Stalin was convinced that the Wehrmacht would strike at Moscow again. The German summer offensive of 1942 was, through Hitler's blind obstinacy, to lead to the battle of Stalingrad.

5   Kozlov's belief that a majority of soldiers did not fire at the enemy in battle is similar to Brigadier General S.L.A. Marshall's controversial 'ratio of fire' theory expounded in *Men Against Fire* (1947). Marshall claimed that between 75 per cent and 85 per cent of men in combat did not fire their weapons at the enemy. The validity of Marshall's research was challenged in the winter of 1988 by Professor Roger Spiller in the *RUSI Journal*, but the basic theory may well be true.

TWELVE

'The Ruthless Truth of War'

Vasily Grossman wrote to his father early in March about the disorientating effects of that winter of war.

> Sometimes it feels that I've spent [so much time] travelling around in trucks, sleeping in sheds and half-burned houses, it's as if I've never really lived any other sort of life. Or was that other life only a dream? I have kept moving all through the winter. I've seen so much it would be enough for anyone. I've become a real soldier, I am sure, my voice has become hoarse from *makhorka* and the cold, and for some reason the hair on my right temple has gone white.

The following day he wrote again.

> Winter has come back to where we are now, the cold is severe . . . And I am longing to warm myself in the sun. I am tired of grabbing my nose the whole time and then my ears – to check whether they are still there, or have fallen off. By the way, I've lost sixteen kilos, and this is very good. Do you remember my fat tummy?

On his return to Moscow at the beginning of April, Grossman went to see Ortenberg, who wrote about their conversation soon afterwards. 'Vasily Grossman came to see me and said without any preamble: "I want to write a novel." He warned me immediately, before I had a chance to reply: "I will need two months' leave to write it." I was not alarmed by this request, as he had obviously expected. There was a relative lull at the front at that moment and I gave my permission.' Grossman wrote to his father immediately.

> I've been given leave for two months' creative work, from 10 April until 10 June. I am overjoyed, I feel just like a schoolboy. Reaching

Moscow made a deep impression on me – the city, the streets and boulevards, they are all like the faces of my dear ones.

I have managed to do something to improve my financial affairs: I've signed a contract for the publication of a small book of my front essays and stories. I will send you some money today . . . It is very cold in our flat. Zhenni Genrikhovna has become so weak.

I haven't been anywhere during my stay here. The editor piled lots of work upon me, and I sat working day and night. Actually, this was not so bad, as it is relatively warm in the editorial office, and they've been feeding me with *kasha* there. I've become so spoilt by the food at the front.

I will be writing a novel during my stay in Chistopol. I am not so well physically. I am overtired and cough a lot. My insides were frozen when I flew over the front in an open aircraft.

Grossman wasted no time in setting off for Chistopol. There, living again with his wife, he worked long hours on his novel about the disasters of 1941, which he decided to call *The People Immortal*. This book, drawing heavily on his notes taken at the front, became a huge success among the soldiers of the Red Army. Grossman, a Jewish intellectual from another world, had not just proved his courage at the front, but above all the accuracy and human sympathy of his observation. Yet despite all his hard work, Grossman also yearned to be back at the front. In fact, he wrote to his father from Chistopol on 15 May that he would leave in the first week of June.

Action has started at the front, and I am listening to the radio greedily. There [at the front] lies the answer to all questions and to all fates.

Three days before, Marshal Timoshenko had attacked with 640,000 men south of Kharkov from the Barvenkovo salient. It was to prove a terrible disaster. The Wehrmacht's Army Group South had been about to launch Operation Fridericus, the preparatory stage before its major summer offensive, Operation Blue, which was to take it to Stalingrad and into the Caucasus. As a result the uninspired Soviet assault found itself surprised between the hammer of Kleist's First Panzer Army and the anvil of General Paulus's Sixth Army. Two Soviet armies were surrounded and virtually annihilated in a little over a week. The Germans took nearly a quarter of a million prisoners. Grossman's enthusiasm for the front appears rapidly to have dissolved, and he returned to work on his novel.

I am doing a great deal of work here [he wrote to his father on 31 May]. It seems to me I've never worked so hard in my life . . . The day before yesterday I was reading out to Aseev what I've written, and he liked it a great deal.

The sort of Red Army soldier whose courage and resilience Grossman evoked in his novel The People Immortal.

Unfortunately, my leave is running out, and I am very tired. I've exhausted myself by writing. However, I've received, completely unexpectedly, a super-liberal telegram from my fierce editor, who wrote that he did not mind me extending my leave to continue my work in Chistopol. So probably with his permission I will stay here for an extra seven or ten days. I am writing about the war during the summer and autumn of 1941.

Another thing that I am suffering from is a terrible shortage of money . . . I've written to Moscow, to all my publishers, but none of these sons of bitches has sent me a kopeck yet . . .

I often think of Katyusha. I would love to see her . . . She must be so grown up now. I've had two letters from her and I felt from those letters that she does not remember me well; they were such cold letters.

In the evenings I sit under the apple tree which is now in blossom, and I look at the lit windows of the house. It is so peaceful and quiet here. This amazes me. There's a general called Ignatiev who once said that correspondents are the bravest people in war, because they have to leave the rear for the front so many times. And this moment is the most unpleasant one, this change from nightingales to aircraft.

I've had a card from the Migration Department, saying that Mama is not on the lists of those evacuated. I knew that she hadn't managed to escape, but still my heart shrank when I read those typed lines.

It appears that Grossman did not need the extra time Ortenberg had allowed him. He delivered the manuscript on 11 June and wrote to his father the following day.

Things seem to be going well with my novel. The editor read it yesterday and approved it passionately. He summoned me at night and embraced me. He said lots of flattering things and promised to publish it in *Krasnaya Zvezda* without any cuts. And the novel is quite long . . . I am anxious about how the readers will receive it . . . By the way, the publication of the novel should greatly improve my financial affairs. I hope you'll be able to see this for yourself in the very near future. This makes me pleased. You must have grown so skinny, my poor man.

At the same time, he wrote to his wife in Chistopol saying much the same as he had written to his father, but added, with touching pride:

I am a key person at the editorial office now. The editor summons me ten times a day. I sleep there in the office, as the proofs are read until two or three in the morning.

Ortenberg himself wrote: '[After] precisely two months, Vasily Semyonovich brought me *The People Immortal*, a manuscript which was about two hundred pages long. I read it, so to speak, without putting it down. Nothing of the sort had been written since the war began. We decided to publish it without delay. The first chapter was sent to the typesetters. When the three-column page was ready, I started proof-reading it. Grossman was standing by my side watching my movements jealously. He feared that I would make unnecessary corrections.'

On 14 July, Grossman wrote in great excitement to his father.

> *Krasnaya Zvezda* started serialising my novel today . . . I wired you 400 roubles the day before yesterday! I will be in Moscow for another three weeks or a month, while the newspaper serialises the novel.

On 12 August, Ortenberg wrote: 'Today we published the final chapter of the novel *The People Immortal* by Vasily Grossman. It was serialised over eighteen issues of the newspaper, and after each one the interest of the readers increased. For eighteen days, and even nights, I stood with the writer by my desk proofreading one chapter after another in order to publish it in the next issue. There were no conflicts with Vasily Semyonovich. Only the end of the novel caused heated discussions: the main character, I. Babadzhanyan, gets killed. When I was reading the manuscript and when I was reading the proofed version of the final chapter, I kept asking the writer whether it wasn't possible to resurrect the main character, of whom the reader had grown so fond? Vasily Semyonovich replied: "We have to follow the ruthless truth of war."'

In fact, Grossman was to face acute embarrassment, the sort that any novelist dreads, even though it had been unusual to give the main char-acter in the novel his real name as well as identity. Babadzhanyan had not been killed, as Grossman had been told. But this future general of tank troops forgave the novelist for his fictional death.

In Moscow, meanwhile, few seemed to have had any idea of the disaster taking place in the south as Hitler's armies advanced on the Don and drove towards the Caucasus. Grossman's letter to his wife on 22 July showed that even those coming back to Moscow from the region appeared oblivious to the dangers.

> Yesterday Kostya Bukovsky returned from Stalingrad by air, and I gave a 'reception'. We drank and sang songs . . . Tvardovsky read

a wonderful chapter from his new work ['Vasily Tyorkin']. Everyone was moved to tears.[1]

Just over three weeks later, on 19 August, Grossman wrote to his father.

> I am leaving for the front in a couple of days. Your parental heart would have rejoiced if you could see how I was welcomed by the Red Army after the novel was published. My God, I was so proud of myself and so touched. And it was received so well at every level, from the top to the bottom of the army. My dear, my situation is better than ever now. I have success and recognition, but there is a heavy, heavy feeling in my soul. My passionate desire is to help all my dear ones, to assemble you all in one place. I am tormented by the thought about Mama's fate . . .
>
> I've had a letter from Vadya's son Yura. He is at the front, a lieutenant. He has fought in many battles and has been wounded.

Grossman's young cousin, Yura Benash, was about to be sent to Stalingrad, which is where Grossman himself was bound.

---

1 Tvardovsky (see note p.63) was best known as the author of 'Vasily Tyorkin', the story of a fictional peasant soldier, a real optimist who always manages to survive. He had begun life in Tvardovsky's newspaper column during the Russian-Finnish War. The character became a folk hero during the Great Patriotic War and won Tvardovsky another Stalin Prize in 1946.

THIRTEEN

The Road to Stalingrad

While Grossman was working on *The People Immortal*, the German general staff had been preparing the plans for Hitler's great summer offensive, Operation Blue. In what was almost a relaunch of Operation Barbarossa, Hitler counted on charging into the Caucasus to seize the oilfields there. He was convinced that securing this source of fuel would enable him to hold out against the 'Big Three' powers now ranged against him. But on 12 May, six days before the German operation was scheduled to start, Marshal Timoshenko launched his own offensive south of Kharkov, as mentioned in the previous chapter. The *Stavka* was hoping to recapture the city. The Soviet attack, however, was doomed. The large concentration of German forces in the area, and their rapid reaction to the new situation led to another disastrous encirclement five days later when General Paulus's Sixth Army sealed the trap on more than three Soviet armies. News of the disaster was a shock, especially for Grossman, who had spent so much time in that area and had met many men involved in the battle.

One important side effect of this engagement was to postpone the main phase of Operation Blue until the end of June. A German staff officer, with all the plans for the offensive in the south, was shot down on Soviet territory when his pilot lost his way, but Stalin refused to believe the evidence. He thought it was a trick, just as he had refused to believe warnings before Barbarossa. He was convinced that Hitler would again attack towards Moscow. It was not long, however, before he realised how serious his obstinacy had been. Timoshenko's South-Western and Southern Fronts, already badly mauled near Kharkov, were soon in headlong retreat. Paulus's Sixth Army pushed into the great bend of the River Don, while three other armies – Fourth Panzer, First Panzer and the Seventeenth Army, approached the lower Don to advance into the Caucasus.

Stalin began to panic. On 19 July, he personally ordered the Stalingrad Defence Committe to prepare the city for war immediately. It had seemed unthinkable that the Germans might reach the Volga, let alone attack the city named after him, for he had bolstered his reputation on a highly inflated version of its defence in the civil war when it was still called Tsaritsyn.

Hitler, meanwhile, began to meddle with the German general staff's operational plan. In the original version, the task of Paulus's Sixth Army had been to advance towards Stalingrad, but not to take it. The idea was simply to guard the whole of Operation Blue's left flank along the Volga as the main thrust went southwards into the Caucasus. But soon the plan changed. The Sixth Army, supported by part of the Fourth Panzer Army diverted back from the Caucasus, was ordered to capture the city which bore Stalin's name.

On 28 July, just after the Germans took Rostov and three of their armies crossed the River Don into the Caucasus, Stalin issued the notorious Order No. 227, known as 'Not One Step Back'. Anyone who retreated without orders or surrendered was to be treated as a 'traitor to the Motherland'. Grossman's daughter later heard of the following exchange in the editorial offices of *Krasnaya Zvezda*. 'When the famous order was issued to shoot deserters, Ortenberg said to my father, Pavlenko and [Aleksei] Tolstoy,[1] who all happened to be in the office at that moment: "Could one of you write a story on this subject, please?" My father replied immediately, without reflecting: "I am not going to write anything of the sort." This made Pavlenko furious. He twisted his body and, hissing like a snake, said: "You are an arrogant man, Vasily Semyonovich, such an arrogant man!" But Tolstoy, who had just stood there and did not take part in this verbal exchange, soon wrote a story about a beast-like deserter who, when fleeing from the Red Army, goes into a house and kills little children there.'

The retreating Soviet armies were in chaos. Thousands of lives were wasted in futile counter-attacks. Many trapped in the bend of the River Don, some sixty kilometres west of Stalingrad, drowned trying to escape. Grossman later interviewed a number of men involved in the disaster.

---

1 Tolstoy, Aleksei Nikolaevich (1882–1945), novelist and playwright, a cousin of Leo Tolstoy, but estranged from the rest of the family. He embraced revolutionary politics before the First World War, yet returned to the Soviet Union only in 1923 when flattered and reassured by the new Bolshevik authorities. His major work was the epic *Peter I*, yet he also wrote science fiction. The survival of his career was assured in 1938 during the Great Terror with his grovelling novel *Khleb*, praising Stalin's defence during the civil war of Tsaritsyn, later renamed Stalingrad. During the war he wrote *Ivan Grozny* in two parts, as well as the sort of 'patriotic articles' described here.

This was the account which Grossman took down from Vassily Georgevich Kuliev, a twenty-eight-year-old military correspondent and former Komsomol head of Young Pioneers, who appointed himself commissar of the group.

'We were retreating from the battle under fire from mortars and machine guns. At the Markovsky farmstead, we squatted in a trench, under a terrible fire, and then slipped through the encirclement. I appointed myself the commissar of a group of eighteen men. We lay down in [a field of] wheat. Germans appeared. A red-haired one shouted: "*Rus, uk vekh!*"[2] We fired bursts from our sub-machine guns and knocked four Germans off their horses. We broke through, shooting with a sub-machine gun and a machine gun. There were about twenty-five Germans. Sixteen of us were left out of the eighteen.

'At night, we walked through the wheat. It was overripe and rustled and Germans fired at us with a machine gun . . . Then I assembled the sixteen men again and took a compass bearing to avoid roads and villages on our way. We spent the night lying on the high bank of the Don.[3] We tied groundsheets together into a rope in order to haul the wounded men across the river, but it wasn't long enough. I suggested we swim the river. We put all our documents inside our forage caps and ammunition into a bag. I got tired halfway across the river and dropped the bag into the water. I kept my notepads in the forage cap.'

Once the Germans had finally cleared the west bank of the Don of Soviet troops, General Paulus redeployed his formations ready for the next leap forward. In the early hours of 21 August, German infantry in assault boats crossed the Don and seized bridgeheads on the east bank. Engineers went rapidly to work, and by the middle of the next day, a series of tank-bearing pontoon bridges were in place across the 'Quiet Don'. Armoured units rapidly filled the bridgehead.

On Sunday 23 August 1942, the 16th Panzer Division led the charge across the steppe to reach the Volga just north of Stalingrad, late that

2   German pidgin-Russian meaning: 'Rus, hands up!'
3   There is an unexplained topological phenomenon in which the great rivers of Russia flowing southwards, especially the Volga and the Don, tend to have very high western banks and flat eastern banks.

same afternoon. Overhead, the bombers of General Wolfram von Richthofen's Fourth Air Fleet waggled their wings in encouragement to the ground forces. Behind them lay the ruins of Stalingrad which they had carpet-bombed in relays. During that day and over the course of the next three, some 40,000 civilians are said to have died in the burning city.

It was also the day that Grossman, on Ortenberg's orders, left the Soviet capital for Stalingrad to report on the approaching battle.

> We left Moscow in the vehicle on 23 August. The chief fitters at the editorial board garage had spent time preparing our vehicle for the thousand-kilometre race from Moscow to Stalingrad. However, we suddenly came to a halt three kilometres outside Moscow. We had flat tyres on all four wheels at the same time. While Burakov, the driver, expressed his surprise at this incident and then started repairing the tyres in a leisurely fashion, we, the correspondents, began interviewing the population of the Moscow area, [in fact] a girl beside the main road. She had a tanned face, aquiline nose and cheeky blue eyes.
>
> 'Do you like colonels?'
> 'Why should I like them?'
> 'And what about lieutenants with their cubes?'
> 'Lieutenants get on my nerves. I like soldiers.'

Despite the urgency of their journey south, Grossman could not forgo a visit to Leo Tolstoy's estate, which he had last seen just before it was occupied by General Guderian the previous October.

> Yasnaya Polyana. Eighty-three Germans were buried next to Tolstoy. They were dug up and reburied in a crater made by a German bomb. The flowers in front of the house are magnificent. It's a good summer. Life seems to be filled with honey and calm.
>
> Tolstoy's grave. Flowers again, and bees are crawling in them. Little wasps are hovering above the grave. And in Yasnaya Polyana, a big orchard has died from the frost. All the trees are dead, dry apple trees stand grey, dull, dead like crosses on graves.
>
> The blue, ash-grey main road. Villages have become the kingdom of women. They drive tractors, guard warehouses and stables, queue for vodka. Tipsy girls are out singing – they are seeing a girlfriend off to the army. Women are carrying on their shoulders the great burden

of work. Women dominate. They are coping with an enormous amount of work and send bread, aircraft, weapons and ammunition to the front. They feed us and arm us now. And we, men, do the second part of the job. We do the fighting. And we don't fight well. We have retreated to the Volga. Women look and say nothing. There's no reproach in [their eyes], not a bitter word. Are they nursing a grievance? Or do they understand what a terrible burden a war is, even an unsuccessful one?

The woman owner of the house where we spend the night is mischievous. She loves silly jokes. 'Ah, it's war now,' she says. 'The war will write everything off.' She looks at Burakov intently, squinting. He is a handsome, good-looking guy. Burakov frowns, he is embarrassed. And she laughs, and begins 'household talk'. She wouldn't mind swapping some butter for a shirt or to buy half a litre [of vodka] from the military.

The woman owner of the house where we spend the next night is cleanliness itself. She rebuffs any dirty talk. At night, in the darkness she tells us trustingly about the household and about her work. She brings chickens and shows them to us, laughs, speaks of children, husband, the war. And everyone submits to her clear, simple soul.

That's how the life of women is going, in the rear and at the front – two currents, one that is clear and bright, and the other a dark, military one. 'Ah, it's war now,' [people say]. But the PPZh is our great sin.

The PPZh was the slang term for a 'campaign wife', because the full term, *pokhodno-polevaya zhena*, was similar to PPSh, the standard Red Army sub-machine gun. Campaign wives were young nurses and women soldiers from a headquarters – such as signallers and clerks – who usually wore a beret on the back of the head rather than the fore-and-aft *pilotka* cap. They found themselves virtually forced to become the concubines of senior officers. Grossman also scribbled down some bitter notes on the subject, perhaps for use in a story later.

Women – PPZh. Note about Nachakho, chief of administrative supplies department. She cried for a week, and then went to him.
'Who's that?'
'The general's PPZh.'
'And the commissar hasn't got one.'

Before the attack. Three o'clock in the morning.

'Where's the general?' [someone asks].

'Sleeping with his whore,' the sentry murmurs.

And these girls had once wanted to be 'Tanya', or Zoya Kosmodemyanskaya.[4]

'Whose PPZh is she?'

'A member of the Military Council's.'

Yet all around them tens of thousands of girls in military uniforms are working hard and with dignity.

Story about a general who escaped from an encirclement leading a goat on a rope. Some officers recognised him. 'Where are you going, Comrade General?' [they asked]. 'Which way will you take?' The general (Efimov) grinned sardonically. 'The goat will show me the way.'

Krasivaya Mecha – the inexpressible beauty of this place. Lamentation over a cow during the night, in the blue light of a yellow moon. The cow had fallen into an anti-tank ditch. Women are wailing: 'There are four children left.'[5] In the blue moonlight, a man with a knife is running to bleed the cow. In the morning, the cauldron is boiling. Everyone has replete faces, red eyes and swollen eyelids.

Thin women and girls wearing shawls on their heads are working on the road, loading earth on wooden handbarrows, levelling uneven places using picks and spades.

'Where are you from?' [we ask]

'We are from Gomel.'

'We were in the fighting near Gomel.'

We look at each other and say nothing. We drive on. It was a

4   Zoya Kosmodemyanskaya, a sixteen-year-old Moscow student, served behind German lines in the province of Tambov with a partisan group and used the nom de guerre of 'Tanya'. She was caught by the Germans, tortured and executed in the village of Petrishchevo on 29 November 1941. Before the Germans hanged her in the village street, she is said to have cried out: 'You'll never hang us all. My comrades will avenge me.' She was awarded posthumously the medal of Hero of the Soviet Union. In more recent years, the story of her heroism has been rather undermined by accounts from local people who blamed her for setting fire to houses, part of Stalin's ruthless order to destroy all shelter so that Germans froze to death, even though probably far more Russian civilians suffered.

5   They are bewailing the fact that there will be four children deprived of her milk.

bit alarming, this encounter near the village of Mokraya Olkhovka, just forty kilometres from the Volga.[6]

Women in the village. The whole heavy burden of work now rests entirely on them. Nyushka – as if made of cast iron, mischievous and whorelike. 'Ah, it's war now,' she says. 'I've already served eighteen [men] since my husband left. We have a cow between three women, but she lets only me milk her. She won't have anything to do with the other two.' She laughs. 'Now it's easier to persuade a woman than a cow.' She grins, offering us her love in a simple and kind-hearted way.

The vastness of our Motherland. We've been driving for four days. The time zone has changed – we are now one hour ahead. The steppe is different. The birds are different: kites, owls, little hawks. Watermelons and melons have appeared. But the pain we see here is still the same.

The village of Lebyazhye. The tall village houses have rooms painted with oil paint. We woke up, it was quiet, the sky was overcast in the morning, it was raining. The distance to the Volga is fifteen kilometres. The deceptive calm and quiet of the village was terrifying.

The Volga. Crossing. A bright day. The enormous size of the river, its slowness, greatness. In short, the Volga. There were vehicles on the barge loaded with aircraft bombs. [Enemy] aircraft are attacking. There is the crackle of machine-gun bursts. And the Volga remains slow and carefree. Boys are fishing from this fire-spitting barge.

There were several airfields in the area, which became important in the battle for Stalingrad. One of them was a melon field next to an open-air market which remained open for business, despite the strafing of German aircraft. The Soviet Union was already receiving a large quantity of Lend-Lease war material from the USA, including Willys Jeeps and the Douglas DC-3 'Dakota', which Russians called the 'Duglas'.

Arrival. Roar of engines, chaos. Cobras, Yaks, Hurricanes. A large Duglas appears, flying effortlessly and smoothly. Fighters are in a

6 This was west of Kamyshin on the Volga, two hundred kilometres by road north of Stalingrad.

frenzy. They are sniffing, running after it in its trace. The Duglas is looking for a place to land, and they are dancing in all directions. The Duglas has landed, with fighters above and around it. This sight is majestic, almost like a movie (with the steppe and the Volga).

Red Army soldiers were watching the scene and discussing it. One of them said: 'Just like bees. Why are they rushing about?'

'Guarding a melon field, apparently.'

The third one, looking at the Duglas which had just appeared: 'Must be the corporal from our company catching up with us.'

The passenger on board would of course have been rather more important. It may even have been General Georgi Zhukov, who flew down on 28 August on Stalin's orders to supervise the defence of the city.[7] 'What's the matter with them?' Stalin exploded on the telephone to General Aleksandr Vasilevsky, the first *Stavka* representative to reach Stalingrad.[8] He was furious with the local military commanders. 'Don't they realise that this is not only a catastrophe for Stalingrad? We would lose our main waterway and soon our oil too!'

Grossman spent at least one night in Zavolzhye.

Spent the night in the house of the RAIKOM chairman. He talks about collective farms, and about the chairmen of collective farms who take their livestock far into the steppe and live like kings there, slaughtering heifers, drinking milk, buying and selling. (And a cow now costs 40,000 roubles.)

Women talking in the kitchen of the RAIKOM canteen: 'Oh this Hitler, he's a real Satan! And we used to say that communists were Satans.'[9]

7 General (later Marshal) Georgi Konstantinovich Zhukov (1896–1974), a cavalry sergeant in the First World War, he was wounded in Tsaritsyn (later Stalingrad) in 1919. In 1939, he won the battle of Khalkin-Gol against the Japanese in the Far East. In 1941, Zhukov was made responsible for the defence of Leningrad and he then masterminded the battle of Moscow.
8 General (later Marshal) Aleksandr Mikhailovich Vasilevsky (1895–1977), the son of a priest, who served as an officer in the Tsarist Army in the First World War. A brilliant staff officer and planner, he escaped the purges, despite his bourgeois origins. He was on Molotov's staff during the November 1940 visit to Berlin, a failed attempt to save the Nazi-Soviet Pact. When the Germans advanced on Moscow, Vasilevsky became, along with Zhukov, one of Stalin's chief advisers and was made a representative of the *Stavka* to be sent to crisis points, such as Stalingrad at the end of August 1942.
9 Such naive remarks, if reported by an informer, could lead to several years in the Gulag, as reports from the Stalingrad Defence Committee make clear.

Land beyond the Volga [i.e. the east bank]. Dust, brown steppe, miserable autumn feather grass, tall weeds, sagebrush. Grass snakes crushed on the roads. Linnets. Camels. Camels' cries. The sun is rising in a pale misty haze. Half the sky is covered with smoke, the smoke of Stalingrad.

The bombing of Stalingrad on 23 August had set the oil storage tanks on fire, and the columns of black smoke, which continued to burn for days, could be seen from far around.

'A German's flying towards us!' [somebody shouts]. Everyone remains sitting.

'He's turning round!' Everyone rushes out from the *izba* and looks up.

Old man, the owner of the *izba*: 'I've got four sons at the war, four sons-in-law, and four grandsons. One son has been done for. They've sent me a notice.'

The kind-heartedness of our people. I don't know if any population could be strong enough to carry this terrible burden. The tragic emptiness of the villages. Girls are driven away in vehicles. They are crying, and their mothers are crying, because their daughters are being taken away to the army.

An old woman goes at night to guard barns at the collective farm. She is armed with a detachable pan handle. When someone approaches her, she shouts: 'Stop! Who's there? I'll shoot!'

Once again, looking across the Volga steppe towards Kazakhstan, Grossman is amazed at the vastness of the country. Yet the very size and depth of the Soviet Union no longer seems to be the defence that it once felt.

This war on the border of Kazakhstan, on the lower reaches of the Volga, gives one a terrifying feeling of a knife driven deep. General Gordov had fought in western Belorussia.[10] Now he is commanding troops on the Volga. The war has reached the Volga.

10 General Vasily Nikolayevich Gordov (1896–1950), the commander of the 64th Army during the retreat across the Don, became commander-in-chief of the Stalingrad Front for a very brief period until replaced by General Yeremenko. Arrested in 1947 during the Lesser Terror, he was executed for treason in 1950.

Grossman finally reached his destination as the German Sixth Army and part of the Fourth Panzer Army approached the northern, the western and the southern suburbs.

Soldiers with letters from home sent folded in a triangle and a copy of Krasnaya Zvezda, *bottom right.*

Stalingrad is burned down. I would have to write too much if I wanted to describe it. Stalingrad is burned down. Stalingrad is in ashes. It is dead. People are in basements. Everything is burned out. The hot walls of the buildings are like the bodies of people who have died in the terrible heat and haven't gone cold yet.

Huge buildings, memorials, public gardens. Signs: 'Cross here.' Heaps of wires, a cat sleeping on a window sill, flowers and grass in flowerpots. A wooden pavilion where they sold fizzy water is standing, miraculously intact among thousands of huge stone buildings burned and half destroyed. It is like Pompeii, seized by disaster on a day when everything was flourishing. Trams and cars with no glass in their windows. Burned-out houses with memorial plaques: 'I.V. Stalin spoke here in 1919.'[11]

Building of a children's hospital with a gypsum bird on the roof. One wing is broken off, the other stretched out to fly. The Palace of Culture: the building is black, velvety from fire, and two snow-white nude statues stand out against this black background.

There are children wandering about, there are many laughing faces. Many people are half insane.

Sunset over a square. A terrifying and strange beauty: the light pink sky is looking through thousands and thousands of empty windows and roofs. A huge poster painted in vulgar colours: 'The radiant way.'

A feeling of calm. The city has died after much suffering and looks like the face of a dead man who was suffering from a lethal disease and finally has found eternal peace. Bombing again, bombing of the dead city.

Although most of the men had been called up and were serving outside the city, the civilian population of Stalingrad had been swollen by refugees from the Don steppe. Grossman tried to interview some of them, including an old woman and a younger one called Rubtseva from a collective farm.

'Where is your husband?'

'No, don't ask,' whispers Seryozha, her boy. 'You'll upset Mama.'

'He's done his share of the fighting,' she replies. 'He was killed in February.' She had received the notice. Her story about Red Army cowards: 'A German [plane] was diving like a spear. Just the right moment to shoot him, but all our "heroes" were lying hidden in the tall weeds. I shouted at them: "Ah, you bastards!"'

'Once, some soldiers were escorting a [German] prisoner through the village. I asked him: "When did you join the fighting?" "In January," he answered. "Then it was you who killed my husband."'

11 The city of Tsaritsyn had been renamed Stalingrad in honour of the grossly exaggerated resistance which Stalin mounted against a marauding force of White Cossacks during the Russian Civil War.

The Palace of Culture in Stalingrad, described by Grossman.

I raised my arm, but the guard didn't let me hit him. "Come on," I said, "let me hit him." And the escort replied: "There's no such law [to permit it]." "Let me hit him without any law, and I'll go away." He wouldn't.

'Of course, one could live under the Germans, but it wasn't the life for me. My husband has been killed. Now all I've got left is Seryozha. He'll become a big person under the Soviets. Under the Germans he'd die a shepherd.

'The wounded men stole so much from us, we couldn't stand it any longer. They dug up all our potatoes, cleaned out all our tomatoes and pumpkins. Now we'll have to live through a hungry winter. They are cleaning out our homes too – shawls, towels, blankets. They've slaughtered a goat, but one feels sorry for them just the same. If a wounded man comes to you and he's in tears, you'll give him your supper and you start crying yourself.'

The old woman: 'These fools have allowed [the enemy] to reach the heart of the country, the Volga. They've given them half of Russia. It is true, of course, that the [Germans] have got a lot of machines.'

Grossman, when visiting the Traktorny, the great tractor works in northern Stalingrad, heard about the attack of the 16th Panzer Division on 23 August from the confusingly named Lieutenant Colonel German commanding the anti-aircraft regiment.

> On the night of the 23rd, eighty German tanks advanced on the Traktorny in two columns, and there were a lot of vehicles with infantry. There are many girls in German's regiment, instrument operators, direction finders, intelligence, and so on. There was a massive air raid at the same time as the tanks came. Some of the batteries were firing at the tanks, others at the aircraft. When the tanks had advanced right to the battery of Senior Lieutenant Skakun, he opened fire at the tanks. His battery was then attacked by aircraft. He ordered two guns to fire at the tanks, and the other two at the aircraft. There was no communication with the battery. 'Well, they must have been knocked out,' [the regimental commander] thought. Then he heard a thunder of fire. Then silence again. 'Well, they are finished now!' he thought again. Firing broke out again. It was only on the night of 24 August that four soldiers [from this battery] came back. They had carried back Skakun on a groundsheet. He had been heavily wounded. The girls had died by their guns.
>
> Golfman's battery was fighting for two days using [captured] German weaponry: 'What are you, infantry or artillery?'
> 'We are both.'

Both sides were using captured weapons and vehicles, which caused great confusion.

> A light tank brigade commanded by Lieutenant Colonel Gorelik was having a break in the area of the tractor plant when some tanks broke suddenly into the area. 'Germans!'
> 'Germans?' The lead tank in the German column was one of our KVs.[12]
> One anti-aircraft subunit had been ordered to retreat, but as they were unable to remove their guns, many of them stayed. Their commander, Lieutenant Trukhanov, took over from the gun-layer

12 The standard Soviet tank by 1942 was the T-34, a medium tank, but there were still a number of the heavy KV tanks in service. KV stood for Kliment Voroshilov, Stalin's old crony who had been minister of defence during the Soviet-Finnish war.

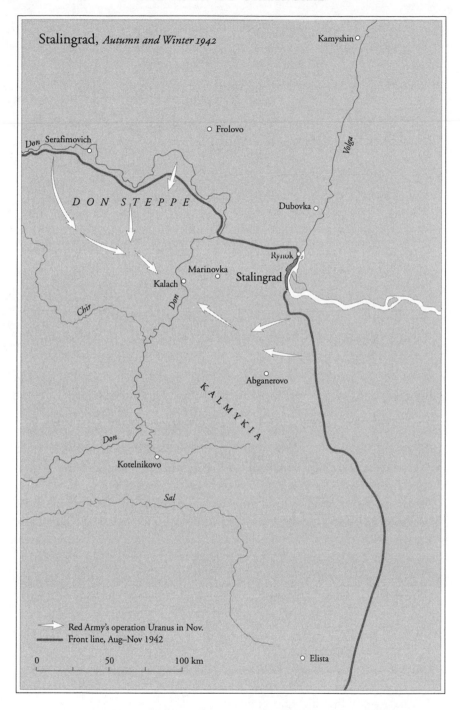

Stalingrad, *Autumn and Winter 1942*

and was firing at point-blank range. He had hit a tank and then was killed himself.

With Gorelik's brigade. People don't realise the importance of the events of 23 August. But they are offended by the lack of attention. No medals have been awarded. And the staff car has been taken away from the brigade commander who is down with typhoid fever.

Sarkisyan. He didn't go to Stalingrad on Sunday, because he knew a woman in the village, and he found out that beer was going to be delivered there. He had jammed himself in the machine of the German military scheme like a simple piece of metal. Perhaps, he caused Hitler insomnia for several days: they hadn't managed to keep up the momentum! And speed is almost the most important thing of all.

Grossman is presumably referring to the battle fought on 23 and 24 August by Captain Sarkisyan and other anti-aircraft gun crews also operated by young women, many of them Stalingrad high school students. Demonstrating an astonishing courage, they held up the 16th Panzer Division until all thirty-seven emplacements were destroyed by tank fire. Sarkisyan, like Colonel German, recounted the battle to Grossman, emphasising that 'the girls refused to go down into their bunkers', and fought the panzers head-on. But the real problem facing General von Wietersheim's XIV Panzer Corps was a lack of fuel.

Using a combination of his own observations and the remarks of those he interviewed, Grossman later wrote an imaginative description of the retreat late in August from the Don to the Volga when headquarters groups from the retreating 62nd and 64th Armies reached Stalingrad.

Those were hard and dreadful days . . . The armies were retreating. Men's faces were gloomy. Dust covered their clothes and weapons, dust fell on the barrels of guns, on the canvas covering the boxes full of headquarters documents, on the black shiny covers of staff typewriters, and on the suitcases, sacks and rifles piled chaotically on the carts. The dry, grey dust got into people's nostrils and throats. It made one's lips dry and cracked.

That was a terrible dust, the dust of retreat. It ate up the men's faith, it extinguished the warmth of people's hearts, it stood in a murky cloud in front of the eyes of gun crews. There were minutes when people forgot their duty, their strength and their weapons, and a murky feeling would come over them. German tanks were moving on the roads with a rumbling noise. German dive-bombers were hanging over the Don crossings by day and by night. 'Messers' were whistling over the supply carts. Smoke, fire, dust, terrible heat. On those days, the faces of the marching soldiers were as pale as those of the wounded men lying on the shaking one-and-a-half-ton trucks. On those days, men marching with their weapons felt like moaning and complaining, just like those who lay on the straw in villages, their bandages bloodstained, waiting for the ambulances to pick them up. The great nation's great army was retreating.

The first units of the retreating army entered Stalingrad. Trucks with grey-faced wounded men, front vehicles with crumpled wings, with holes from bullets and shells, the staff Emkas with star-like cracks on the windscreens, vehicles with shreds of hay and tall weeds hanging from them, vehicles covered with dust and mud, passed through the elegant streets of the city, past the shining windows of shops, past kiosks painted light blue and selling fizzy water with syrup, past bookshops and toyshops. And the war's breath entered the city and scorched it.

One has to be honest. On those anxiety-filled days, when the thunder of fighting could be heard in the suburbs of Stalingrad, when at night one could see rockets shot far away into the sky, and pale blue rays of searchlights roamed the sky, when the first trucks, disfigured by shrapnel, carrying the wounded and the belongings of retreating head-quarters appeared in the streets of the city, when front-page articles announced the mortal danger for the country, fear found its way into a lot of hearts, and many eyes looked across the Volga. It seemed to these people that they didn't have to defend the Volga, that it was the Volga that had to defend them. These people were saying a lot about the evacuation of the city, about transport, about steamers going to Saratov and Astrakhan; it seemed to them that they cared for the city's fate, while in fact, unwillingly, they made the city's defence more difficult by silently indicating, with their fears and anxiety, that Stalingrad had to be surrendered.

FOURTEEN

The September Battles

The city of Stalingrad, some forty kilometres long, follows the western bank of the great Volga. After the sudden rush of XIV Panzer Corps to the northern tip of the city on 23 August, the Sixth Army's advance on the city slowed. The *Stavka*, under tremendous pressure from a very nervous Stalin, ordered attacks from the open steppe to the north against the left flank of XIV Panzer Corps. These were hurried and ill-prepared, leading to terrible losses of men and equipment, but they made Paulus cautious, diverted the Luftwaffe from the city, and provided more time for the *Stavka* to rush reinforcements forward.

To the south-west, part of General Hoth's Fourth Panzer Army advanced on Stalingrad relentlessly, even though Yeremenko had concentrated the bulk of his forces in that direction. Yeremenko's 'member of the Military Council', which meant chief political officer, was Nikita Khrushchev, who had been in charge of the evacuation of Soviet industry from the Ukraine.[1] Grossman later crossed the Volga to visit Yeremenko and Khrushchev in the new headquarters of the Stalingrad Front.

The exhausted and demoralised remnants of the 62nd and 64th Armies had retreated across the last of the Don steppe in towards the city itself. By 12 September, the 62nd Army was reduced to a perimeter which was three kilometres deep at the southernmost point of the city and up to fifteen kilometres deep at the point of the northern suburbs. By the end of the month, the defensive perimeter was reduced to a strip of the

---

1   Khrushchev, Nikita Sergeyevich (1894–1971), a commissar in the civil war, he rose in influence by supporting Stalin against Trotsky. He oversaw much of the construction of the Moscow metro and played a leading part in the destruction of the Ukrainian intelligentsia during the Great Terror. In 1939, he became head of the Communist party in the Ukraine and, in 1941, organised the evacuation of factories to the east as the Germans advanced. After the war, following the death of Stalin in 1953, he led the coup against Beria and took power. He denounced Stalin at the XX Party Congress in 1956, but his attempts at liberalisation were inconsistent with other actions, such as the suppression of the Hungarian uprising in 1956.

northern part of the city, some twenty kilometres long and between one and five kilometres deep.

Without any sort of diary, it is hard to follow Grossman's movements precisely. One can, however, deduce from his notebooks that initially he seems to have been billeted in Dubovka, on the west bank of the Volga less than forty kilometres upstream from the northern part of Stalingrad. The west bank of the river, with a steep bank and sometimes with small cliffs, was much higher than the flat eastern side. The very idea of the German invaders reaching the Volga, the 'heart of Russia', did much to create a defeatist mood, as Grossman encountered in many conversations.

Now, there is nowhere further to retreat. Every step back is now a big, and probably fatal, mistake. The civilians in the villages beside the Volga feel it, as well as the armies that are defending the Volga and Stalingrad.

It is a joy and a pain at the same time to look at this most beautiful of rivers. Steamers painted grey green, covered with wilted branches, were standing by piers, with barely a light smoke rising from their smokestacks . . . Everywhere, also on the bank, there are trenches, bunkers, anti-tank ditches. The war has reached the Volga.

We are staying in the house of a dispossessed kulak. Only we suddenly see that the old owner of the house has returned, God knows from where. She watches us day and night and says nothing. She is waiting. And there we are, living under her stare.

An old woman sits all night in the slit trench. The whole of Dubovka sits in slit trenches. A *kerosinka* is flying overhead.[2] It rattles, lights candles[3] and drops little bombs.

'Where's the babushka?'

2 A *kerosinka* (a 'kerosene lamp' or 'Primus') was the nickname for a very simple, canvas-covered biplane, the Polikarpov U-2, which had been designed as a training aircraft and was also used as a crop sprayer. They were called a *kerosinka* because they could catch fire in no time. At Stalingrad, they were often piloted by young women between eighteen and twenty years old. They would fly across the front line during the night, stopping their engines and dropping small bombs on German lines. The bombs were ineffective, but the tactic terrified and wore the Germans down. They called the aircraft 'coffee grinders' and referred to the young women pilots as 'night witches'.
3 Presumably this means that it dropped a recognition flare to warn Red Army soldiers in the front line not to fire at them.

'She's in the trench,' laughs the old man. 'She sometimes looks out like a *suslik*[4] and then rushes back.'

'It's the end for us. That trickster [Hitler] has reached the heart of our land.'

A soldier with an anti-tank rifle is driving a huge flock of sheep through the steppe.

In the following description, Grossman appears to be close to the northern edge of the city near Rynok, where the parks and allotments full of ripening fruit appeared like a minor Garden of Eden to the men of the 16th Panzer Division who had spent the last two months crossing the sun-baked steppe.

Aircraft roar all night over our heads. The sky is humming day and night, as if we were sitting under the span of a huge bridge. This bridge is light blue during the day, dark blue at night, arched, covered with stars – and columns of five-ton trucks are thundering over this bridge.

Fire positions on the other side of the Volga, in a former sanatorium. A steep cliff. The river is blue and pink, like the sea. Vineyards, poplars. Batteries are camouflaged with vine leaves. Benches for the holidaymakers. A lieutenant is sitting on a bench, with a little table in front of him. He shouts: 'Battery fire!'

Beyond is the steppe. The air coming from the Volga is cool, and the steppe smells of warmth. Messers are up there. A sentry shouts: 'Air!' and the air is clear and smells of sagebrush.

Wounded men in their bloodstained bandages are walking along the Volga, right by the water. Naked people are sitting over the pink-evening Volga crushing lice in their underwear. Towing vehicles are roaring and skidding on the gravel by the bank. And then the stars at night. All one can see is a white church beyond the Volga.

A clear, cold morning in Dubovka. There is a bang, clinking of broken glass, plaster, dust in the air, haze. Screams and weeping over the Volga. Germans have dropped a bomb killing seven women and children. A girl in a bright yellow dress is screaming: 'Mama, Mama!'

4 A steppe ground squirrel, or gopher.

A man is wailing like a woman. His wife's arm has been torn off. She is speaking calmly, in a sleepy voice. A woman sick with typhoid fever has been hit in the stomach by a shell fragment. She hasn't died yet. Carts are moving, and blood is dripping from them. And the screaming, the crying over the Volga.

Grossman managed to get permission to cross the Volga from the east, or left, bank over to the burned-out city on the west bank. The crossing points were strictly controlled by troops from the 10th NKVD Rifle Division to catch deserters and even prevent civilians from fleeing the city. Stalin felt that their presence would oblige the Soviet troops to fight harder to save the city. Grossman was accompanied by Kapustyansky, another correspondent from *Krasnaya Zvezda*. Just crossing the Volga was dangerous as the Luftwaffe continually targeted the crossing points.

A terrifying crossing. Fear. The ferry is full of vehicles, carts, hundreds of people crowded together, and it gets stuck. A Ju-88 drops a bomb from high above. A huge spout of water, upright, bluish-white in colour. The feeling of fear. There isn't a single machine gun at the crossing, not a single little anti-aircraft gun. The quiet, clear Volga is terrifying like a scaffold.

The city of Stalingrad, the last days of August, beginning of September, after the fire. Crossing the river to Stalingrad. At the start, for courage, we drink a huge amount of apple wine at a collective farm on the left bank.

Messers are howling over the Volga, there is haze and smoke over it, smoke canisters are burned constantly to camouflage the crossing.

The burned, dead city, the square of Fallen Warriors. Dedications on memorials: 'From the Proletariat of Red Tsaritsyn to the Fighters for Freedom who died at the hands of Wrangel's henchmen in 1919.'

Inhabitants of a burned building are eating shchi[5] in a gateway, seated upon a heap of belongings. A book entitled *The Insulted and the Injured*[6] is lying on the ground nearby. Kapustyansky says to these people: 'You, too, are insulted and injured.'

'We are injured, but not insulted,' a girl replies.

---

5 Traditional Russian cabbage soup.
6 *The Insulted and the Injured* (1861) by Fyodor Dostoevsky.

The two correspondents made their way beyond the western edge of Stalingrad where the right-hand corps of Paulus's Sixth Army was joining up with Hoth's Fourth Panzer Army advancing from the south-west. On this side, the Germans, with nine divisions, heavily outnumbered the 40,000 exhausted Soviet troops of the 64th and 62nd Armies, retreating back into the city.

> Varapanovo, where there are old trenches overgrown with grass. The most severe battles of the civil war had taken place here, and now, once again, the heaviest enemy attacks are directed at this place.

Grossman and Kapustyansky appear, however, to have spent most of this visit in the city. They heard about the first worker battalions to be raised from various factories in the city. They were under the command of Colonel Sarayev of the 10th NKVD Rifle Division. The shock of battle proved too much for many in their ranks, so NKVD and Komsomol blocking detachments were used to prevent them running away. Political officers gave the correspondents stories of the determination of their troops.

> A soldier shot his comrade who had been carrying a wounded man back from the battlefield and had raised his hands in surrender. After this the soldier brought the wounded man back himself. His father, when saying goodbye to him, had given him a towel his mother had embroidered as a girl and his four crosses from [the First World War].

> Night in Stalingrad. Vehicles are waiting at the crossing point. Darkness. Fires are burning in the distance. A batch of reinforcements that has just crossed the Volga is moving slowly up [the steep river bank]. Two soldiers walk past us. I hear one of them say: 'They like an easy life, they hurry to live.'[7]

Grossman used some of these notes as well as material from the previous visit in his article for *Krasnaya Zvezda* which was published on 6 September.

> We arrived in Stalingrad soon after an air raid. Fires were still smoking here and there. Our comrade from Stalingrad who came there with

7 This means that they are taking all they can from life while they still have a chance.

*Grossman on the banks of the Volga with Kolomeitsev,
another correspondent. The burning oil tanks
can be seen in the background.*

us showed us his burned house. 'Here was the children's room,' he says. 'And here stood my bookcases, and I worked in that corner, where the distorted pipes now are. My desk stood there.' One could see the bent skeletons of children's beds under a pile of bricks. The walls of the house were still warm, like a dead man's body which hadn't had time to go cold.

Walls and the colonnade of the Physical Culture Palace are covered with soot after a fire, and two sculptures of naked young men are blindingly white on this velvet-black background. Sleek Siberian cats are sleeping on the windows of empty buildings. Near the statue of Kholzunov, boys are picking up fragments of bombs and anti-aircraft shells. On this quiet evening, the pink beautiful sunset looks so melancholy through hundreds of empty eye sockets of windows.

Some people have instantly accustomed themselves to the war. The ferry which transports troops to the city is frequently attacked by enemy fighters and bombers. The crew are eating juicy water-melon slices, looking into the sky now and then. A boy is looking attentively at the float of his fishing angle, dangling his feet outside. An elderly woman is sitting on a little bench knitting a stocking during bursts of machine-gun fire and anti-aircraft guns firing away.

We entered a destroyed house. The inhabitants of the building were having dinner, sitting at tables made from planks of wood and boxes, children were blowing at hot *shchi* in their bowls.

For the Soviet military authorities, it seemed that the only way to save Stalingrad was to launch attack after attack against the northern flank of XIV Panzer Corps. But the three infantry armies involved, the 1st Guards, the 24th and the 66th, stood little chance, even though they vastly outnumbered their opponents. They were short of ammunition, had hardly any artillery and their ranks consisted mainly of reservists.

Stalin's furious orders urging speed led to total chaos. Divisions became confused as they marched forward from the railhead at Frolovo, north of the Don bend, with no idea of which army they were supposed to join or where they were going. The Luftwaffe strafed and bombed them on the open steppe, while the superiority of German tank-crew training made it an unequal struggle. Grossman, at Dubovka, was close to the forming-up areas for these ill-fated attacks.[8]

Divisions on the move. People's faces. Engineers, artillery, tanks. They are moving day and night. Faces, faces, their seriousness, they are the faces of doomed people.

Before the advance began, Donbass proletarian Lyakhov, soldier from the motorised infantry battalion of a tank brigade, wrote this note to his commanders: 'Let Comrade Stalin know that I will sacrifice my life for the sake of the Motherland, and for him. And I won't regret it even for a second. If I had five lives, I would sacrifice them all for his sake, without hesitating, so dear is this man to me.'

Grossman was interested in the daily grumbles of soldiers. In the following case, a soldier talked about the open steppe, where Luftwaffe pilots could spot field kitchens easily, and then moved on to that other soldierly preoccupation: boots.

8 The beginning of this notebook, entitled 'North-West of Stalingrad, September 1942', has been lost or destroyed.

'Most men got killed because of kitchens. Corporals "get tanned" by the kitchens, waiting for food. It's usually gone off by the time we get it. I've suffered so much because of my boots. I've been walking with blood blisters. I took the boots off a dead man because they didn't have any holes, but they were too small for me.'

'We, young soldiers, don't even think of home, it's mostly older soldiers who do . . . A corporal from the 4th Company called Romanov has let us down on the battlefield. We, the young soldiers who are properly brought up and conscientious, we endure all this with patience, but the moods of older soldiers are worse than ever.'

Grossman was particularly taken with Red Army soldier Gromov, an anti-tank rifleman, who at thirty-eight must have appeared ancient to the young conscripts. According to Ortenberg, Grossman spent a week with the anti-tank unit. 'He was not a stranger any more in their family,' he wrote. Ortenberg claimed the credit for the idea of writing about him, perhaps because Grossman's portrait of Gromov was later hailed as a masterpiece, particularly by Ilya Ehrenburg. These were Grossman's notes on what he called Gromov's story:

'When you've hit it, you see a bright flash on the armour. The shot deafens one terribly, one has to open one's mouth. I was lying there, I heard shouts: "They're coming!" My second shot hit the tank. The Germans started screaming terribly. We could hear them clearly. I wasn't scared even a little. My spirits soared. At first, there was some smoke, then crackling and flames. Evtikhov had hit one vehicle. He hit the hull, and how the Fritzes screamed!' (Gromov has light green eyes in a suffering, angry face.) 'The number one carries the anti-tank rifle. The number two carries thirty cartridges for it, a hundred cartridges for [an ordinary] rifle, two anti-tank grenades, and a rifle. What a noise the [anti-tank rifle] makes. The earth trembles from it.'

'Our main losses occur because we have to go and get breakfast and dinner ourselves. We can only go and get them at night. There are problems with dishes, we should get hold of buckets.'

'We used to lie down during the night and advance during the day. The ground's as flat as a tabletop.'

These notes, including Gromov's words, were then refashioned into the piece for *Krasnaya Zvezda*, which so impressed Ehrenburg and others.

When on the march, one's shoulder bone aches like hell from the anti-tank rifle, and the arm becomes numb. It's difficult to jump with the anti-tank rifle and difficult to walk on slippery ground. Its weight slows you down and upsets your balance.

Anti-tank riflemen walk heavily, in broad steps, and seem slightly lame – on the side where the rifle's weight is. [Gromov] was filled with the anger of a difficult man, a man whom the war has taken away from his field, from his *izba*, and from his wife who had given birth to his children. This was the anger of a doubting Thomas who saw with his own eyes the huge troubles of his people . . . Walls of white and black smoke and grey-yellow dust rose in front of the anti-tank riflemen and behind them. This was what one usually calls 'hell' . . . He was lying on the bottom of the slit trench. The hell was howling with a thousand voices, and Gromov was dozing, stretching his tired legs: a soldier's rest, poor and austere.

'I fired at [the tank] again,' [said Gromov]. 'And I saw at once that I'd hit it. It took my breath away. A blue flame ran over the armour, quick like a spark. And I understood at once that my anti-tank shell had got inside and gave off this blue flame. And a little smoke rose. The Germans inside began to scream. I'd never heard people scream this way before, and then immediately there was a crackling inside. It crackled and crackled. The shells had started to explode. And then flames shot out, right into the sky. The tank was done for.'

Regimental commander Savinov, a wonderful Russian face. Blue eyes, red tan. There's a dimple from a bullet on his helmet. 'When the bullet hit me,' Savinov said, 'I became drunk and lay for fifteen minutes unconscious. A German had got me drunk.'

Civilians too were caught up in what was seen by both sides as the key battle of the war.

Spies. A twelve-year-old boy who could report on where [German] headquarters had been situated by its signal cables, kitchens and dispatch riders. A woman, to whom the Germans had said: 'If you don't go and don't come back, we are going to shoot your two daughters.'

Soviet pitilessness more than matched that of the Germans, when it came to forcing their own men into the attack. Stalin's Order No. 227 – 'Not One Step Back' – included the instruction to each army command to organise 'three to five well-armed [blocking] detachments (up to two hundred men each)' to form a second line to 'combat cowardice' by shooting down any soldier who tried to run away. In the factory district of northern Stalingrad, Grossman came across Colonel S.F. Gorokhov, then commanding the 124th Brigade.

> After the seventh attack, Gorokhov said to the commander of the blocking detachment: 'Come on, that's enough shooting at their backs. Come on and join the attack.' The commander and his blocking detachment joined the attack, and the Germans were thrown back.

The defence of Stalingrad was stiffened by the most terrifying discipline. Some 13,500 soldiers were executed during the five-month battle. Most of these were during the earlier days when many men broke. Grossman heard about an 'extraordinary event', which was the official Soviet term for 'betrayal of the Motherland', a very broadly defined crime.

> An extraordinary event. Sentence. Execution. They undressed him and buried him. At night, he came back to his unit, in his blood-stained underwear. They shot him again.

This may possibly refer to another case, but it is almost exactly what happened in the 45th Rifle Division, when the execution squad from the NKVD Special Department attached to the division failed to kill the condemned man, perhaps because their aim was affected by alcohol.[9] This soldier, like so many others, had been condemned to death for a self-inflicted wound. After shooting him, the execution squad buried him in a nearby shell-hole, but the condemned man dug himself out and returned to his company, only to be executed a second time. Usually, however, the prisoner was forced to undress before being shot so that his uniform could be issued to somebody else without too many discouraging bullet-holes.

---

9   The 45th Rifle Division became the 74th Guards Rifle Division on 1 March 1943 as a tribute to its role at Stalingrad. It stayed with the 62nd Army, later the 8th Guards Army, until the end of the war.

A number of Soviet generals did not shrink from hitting even quite senior subordinates, although the striking of soldiers by officers and NCOs had been one of the most hated characteristics of the Tsarist Army.

> Conversation of Colonels Shuba and Tarasov with the army commander:
> '"What?"'
> '"May I say again . . . ?"'
> '"What?"'
> '"May I say again . . . ?"'
> 'He hit Shuba in the mouth. I [presumably Tarasov] stood still, drew my tongue in and clenched my teeth, because I was afraid to bite my tongue off or be left with no teeth.'

At this critical moment of the war, Grossman recorded in his notebooks a number of stories about Soviet and military bureaucracy.

> Aircraft had been bombing our tanks for three days, and all this time telegrams about it were travelling through different chains of command.

> Provisions for an encircled division were to be dropped by parachute, but the quartermaster didn't want to issue the foodstuffs, because there was no one to sign the invoice.

> A chief of reconnaissance could not get permission for half a litre of vodka, nor could he get a badly needed piece of silk which cost eighty roubles fifty kopecks.

> Information on take-off. Applications for bombing missions.

> A plane caught fire. The pilot wanted to save it and didn't bail out by parachute. He brought the burning plane back to the airfield. He was on fire himself. His trousers were burning. The quartermaster, however, refused to issue him with new trousers because the minimum period hadn't elapsed before a replacement could be provided for the old ones. The red tape lasted for several days.

> A Yu-53 with a full load of fuel was burning in the clear evening sky. The crew bailed out with their parachutes.

Stalin was beside himself with rage when he heard on 3 September that Stalingrad was encircled on the western bank. For General Yeremenko, the commander-in-chief of the Stalingrad Front, and Nikita Khrushchev, the member of his Military Council and thus chief commissar, the key question was who should be given the responsibility of defending the city itself. The candidate would have to take over the thoroughly demoralised and battered 62nd Army, which was cut off from its neighbour to the south, the 64th Army, on 10 September.

On the following day, 11 September, Yeremenko's headquarters in a complex of tunnels in the Tsaritsa gorge came under direct fire. Grossman's editor, Ortenberg, accompanied by the writer Konstantin Simonov, reached the headquarters that day. They spoke to a 'gloomy' Khrushchev, who found it hard to light a cigarette due to the lack of oxygen in the tunnel. When Ortenberg and Simonov woke the next morning, they found that the headquarters had departed while they slept. Stalin, still in a foul temper, had been forced to agree that Yeremenko must withdraw Stalingrad Front headquarters across the Volga. General Vasily Chuikov, a tough and thoroughly ruthless commander, was summoned

Ortenberg (centre) and Konstantin Simonov (right) sending despatches back to Moscow from Stalingrad Front HQ, September 1942.

to take command of the 62nd Army left on the west bank.[10] Grossman later interviewed all those involved.

> Khrushchev – Tired, white-haired, bloated. Looks perhaps like Kutuzov. Yeremenko – He has been wounded seven times in this war.

Yeremenko claimed the credit for selecting Chuikov.

> 'It was I who promoted Chuikov. I knew him, he was never prone to panic . . . I knew Chuikov from peacetime. I used to drub him during manoeuvres. "I know how brave you are," [I told him], "but I don't need that sort of courage. Don't make hasty decisions, as you tend to."'

According to Chuikov, the interview with Yeremenko and Khrushchev went as follows:

> 'Yeremenko and Khrushchev said to me:
> '"You have to save Stalingrad. How do you feel about it?"
> '"Yes, sir."
> '"No, it isn't enough to obey, what do you think about it?"
> '"It means to die. So we will die."'

In his memoirs written during the Khrushchev era, Chuikov recounted the conversation in a slightly different way:

> 'Comrade Chuikov,' said Khrushchev, 'how do you interpret your task?'
> 'We will defend the city or die in the attempt,' came Chuikov's reply.
> Yeremenko and Khrushchev looked at him and said that he had understood his mission correctly.

---

10   General Vasily Ivanovich Chuikov (1900–1982) commanded the 4th Army in the invasion of Poland in 1939, then the 9th Army in the Russo-Finnish War. From 1940–2 he served as military attaché in China. After Stalingrad, his 62nd Army became the 8th Guards Army and he commanded it all the way to victory in Berlin where he conducted surrender negotiations with General Hans Krebs. From 1949–53 he was Commander-in-Chief Soviet Forces in East Germany and from 1960–61, he served as Deputy Minister of Defence.

As will be seen later, Grossman became disillusioned by the vanities and jealousies of the Stalingrad commanders after the battle, all of whom felt that their role had been insufficiently appreciated. Yeremenko was quite open in his boasting and his attempts to undermine Khrushchev.

'I was a corporal during the last war and killed twenty-two Germans . . . Who wants to die? No one is particularly eager . . . I had to take terribly cruel decisions here: "Execute on the spot."

'Khrushchev proposed that we should mine the city. I telephoned Stalin [about it]. "What for?" [Stalin] asked.

"I am not going to surrender Stalingrad," I said. "I don't want to mine the city."

'"Tell him to fuck off, then," [Stalin replied].'

'We have held on thanks to our [artillery] fire and thanks to the soldiers. The fortifications were fucking bad.'

The inadequacy of Stalingrad's defences was just about the only matter on which all the senior officers agreed. Chuikov observed that the barricades could have been pushed over with a truck. Gurov, the chief commissar of the 62nd Army, said that no fortifications had existed, and Krylov, the chief of staff, said they were laughable. 'In the defence of Stalingrad,' Chuikov said later to Grossman, 'divisional commanders counted on blood more than on barbed wire.'

Chuikov, whom Grossman came to know very well during the course of the war, also liked to expound on his past experience and his role at Stalingrad. 'I commanded a regiment at the age of fifteen,' he said to Grossman of his time in the Russian civil war. 'I was the chief adviser to Chiang Kai-shek,' Chuikov added when talking of 1941. He did not mention that it was a great advantage to have been absent in China during that first disastrous summer of the war.

Chuikov's army was not only exhausted and demoralised. Reduced to fewer than 20,000 men, it was heavily outnumbered and outgunned on the key sector of central Stalingrad, where four German infantry divisions, two panzer divisions and a motorised division attacked from the west towards the Volga. The two key objectives for them were the Mamaev Kurgan, a Tartar mound 102 metres high (and known as Point 102), and the Volga crossing point just beyond Red Square. Chuikov reached this landing stage on the night of 12 September immediately after his appointment as commander of the 62nd Army had been confirmed by Yeremenko and Khrushchev.

By the light from blazing buildings, he made his way to the Mamaev Kurgan where 62nd Army headquarters was temporarily established. The situation was even more desperate than he had feared. 'I see Mamaev Kurgan in my dreams,' Chuikov told Grossman later.

The only unmauled formation under his command was Colonel Sarayev's 10th NKVD Rifle Division, but its units were dispersed and Sarayev, who reported to the NKVD chain of command, was more than reluctant to put his men under Red Army control. Chuikov's commissar, Gurov, was scathing about the NKVD division.

> 'The Sarayev division was scattered all over the front, and therefore there was practically no control over it. The Sarayev division did not fulfil its function. It hadn't held its defensive positions, and didn't maintain order in the city.'

The previous year, no military commander had had the courage to face up to one of Beria's officers. But Chuikov, facing disaster, had no qualms. Evidently, his threat to Sarayev about Stalin's anger if the city fell had the required effect. Sarayev followed orders and placed one of his regiments in front of the vital landing stage, as instructed.

Grossman only discovered later that Chuikov was another commander who used to punch his subordinates when in a foul mood. Chuikov was indeed ruthless, as ready to execute a brigade commander who failed in his duty as a simple soldier who turned tail in battle, but his own physical bravery was beyond question.

> 'A commander must feel that it is better for him to lose his head than to bow to a German shell. Soldiers notice these things.'

> 'The first task was to instil in your [subordinate] commanders the idea that the Devil is not so terrible as he is painted.'

> 'Once you are here, there is no way out. Either you will lose your head or your legs . . . Everyone knew that those who turn and run would be shot on the spot. This was more terrifying than the Germans . . . Well, there is also Russian zeal. We adopted a tactic of counter-attack. We attacked when they became tired of attacking.'

In his memoirs, Chuikov openly acknowledged that when defending Stalingrad, he had followed the precept that 'Time is Blood'. He had to hold the Germans at all costs and that meant throwing fresh regiments and divisions into the hell of the city as soon as they reached the eastern bank and were ready to be ferried across.

The Sixth Army's major offensive into the city was launched just before dawn on 13 September. Chuikov had not even had time to meet his formation commanders when the German 295th Infantry Division came straight for the Mamaev Kurgan. Two other infantry divisions headed for the main station and the landing stage. Chuikov could only watch events from a slit trench through periscopic binoculars.

That evening, Führer headquarters celebrated the success of the 71st Infantry Division reaching the centre of the city. Stalin heard the same news in the Kremlin when Yeremenko telephoned him and warned that another major attack could be expected the next day. Stalin turned to General Vasilevsky. 'Issue orders immediately for Rodimtsev's 13th Guards Division to cross the Volga and see what else you can send over.' Zhukov, who was also with them, poring over a map of the area, was told to fly down again immediately. Nobody was in any doubt that the moment of crisis had arrived.

Chuikov's army headquarters now found itself in the front line, following the attack on the Mamaev Kurgan the day before. In the early hours they moved south to the tunnels of the Tsaritsa gorge, which Yeremenko and Khrushchev had so recently abandoned. Gurov told Grossman: 'When we were leaving Height 102, we felt that the worst thing of all was uncertainty. We didn't know how all this was going to end.'

The battle on 14 September went badly for the defenders. The German 295th Infantry Division captured the Mamaev Kurgan as Chuikov had feared, but the biggest threat came in the centre of the city, where one of Sarayev's NKVD regiments was thrown into a counter-attack on the main station. It changed hands several times during the day.

The key event, according to the Stalingrad legend, was the crossing of the Volga under fire by General Aleksandr Rodimtsev's 13th Guards Rifle Division.[11] This formation had been hurried down by forced marches. Grossman recreated the march and the arrival on the bank of the Volga from participants.

11 The 13th Guards Rifle Division was founded on 19 January 1942, on a basis of the 87th Rifle Division. General Aleksandr Ilyich Rodimtsev (1905–1977) had won the gold star of Hero of the Soviet Union as an adviser in the Spanish Civil War, particularly for his role at the Battle of Guadalajara in 1937, when Mussolini's blackshirt divisions were put to flight.

The road turned south-west, and soon we began to see maples and willows. Orchards with low apple trees in them stretched around us. And as the division was approaching the Volga, we saw a tall, dark cloud. One couldn't possible mistake it for dust. It was sinister, quick, light, and black as death: that was the smoke from burning oil-storage tanks rising over the northern part of the city. Big arrows nailed to the trunks of trees said 'Crossing'. They pointed towards the Volga . . . The division couldn't wait until night to cross the river. Men were hastily unloading crates of weapons and ammunition, and sugar and sausage.

Barges were rocking on the waves, and men from the rifle division felt frightened because the enemy was everywhere, in the sky, on the opposite bank, but they had to encounter him without the comfort of solid earth under their feet. The air was unbearably transparent, the blue sky was unbearably clear, the sun seemed relentlessly bright and the flowing flat water seemed so tricky and unreliable. And no one felt happy about the clarity of the air, about the coolness of the river in the nostrils, about the tender and moist breath of the Volga touching their inflamed eyes. Men on the barges, ferries and motor boats were silent. Oh, why isn't there that suffocating and thick dust over the river? Why is the bluish smoke of the smoke-screen canisters so transparent and fine? Every head was turning from side to side in anxiety. Everyone was glancing at the sky.

'He's diving, the louse!' someone shouted.

Suddenly, a tall and thin bluish-white column of water sprang up about fifty metres from the barge. Immediately after it another column grew and collapsed even closer, and then a third one. Bombs were exploding on the surface of the water, and the Volga was covered with lacerated foamy wounds; shells began to hit the sides of the barge. Injured men would cry out softly, as if trying to conceal the fact of being wounded. By then, rifle bullets had already started whistling over the water.

There was one terrible moment when a large calibre shell hit the side of a small ferry. There was a flash of flame, dark smoke enveloped the ferry, an explosion was heard, and immediately afterwards, a drawling scream as if born from this thunder. Thousands of people saw immediately the green helmets of the men swimming among the wreckage of wood rocking on the surface of water.

Chuikov told Rodimtsev, who crossed to the west bank during the afternoon of 14 September to receive his orders, that the situation was so desperate that his men should leave behind all their heavy equipment, bringing just grenades and personal weapons. Rodimtsev described it to Grossman at a later stage in the battle.

> 'We began the crossing at 1700 hours on 14 September, preparing weapons as we went along. One barge was destroyed [by bombing] during the crossing; forty-one men were killed and twenty survived.'

Much has been written of the 13th Guards Rifle Division charging up the steep bank of the Volga and straight at the Germans, who had advanced to within two hundred metres of the river's edge. But Grossman heard about a special mission assigned to a small group of six men from the division.

> Sapper Lieutenant Chermakov, Sergeants Dubovy and Bugaev, and Red Army soldiers Klimenko, Zhukov and Messereshvili carried out the task of blowing up a sealed building of the State Bank. Each carried 25kg of explosives. They made it to the bank and blew it up.

Inevitably, there was a less heroic aspect to the crossing of the river, which Soviet official accounts always suppressed.

> Seven Uzbeks were guilty of self-inflicted wounds. They were all shot.

The exploits of the 13th Guards Rifle Division attracted a great deal of attention in the Soviet and international press. Rodimtsev, to Chuikov's furious jealousy, became a world-famous hero. Grossman, however, was more interested in the bravery of the soldiers and junior officers than in the squabbles of the commanders. He persuaded Rodimtsev's headquarters to let him have the report below, and he carried it with him in his field bag all through the war. He mentioned it in his essay 'Tsaritsyn-Stalingrad' and included it in the novel *For a Just Cause*.

> [Report]
> Time: 11.30 hours, 20.9.42
> To: Guards Senior Lieutenant Fedoseev (Commander of the 1st Battalion)
>
> May I report to you, the situation is as follows: the enemy is trying to encircle my company, to send sub-machine-gunners round to

our rear. But all their efforts have so far failed in spite of their superior strength. Our soldiers and officers are displaying courage and heroism in the face of the fascist jackals. The Fritzes won't succeed until they've stepped over my corpse. Guards soldiers do not retreat. Soldiers and officers may die like heroes, but the enemy mustn't be allowed to break our defence. Let the whole country learn about the 3rd Rifle Company of the 13th Guards Division. While the company commander is alive, not a single whore will break through. They might break though if the company commander is killed or heavily wounded. The commander of the 3rd Company is under stress and unwell physically himself, deafened and weak. He gets vertigo, is falling off his feet, his nose bleeds. In spite of all the hardships, the Guards, namely the 3rd and 2nd Companies, will not retreat. We will die like heroes for Stalin's city. Let the Soviet land be the [enemy's] grave. Commander of the 3rd Company Kolaganov has himself killed two Fritz machine-gunners and took from them a machine gun and documents which he has presented to the HQ of the battalion. [Signed] Kolaganov

The 62nd Army, continually outnumbered, held on as best it could within an ever diminishing perimeter along the west bank. Rodimtsev told Grossman: 'We operated with no reserves. A thin defence line, that was all we had.'

Yeremenko told him: 'I was sweating, [The Germans] were pressing hard, and we had positioned our troops stupidly. I felt hot all the time, [even though] I am a very healthy man. We were just feeding soldiers [into the battle]. That was it.'

Gurov, the chief commissar of the 62nd Army, pointed out: 'There were days when we evacuated 2,000–3,000 injured men.'

Krylov, the chief of staff of the 62nd Army, remarked on the German conduct of the battle.

'They rely on the massive use of fire-power, to stunning effect. Their powerful materiel is in inverse proportion to the potential of German infantry. German middle-rank commanders completely lack initiative.

'The first days of September were particularly hard, the beginning of chaos. In the evenings I could pull myself together in order to give instructions to the troops. During the day, we just counted down minutes till the evening.'

The Germans knew only too well that they needed to break the 62nd Army's life lines across the Volga, using artillery as well as the Luftwaffe. That was why there were so many struggles back and forth to secure the Mamaev Kurgan, the one hill from which direct fire could be concentrated on the landing stages. The river-transport troops, many of them Volga boatmen and fishermen, faced dangers as great as those of the *frontoviki* on the west bank.

> The officer in charge of the crossing, Lieutenant Colonel Puzyrevsky, has been here about two weeks. His predecessor, Captain Eziev, a Chechen, was killed by a bomb on a barge. Perminov, the military commander, has been here for fifty-seven days. Deputy Battalion Commander Ilin has been taken away by air, heavily wounded. Smerechinsky – killed – was the chief of the crossing before Eziev. The battalion commander, who set up the Volga crossing, was killed by a bomb splinter. Sholom Akselrod, commander of the technical platoon, was killed on a barge by a mine. *Politruk* Samotorkin was wounded by a mine. *Politruk* Ishkin's leg was torn off by a shell.

For the reinforcements assembling on the west bank opposite, the 1,300 metres of open water was enough to break anyone's nerve. But Chuikov, with his characteristically brutal humour, observed that the crossing was just the start.

> 'Approaching this place, soldiers used to say: "We are entering hell." And after spending one or two days here, they said: "No, this isn't hell, this is ten times worse than hell." [It produced] a wild anger, an inhuman anger, towards Germans. [Some Red Army soldiers] were escorting a prisoner, but he never reached his destination. The poor chap died from fear. "Would you like to drink some water from the Volga?" [they asked], and they rammed his face into the water ten or twelve times.'

Suffering seemed to have become a universal fate. Towards the end of the month, Grossman received a letter from his wife, Olga Mikhailovna, in which she recounted the death of her son, Misha, who had been killed by a bomb. He wrote back in a clumsy attempt to mitigate her despair.

> My own one, my good one. Today I received your letter which someone had brought from Moscow. It grieved me deeply. Don't

Grossman with Vysokoostrovsky (centre) at Stalingrad, September 1942.

let your spirits sink, Lyusenka. Don't give way to despair. There is so much sorrow around us. I see so much of it. I've seen mothers who have lost three sons and a husband in this war, I've seen wives who've lost husbands and children, I've seen women whose little children have been killed in a bombing raid, and all these people don't give way to despair. They work, they look forward to victory, they don't lose their spirits. And in what hard conditions they have to survive! Be strong, too, my darling, hold on . . . You've got me and Fedya, you have love and your life has a meaning.

'I've been recommended for the Order of the Red Star for the second time, but to no effect so far, just as before. I've got this letter taken from a dead soldier; it's written in a child's scribble. There are the following words at the end: 'I miss you very much. Please come and visit, I so want to see you, if only for one hour. I am writing this, and tears are pouring. Daddy, please come and visit.'

He also wrote to their old German-speaking nanny, Zhenni Genrikhovna Henrichson, whom many years later he put into his novel *Life and Fate*.

You already know about our terrible grief: the death of Misha. Sorrow has come to our family too, Zhenni Genrikhovna. Please write to me at my new address: 28 Field Post, 1st Unit, V.S. Grossman (don't mention my position in the address). Have you heard from Papa? Where is he now? I don't know at what address to write to him.

Grossman at this point had no idea that his nephew, Yura Benash, a young lieutenant in Stalingrad who had been trying to contact him having read his articles, had been killed in the fighting.

FIFTEEN

The Stalingrad Academy

It was General Chuikov who coined the phrase the Stalingrad Academy of Street-Fighting. Chuikov's idea was to keep the Germans constantly engaged. He ordered his troops to site their trenches as close to the enemy as possible, because that would make it harder for the Luftwaffe, which enjoyed air supremacy by day, to distinguish between the two opposing forces. Chuikov boasted to Grossman:

> 'During air raids our soldiers and Germans ran towards each other to hide in the same holes. [The Germans] could not strike our front line with their air attacks. At the Red October plant they demolished a fresh division of their own.'

Grossman emphasised this proximity in an essay written towards the end of the battle.

> Sometimes, the trenches dug by the battalion are twenty metres from the enemy. The sentry can hear soldiers walking in the German trench, and arguments when Germans divide up the food. He can hear all night the tap dance of a German sentry in his torn boots. Everything is a marker here, every stone is a landmark.

The way to wear the Germans down was by small-scale night attacks, to prevent them sleeping, and playing on their fear of darkness, and of the hunting skills of the Siberian troops. Snipers also provided a powerful psychological weapon as well as a boost to Soviet morale.

Chuikov could be as wasteful of lives as any Soviet general – especially in the early days when he ordered one counter-attack after another to blunt the German advance – but he also quickly recognised the advantage of close-combat engagements, using small groups armed with grenades, sub-machine guns, knives, sharpened spades and a flame-thrower. This savage system of fighting in cellars, sewers and in the ruins of apartment blocks became known to the Germans as *Rattenkrieg*. Chuikov told Grossman later in the battle:

> 'Stalingrad is the glory of the Russian infantry. Our infantry has taken and made use of German weapons and ammunition. We didn't just receive attacks, we had to attack. Retreat meant ruin. If you retreated, you'd be shot. If I did, I'd be shot . . . A soldier who'd spent three days here considered himself an old-timer. Here, people only lived for one day . . . Weapons for close-quarter combat have never been used as they have in Stalingrad . . . [and our men] didn't fear tanks any longer. Our soldiers have become so resourceful. Even professors wouldn't be able to think up their tricks. They can build trenches that are so good you wouldn't notice soldiers in them even if you step on their heads. Our soldiers were on an upper floor [in a building]. Some Germans below them wound up a gramophone. Our men made a hole in the floor and fired [through it] with a flame-thrower . . . "Oh, may I report to you, comrades, what a fight it was!"'

Grossman was fascinated by the way soldiers watched, learned and improvised new methods to kill the enemy. He was especially interested by the snipers and got to know the two star snipers in Stalingrad quite well. Vasily Zaitsev, who was made the biggest star by Soviet propaganda – the character played by Jude Law in the film *Enemy at the Gates* – had been a sailor with the Pacific Fleet based in Vladivostok. He belonged to General Nikolai Batyuk's 284th Division of Siberians.[1] Anatoly Chekhov, whom Grossman accompanied on a sniper mission to observe him at work, was part of Rodimtsev's 13th Guards Rifle Division. It may well have been the case that Chuikov's jealousy of Rodimtsev and the press coverage of his Guards Division led to Chekhov's exploits being subordinated to those of Zaitsev. Rodimtsev told Grossman about Chekhov during his October visit. 'Red Army soldier Chekhov killed thirty-five fascists [during the fighting]. I wanted to give him some leave. He's killed enough Germans to deserve a lifetime's leave.' Grossman then went to interview Chekhov.

---

1 The 284th Rifle Division became the 79th Guards Rifle Division on 1 March 1943 in honour of its role at Stalingrad.

Chekhov, Anatoly Ivanovich. Born 1923. 'We moved to Kazan in 1931. I was at school there for seven years. Then my father took to drinking, and left my mother. There were also my two sisters. I had to leave school although I was a top pupil. I liked geography very much, but I had to stop . . . A notice appeared on 29 March 1942, and I volunteered for sniper school. In fact, I had never shot anything as a child, not even with a slingshot. My first experience of shooting was from a small-calibre rifle. I scored nine out of fifty. The lieutenant got very angry: 'Excellent marks in all subjects, but you shoot badly. We'll never make anything of you.' But I wasn't dismayed. I began to study theory and weapons. First, the experience of shooting with a proper rifle – chest shots and head shots. We were given three rounds and I hit the target [each time]. And from then on I became the best shot. I volunteered for the front.

'I wanted to be someone who destroyed the enemy on his own. I first thought about it when I read the newspaper. I wanted to be famous. I learned to judge distances by sight. I don't need an optical device. My favourite books? I didn't read much, actually. My father would get drunk and we would all scatter, sometimes I couldn't even do my homework. I never had my own corner.

'I took part in the attack on the morning of 15 September. I was advancing to Mamaev Kurgan . . . I had the feeling that this wasn't war, that I was simply teaching my section to camouflage in the field and to shoot. We shouted "*Urra!*" and ran about two hundred metres. Then their machine gun opened up and wouldn't let us work. I crawled as I had been taught, and slithered. And I fell into a trap. There were three machine guns around me, and a tank. I'd set myself a task, so I didn't look back. I knew that my section wouldn't desert me. I was shooting point-blank, at a range of five metres. [The machine-gunners] were sitting side-on to me. I knocked both of them down. Then three machine guns, a tank and a mortar began firing at me at the same time. I and my four soldiers lay in a crater from nine in the morning till eight in the evening . . . After this I was appointed the commander of a mortar platoon.

'When I was given a sniper's rifle, I chose a place on the fifth floor. There was a wall and its shadow concealed me. When the sun came out, I slipped downstairs. From there I saw the German house a hundred metres away. There were sub-machine-gunners and machine-gunners there. They were there during the day, they sat in basements. I went out at four in the morning. It starts to get light at this time. The first Fritz ran to get some water for the chiefs to have a wash. The sun was already rising. He ran side-on to me. I didn't look at their faces much, I looked at their uniforms. Commanders wear trousers, jackets, caps and no belts, privates wear boots.

'I sat on the landing of a staircase. I'd arranged my rifle behind the grill so that the smoke would drift along the wall. At first they walked. I knocked down nine on the first day. I knocked down seventeen in two days. They sent women, and I killed two out of five.[2] On the third day I saw an embrasure! A sniper. I waited and fired. He fell down and cried out in German. They stopped carrying mines and getting water. I killed forty Fritzes in eight days.

'When it was sunny, there was a shadow on the wall when I moved [so] I didn't shoot them when it was sunny. A new sniper appeared by the open window . . . This sniper had me cornered. He fired at me four times. But he missed. Of course, it was a pity to leave. Well, they've never drunk from the Volga. They went to get water, and they carried reports, dinner and ammunition . . . They drank filthy water from locomotives. They went to get water in the morning, with a bucket.

It is more convenient for me to shoot [a man] when he is running. It's easier for my hand and eye. It's more difficult when he is standing still. The first one appeared. He walked five metres. I took aim at once, a little in front of him, about four centimetres from his nose.

'When I first got the rifle, I couldn't bring myself to kill a living being: one German was standing there for about four minutes, talking, and I let him go. When I killed my first one, he fell at once. Another one ran out and stooped over the killed one, and I knocked him down, too . . . When I first killed, I was shaking all over: the man was only walking to get some water! . . . I felt scared: I'd killed a person! Then I remembered our people and started killing them without mercy.

'The building [opposite] has collapsed inside down to the second

2 There were no German servicewomen in the front line, so one assumes that these were Russian civilians recruited or forced to act as auxiliaries. Under Stalin's personal order, they were to be treated as traitors even if they had been compelled to work for the Germans at gunpoint.

floor. Some [Germans] sit on the staircase, others on the second floor. There are safes, all the money in them has been burned.[3]

'Some girls are living on the Kurgan. They make bonfires and cook. [German] officers go to see them.

'Sometimes you see the following picture: a Fritz is walking and a dog barks at him from a yard, and he kills the dog. If you hear dogs barking at night, this means the Fritzes are doing something there, roaming about, and the dogs bark.

'I've become a beast of a man: I kill, I hate them as if it is a normal thing in my life. I've killed forty men, three in the chest, the others in the head. When you fire, the head instantly jerks back or to the side. He throws up his arms and collapses . . . Pchelintsev, too, had been sorry to kill: his first one, and the second, 'How could I?'

'I've killed two officers. One on a hill, the other one by the State Bank. He was dressed in white. All the Germans sprang to their feet and saluted him. He was checking on them. He'd wanted to cross the street, and I hit him in the head. He fell down at once, raising his feet with shoes on them.

'Sometimes I come out of the basement in the evening, I look around and my heart sings, I would love to spend half an hour in a city which is alive. I come out and think: the Volga is flowing so quietly, how come such terrible things are happening here? We had a man from Stalingrad here. I kept asking him where all clubs and theatres were, and about going for strolls by the Volga.'

The editorial staff at *Krasnaya Zvezda* could hardly believe it when they received the full text of this article in a signal more than four hundred pages long brought over from the *Stavka*, the general staff headquarters attached to the Kremlin. Grossman had persuaded the signals detachment of Stalingrad Front to transmit it to Moscow. That they agreed to such a request in the middle of the battle of Stalingrad is sufficient proof of the regard in which he was held. Ortenberg was the first to acknowledge that the effort and risk to which Grossman subjected himself was worth it. 'It was probably because Grossman

---

3 In his *Krasnaya Zvezda* article, Grossman added extra detail. 'Sometimes it is very quiet, and then one can hear small pieces of plaster fall in the house opposite where Germans are sitting. Sometimes one hears German speech and the creaking of German boots. And sometimes the bombing and shooting gets so strong that one has to lean to the comrade's ear and shout as loudly as one can, but the comrade answers with gestures: "I can't hear."'

had got close to [Chekhov],' he wrote, 'and had shared the hardships and dangers of fighting, that he succeeded in creating such an expressive portrait of a warrior, going so deep into the world of his thoughts and sentiments.'

The exploits of snipers were talked about and admired almost like those of football players. Each division was proud of its star, and the Siberians of the 284th Rifle Division were convinced that they had the greatest star of all in the form of Vasily Zaitsev. But the compulsion of propaganda exaggeration made the scores achieved by these Stakhanovites of the urban battlefield somewhat suspect.

> Zaitsev is a reserved man, about whom soldiers in the division say: 'Our Zaitsev is cultivated and modest. He has already killed 225 Germans.'[4] His other snipers are [known as] young hares.[5] Batyuk says: 'They obey him, just like little mice. He asks: "Am I saying the right things, comrades?" Everyone answers: 'Yes, Vasily Ivanovich.'''

There is a striking entry in Grossman's notebook, which is hard to verify.

> Murashev and medical orderly Zaitsev had been sentenced to be executed. Murashev for shooting himself through the hand, the other, because he had killed a famous pilot, who was coming down by parachute from a shot-up aircraft. [The sentence of] execution was commuted for both of them. And now they are both the best snipers in Stalingrad. (Murashev is nineteen.)

Zaitsev was the only well-known sniper of that name in Stalingrad, and there is no other account that he was ever a medical orderly, or had shot a 'famous pilot' coming down by parachute. Perhaps Grossman was the only person to have recorded this story before the Soviet propaganda machine rewrote his life into a legend.

---

4 It is impossible to judge the claimed kill scores of snipers in Stalingrad, especially Zaitsev's, since according to his own account, he did not become a sniper until 21 October, when he shot three men, one after another. Colonel Batyuk is said to have seen this feat and ordered that he be made a sniper. So how Zaitsev achieved such a stupendous score when the most intense phase of the battle was over is hard to tell.

5 'Zaitsev' in Russian means hare, so Zaitsev's apprentice snipers were known as *zaichata*, or leverets.

Like the other snipers, Zaitsev seemed to be proud of taking revenge on any Russian woman seen associating with a German.

> Zaitsev has killed a woman and a German officer: 'They fell across each other.'

Several of the leading snipers at Stalingrad, including Chekhov and Zaitsev, reported brief duels with German snipers. This was hardly surprising since counter-sniper actions were regarded as their highest priority.

> A single combat between Zaitsev and a German sniper: 'He had killed three of our men. He waited for fifteen minutes. Our little gully was empty, and he started to get up. And I saw that his rifle was on the ground. And I stood up upright. He saw me and understood. And I fired.'

This brief, but deadly encounter was probably the one seized upon later by Soviet propaganda. It was blown up into the epic saga of a protracted duel between Zaitsev and the untraceable 'Major Koenig', the chief of an equally unidentifiable 'Berlin Sniper School', who had been flown in to track down Zaitsev and kill him. There is, however, no mention of any of this in any German source. Zaitsev's claim that they both stood up is also highly unconvincing. Snipers on both sides tended to work in pairs, and a victorious sniper who indulged in such a boastful gesture would have been shot down immediately.

To judge by the way General Chuikov played up the story in his memoirs, he may well have been the one who had the idea of promoting the myth, especially since Zaitsev belonged to Batyuk's division and not to Rodimtsev's. It is intriguing that Grossman, who reproduced in *Life and Fate* his wartime notes about the sniper meeting almost as he had written them at the time, makes one change. The duel, which Zaitsev had described so perfunctorily at the meeting recorded in Grossman's notes, lasts 'for days' in the novel. Grossman, for once, appears to have preferred the propaganda version.

Zaitsev's subsequent memoirs (almost certainly written with heavy assistance by Soviet propaganda experts) recount the same exciting, but ultimately unconvincing, story of a duel over several days. A German telescopic sight, with a label stating that it had been recovered from the corpse of the German major, is displayed to this day in the Armed Forces

Museum in Moscow. Yet, most telling of all, there is no mention whatsoever of the famed duel in any of the accounts of the Stalingrad Front political department sent back to Moscow during the battle, even though every detail on sniper activities which could be used for propaganda was reported.

Colonel Batyuk was equally proud of their other weapon stars.

'In our division, we have the best sniper on the [Stalingrad] Front, Zaitsev; the best mortar man, Bezdidko; and the best artillerist, Shuklin, commander of the 2nd Battery (who destroyed fourteen tanks with one gun from a pillbox). Bezdidko remarked: "He hit them all with one gun because he's only got one."

'Here one likes to make fun of the legendary heavy-mortar sniper Bezdidko. When German mortar bombs fall by the command post, the divisional commander says: "Oh, that son of a bitch, Bezdidko, why haven't I taught him to shoot like this?" And Bezdidko, who never misses his aim, which is accurate to a centimetre, laughs and frowns. And Bezdidko himself, a man with a melodious soft little tenor voice and a sly Ukrainian smile, who has 1,305 German kills noted in his scorebook, affectionately teases Shuklin, the skinny commander of the 2nd Battery.'

Bezdidko also appears in the sniper meeting recounted in *Life and Fate*, and the conversation left virtually unchanged from the original notes.

'Comrade Colonel, I've killed five Fritzes today, and used four bombs.'

'Bezdidko, tell them how you destroyed that little brothel.'

'I regard it as a bunker,' Bezdidko answered modestly.

Some improvisations were less successful. Zaitsev tried attaching a sniper scope to an anti-tank rifle, thinking he could put a round through a gun-slit in an enemy bunker, but the quality of the ammunition was so unpredictable that no two rounds came close to the same target. Grossman noted another invention, which was in fact less perfect than is implied here.

The brains of the Red Army have finally turned to the anti-tank rifle . . . [using] a cart wheel, fastened to a picket and rotating [through] 360°. Seven aircraft have been hit.

Battalion Commander Captain Ilgachkin had a problem: he never could manage to hit an aircraft with a rifle. He made theoretical calculations of the speed of the bullet from an anti-tank rifle (one thousand metres per second), made a table, supplemented it with information on whether an aircraft is moving towards the firing point or away from it. Having made this table, he hit an aircraft immediately. After that, he fastened a stake in the ground, made an axle, put a wheel on it and they attached an anti-tank rifle to the spokes.

Batyuk also recounted how the Germans tried to taunt them on the radio or just make jokes.

"'Rus, have you had dinner? . . . I've had butter, I've also had eggs, Rus. But not today. Today I've eaten nothing."
  "'Rus, I am going to get some water. Please shoot at my legs, not at my head. I've got children, I've got a mother."
  "'Rus, do you wanna swap an Uzbek for a Romanian?'"[6]

Batyuk, known to his soldiers as 'Bulletproof Batyuk', appears to have been one of those commanders genuinely impervious to danger.

Batyuk: 'In this very bunker, the door used to crash down inside and fall on to the table.' While the Germans were shelling the bunker of the artillery commander, Batyuk stood outside the entrance of his bunker laughing, and [pretending to] correct them: 'Further right, further left.'

Artillery, as Chuikov had realised right from the start of the battle, would be their only hope. As there was little room for deploying heavy artillery among the ruined buildings of the west bank, he had withdrawn all guns and howitzers over 76mm to the east bank. The key people were the gun batteries' forward observation officers, often concealed in high buildings like snipers. They relayed target details back by radio or by landline. 'Artillery on the battlefield must be like a kite,' General

6   Uzbeks had the reputation of being the least reliable members of the Red Army while the Germans were openly contemptuous of their Romanian allies of the Romanian First and Third Armies which were supposed to secure the north-western and the southern flanks of the German Sixth Army at Stalingrad.

Yeremenko observed to Grossman. But he had no illusions about the frequent danger of 'friendly fire'. 'In Stalingrad, when our artillery fires at our soldiers, they joke bitterly: "Here we are, the second front has opened at last."'

Chuikov's main tactic for blunting heavy German assaults was to create 'breakwaters' with defended houses. Fighting patrols would slip forward at night towards a chosen target, then be reinforced.

> Seizure of a house. The assault group of ten men, [followed later by] a consolidation group, [with] ammunition and food for six days. [They would dig] trenches ready in case they were surrounded.

Resupplying forward and isolated units was a major problem. The 62nd Army often resorted to U-2 biplanes, mostly flown by the young women pilots, who could switch off their engines and glide silently either over German trenches to drop bombs, or over Soviet positions to drop supplies.

> During the night, U-2s drop food for our troops. We mark the front line with oil lamps (flat dishes), which the soldiers light on the bottom of trenches. Company Commander Khrennikov once forgot to do this, and suddenly he heard a hoarse voice coming from the dark sky above: 'Hey, Khren![7] Are you going to light those lamps or not?' That was the pilot. The engine had been switched off. Khrennikov says this made a terrifying impression on him: a voice from the sky calling his name.

General Rodimtsev said to Grossman:

> 'My division and the Germans are stationed in houses next to each other, like pieces on a chessboard . . . They are living in basements, apartments and trenches . . . Four [soldiers] held a house for fourteen days. Two would go to get some food, the other two stayed to guard the house . . . Reconnaissance became very complicated . . . All anti-tank defence crews have been killed or wounded, to the last man . . . Moods – [the men were] tired, but spirits were high . . .

---

7 'Khren' in Russian means horseradish, but it is also a euphemism for an insult similar to 'motherfucker'. So when the pilot shouted: 'Hey, motherfucker!' Khrennikov was astonished at hearing what he thought was his own name.

Lice – we got hold of Primus stoves and irons, and squashed them. [That] got rid of them.

And once again, jokes and insults would be hurled between trenches or even floors of the same house, often with heavy German humour: 'Rus, give me your hat, and I'll give you my tommy gun!'

Grossman was slightly perplexed by the 'strange anxiety' of the soldiers and officers he talked to. They seemed to be unusually concerned about the outside world.

'And what do they say about us there? What do they think about us?' There is a terrible lack of confidence.

Generals, especially Yeremenko, liked to pontificate on war and soldiering, but they often brought the subject back to themselves.

'Young people have little experience of life, they're like children. They die where they are sent . . . The cleverest soldiers are those aged between twenty-five and thirty. Older soldiers are "not exactly healthy men, tormented with worries about their families". And I am tormented by my leg. I was under a terrible strain in Smolensk, and then at the Bryansk Front. Once, at the North-Western Front, I never went to bed for five days.'

'Yes, when two generals fight each other, one of them will definitely turn out a clever man, and the other a fool. Although they are both fools,' he added, laughing.

Gurov, the chief commissar of the 62nd Army, made similar sweeping statements.

'The men, the soldiers, are all alike. Only commanders are different.'

If there was one area where Soviet commanders had little influence over events, it was on the vital Volga crossings. Everything depended on the men of the river-transports battalions – many of them Volga boatmen from Yaroslavl.

General Rodimtsev gave Grossman the official – and therefore optimistic – view.

'We've been collecting boats from all over the river. Now we've got quite a fleet: twenty-seven fishing boats and motor boats. We raised a launch from the bottom of the Volga, but it was destroyed by a direct hit. The division is fully supplied: there is hot food, a spare set of underwear, chocolate and condensed milk. The evacuation of the wounded is exemplary. We have enough supplies for three days.'

Grossman, however, spent enough time with the boatmen, who had been conscripted into the army, to form a more accurate picture.

The Volga is 1,300 metres wide here . . . The boat has been hit. It was loaded with flour. Soldier Voronin didn't lose his head. He emptied the flour from one sack, plugged the hole with the sack and blocked other holes with glue made from flour. There were seventy-seven holes in the boat. The soldier plugged them all in one day.

Corporal Spiridonov's rear end has got smashed up. He is asking for some alcohol. Two heavily wounded men, Volkov and Lukyanov, barge in. They had walked thirty kilometres from the hospital. They'd escaped from the hospital. When put on a vehicle and driven back, they were both crying: 'We won't leave the battalion.'

When Eziev and Ilin were wounded, Red Army soldier Minokhodov dragged both of them from the barge and bandaged them. He himself was wounded in the back. He ran a kilometre back to the second echelon and told them that the battalion commander had been wounded, and he fell down unconscious. They were all taken to hospital together.

Sergeant Vlasov, forty-eight, an old man, from Yaroslavl. The barge was holed by a shell. While one man held his legs, Vlasov plugged the hole with his coat and nailed planks over it. There was four hundred tons of ammunition on the barge. [Vlasov] had been the chairman of a collective farm. His two sons are at the front, his wife is back home with three other children.

After the commissar's speech, Vlasov shot a coward, the helmsman of a motor launch, the driver Kovalchuk. Kovalchuk had been ordered to take soldiers across to the Red October factory. There was a heavy bombardment, he got frightened and took them to an island instead, saying: 'Life is more important to me . . . You can transfer me, or shoot me, but I'm still not going to do it. I'm an old man.' He was simply afraid, and he was swearing. He wouldn't recognise anyone, and he said about the general's order: 'To hell with generals!'

The battalion was formed up for Kovalchuk's execution in front of the ranks. 'At a time when hundreds of thousands of soldiers are fighting for Stalingrad, he has betrayed the Motherland,' [the commissar proclaimed]. 'Who would like to shoot him?' Vlasov stepped forward. 'Allow me, Comrade Commissar.'

[Kovalchuk] cringed. He cried: 'Have mercy on me, Comrade Commissar, I will reform.' [The commissar] embraced Vlasov in front of his company.

The battalion commissar clearly had considerable respect for Vlasov.

'The most terrible thing I've been through was when a barge [was hit]. There were about four hundred men on it. There was panic, and cries. "We are sinking, we are lost!" Vlasov came up to me: "It's ready, Comrade Commissar." [i.e. the barge was already patched up.] And just then a fire broke out. A soldier, the son of a bitch, had taken a bottle of KS[8] and started drinking, and a fire began. We put it out with a groundsheet. At any moment they could have started jumping in the water! Old man Muromtsev was there with us as well. He found two holes and plugged them. Everyone can get scared, can't they? I got frightened myself, everyone is prone to it, but some can keep this fear under control. Now we are so used to it that when it becomes quieter, they say: "It's a bit boring!"'

Grossman did a full interview with Vlasov.

Vlasov, Pavel Ivanovich, forty-eight years old, from the area of Yaroslavl. He has a family of five. One of his sons is a guards mortarman. Vlasov was drafted in August 1941. To begin with he guarded depots.

'We have been here on the Volga since 25 August. The barge was

8   KS was an industrial mixture containing unpurified spirit.

large, about four thousand tons of amunition. A bombardment began while we were loading it, but we paid no attention to it. We cast off. I was in the front of the boat, that was my place. They opened fire. I had to watch out. A hole appeared in the deck and in the side of the boat, one metre below the waterline. The wood was splintered. We heard the noise of water [pouring in]. People began to cry out.

'I snatched a groundsheet from one of them and ran into the hold. It was light [enough to see] there because the deck was broken. We crammed the big hole with the groundsheet and a greatcoat. And the small holes, we filled them from the outside. They held me by the legs, and I leaned over.'

About the cowardly driver of the motor launch. 'That was at the beginning of October. We had received an order to cross over to the other [western] side and mend the mooring. He took us to an island and said: "For me, life is more important." We started cursing him in foul language.

'A report was made to the commissar about it. We were formed up, the whole battalion. The commissar read out the order, and he, Kovalchuk, was not behaving well. He was crying and pleading to be sent back to his post. But he was a bad offender already: he'd said that he'd desert. I had the feeling that, if I could, I'd tear him to pieces, even without that [death] sentence. Then the commissar said: "Who would like to shoot him?" I stepped out of the line, and [Kovalchuk] collapsed. I took a rifle from my comrade and shot him.'

'Did you feel any pity for him?'

'How can one speak of pity?'

'I received my call-up papers on the night of 28 August [1941]. I don't drink much normally, I am not used to it. I don't write much [in letters home]: "I am still alive," and I ask them to describe how they are managing the household. The kids aren't spoilt, I don't know how they are behaving in my absence, but they did help when I was there. There's a lot of work. One has to work night and day. Of all crops, flax is the most labour-intensive. You need to weed it, and weed again, to pull it by hand, to dry it in stooks, then beat it down, spread it and then lift it . . . In general, the work here is not so hard as back home, although we had to go three days without sleep while we were making a bridge. If you get tired well and truly, you sleep. If you haven't slept one night, you'll sleep the following one.

'Our anti-aircraft guns aren't doing a good job. So far, I have only seen three aircraft knocked down by them. They don't deserve any praise.

'The youngsters obey me. Sometimes I am strict with them, but it's necessary. If one shows a weak spot, it's no good, either at home or at war . . . I handed everything over when I was leaving for the war. I have no debts. If I get killed, there'll be no debts left unpaid . . . One carries all one's belongings on oneself: a mug, a pot, a spoon. Money we send home, there's nothing to buy.

'In my section there's Moshchav and Malkov. There's no one else. Everyone else has been killed or wounded . . .

'We catch fish. The Germans stun 'em for us. I caught a sterlet, then an ide, and we made soup.[9]

'There are dogs who know aircraft very well. They pay absolutely no attention when one of our aircraft is flying over, even if it roars across right above their heads. But they start to bark immediately at German planes. They start to howl and hide, even when one of their aircraft is flying very high.'

'Shells and bombs send off no shrapnel or splinters when they explode in the water. Only a direct hit is dangerous. Yesterday a trawler was hit. It went to the bottom with seventy-five wounded men.'

In his article 'The Stalingrad Crossing', Grossman wrote:

The earth around the landing point was ploughed up by their evil metal . . . And German fire never stopped even for a minute . . . Between the piers on the bank and Stalingrad lay 1,300 metres of the Volga's water. Soldiers from the pontoon battalion had heard many times, in brief moments of silence, a distant sound of men's voices. At that distance it sounded sad: 'A-a-a . . .' That was our infantry rising for a counter-attack.

The [Germans have a] timetable: [Artillery] fire until midnight. From midnight until two in the morning – quiet. From 2 a.m. until 5 a.m. – they fire again. From five till noon – quiet. The [Luftwaffe]

9 *Acipenser ruthenus*, or freshwater sturgeon, and *Leuciscus idus*, sometimes known as the orfe.

works from nine in the morning until five in the afternoon, as if it were a regular job. They aim at the bank. They don't waste bombs in the river.

'The crossing operates from six o'clock in the evening until four thirty in the morning . . . [one of the men said] We camouflage [the boats], bringing them under cover of the bank and trees. The steam pinnace *Donbass* is hidden inside a destroyed barge . . . It's very hard when there's a moon. It's beautiful, but damn the beauty.'

A welder at the west bank crossing point soon found himself mending more than battered boats.

Welder Kosenko was so good people came to him from the front and asked him to mend their Katyushas. 'You do it better than at the front.' Two tanks rushed back from the front. 'Quick, we've got to go back and fight.' He fixed them and they went back into the battle.

Everyday life. The [transport troops] have their own bakery, *banya* and delousing facility. The *banya* is dug out of the earth. The soldiers like to go there with birch twigs. They would stay there all the time if they could. Its chimney has been knocked down by an explosion. The bakery is a Russian stove, dug into the earth. They bake a wonderful, light hearth bread. They are excellent bakers, but the whole bakery was smashed by the latest bombing! The 2nd Company's kitchen [suffered] a direct hit too. 'May I report? The kitchen has been blown up, together with the *shchi*!'
    'Well, go and cook more dinner, then.'

Grossman, although only a correspondent, evidently pitched in when the situation demanded.

[A supply of] Katyusha rockets caught fire. There was one truck-load of them and dozens of vehicles around it. We dragged them away.

But above all, he was pleased that his articles meant so much to the men.

They all liked my piece very much about the soldiers from Yaroslavl. They were as proud as peacocks: 'This is written about us!'

SIXTEEN

The October Battles

General Chuikov's headquarters had been less than a week in the Tsaritsa tunnel when another German offensive crushed the centre of Stalingrad. Chuikov and his staff moved some four kilometres north to the Red October works. The factory district of northern Stalingrad soon proved to be the focus of German attacks, with the first major offensive starting on 27 September. These attacks were heralded by squadrons of Stukas, which Red Army soldiers dubbed 'screechers' or 'musicians' because of their screaming sirens as they dropped towards their target.

The fighting was equally desperate on the northern flank where the 16th Panzer Division had captured Rynok and Spartakovka and advanced towards the tractor works from the north.

> Bolvinov's 149th Brigade – probably, one of the best units . . . was sent to fight under Gorokhov [commanding the 124th Brigade], and Gorokhov pushed Bolvinov into the backgound. But Bolvinov was doing what he had to. He crawled, armed to the teeth with grenades, from one fire point to another, and Red Army soldiers loved him.

For all headquarters on the west bank, the major problem was communications. Signal cables were forever being broken by shellfire and runners were cut down. Chuikov described to Grossman the feeling of frustration and fear.

> '[It was] the most oppressive sensation. There's firing and thunder all around. You send off a liaison officer to find out what's happening, and he gets killed. That's when you shake all over with tension . . . The most terrible times were when you sat there like an idiot, and the battle was boiling around you, but there was nothing you could do.'

The most direct threat to Chuikov's headquarters came on 2 October. The headquarters of 62nd Army had been sited on the steep bank of the Volga just below some fuel storage tanks which everyone had assumed to be empty. This was a dangerous mistake. The Germans targeted the tanks successfully and suddenly the headquarters was engulfed in burning oil, as Chuikov later described to Grossman.

'Oil was flowing in streams to the Volga through the command post. The Volga was in flames. We were only some fifteen metres from the river's edge . . . The only way out was to move towards the enemy . . . The fuel tanks were on fire. A fountain of smoke eight hundred metres high. And the Volga. All this stuff was flowing with roaring flames down to the river. They dragged me out of the river of fire and we stood on the water's edge until morning. Some men who had been asleep burned to death . . . Up to forty men were killed at the headquarters.'

Chuikov's chief of staff gave his own version.

Then [headquarters] moved into a tunnel by the Barrikady plant and was there from 7 to 15 October. There we were being forced away from the main forces, [so] from there, we moved to the Banny gully, into the tunnel headquarters of the 284th Rifle Division which had left there and moved towards the bank. Here one often hears of the Banny gully.
   "'The Army Command Post has disappeared!'"
   "'Where to?'"
   "'It's not gone to the left bank, it's moved closer to the front line.'"

On 6 October, General Paulus sent two divisions against the huge Stalingrad tractor plant on the northern edge of the city. Paulus was under heavy pressure from Hitler to finish off the pocket of Soviet resistance on the west bank. Meanwhile, Yeremenko was being urged by Stalin to counter-attack and throw the Germans back. Chuikov ignored this unrealistic order. He could barely hold on as it was, and then only thanks to the Soviet heavy artillery positioned on the east bank, firing over their heads into German forming-up areas to disrupt their preparations for an attack.

The Stalingrad Tractor Plant was the scene of nightmare fighting as the tanks of the 14th Panzer Division smashed like prehistoric monsters into workshops, their tracks crunching the shards of glass from the shattered skylights above. The remains of the 112th Rifle Division and Colonel Zholudev's 37th Guards Rifle Division could not withstand the force, but although their defence lines were broken, they fought on in isolated pockets.[1]

> Zholudev's division. Commissar Shcherbina. Tractor plant. The command post was buried by an explosion. It became quiet at once. They were sitting there for a long time, then they began to sing: '*Lyubo, bratsy, lyubo.*' ['Life is great.'] A sergeant dug them out under fire. He worked like a madman, frenziedly, with bubbles on his lips. An hour later, he was killed by a shell. A German 'sneezed' with his sub-machine gun. He had crept into the 'tube' [tunnel] and opened fire when there was noise from mortars and guns. They dragged him out. He was all black, and they tore him to pieces.
>
> When the Germans captured one workshop, they even managed to raise a disabled tank up to a certain height and fire from the window.

Grossman crossed once more to the west bank just as the battle erupted again with a renewed German offensive. He wrote to the editor of *Krasnaya Zvezda* to inform him of his movements.

> Comrade Ortenberg, I arrived on the 11th with Vysokoostrovsky [another *Krasnaya Zvezda* correspondent], and crossed the river to Stalingrad during the night. I've done thorough interviews with soldiers, officers, and with General Rodimtsev.

Grossman overheard two Red Army soldiers talking on the way to the Volga crossing point:
'It's been a long time since I last had hot food.'
'Well, we'll soon be drinking our own hot blood over there,' the other one answered.
Rodimtsev's 13th Guards Rifle Division had almost been destroyed in a surprise attack. On 1 October, groups from the the German 295th Infantry Division had infiltrated gullies on Rodimtsev's right flank and

---

1 The 37th Guards Rifle Division was formed from I Airborne Corps in August 1942, and later became part of the 65th Army once it had been re-formed after its heavy losses in Stalingrad.

nearly managed to cut off the division from the rest of the 62nd Army. Rodimtsev's guardsmen had reacted with furious counter-attacks and only just managed to force the Germans back. Grossman spent the 12 and 13 October with the division.

Funeral by the Volga. Speeches, salute. A memorial was put on the grave, stating when they were killed and under what circumstances. Funerals are done at night, always with a salute.

The salute in Stalingrad consisted not of a volley fired in the air, but towards the Germans.

Charming and sad. Mamaev Kurgan – here is the command post of the battalion. Men from the mortar company are playing a record all the time with the song 'No, friends, please not now, don't put me yet on this bed of frost.'
There was never another place with so much music. This ploughed-up clay, stained with shit and blood, was ringing with music from radios, gramophone records and from the voices of company and platoon singers.

'We also had two concerts here,' [Rodimtsev told him]. 'Hairdresser Rubinchik played the violin in our tunnel. And everyone began to smile remembering the concert.'

Rodimtsev also recounted an anecdote rather more representative of soldiers' priorities.

'Today, for example, two soldiers came to me. It turned out that they had been fighting for fourteen days in a house surrounded by German houses. And these two, so quietly, you know, demanded rusks, ammunition, sugar, tobacco, loaded it all in their rucksacks, and went off. They said: "There are two more of our men there, guarding the house, and they need a smoke." Actually, it is such a peculiar affair, this war in houses,' he smiled. 'I don't know whether I should tell this to you, but a funny incident happened yesterday. The Germans captured a house, and there was a barrel of spirits in its basement. And our guards soldiers became angry about [the idea of] the Germans drinking this barrel, so twenty men attacked the house, seized it back and rolled the barrel away, while almost the whole street was held by the Germans. All this caused a great sense of triumph . . .

'I'm not afraid,' he said. 'It's the only way. I think I've seen everything. Once, a German tank was ironing flat my command post, and then a sub-machine-gunner threw a grenade, just to be sure, and I threw the grenade back . . .'

Grossman also went on another occasion with Efim Gekhman to see Rodimtsev on the west bank. The Guards general said that he was getting uneasy about interviews. 'You know, I am a superstitious man. I remember how [*Krasnaya Zvezda*] published a leader about Dovator. He was killed on the very same day.'[2]

Grossman, with typical generosity, always praised the courage of others. 'Gekhman is extremely brave,' Ortenberg remembers him saying. 'Once, on a dark October night, we had to leave Rodimtsev's tunnel in Stalingrad and cross the Volga in a boat. Rodimtsev was listening anxiously to the thunder [of fire] outside. He shook his head and said to us: "Comrades, have a glass before you go, it is too hot out there, crossing the water." Gekhman shrugged his shoulders and answered: "No, thanks. I would rather have another piece of sausage." He said this so calmly and ate the sausage with such good appetite that everyone couldn't help laughing.'

At dawn on Monday, 14 October, the German Sixth Army began what General Paulus hoped was the last offensive to push the 62nd Army from the west bank. Every available Stuka in General Wolfram von Richthofen's Fourth Air Fleet was used to soften up Soviet positions. It was the most intensive bombardment yet. Chuikov had sensed that the climax of the battle was approaching.

'The press[3] was teasing Hitler [about his failure to take Stalingrad], and we were terrified. We were sitting here, knowing, feeling, realising that Hitler has sent his main forces here.

'After the 14th, I decided to send all the women back to the opposite bank. There were many tears. Courage is infectious here, just like cowardice is infectious in other places. Take my word for it,

2   Major-General L.M. Dovator, the commander of the II Guards Cavalry Corps in the battle for Moscow, was killed on 20 December 1941.
3   The international press was more likely to have had an effect than the Soviet press.

Levkin (left), Koroteev (centre right), and Grossman
(right) talk to civilians, October 1942.

we were living by the hour, by the minute. One waited for the dawn. Well, it all started again then. And in the evening, one thought: "Well, thank God, another day is gone, how surprising." Yes, if someone had told me that I would [live to] celebrate the new year, I would have laughed.'

On the night of 15 October, 3,500 wounded men were evacuated across the river. Many had to crawl to the river bank because there were not enough medical orderlies. In the early hours of 16 October, General Yeremenko himself crossed the river to see Chuikov. He needed to know for certain whether they could hold on. 'Yeremenko arrived during the night[4] . . . Gurov and I went out to meet him.

'There was a hellish fire, an air raid.' Chuikov did not explain that he and Gurov could not find Yeremenko on the river bank, but Yeremenko stumbled across their headquarters and waited for them there. Yeremenko told Grossman how he encountered a soldier on the river bank: '"I recognise you, Comrade Commander-in-Chief".' He told me where he had been, where he had fought, how many Germans he had killed.'

---

4   Grossman notes this as the night of 13 October, but most accounts put Yeremenko's visit to the embattled west bank as taking place in the early hours of 16 October.

After the battle was over, Chuikov's version of events tended to make light of the reality, but this obscured the fact that during the crisis of mid-October, the 62nd Army's bridgehead was down to less than a thousand metres deep, and would soon be squeezed even further.

'German attacks: they smash everything into the earth, send in their tanks, and after this mad chaos our infantry come out of their trenches and cut their infantry off from the tanks . . . There are shouts: "Tanks at the command post!"
'And infantry?'
'We've cut 'em off.'
'Everything's all right, then.'

Grossman asked Chuikov what he thought of the Germans' performance. 'Not particularly brilliant. But we must do them justice concerning their discipline. An order is the law for them.'

His chief of staff, Krylov, who had suffered the terrible siege of Sebastopol, compared the battle there with Stalingrad. 'There, our force was melting away, while here it was replenished. There was a lot in common. It seemed to us sometimes as if we were still continuing the same battle. But we did not feel doomed, like we did in Sebastopol.'

The loss of the tractor works had meant that Gorokhov's 124th Brigade was cut off in Spartakovka.

On the day of glory, I remembered the battalion which crossed the river and reached Gorokhov in order to divert the main blow on to themselves.[5] They all died. Not a single man survived. But has anyone remembered this battalion? No one has thought of those who crossed the river on that rainy night in the latter part of October. (Two days later, I saw a captured Georgian from this battalion. He had deserted and surrendered. He said that there were many who surrendered.)
A man from Ossetia, Alborov, was killed at his post (a bomb). He was still holding in his hand the butt of his rifle, the barrel had been torn off by the explosion, his pulse was still throbbing. His friend was sobbing, and he cried: 'My comrade is killed.'

5 Grossman is probably referring to 17 October, when all the west bank bridgeheads faced the most intense onslaught. The battalion was from Lyudnikov's 138th Division, a fresh batch of reinforcements which Chuikov brought across the Volga at the critical moment.

Grossman spent time with Colonel Gurtiev's 308th Rifle Division of Siberians who had been defending the silicate works just north of the Barrikady factory complex.[6] They had crossed the Volga on 30 September, and went straight into action. This is his compilation of what had happened to them since the last day of September, when they crossed to the west bank.

The first line went in, the second, and the third. Thirteen attacks were thrown back on that day. [The Germans] were struggling to reach the crossing point. Our artillery played a major role.

On 1 [October], four artillery regiments and Katyusha batteries fired for half an hour. Everything froze. Germans were rooted to the spot. Everyone was watching and listening.

Germans were on the edge of the plant. That was in the afternoon of the 2nd. Some of them took cover, others ran away. A Kazakh was escorting three prisoners. He was wounded. He took out a knife and stabbed the three prisoners to death. A tankist, a big red-haired man, jumped out of his tank in front of Changov's command post when he ran out of shells. He grabbed some bricks and [started throwing them at] the Germans, effing and blinding. The Germans turned on their heels and ran.

The men's spirits were high, they had had some experience of fighting. Their ages ranged from twenty-three to forty-six. Most of them were Siberians, from Omsk, Novosibirsk and Krasnoyarsk. Siberians are more stocky, more reserved, more stern. They are hunters, they are more disciplined, more used to cold and hardship. There wasn't a single case of desertion [en route to Stalingrad]. When one of them dropped his rifle, he ran three kilometres after the train and caught up. They aren't talkative, but are witty, and have sharp tongues.

'We're used to "whistlers" [Stukas]. We even get bored when the Germans aren't whistling. When they are whistling, this means they aren't throwing anything at us. They started attacking the silicate plant on the night of 2 October. The whole of Markelov's regiment was killed or wounded. There were only eleven men left. The Germans had taken the whole plant by the evening of the 3rd. Our instruction was: not one step back. The commander was wounded heavily, the commissar was killed.

6   The 308th Rifle Division became the 120th Guards Rifle Division with the 3rd Army. Like almost all the divisions at Stalingrad, it fought all the way to Berlin.

'We began to defend a destroyed and burning street in front of the sculpture garden. No one came back from the fighting. They all died on the spot. The climax came on 17 October. The enemy kept bombing us day and night on the 17th, 18th and 19th. Two German regiments started to advance.

'The attack began at five in the morning and the battle went on for the whole day. They broke through on a flank and cut off the command post. The regiment fought for two to three days from house to house, and the command post was in the fighting, too. The commander of the 7th Company with twelve men took out a company of Germans in a gully. They got out of there during the night, then they occupied a house. There were twenty of them in a grenade battle, fighting for floors, for stairs, for corridors, for rooms.

'Kalinin, the deputy chief of staff, killed twenty-seven men and hit four tanks with an anti-tank rifle. There were eighty workers and a security company at the plant. Only three or four of them survived. They had never received any military training. Their commander was a young worker, a communist, and they were attacked by a regiment of Germans.

'On 23 October, fighting began inside the plant. Workshops were on fire, as well as railways, roads, trees, bushes and grass. At the command post, Kushnarev and the chief of staff, Dyatlenko, were sitting in the "tube" with six sub-machine-gunners. They had two boxes of grenades and they beat the Germans off. The Germans had brought tanks to the plant. The workshops changed hands several times. Tanks destroyed them, firing at point-blank range. Aircraft were bombing us day and night. A captured German, a teacher, told us on the 27th about the strict order to reach the Volga. His hands were black, there were lice in his hair. He began to sob.'

Mikhalyev, Barkovsky, Chief of Staff Mirokhin have all been killed. They all received posthumous awards . . . Sub-machine-gunner Kolosov was buried up to his chest in earth. He was stuck there laughing: 'This makes me mad!' The signals platoon commander, Khamitsky, was sitting by the entrance of his bunker reading a book during a heavy bombing raid. Gurtyev [the divisional commander] became angry.

'What's the matter with you?'

'I've nothing else to do. He's bombing and I read a book.'

Mikhalyev was very much loved. When someone now asks: 'How are things?' 'Well, what can I say?' [comes the answer]. 'It's as if we'd lost a father. He had pity for his men. He spared them.'

Liaison Officer Batrakov, a chemist, black-haired and wearing spectacles, walked ten to fifteen kilometres every day. He would come in to headquarters, clean his glasses, report on the situation and go back. He arrived at exactly the same time every day.

'It was quiet on the 12th and 13th [October], but we understood what this quietness meant. On the 14th, [the enemy] began firing at the divisional command post with a *Vanyusha*.[7] [The bunker] became blocked up with earth, but we got out. We lost thirteen or fourteen men at the command post. A thermite shell makes a hollow noise. It hits one's ears. At first, there's a creaking noise: "Aha! Hitler's started playing [his violin]," and one has time to hide. Vladimirsky was dying to go to the toilet, he suffered so much until nightfall. He wanted to take a mess tin from a soldier.'

Workshop No. 14 started to burn from the inside. When Andryushenko was killed, the regimental commissar (holder of four medals, Lieutenant Colonel Kolobovnikov, a man with a face of stone) telephoned the command post and started to speak: 'Comrade Major-General, may I report?' He stopped, then said, sobbing: 'Vanya is dead,' and hung up.

A 'hired' tankist [i.e. the commander of a tank attached to the infantry]: they gave him chocolate, vodka, and collected his ammunition for him. And he worked like an ox. They thought the world of him in the regiment.

'We had grenades, sub-machine guns, and 45mm [anti-tank] guns. Thirty tanks attacked. We were scared. This was the first time it happened to us! But no one ran away. We started firing at the armour. The tanks were crawling over deep slits. A Red Army soldier would take a look and laugh: "Dig deeper!"'

---

7 A *Vanyusha* was their nickname for the German Nebelwerfer multi-barrelled mortar. This less effective counterpart to the Katyusha was originally called a *Vanya*, and then the joke arose about what would happen to little *Vanya* if he married the rather more powerful *Katyusha*. It was sometimes known also as the 'braying donkey' because of the noise the mortar bombs made in the air.

Postmen: Makarevich, with a little beard, a peasant, with his little bag, with little envelopes, postcards, letters, newpapers. Karnaukhov has been injured. There are three wounded and one killed . . . When he was wounded, Kosichenko tore the pin from the grenade with his teeth.

Grossman wrote up the the story of the attack on the 308th Rifle Division for *Krasnaya Zvezda* and it was published just over a month later under the title 'Axis of the Main Attack'. Ortenberg wrote a little later about Grossman's interviewing technique. 'All the correspondents attached to the Stalingrad Front were amazed how Grossman had made the divisional commander, General Gurtiev, a silent and reserved Siberian, talk to him for six hours without a break, telling him all that he wanted to know, at one of the hardest moments [of the battle].'

Grossman may have been influenced by the superstitions of the *frontoviki*, the result of living constantly with death in its most unpredictable form, but he also had his own as a writer. His editor was entertained to find that Grossman believed it was bad luck to seal up your own letters and packages. 'When he wrote another of his essays, he would ask Gekhman, who often accompanied him on trips to the front: "Efim, you've got a light hand. Could you take my material, seal the envelope with your own hands and send it to Moscow?"'

Ortenberg, a hardened Party journalist, was also amused by how carefully Grossman checked the final printed version of his articles. 'I remember how he would change when a newspaper with his essay in it arrived. He was so happy. He would reread his essay, checking how one or another phrase sounded. He, an experienced writer, simply worshipped the printed word.' Ortenberg may well have been a little disingenuous in this description. Grossman was often furious at the way his articles were rewritten and chopped about. He wrote in a letter to his wife, Olga Mikhailovna, on 22 October:

I've written an angry letter to the editor and now await his reply not without interest. I wrote about a bureaucratic attitude and officials' tricks on the editorial board.

In fact, Grossman's prose was probably interfered with less than that of most other journalists'. Ortenberg openly acknowledged that much of the newspaper's popularity was due to Grossman. Even the Party hacks in Moscow were well aware of the determination which his prose

gave to the soldiers of the Red Army, to say nothing of the whole population. It had far more effect than the most impassioned Stalinist
clichés.

It is only here that people know what a kilometre is. A kilometre
is one thousand metres. It is one hundred thousand centimetres.
Drunken [German] sub-machine-gunners pushed on with a lunatic
stubbornness. There is no one now who can tell how Markelov's
regiment fought . . . Yes, they were simply mortals and none of
them came back.

Several times during the day, German artillery and mortars would
suddenly fall silent, and the squadrons of dive-bombers would
disappear. An incomprehensible quietness would ensue. It was then
that the lookouts would shout: 'Watch out!' and those in forward
positions would grip their Molotov cocktails, men in anti-tank units
would open their canvas ammunition bags and sub-machine-gunners
would wipe their PPSh with the palms of their hands. This brief
quietness preceded an attack.

It wasn't long before the clang of hundreds of caterpillars and
the low humming of motors would announce the movement of
tanks. A lieutenant shouted: 'Watch out, comrades! Sub-machine-
gunners are infiltrating on the left!' Sometimes the Germans got so
close that the Siberians saw their dirty faces and torn greatcoats,
and heard their guttural shouts . . .

Looking back now, one can see that heroism was present during
every moment of daily life for people in the division. There was
the commander of a signals platoon, Khamitsky, who was sitting
peacefully on a hillock reading a novel while a dozen German Stukas
dived down roaring, as if about to attack the earth itself. And there
was liaison officer Batrakov, who would carefully clean his glasses,
put reports into his field bag, and set out on a twenty-kilometre
walk through the 'death ravine' as if it were a Sunday walk in the
park.[8] There was the sub-machine-gunner Kolosov who, when an
explosion buried him in a bunker up to his neck, turned his face
to Deputy Commander Spirin and laughed. There was a typist at
the headquarters, Klava Kopylova, a fat red-cheeked girl from Siberia,
who had begun typing a battle order at the headquarters and was

8   In the final article, the daily walk appears to have grown from Grossman's original ten to fifteen
kilometres a day all the way to twenty kilometres a day.

buried by an explosion. They dug her out and she went to type in another bunker. She was buried again and dug out again. She finally finished typing the order in the third bunker and brought it to the divisional commander to sign. These were the people fighting on the axis of the main attack.

The *balkas*, or ravines, many of them running at right angles to the Volga river bank, provided shelter as well as danger if the enemy managed to slip into them unnoticed.

> The *balka* has a great influence, particularly here in Stalingrad. [It provides] good approaches, [being] narrow and deep. Command posts or mortar units use it. It is always under fire. Many people have been killed here. Wires go through it, ammunition is carried through it. Aircraft and mortars have levelled it with the surrounding area. Chamov was buried there, too [by an explosion]. They had to dig him out. Spies have walked through it.

Grossman observed life at Gurtiev's command post.

> Reports [written] on forms, scraps of sheets from plant, party papers, etc. The return of Zoya Kalganova. She had been wounded twice. The divisional commander [greeted her]: 'Hello, my dear girl.'

The courage of the young women medical orderlies was respected by everyone. Most of those in the 62nd Army's Sanitary Company were Stalingrad high school students or graduates, but the 308th Rifle Division had brought some of their own female medics, clerks and signallers all the way from Siberia. The medical orderlies went out under heavy fire to collect the wounded and carry or drag them to safety. They would also take rations forward.

> Our girls, with thermos flasks on their shoulders, bring us breakfast. Soldiers speak of them with so much love. These girls have not dug themselves any slit-trenches.

One of the young women later provided an improvised casualty list for him of those who had come with her from Siberia.

'Lyolya Novikova, a cheerful nurse afraid of nothing, was hit by two bullets in the head. Lysorchuk, Nina, wounded. Borodina, Katya, her right hand was smashed. Yegorova, Antonina, she was killed. She went into an attack with her platoon. She was a junior nurse. A sub-machine-gunner shot her through both legs and she died from loss of blood. Arkanova, Tonya, accompanied wounded soldiers and was posted missing. Kanysheva, Galya, killed by a direct hit from a bomb. And there are just two of us left: Zoya and I . . . I was wounded by a mortar-bomb fragment near the bunker, and then by a shell splinter near the Volga crossing.

'We studied at School No. 13 in Tobolsk. Mothers were crying: "How come you're going [to the front]? There are only men there." We imagined war very differently to how it's turned out. Our battalion was in the advance guard of the regiment. It went into battle at ten in the morning. Although it was frightening, it was very interesting for us. Thirteen girls survived out of eighteen.

'I had long been afraid of dead men, but one night, I had to hide behind a corpse when a sub-machine-gunner blazed away. And I lay behind this corpse. I was so afraid of blood on that first day that I didn't want to eat anything, and I saw blood when I closed my eyes.

'We had marched for eight days, 120 kilometres, without sleep and without food. I had been imagining what war was like – everything on fire, children crying, cats running about, and when we got to Stalingrad it really turned out to be like that, only more terrible.

'I was peeling potatoes with the cook. We were engrossed in a conversation about soldiers. Suddenly, smoke covered everything, and the cook was killed, and a few minutes later, when the lieutenant came, a mortar bomb exploded and we were both wounded.

'It's particularly frightening to move during the night when Germans are shouting not far away, and everything is burning all around. It's very hard to carry the wounded. We made soldiers carry them.

'I cried when I was wounded. We didn't collect the wounded in the daytime. Only once, when Kazantseva was carrying Kanysheva, but a sub-machine-gunner shot her in the head. In the daytime, we put them into a shelter, and collected them in the evenings, helped by soldiers.

'There were moments sometimes when I regretted having

volunteered, but I consoled myself saying to myself that I was not the first one, and not the last. And Klava said: "Such wonderful people get killed, what difference would my death make?" We received letters from our teachers. They were proud of having brought up such daughters. Our friends are jealous of us, that we have the chance to bandage wounds. Papa writes: "Serve with honesty. Come back home with victory." And Mama writes . . . Well, when I read what she writes to me, tears start streaming.'

Klava Kopylova, clerk: 'I was buried in the bunker while I was typing an order. The lieutenant shouted to us: "Are you alive?" They dug me out. I moved to a bunker next door, and was buried there once again. They dug me out again, and I started typing again, and typed the document to the end. I will never forget it if I manage to stay alive. There was a bombardment that night. Everything was on fire. They woke me up. All were Party members in the bunker. They congratulated me so warmly, so nicely. On 7 November, I was given my Party card. They tried to photograph me several times for the Party identity card, but shells and mortar bombs were falling all the time. On quiet days, we tap dance and sing "The Little Blue Shawl".[9] I read *Anna Karenina* and *Resurrection*.'

Lyolya Novikova, junior nurse: 'Galya Titova's friends told me that once when she was bandaging someone, there was heavy firing, the soldier was killed, and she was wounded. She stood up straight and said: "Goodbye, girls," and fell. We buried her . . . The wounded soldiers write mostly to their commissars . . .[10] Although I speak German, I never speak to the prisoners, I don't want even to speak to them.

'My favourite subject was algebra. I had wanted to study at the Machine Manufacturing Institute . . . There are just three of us left, out of eighteen girls . . . We buried Tonya Yegorova. After the

9 'The Little Blue Shawl' had such a powerful influence that some soldiers even added the song's title to the official battle cry so that it became: '*Za Rodinu, za Stalina, za Siny Platochek!*' – 'For the Motherland, for Stalin, for the Blue Shawl!'
10 A good soldier when wounded feared, with justification, that he would never be allowed to return to his comrades. The authorities in the rear would just make up a batch of those deemed to be battleworthy again and send them off to any regiment. This was why they were writing to their political officers.

first battle, we lost two girls. We saw the corporal who said that Tonya had died in his arms. She had said to him: "Ay, I am dying. I am in such pain, I don't know whether these legs are mine, or not." He said: "They are yours." It was impossible to get close to the tank for two days. When we finally got there, we found her lying in the trench. We dressed her, put a handkerchief there, covered her face with a blouse. We were crying. There was myself, Galya Kanysheva and Klava Vasilyeva. They are both dead now. In reserve, we didn't get on well with the soldiers. We checked them for lice and quarrelled with them all the time. And now the soldiers are saying: "We are very grateful to our girls."

'We have gone into the attack with our platoon, and crawled side by side with them. We have fed soldiers, given them water, bandaged them under fire. We turned out to be more resilient than the soldiers, we even used to urge them on. Sometimes, trembling at night, we would think: "Oh, if I were at home right now."'

Sergeant Ilya Mironovich Brysin: 'In the evening we began to carry shells from the crossing. It was six kilometres, first along the bank, then through a *balka*, then the city, and then to the plant. We carried sixteen kilos each. We carried them in groundsheets, eight at a time. We had to walk along the bank under mortar fire. One didn't look in front of one's feet any longer. Everyone looked up into the sky. Bombs were falling about five metres from us. We would leave the wounded with someone to take care of them and carry on. In the ravine, sub-machine-gunners and mortars fired at us. We gave it a name, the Ravine of Death. It was about four hundred metres long. One would walk [only about] five steps and then have to get down. Twenty-two men brought two hundred shells. Ten were killed or wounded. When we reached a street, we somehow managed to move forward between the buildings. Once, we stockpiled three hundred rounds and the enemy blew them up with a direct hit. Oh, how infuriated we were, to have to start again from the beginning.

'We were firing all day. The Germans were about seventy metres from us. With me were Dudnikov, Kayukov, Pavlov, Glushakov and Pinikov. Before morning on the 28th, a lieutenant had crawled out to us, but his eyes were injured by a mortar bomb at dawn. I had to send him away. I sent Pavlov with him. There were four of us left. The Germans were advancing in a column, standing upright.

'We kept beating them off all day. Pavlov called to me: "Let's attack." I asked: "How many people have you got?" "Ten. And you?" "Four." "Well, let's attack!" And there were about a hundred Germans, two companies of SS.[11] Well, we went for them.

'I leaped out and ran upright. "Follow me! *Ura!*" I ran to the second house alone. There were Germans about fifteen metres from me. It was quiet, and dawn was breaking. I felt a little scared. I ran into the house, into its first room and listened. Germans were firing from behind walls, from corners. I threw a grenade at one corner from the window, and from the door, at another. It's hard to express how I was feeling, I wanted to get closer to the Germans, but they had disappeared behind an earth wall and I couldn't reach them.

'I climbed to the next floor up a smashed wall. I had hidden eight grenades there the afternoon before. We referred to them as "sausages".[12] I was standing there as if behind bars in a prison, armaments were hanging there, but there were no walls. I threw those eight grenades at them. They began firing at me with two machine guns and a mortar. I wasn't in fact afraid. I tied together two groundsheets, fastened them to a bar and got down to the ground floor through a shell-hole. I managed to crawl back to my men in the first house. I was told: "Kayukov has been mortally wounded."

'The company commander summoned me: "Can you recce the slag heap behind the [railway] line? There's a wooden house there." I said: "I must eat. And what about some sleep?" "To hell with sleep." The lieutenant gave me some bread and sugar, but then the shells began to fly. So I didn't manage to eat anything. I just went without eating. Well, I set off . . . I went to the slag heap. I spotted two machine guns and a mortar. I came back and reported. "Well," said my lieutenant, "you've spotted them, and you will destroy them."'

11 Almost every account by a Red Army soldier at Stalingrad talks of fighting SS soldiers, but in fact there were no SS formations serving there at all. It had tended to become a figure of speech for well-armed and disciplined German soldiers.
12 The standard grenade of Soviet manufacture was known as a 'sausage'. The American hand grenade, supplied through Lend-Lease, was known as a 'pineapple'.

'When Germans had pushed us right back to the Volga, their sub-machine-gunners were shouting: "Rus, glug-glug!" And we shouted back: "Hey, come here, you're thirsty, aren't you?"'[13]

Soldiers burned to death in the houses. Their charred corpses were found. Not one of them had fled. They burned holding out.

One of Grossman's most celebrated articles in _Krasnaya Zvezda_ was entitled 'The Stalingrad Battle', a collection of descriptions, some just vignettes.

In the light of rockets one sees the destroyed buildings, the land covered with trenches, the bunkers in the cliff and gullies, deep holes protected from bad weather by pieces of tin and planks of wood.
    'Hey, can you hear me? Have they brought dinner yet?' asks a soldier, who is sitting by the entrance of the bunker.
    'They left a long time ago to fetch it, and look, they haven't returned yet,' a voice anwers from the darkness.
    'They either had to shelter somewhere, or they're never coming back. [Enemy] fire around the field kitchen is too heavy.'
    'What louses! I badly want my dinner,' says the sitting soldier in an unhappy voice, and yawns . . .

Germans sitting in one of the buildings were resisting so stubbornly that they had to be blown up together with the heavy walls of the building. Under a fierce fire from the German defenders who could sense their own death, six sappers carried up by hand ten poods[14] of explosive and blew up the building. And when I imagine for a moment this picture – Sapper Lieutenant Chermakov, Sergeants Dubovy and Bugaev and Sappers Klimenko, Zhukhov and Messereshvili crawling under fire along the destroyed walls, each with 1.5 poods of death, when I picture to myself their sweaty, dirty faces, their shabby army shirts, when I remember how Sergeant Dubov shouted: 'Hey, sappers, don't be scared!' And Zhukhov

13 As mentioned in the previous chapter, Soviet snipers had been killing all their water carriers. Germans, desperate for water, had even resorted to tempting Stalingrad children with crusts of bread to go and fill their water bottles in the Volga, but snipers had orders to shoot down any civilians, including children, who assisted the enemy for whatever reason.
14 A pood was the equivalent of 16kg, so ten poods of explosive was 160kg, a huge charge.

answered, twisting his mouth and spitting dust out: 'There's no time to be scared now. We should have been before!' – I feel a great pride for them.

Here, where the meaning of measurement has shifted, where an advance of only several metres is as important as many kilometres under [normal] battle conditions, where the distance to the enemy sitting in a house next door is sometimes counted in dozens of steps, the location of divisional command posts has also changed accordingly. Divisional headquarters is 250 metres from the enemy; command posts of regiments and battalions are correspondingly closer. 'If communications are broken, it is easy to communicate with regiments using one's voice,' a man from the headquarters says jokingly. 'You shout, and they'll hear you. And they'll pass the order on to their battalions, also by voice.' . . . And in this catacomb where everything is shaking all the time from explosions of bombs and shells, the staff and commanders are sitting bent over the maps, and a signaller, who is always present in all essays from the war, is shouting: '*Luna, luna!*' And here, a runner is sitting shyly in the corner, holding a *makhorka* cigarette in his hand, averting his eyes and trying not to exhale in the direction of his chiefs.

After the battle, Grossman heard this story of Gurtyev, the commander of the 308th Rifle Division, and Zholudev, the commander of the 37th Guards Rifle Division. They had been neighbours in the terrible battle for the tractor works when Zholudev's guardsmen were crushed.

Gurtyev telephoned Zholudev and said: 'Courage, I can't help. Stand firm!' When Zholudev was ordered to move to the left bank, [i.e. withdrawn entirely from the battle] he said to Gurtyev: 'Stand firm, old man! Courage!' and they both laughed.

Ortenberg also recounted a bizarre event, which took place during one of Grossman's trips to Stalingrad from Akhtuba, the base on the east bank of the Volga. 'Once, in mid-October, he told officers from the Political Department of the front that he was going to visit [General] Rodimtsev the next day. They had two well-packed parcels with presents sent by an American women's organisation. Grossman was asked to deliver these presents to the two "most courageous women defending Stalingrad". The Political Department had decided that the two most courageous women could be found in Rodimtsev's division, and that Grossman was a suitable person to deliver these presents to them. Although he did not like official ceremonies, Vasily Semyonovich reluctantly agreed. He crossed the Volga in a motor boat, and joined Rodimtsev. The two girls stood in front of him. They were very excited about the famous writer and the heroic general presenting them with gifts. They said a formal thank you and started unwrapping the packages at once. Inside were ladies' swimming costumes and slippers to go with them. Everyone was extremely embarrassed. The luxurious swimming costumes looked so strange in this environment, under a thundering cannonade of the Stalingrad battle.'

SEVENTEEN

The Tide Turned

The October battles petered out at the end of the month, mainly due to exhaustion and a shortage of ammunition. The reorganised Soviet artillery across the river was now able to hammer German concentrations even more effectively as they prepared to attack. Paulus, under pressure from Hitler, still mounted assaults, but they were much smaller in scale to avoid the Soviet artillery and Katyusha batteries and because the German divisions were so short of men. Most dangerously of all, Paulus accepted Hitler's order to use panzer troops as infantry. It meant that he had no armour in reserve in case of surprise attack.

Hitler's obsession with taking Stalingrad – an ersatz victory to compensate for his failure to seize the oilfields of the Caucasus – had not slackened. He talked about it on 8 November in a broadcast speech from Munich. 'I wanted to reach the Volga,' he declared with unsubtle irony, 'to be precise at a particular spot, at a particular city. By chance it bore the name of Stalin himself.' He then boasted that 'time is of no importance'.

Hitler could not have been more wrong. Time was of great importance. Winter was approaching rapidly, and so, therefore, was the season of Soviet offensives. German soldiers called the worst climatic conditions 'weather for Russians' for that very reason. Grossman, unaware of any plans, wrote to his father on 13 November, just under a week before the great attack.

> I work a lot, the work is stressful, and I am pretty tired. I have never been to such a hot spot as this one. Letters don't reach me here, only once they brought me a whole bundle of letters, among them was a letter and a postcard from you . . . It is quite frosty here now, and windy.

Neither Hitler's headquarters in East Prussia nor the German Sixth Army had fully realised that the *Stavka* in Moscow was using the 62nd Army as the bait in an enormous trap. The Germans knew that there was a threat to their flanks – the left rear along the River Don was manned by the Third Romanian Army and the front to the south of Stalingrad was held by the Fourth Romanian Army. A Soviet build-up was spotted, but the scale and the ambition of the operation was grossly underestimated. Any suggestion that the Red Army could carry out a huge encirclement of the Sixth Army in the way that German panzer groups had surrounded Soviet armies the year before was considered unthinkable.

General Chuikov, still holding on in Stalingrad itself, had his own problems. The Volga was freezing over but had not yet frozen solid. The large ice floes coming down the river meant that taking supplies across was now extremely hazardous. But on 19 November, Operation Uranus began 150 kilometres north-west of Stalingrad, with a massive assault on the Romanian Third Army. The next morning, another attack fifty kilometres south of Stalingrad smashed open the Fourth Romanian Army. It took the Germans until midday on 21 November to appreciate that the 300,000 men of the Sixth Army were about to be cut off and that there was nothing that they could do about it.

Grossman had managed to have himself attached to IV Cavalry Corps which protected the left and outer flank of the two attacking mechanised

Soviet troops prepare for Operation Uranus
round Stalingrad, November 1942.

corps. According to Ortenberg, Grossman 'watched the beginning of the advance from the observation post of the division, and then, walking with the advancing troops, he described expressively all that he had seen on the way'.

A soldier who had been a prisoner of war during the last war looks at a diving plane: 'Must be my lad bombing,' he says.

They run into the attack protecting their faces with sapper spades. In the attack, a rifle is better than a sub-machine gun.

The Romanian troops, dressed in brown uniforms and Balkan sheepskin caps, lacked modern equipment, leadership and anti-tank guns. They soon threw down their rifles and shouted '*Antonescu kaputt!*',[1] but surrender did not save them. Thousands of prisoners were shot out of hand, and the frozen roads were littered with the detritus of a defeated army.

Troops are marching. Their spirits are higher now. 'Ah, it would be great to get to Kiev.' Another man: 'Ah, I'd like to get to Berlin!'

An image: a strongpoint destroyed by a tank. There is a flattened Romanian. A tank has driven over him. His face has become a bas-relief. Next to him, there are two crushed Germans. There is one of our soldiers, too, lying in the trench half buried.

Empty cans, grenades, hand grenades, a blanket stained with blood, pages from German magazines. Our soldiers are sitting among the corpses, cooking in a cauldron slices cut from a dead horse, and stretching their frozen hands towards the fire.

A killed Romanian and a killed Russian were lying next to each other on the battlefield. The Romanian had a sheet of paper and a child's drawing of a hare and a boat. Our soldier had a letter: 'Good afternoon, or maybe good evening. Hello, Daddy . . .' And the end of the letter: 'Come and visit us, because when you aren't here, I come back home as if to a rented flat. I miss you very much. Come and visit, I wish I could see you, if only for an hour. I am

---

1   Marshal Ion Antonescu (1882–1946), the Romanian dictator, had been Germany's staunchest supporter in the invasion of the Soviet Union, but the collapse of his ill-equipped forces in the Stalingrad campaign produced intense German resentment against their unfortunate ally.

writing this and tears are pouring. That was your daughter Nina writing.'

During the rapid advance, when there was no clear front line, Grossman found himself in unexpected danger. He was accompanied by Aleksei Kapler, the film director who became the first love of Svetlana Stalin. For daring to fondle the tyrant's young daughter, Kapler was beaten up by Beria's men and sent to the Gulag for ten years in 1943. After Stalin's death, Kapler recounted his adventure with Grossman during this advance. 'We wandered into an empty house and decided to stay there for the night. Then some soldiers appeared. We saw their shadows on the ceiling and realised that they were not our soldiers, because their helmets were different from ours. They turned out to be Romanians. Fortunately they did not spot us and went away.'

Red Army soldiers were furious to find what their Romanian prisoners had looted from the homes of the local population. 'Old women's kerchiefs and earrings, linen and skirts, babies' napkins and brightly coloured girls' blouses. One soldier had twenty-two pairs of woollen stockings in his possession.'

The greatest joy was that of liberated civilians.

'How did we find out that our troops had arrived? We were listening by the window: "Yegor, crank the engine!" [we heard] "Ours!" we cried.'

They soon expressed their loathing of the Romanians who, following the German example, had whipped or beaten civilians until they revealed where they had hidden their food.

Romanians. An old man called them 'turkeys'. Real Gypsies. They kept saying all the time: 'War is bad, we should go home.' [Yet] they whipped the old man four times. They forced him to go and harvest cereals, and took the grain. They had fruit drops and canned food to eat.

Some civilians had also suffered from Soviet military action.

A babushka told us how one of our own pilots wounded her: 'He dropped a bomb, the son of a bitch, fuck him,' she says angrily, then looks at the commander who is changing his boots and corrects herself: 'Son of a bitch, sonny. There are no cows, no cows to drive to the pasture, no cows to let back in. There is no life [left] for us.'

Grossman's notes contributed to his article 'On the Roads of the Advance' about the offensive south of Stalingrad.

Ice is moving down the Volga. Ice floes are rustling, crumbling, crushing against one another. The river is almost wholly covered with ice. Only from time to time can one see patches of water in this wide, white ribbon floating between the dark snowless banks. The white ice of the Volga is carrying tree trunks, wood. A big raven is sitting sulkily on an ice floe. A dead Red Fleet soldier in a striped shirt floats past. Men from a freight steamer take him from the ice. It is difficult to tear the dead man out of the ice. He is rooted in it. It is as if he doesn't want to leave the Volga where he has fought and died.

Barges full of captured Romanians pass us. They are standing in their skimpy greatcoats, in tall white hats, stamping their feet, rubbing their frozen hands. 'They've seen the Volga now,' say the sailors.

A group of two hundred prisoners usually marches under the guard of two or three soldiers. The Romanians march in an organised manner, some groups are even lined up and keeping in step, and this makes those who see them laugh . . . Prisoners move on and on in crowds, their mess tins and flasks rattling, belted with pieces of rope, or wire, blankets of different colours upon their shoulders. And women say, laughing: 'Oh, these Romanians are travelling just like Gypsies.'

Romanian corpses are lying along the roads; abandoned cannons camouflaged with dry steppe grass point eastwards. Horses wander about in *balkas* dragging behind them broken traces, vehicles hit by shellfire are giving off a blue-grey smoke. On the roads lie helmets decorated with the Romanian royal coat of arms, thousands of cartridges, grenades, rifles. A Romanian strongpoint. A mountain of empty, sooty cartridges by the machine-gun nest. White sheets of writing paper are lying in the communication trench. The brown winter steppe has turned brick red from blood. There are rifles with butts splintered by Russian bullets. And crowds of prisoners are moving towards us all the time.

They are searched before being sent off to the rear. Heaps of peasant women's belongings that were found in rucksacks and pockets of Romanians look comic and pitiful. There are old women's shawls, women's earrings, underwear, skirts, swaddling clothes. The further on we move, the more abandoned vehicles and cannons we see. There are trucks, armoured vehicles and staff cars.

We enter Abganerovo. An old peasant woman told us about the three months of the occupation. 'It became empty here. Not a single hen to cackle, not a single cock to sing. There isn't a single cow left to let out in the morning and let in in the evening. Romanians have pinched everything. They whipped almost all our old men: one didn't report for work, another one failed to hand in his grain. The starosta in Plodovitaya was whipped four times. They took away my son, a cripple, and with him a girl and a nine-year-old boy. We've been crying for four days, waiting for them to return.'

Abganerovo station is full of captured materiel. The Germans had already managed to alter the railway track.[2] There are French and Belgian freight carriages here, and Polish ones, too. There are whole trains loaded with flour, corn, mines, shells, fat in big square tins, freight cars full of ersatz *valenki* with thick wooden soles, sheepskin hats, equipment, searchlights. Our medical *teplushkas* look pitiful and destitute with their hastily made bunk beds covered with dirty rags. Soldiers grunt as they carry paper sacks of flour out of the freight cars and load them on to trucks. A [Nazi] eagle is printed boldly on each sack.

The faces of Red Army soldiers have become bronze red from the severe winter winds. It isn't easy to fight in this kind of weather, to spend long winter nights out in the steppe under this icy wind that penetrates everywhere, yet the men are marching cheerfully. This is the Stalingrad advance. The army is in exceptionally high spirits.

By 26 November, over a quarter of a million men from Paulus's Sixth Army, the largest formation in the Wehrmacht, had been surrounded between the Volga and the Don. The Red Army, underestimating the size of the force it had surrounded, immediately launched a series of attacks to smash the perimeter, but the Germans, believing that Hitler would never abandon them, resisted fiercely.

A happy, bright day. Preliminary bombardment. *Katyushas*. Ivan the Terrible. Roaring. Smoke. And failure. The Germans have dug themselves in, we couldn't hunt them out.

2   The Russian gauge railway track was different to that of Western Europe.

Grossman reads a newspaper, perhaps checking one of his own articles in Krasnaya Zvezda. *The camel in the background may be the famous Kuznechik who accompanied the 308th Rifle Division all the way from Stalingrad to Berlin.*

The weather became increasingly harsh, with snow and hard frosts, which reduced the chances of the Sixth Army being able to fight its way out. The Red Army was far more used to such conditions.

At the front line out in the steppe, winter. A hole covered with a groundsheet. A stove made from a helmet. A chimney from a brass shell. The fuel [consists of] tall weeds. On the march, one soldier carries an armful of tall weeds, another one a handful of chips, the third one a shell, the fourth one the stove.

At the beginning of December, Grossman returned to the east bank opposite Stalingrad. He wrote to the editor of *Krasnaya Zvezda*.

Comrade Ortenberg, I am planning to leave for the city tomorrow. I had wanted to start a big essay,[3] but I realise that I have to post-

3   Grossman is almost certainly referring to 'Stalingrad Army'.

pone writing and spend some time collecting material in the city. As the crossing is complicated now,[4] my trip is going to take at least a week. This is why you should not be angry if there is a delay in sending you my work. In the city, my plan is to have conversations with Chuikov and divisional commanders and to visit the front units. Also I would like to inform you that I will need to visit Moscow, approximately in January. I would be very grateful, if you could summon me back. In fact, I feel somewhat overloaded with impressions and overexhausted after the three months of tension in Stalingrad. If something unfortunate and unexpected happens during my visit to the city, could you please help my family? Vasily Grossman.

Grossman managed to get across and went to 62nd Army headquarters. Life was much quieter, since the now besieged Germans were short of ammunition as well as food. Their survival depended entirely on resupply by air to Pitomnik airfield, in the centre of the encircled area. Goering had told Hitler it was perfectly possible to resupply the Sixth Army by air, even though his own Luftwaffe generals had warned him that such a huge task was impossible. The soldiers of the Sixth Army were encouraged to hold out with vain stories of an SS panzer army coming to their aid. General Chuikov told Grossman: 'There was a rumour among Germans that Hitler himself had visited Pitomnik and that he had said: "Stand firm! I am leading an army to rescue you." (He was dressed as a corporal).'

This battlefield legend bore a resemblance to the equally untrue story on the Soviet side during the desperate September days that Stalin himself had been seen in Stalingrad.

Chuikov also outlined the situation his own 62nd Army faced due to virtual impossibility of resupply across the half-frozen Volga. They had to rely almost entirely on radio communications with the east bank, because all the land-lines had been snapped by the ice. Their one great advantage, however, remained the artillery positions concentrated on the west bank. Their resupply of ammunition was not affected.

Grossman described Chuikov's bunker in an article entitled 'Military Council'.

When one enters a bunker and the underground quarters of officers and soldiers, one feels again an ardent wish to retain for ever

4　The Volga had still not frozen solid, so crossing the river was extremely dangerous and unpredictable.

in one's memory the remarkable traits of this unique life. The lamps and the chimney made from artillery shell cases, cups made of brass shell bases standing on tables near crystal glasses. Next to an anti-tank grenade sits a china ashtray on which is written 'Wife, don't make your husband angry'. There is a huge dull electric bulb in the commander-in-chief's bunker, and a smile from Chuikov, who says: 'Yes, and a chandelier. Aren't we living in a city?' And this volume of Shakespeare in General Gurov's underground office . . . All these samovars and gramophones, blue family sugar bowls and round mirrors in wooden frames on the clay walls of basements. All this everyday life, with peaceful household things rescued from the burning buildings.

Grossman, although fiercely satisfied by the inevitable victory over the Sixth Army, became increasingly depressed by the way his work was rewritten in the editorial offices of *Krasnaya Zvezda* and wrote about it to his wife on 5 December.

I work a lot. You can probably see that from the newspaper. If you saw how they cut and distort [my writing], and not only that, they also add new phrases to my poor pieces, you would probably be more upset than happy about the fact that my writing sees the light at all. The editorial office has adopted a rule of cutting off the end of any essay, replacing dots with commas, crossing out the descriptions that I particularly like, changing titles and inserting phrases like: 'This faith and love virtually made miracles.' This editing is done in haste by professional editors, and sometimes I have to read a phrase several times to understand its meaning. All this upsets me very much because I am working in very difficult conditions . . .

Chuikov's 62nd Army remained on short rations – including *makhorka* and vodka – during the slow freezing of the Volga. Finally, on 16 December, the river froze solid. First, a footbridge across the ice was made with planks. Then, a proper route across the river could be laid, with branches and twigs doused in water to strengthen the surface. This meant that it could soon take trucks and even heavy artillery. 'Good frosts!' Red Army soldiers wrote home in satisfaction. In less than two months, 18,000 trucks and 17,000 other vehicles are said to have driven across the ice. Grossman celebrated this development in an article entitled 'The New Day'.

All those who, for a hundred days, held on to the Volga crossing and crossed the dark grey icy river, looked into the eyes of a quick, pitiless death. One day someone will sing a song about those who are now asleep on the Volga's bed . . .

At night, we could walk upon the Volga. The ice was two days old and did not bend any longer beneath our feet. The moon lit the network of paths, uncountable tracks of sledges. A liaison soldier was walking in front of us, quickly and confidently as if he'd spent half of his life walking on these intermingling paths. Suddenly the ice started cracking. The liaison soldier came to a wide ice clearing, stopped and said: 'Aha! We must have taken the wrong path. We should have stayed to the right.' Liaison men always utter this sort of consoling phrase, no matter where they take you.

Barges smashed by shells have frozen into the ice. There's a bluish glistening of ice-covered hawsers. Sterns rise steeply up, so do the bows of sunken motor boats.

Fighting is still going on in the factories . . . Guns fire with hollow bangs, rumblings, and the explosions of shells resound drily and clearly. Often, bursts of machine-gun and sub-machine-gun fire can be heard distinctly. This music is fearfully similar to the peaceful work of the plant, like riveting or steam hammers beating steel bars, and flattening them. It is as if liquid steel and slag pouring into a mould are lighting the fresh ice on the Volga with a pink, quick glow.

The sun rises and illuminates the edges of large holes made by heavy bombs. The depths of these frightening holes are always in a gloomy penumbra. The sun is afraid to touch them . . .

The sun shines over hundreds of railway tracks where tanker wagons are lying like killed horses, with their bellies torn open; where hundreds of freight carriages are jammed one on top of another, blasted there by the force of an explosion, and crowded around cold locomotives like a panic-stricken herd huddling around its leaders.

We are walking on a wasteland covered with holes from bombs and shells – German snipers and lookouts can see the place well, but the skinny Red Army soldier in a long trenchcoat is walking by my side calmly and without haste. He explains soothingly: 'You wonder whether he can't see us? Well, he can. We used to crawl here at night, but now it is different: he is saving rounds and shells.'

Past a heap of rust-coloured metal rubbish, past the colossal steel-pouring ladles, past steel plates and broken walls. Red Army soldiers are so used to destruction here that they fail to notice all this. On the contrary, an item of interest here is an intact glass in a window of the destroyed factory office, a tall chimney, or a wooden house that has miraculously survived. 'Please look. That house is still alive,' passers-by say, smiling.

Not surprisingly, Grossman was suffering from severe strain by mid-December, when he wrote again to his father.

I think I will be in Moscow in January. I am well, but my nerves have suffered a lot. I've become angry and irritable, I keep attacking my colleagues. They are frightened of me now. I cannot leave this place right away and I don't want to. You see, now that fortune has turned in our direction, one does not want to leave the place where one had seen the hardest possible moments.

As his departure from Stalingrad approached, Grossman became increasingly preoccupied with his experiences there.

Red Army soldiers wound the gramophone up. 'What record shall we put on?' one of them asked. Several voices spoke up at once. 'Our one. That one.'

Then a strange thing happened. While the soldier was looking for the record, I thought: It would be so wonderful to hear my favourite song in this black, destroyed basement. And suddenly, a solemn, melancholy voice began to sing: 'A snowstorm is howling outside the windows . . .' The Red Army soldiers must have liked this song very much. Everyone sat in silence. We must have heard the same refrain of the song a dozen of times:

> 'My Lady Death, we beg you,
> Please wait outside.'

These words and Beethoven's immortal music sounded indescribably powerful here. For me, this was probably one of the most emotional moments in the whole war . . . And I remembered a little letter written in a child's hand, which was found by a dead soldier in a strongpoint. 'Good afternoon, or maybe good evening. Hello, *Tyatya* [Daddy] . . .' And I remembered this dead *Tyatya*, who was probably reading the letter when he was dying, and the crumpled sheet lay by his head.

PART THREE

Recovering the Occupied Territories
1943

EIGHTEEN
After the Battle

The battle of Stalingrad had wound down in the city itself during December 1942. Fierce fighting took place only out in the frozen wastes of the Volga–Don steppe where seven encircling Soviet armies were trying to crush the diseased and starving Sixth Army. But the Wehrmacht at bay was still a formidable force. In the city, there was a slight sense of anti-climax which came from a mixture of exhaustion, relief and sadness at the terrible losses. Grossman was profoundly moved when he discovered his nephew's grave on 29 December.

> Grave of Yura Benash by Mikhailov's command post – you have to go up just behind it. The commanding heights. There are four graves right above the cliff.

He wrote about it to his wife as soon as he was back on the east bank.

> My dearest Lyusenka, I've just come back from the city, in order to write things up. I crossed the river walking over the ice. This recent excursion has caused me a lot of deep impressions. Imagine, my darling, there is the grave of Yura Benash, Vadya's son, on the cliff above the Volga. I found his regimental commander, and he told me in detail about Yura. Yura was a battalion commander. He was fighting like a hero. His anti-tank company had hit sixteen enemy tanks. He led crazy attacks. Everyone talked of him with admiration. He knew that I was here, he kept trying to get in touch with me through people from the front editorial office, he wrote letters to me, but I never received a single one of them. Well, I've found him now.
> . . . Lyusenka, so much has passed before my eyes, so much that it's hard to comprehend how my soul, my heart, my thoughts and my memory can still take all this in. I feel as if I am full to the brim with all this . . . Tomorrow I am going to sit down and write a very long essay.

203

At the same time he wrote a similar letter to his father, recounting that Yura had received the Order of the Red Star and had been killed in an explosion a month before.

> There is no one to cry for him – neither mother nor a grandmother . . . I've wandered a lot over the last few days, I've seen a lot of interesting things, now I will sit down and write. I'd like to scribble something serious and big . . . I don't know what to write about, there are so many thoughts and impressions, I wouldn't know where to start. When I see you and we sit together, I'll sit down in the red armchair and we will talk and talk.

After the intensity and importance of the battle of Stalingrad, Grossman found it was hard to accept that life moved on in its usual way, that goodbyes could be hurried and casual after such momentous events.

> A commander leaves his regiment. Empty goodbyes: 'Write,' 'All right, all right.' Haste. And the man has been through all the hardships of fighting in Stalingrad.

His own farewell to the place was made in his article for *Krasnaya Zvezda* entitled 'Today in Stalingrad'.

> The winter sun is shining over mass graves, over handmade tombstones at the places where soldiers had been killed on the axis of the main attack. The dead are sleeping on the heights by the ruins of factory workshops, in gullies and *balkas*. They are sleeping now right where they had been fighting when alive. These tombstones stand by the trenches, bunkers, stone walls with embrasures, which never surrendered to the enemy, like a great monument to a simple, blood-washed loyalty.
> The Holy Land! How one wants to keep for ever in one's memory this new city which gives its people a triumphant freedom, a city that has grown up among the ruins, to absorb it all – all the underground lodgings with chimneys smoking in the sun, nets of paths and new roads, heavy mortars raising their trunks among the bunkers and dugouts, hundreds of men wearing quilted jackets, greatcoats, *ushanka* hats, doing the sleepless labour of war, carrying mines under their arms like loaves of bread, peeling potatoes by the pointed trunk of a heavy gun, squabbling, singing in low voices,

telling about a grenade fight during the night. They are so majestic and matter-of-fact in their heroism.

Grossman was surprised by his own sense of pain when Ortenberg ordered him down to the Southern Front away from Stalingrad.

We were leaving Stalingrad on New Year's Eve. We are moved to the Southern Front. What sadness! Where did it come from, this feeling of parting, I never had it before during this war.

Ortenberg had decided to replace him with Konstantin Simonov, who would have the glory of covering the final victory. Simonov had visited Stalingrad with Ortenberg in the September days (when they had fallen asleep in Yeremenko and Khrushchev's bunker on the west bank and awoken to find that the whole headquarters had disappeared in the night to transfer to the east bank). Grossman was the *Krasnaya Zvezda* correspondent who had spent by far the longest in the city and Ilya Ehrenburg was one of those who thought this decision unjust and illogical. 'Why did General Ortenberg order Grossman to go to Elista and send Simonov to Stalingrad instead? Why was not Grossman allowed to see the ending? This I still cannot understand. Those months that he spent in Stalingrad and all that was associated with them remained in Grossman's soul as the most important impressions.'

Grossman wrote to his father just before leaving Stalingrad.

Well, my [dear Father], I will say goodbye to Stalingrad tomorrow and travel towards Kotelnikovo [and then] Elista. I am leaving with a feeling of sadness, you know – as if I were leaving some person dear to me, as so many memories, so many thoughts and feelings, depressing and significant, exhausting, unforgettable are associated with this city. This city has become human for me. Father, things are going well at the front, and my spirits are now higher.

The Southern Front extended through Kalmykia from the empty steppe south of Stalingrad, right into the northern Caucasus, from where Field Marshal von Manstein was withdrawing Army Group A in great haste. A second major Soviet offensive in the second half of December, Operation Little Saturn, threatened the Germans' route of withdrawal around the Sea of Azov. This rapid retreat allowed Grossman to study what life had been like under German occupation, especially in Elista, the main town of the region some three hundred kilometres west of Astrakhan.

Kalmykia. The steppe. Snow and yellow dust and whitish-yellow drifting snow whipped up by the wind on a road. Empty houses. Silence. There's no silence quite like it anywhere else. The roads are mined. 'You go first,' [people say, playing their] tricks: 'We'll have a smoke and breakfast.' 'And we'll put some more oil into the tank!' 'And we'll melt some snow to top up the radiator.' [Such is the] terror of a mined road. An armoured vehicle, a truck, another truck a little further on, each one destroyed by an explosion. The dead bodies of soldiers have been blasted out of trucks by the force of the explosion. Horses with their bellies ripped out. They are lying side by side, just like when they were drawing the cart. Another truck. The fear of mines – it's a disease.

It's empty and quiet. A dog is running along the road, a human bone between its teeth. Another one is running after it, its tail between its legs. Villages – the men have left . . . A Russian house. Komsomol member Bulgakova [lives there] with her baby. She is the only one in the whole area who kept her Komsomol identity card, which she hid under *kizyaks*.[1]

Gramophones, cosiness and fear. There are gangs all around. A man who has come back from prisoner-of-war camp. Who is he? A spy or a reliable man? It's a mystery. There's a shadow over him. He is an unknown quantity. He says he has walked 4,000 kilometres. He had escaped three times. Death was never far away, and with death hovering over him his suffering was great: he had been captured near Smolensk, and escaped from prison near Elista. One cannot believe him, but one cannot disbelieve him either. A tragic figure.

There isn't a single cock in the village: women killed them all, because Romanians discovered where chickens had been hidden by the cries of the cockerels. The steppe – its smoothness and waves, fog, dust, snow, hoarfrost, frozen sagebrush, horsemen in the fields.

Elista. [The Germans] burned Elista, and once again, like fifteen years ago, Elista is a village. There isn't a town here any longer . . . The town commandant of Elista was a Major Ritter.

1 Compressed dung used as fuel in stoves.

Grossman interviewed the schoolteacher who had continued to work under the Germans throughout the occupation. 'I was tormented by the feeling that it was wrong to work for them,' the teacher told him.

Lavrenty Beria's NKVD, which descended on Kalmykia soon afterwards to root out traitors, would have been pitiless. Grossman named the teacher in an article (see below) as Klara Frantsevna, but we do not know if that was her true name or not. The Kalmyks suffered terribly in the Stalinist wartime purge of the southern nationalities, but not quite as badly as the Chechens and Crimean Tatars. Many Kalmyks had welcomed the Germans as liberators, and proudly wore the green uniform of Kalmyk auxiliary police.

School. History had been removed from the curriculum as a subject. Geography of the USSR was replaced by a physical study of Europe as a part of the world (without any countries), the position of Europe, the borders of Europe, the seas surrounding Europe, islands, peninsulas, climatic conditions, mountains, surface.

Russian language: [the Germans] didn't give us a new textbook, they just amended the old one by tearing out all the pages to do with the politics of the USSR. They suggested to children that they should tear out those pages themselves. A German officer spoke to the children. (He had studied in a classical school in Odessa and was a teacher of chemistry for senior pupils).

Reading: the reading book was banned ('Gorky isn't a writer, he is a charlatan').[2] They introduced a book [entitled] *What Will Happen After?* and the magazine *Hitler the Liberator*. (Albrecht's 'In the basements of the GPU'.)[3]

Maths: they removed from the textbook all the questions to do with Soviet affairs [and replaced them with]: this number of Soviet aircraft has been shot down, etc.

The German language was included in the curriculum. An officer searched children's schoolbags looking for pages that they didn't tear out. A book by Lenin was found in the bag of one girl. There was a great deal of shouting, but the girl was not expelled.

Natural science: the last chapter, 'On the Origins of Humans', was banned.

2   Gorky, of course, had helped Grossman at the start of his literary career.
3   This long article by a renegade communist was published in Nazi Germany in Karl Albrecht's book *Der verratene Sozialismus* (1941).

They had two hours of German every week. Punishments were introduced: 'You could even beat children.'

Singing: Russian folk songs, 'Ripe apple'. 'Children, get ready for school.'

This school was not typical for the occupied territory – the Germans [on the spot] were acting on their own authority. 'One German asked: "And could they read from *War and Peace*?"[4] I said: "They are too young for that."'

Library. All books on politics were removed, as well as Heine and all Soviet writers.

Metises (half-Germans) received German food rations. There was an announcement: 'All *metises* must register at the commandant's office. It is in their own interests.' They were given a pure-bred cow which cost a thousand roubles, chocolate, white flour, sweets. Some Russians were given the same status as *metises*.

'A [German] soldier came and found sugar. He sucked a piece of sugar. I pointed at the baby, he smiled and went away. They love sweet things, they always suck sugar.'[5]

Sign on the lavatory: 'Entrance forbidden to Russians.'

Germans in Elista. In August, they were walking around and riding motorbikes in their underpants.[6]

Grossman also heard of atrocities against the Jewish population, which were presumably carried out by the short-lived SS *Sonderkommando Astrachan*, formed in October 1942 and disbanded in December soon after the front collapsed. Despite its name, this *Sonderkommando* was based in Elista.

Death of ninety-three Jewish families. They'd smeared the children's lips with poison.

4 Presumably the German wanted to know whether Tolstoy was seen by the Soviet state as a tsarist writer.
5 Burial parties could soon distinguish a German skull from a Soviet one simply by the teeth. The Soviet skulls contained much healthier teeth and lacked amalgam fillings.
6 The German motorcyclists were almost certainly wearing shorts, an article of clothing seldom seen in out-of-the-way places.

It is hard to know exactly what he meant about the death of the children, a term in Russian which includes babies and infants. The implication seems to be that the SS was experimenting with a new poison.

He also interviewed a teacher who had been raped by a German officer.

> Teacher (I decided not to ask her name and surname). At night, an officer, helped by his orderly, raped her. She was holding a six-month-old baby in her arms. He fired at the floor, threatening to kill the baby. The orderly went away and locked the door. Some of our prisoners of war were in the next room. She cried out and called, but there was dead silence in the next room.

Using his interviews in Elista, Grossman tried to recreate what it was like to be occupied by the Germans. It is hard to imagine that Grossman would have been able to publish it, considering that it deals with the taboo subject of collaboration with the enemy.

> The old teacher . . . On 5 June 1942, he was sitting in the yard. Dogs, who had already experienced many air raids, went into the slit trenches after the women, their tails between their legs. The women kicked them and screamed: 'We are sick even without you! Do you think we want you here with your fleas! Get out, cholera take you!' But the dogs rolled on to their sides and refused to leave.

> Voronenko announced that Germans had dropped a two-hundred-kilo bomb, and anti-aircraft guns were missing their targets at about five hundred metres. Old woman Mikhailyuk was muttering: 'If only the Germans could come quicker and end all this nightmare. During yesterday's alarm some parasite stole a pot of borscht from my stove.'
> Boys would appear first, they would run in, with exact information: 'A bomb fell right opposite Rabinovichka's house, Zabolotsy's goat killed, old Miroshenko's leg was torn off, they took her to a hospital on a cart, and she died on the way, her daughter is mourning so much that one can hear her from four blocks away.'
> 'There's one thing that I fear most of all,' the teacher said, 'and that's the people with whom I've lived my whole life side by side, whom I love, whom I trust, that they would give in to a dark, mean provocation.'

It was only at noon that German motorcyclists appeared. They were wearing forage caps, shorts and gym shoes, and had a dark tan. Each of them had a wristwatch. An old woman looking at them said: 'Ah, my God, they are shameless, naked in the main street. Such godlessness!'

The motorcyclists poked round the houses, took the priest's turkey who came out to pick through some horse dung, hurriedly ate two and a half kilos of honey at the church starosta's house, drank a bucket of milk and moved on, having promised that the commandant would arrive in about two hours.

During the day, two of Yashka's friends, deserters, came to visit him. They were all drunk and sang in a chorus: 'Three tankists, three jolly friends.' They probably would have been singing a German song if they knew one. The agronomist was walking around the yard and asking women with an arch smile: 'So, where are all our Jews? I saw neither children nor old people for the whole day today, as if they'd never existed. And only yesterday they were carrying five-pood baskets from the bazaar.'

Days passed. The agronomist was made the person responsible for the block. Yashka was serving in the police, the most beautiful girl in town played the piano at the officers' café and lived with the commandant's orderly. Women went to villages to swap their belongings for wheat, potatoes, millet, and they were cursing German drivers who demanded an enormous fee for transporting the stuff. The employment office was sending out hundreds of call-up notes, and girls and boys walked to the station with backpacks and boarded freight cars. A German movie theatre, an officers' brothel and a soldiers' brothel were set up in the town. A big brick toilet was built in the main square, with the sign 'For Germans only' in Russian and Italian. At the school, teacher Klara Frantsevna set first-year pupils the problem: 'Two Messerschmitts have shot down eight Red fighters and twelve bombers, and an anti-aircraft gun shot down eleven Bolshevik attack aircraft. What is the total of Red aircraft shot down?' Prisoners of war were marched through the town. They were ragged and they staggered from starvation. Women ran to them and gave them pieces of bread and boiled potatoes. The prisoners fought over the food, and the guards were beating them to establish order.

Yashka said, mockingly and with an air of mystery: 'You'll soon have a lot of space for living. I've seen towns which have been cleared completely . . . Down to the last little root.'

The old woman, Weisman, started to cry for her granddaughter. 'Dasha,' she said, 'I'll leave my wedding ring to you, and then you'll be able to get about fifteen poods of potatoes from our vegetable garden, as well as pumpkins and beets. You'll be able to feed my girl somehow until the spring. I've also got a piece of cloth for a lady's coat. You can exchange it for bread.' She eats very little, she has got no appetite.

On 17 February, Grossman wrote to his wife about his longing to be back in the centre of things after his time in the wastes of Kalmykia.

I am waiting for the plane with a lot of nervousness . . . Grandiose events are taking place, I've already missed Kharkov. I was going to be there during the assault . . . My essays on Stalingrad are enjoying a great success.

Grossman was still unaware that the over-optimistic advance following Operation Little Saturn was a repeat of Stalin's blunder the previous January, when the success around Moscow was turned into a general offensive. In the south, the Red Army faced the formidable talents of Field Marshal von Manstein who was preparing a counter-offensive which would retake Kharkov. Grossman, however, had his own disappointment, as he explained in a letter to his wife.

I was very disturbed and offended by this thing about the prize. Never mind, this has not reduced respect for me in literary circles and among readers. Please don't get upset about it. It is all in the past now.

The commission which chose the winner for the Stalin Prize in 1942 had voted unanimously for *The People Immortal*, but Stalin crossed out Grossman's name. Perhaps the subject matter, dealing with the disaster of 1941, was an uncomfortable subject for the Great Leader who had made such catastrophic mistakes. The winner as a result of Stalin's intervention was Ilya Ehrenburg's *The Fall of Paris*. In December 1944, during de Gaulle's visit to Moscow, Stalin mischievously told Ehrenburg to present the French leader with a copy.

Ehrenburg himself seemed uneasy in that Stalingrad winter at his own fortune and Grossman's misfortune. 'People say that some are born under a lucky star,' he wrote. 'But the star under which Grossman was born was definitely an unlucky one. I was told that Stalin had deleted his novel, *The People Immortal*, from the list of those proposed for the prize.'

Grossman had hardly endeared himself to the political controllers of Soviet literary life. Ortenberg noted that in the summer of 1942 'we received a note from Vasily Grossman. He asked me to "give refuge" to his friend Andrey Platonov.[7] "He is defenceless and unsettled." This was a difficult task. Platonov at the time was *persona non grata* in our literature.' But Grossman got his way, and Platonov was given a job at *Krasnaya Zvezda*.

---

7   Platonov, Andrey Platonovich (1899–1951), writer, poet and literary critic, was a special correspondent of *Krasnaya Zvezda* from October 1942 to the end of the war.

NINETEEN

Winning Back the Motherland

Stalin's misplaced certainty that the Germans were about to collapse after the Stalingrad campaign led to overextended Red Army advances and sharp reverses. Field Marshal von Manstein's timing was impeccable. He struck just as the Soviet armoured columns were exhausted and low on fuel. The XXV Tank Corps had to abandon their vehicles near Zaporozhe and flee on foot through the snow.

The main setback to Manstein's plans, however, came in early March when, against his orders, General Paul Hauser took the SS Panzer Corps into what was known as the third battle of Kharkov, a rash and costly recapture of the city. In the latter part of March, after this swirling campaign in which Manstein had managed to stave off disaster, largely by ignoring Hitler's orders, both sides went on the defensive to recuperate and reorganise. Perhaps the most important consequence of this toing and froing was the large Kursk salient, a great chunk of Soviet territory more than eighty miles square, sticking into the German front. It was to obsess Hitler in the coming months, with results that would prove fatal for his armoured forces.

Grossman found himself back in the familiar territory of the eastern Ukraine, at Starobelsk, just north of the River Donets. Ortenberg noted how Grossman had adapted to military life. 'Months of war passed one after another, and Grossman, who was utterly civilian by nature and who had not been liable for call-up because of health problems, had made himself at home in the war. He did not change much on the outside, except perhaps his tunic did not ride up so much as before, and his great-coat had shrunk a bit from rain and snow. There were still no commanding intonations in his voice, in spite of his lieutenant colonel's shoulder-boards.'

Grossman, attached to the 3rd Guards Army in the northern Donbass, found the military situation rather like the year before. In his notebook, he wrote: 'Early spring. Complete lull at the front.'

In Starobelsk, he encountered strange echoes of the pre-revolutionary past.

> I gave a lift in my truck to a priest, his daughter and granddaughter, with all their belongings. They received me [at home] as if I were royalty, with a supper and vodka. The priest told me that Red Army soldiers and officers come to him to pray and to talk. One major came to see him not long ago.

Grossman at the headquarters in Svatovo, April 1943.

> Story about the Tsar's sister Kseniya, who lives in Starobelsk. She had protected Soviet people from the Germans. People say that she had returned from abroad with Dzerzhinsky's permission some time ago, in order to find her son.[1]

1 Dzherzhinsky, Feliks (1877–1926), the son of a Polish landowner, became in December 1917 Commissar for Internal Affairs and chief of the Cheka, the All-Russian Extraordinary Committee for Combating Counter-Revolution and Sabotage, which became the GPU (State Political Administration) in 1922.

This is a complete myth. The Grand Duchess, who had left the Crimea in 1919 with the Dowager Empress and other members of the imperial family on board the battleship HMS *Marlborough*, never returned to Russia. During the Second World War she was living at Balmoral, not in Starobelsk.

An attempt to fish, [but] a Messer attacked suddenly, firing at us.

The Ukrainian government has accommodated itself on a scrap of liberated Ukrainian land, in the tiny town of Starobelsk, in a tiny white building. A talk with Bazhan.[2] He complained about our great-power chauvinism. A guard standing at his door has one of those inhuman faces that takes one back immediately to the time of peace.

A war correspondent, the Ukrainian writer Levada, is terribly upset because he has been given a medal instead of a [military] order.[3] After receiving it, he returned to the *izba* where he was based. A little girl shouted, looking at the medal: 'A kopeck!' The boy corrected her: 'That isn't a kopeck, you fool, that's a badge.' This was the last straw for Levada.

Starobelsk had been occupied by remnants of the Eighth Italian Army after it was shattered on the Don by Operation Little Saturn in the second half of December.

People, especially women, speak well of the Italians. 'They sing, they play, "O mia donna!"' However, people disapprove of them for eating frogs.

How agonising, how alarming this lull at the front is! There's already dust on the roads.

The rainy period of deep mud, the *rasputitsa*, was over, as the dust showed, which indicated that the ground was already hard enough for all vehicles, yet nothing had happened.

---

2 Bazhan, Mykola Platonovich (1904–1983), poet, critic and subsequently member of the Ukrainian Academy of Sciences, he was later forced by the Soviet authorities to refuse his candidature when nominated for a Nobel Prize.
3 Levada, Aleksandr Stepanovich (1909–), Ukrainian writer and poet.

Grossman interviewed General Belov.[4]

'A German division's area of responsibility is eight kilometres deep. If we break through to a depth of eight kilometres, we will paralyse the front to a depth of thirty kilometres. If we break through thirty kilometres, we would paralyse a hundred kilometres. If we break through a hundred kilometres, we would paralyse the command [and control] of the whole front.

'We made one mistake on the Don: I was told that the men were tired. I lost two hours while they rested, and the [Luftwaffe] had the opportunity to attack and [the German ground forces] pulled in their reserves. If we hadn't had that rest, we would have made it. One must act boldly. If you look over your shoulder, you get squashed.

'There are commanders who show off: "I am facing the [enemy's] fire. I've halted, I am carrying out reconnaissance." What nonsense! What else can you face? Of course [it's going to be] fire. Are they going to throw apples at you, or what? You must break through even more deeply and suppress their fire. The deeper you break through, the weaker and more confused the enemy will be . . . Yet both in the battle and in the whole operation there's a moment when one should think things over, whether to rush forward, throw all your reserves into fighting, or, on the contrary, to stop. Our commanders sometimes love ordering: "Forward, forward!"

'There should be an operational pause, after about five days, when you've run out of all ammunition, the rear echelon is left far behind, and soldiers are so tired that they cannot carry out their tasks. They drop into the snow and fall sleep. I've seen an artillerist who was asleep two paces away from a firing gun. I stepped on a sleeping soldier, and he didn't wake up. They need rest. Twenty-four hours – well, even eight hours would be good. Let the reconnaissance company advance.

'The men in one of my companies were so fast asleep that they didn't want to wake up even when the Germans were pricking them with their bayonets. The company commander was awake and with his sub-machine gun managed to hold the Germans off. That's why it's clear, one shouldn't overstrain the men, no good will come of it.

4 No less than eleven generals of the name of Belov served in the Red Army during the Second World War, so it is hard to be certain, but Grossman is probably referring to General (later Colonel-General) P.A. Belov, soon to become the commander of 61st Army.

'One should evaluate absolutely clearly, soberly, what one has done to the enemy: defeated them, or just pushed them back. Don't announce that you've defeated the enemy. They might retreat a bit, and then hit you hard right in the face.

'I could see that the enemy was strong, rear echelons were left behind, and [front headquarters] was telling me: "Forward, Forward!" That way ruin lies. That's what happened to Popov.'[5]

'We don't really know [enough about] the enemy, and sometimes reconnaissance disorientates us.[6] Where the enemy is, what they are doing, where their reserves are, where they are going. One has to fight blind without all this information.

'The main conflict with higher commanders occurs because they always think that the enemy is weaker than the enemy really is, but I, I do know what strength the enemy really possesses. There I was, with fifteen machine guns facing me, and they were shouting at me: "Go forward!" And I knew that there were fifteen machine guns that I had to suppress. But it also happens that a commander shouts: "I am up against thirty tanks," when in fact there's just one tank. That's why there is mistrust.

'There are young commanders who have seen nothing but the offensive,[7] so when they had to organise defensive positions, they didn't know how to dig trenches or even why they should dig them at all, how to organize fire, etc. We also have another type of commander – those who were always on the defensive and are afraid to advance.

'A bad thing about defensive battles is that people lose confidence in their strength, and they become depressed. In defence, the faith in victory becomes weaker, as well as faith in one's strength. In defence, troops need more moral strength, while in the advance, more physical effort is required, and spirits are high . . .

'Once we had dug in, men became used to German tanks

5   General M.M. Popov's 'Front Mobile Group' was ordered by General Vatutin to keep advancing, towards Stalino and Mariupol even though he had lost most of his tanks and was low on fuel. Meanwhile, XXV Tank Corps, which did run out of fuel, was within fifty miles of Zaporozhe on 19 February, just as Hitler was leaving Manstein's headquarters there. It was during this meeting that the basic plan for Operation Citadel, the attack on the Kursk salient, was conceived.
6   The Red Army used the term 'reconnaissance' to cover both the Western military idea of reconnaissance and also military intelligence as a whole.
7   Belov means since 19 November 1942, when Operation Uranus turned the tables on the Germans.

[attacking them]. You know, when I was sitting in the trench I felt I would have run away, but there was nowhere to run away to. Three or four men sit in a trench at a time, the rest are in *zemlyankas*, in "Lenin tents".[8] If the enemy stirs just a little, I give a ring and everyone jumps out.'

The need to resist the fear of tanks was vital on the Eastern Front. The Germans even had a special name for the phenomenon – *Panzerschreck*. Before his Siberian troops crossed the Volga to defend the factory district of Stalingrad, General Gurtyev made them dig practice trenches on the west bank and then ordered some tanks to run over the trenches with the men in them. A tank running over a trench was known as 'ironing'. The vital lesson was to dig deep, so that the trench would not collapse, and the soldiers in it would keep their nerve. There were many stories about such incidents.

An enemy tank had ironed the trench of machine-gunner Turiev, but he began to fire at the slits, and then at the file of enemy infantry, which dropped flat under his fire. When the men in the tank noticed this, they turned the tank back, and drove it over Turiev's trench. Then this brave soldier took his machine gun, crawled from under the tank, settled by a haystack and began to mow the Germans down. This way hero Turiev went on fighting until he died, crushed by the tank.

Grossman also talked to one of Belov's subordinate commanders, Martinyuk.

Once, I nearly shot him [Zorkin] when his regiment started to run away and he lost control, lost his head and did not take measures. Zorkin changed by December. They now call him the "professor", he sits over maps, thinking, while German tanks are advancing. Now, after the advance battles, the middle-rank commanders are mostly those promoted [from soldiers and sergeants].
    'Commanders are being pushed aside from the political work while deputy commanders [i.e. commissars] are occupied entirely with political work.'

---

8   A *zemlyanka* was a dugout bunker, usually reinforced with beams and earth overhead. It was also the name of one of the favourite songs of the war, about a soldier in a snow-bound *zemlyanka* thinking of his girlfriend.

This was a rather euphemistic observation on the situation following Stalin's Decree No. 307 of 9 October 1942, which re-established the single command and downgraded commissars to an advisory and 'educational' role. Commissars were shaken to find in many cases how much Red Army officers loathed and despised them. The political department of Stalingrad Front, for example, complained bitterly to Aleksandr Shcherbakov, the head of the Red Army's political arm, GLAVPURRKA, about the 'absolutely incorrect attitude' which had emerged.

'There's a lack of affection and care towards Red Army soldiers; on the other hand, our commanders aren't [sufficiently] demanding. This comes from the lack of culture. Why did Red Army soldiers love Lieutenant Kuznetsov? Because he cared about them; he lived with them. They would come to him with both bad and good letters from home, he promoted men, he wrote about his soldiers to the newspaper. Yet he punished negligent soldiers. He never over-looked the smallest sign of negligence: a button missing, someone coughing on a reconnaissance mission. Care [also means checking]: have you got cartridges, have you got dry foot bandages? It often happens that because of giving our work insufficient thought we lose people and don't accomplish our mission.

'Soldiers who have been promoted as officers fulfil their tasks extremely well and are very attentive towards their men. As far as everyday life is concerned, combatant officers are usually upright characters. In rear units, corporals, orderlies of regiment commanders, quartermasters in regiments and battalions – these are the most susceptible to moral degeneration in everyday life.

'The phrasing of an order – "If you don't go forward now, mother-fucker, I'll shoot you" – comes from a lack of will. This does not persuade anybody, this is weakness. We are trying to reduce such cases, and there are fewer and fewer of them. However, it would be very, very useful to raise this problem.

'The nationality issue is quite all right. There are individual cases when it isn't, but they are exceptions.'

This is an optimistic view of the nationality question, to say the least. The sometimes arrogant attitude towards ethnic minorities within the Red Army, particularly those from Central Asia, made notions of 'Soviet brotherhood' sound very false. Although no figures are available, the rate of desertion and self-inflicted injuries appears to have been much higher among soldiers from Central Asia. The only solution of the political department was: 'To indoctrinate soldiers and officers of non-Russian nationality in the highest noble aims of the peoples of the USSR, in the explanation of their military oath and the law for punishing any betrayal of the Motherland.'

'There are lots of people who come to us from the occupied territory; they believe in the strength of the Red Army and are witnesses, sober and useful to us, of the occupation regime.'

Once the Germans began to retreat, many more stragglers and civilians from the occupied territories were incorporated into the Red Army. They were indeed useful to political officers in their propaganda sessions calling for revenge on the violators of the Motherland, but many were arrested by the NKVD or SMERSh as deserters or potential traitors.

Meeting of snipers at corps headquarters.

Solodkikh: 'Actually, I am from Voroshilovgrad myself, but I've become a sniper instead of a collective farmer.'

Belugin: 'I am from the occupied territory. I used to be nothing, but now, in defence, we aren't [a waste of rations]. I was sitting, observing. Strizhik said to me: "No nonsense, all right?" The regimental commander, a clever chap, said: "Get a tongue.[9] It's not so good to have to report at divisional headquarters without one." Even if there were to be a hundred Germans against me, and I'm on my own, I would fight just the same, I'll get killed anyway. I had been dying in prison for ten months, I jumped from the train which was moving at full speed, in order to get back to our people. My boy was killed because he was called Vladimir Ilich.'[10]

Khalikov: 'I've killed sixty-seven people. I arrived at the front speaking not a single word of Russian. My friend, Burov, he taught me Russian, I taught him Uzbek. On one occasion, no one wanted to eliminate a machine-gun pillbox. I said, I'll knock it out. [I found

9   A 'tongue' was slang for an enemy soldier snatched for interrogation.
10   Vladimir Ilich was, of course, Lenin's first name and patronymic. First names were even invented acronyms, such as Lemar, standing for Lenin and Marx. To give a son a conspicuously political name was a sign of communist devotion and thus a target for Nazi anti-Bolshevik fervour.

that] there were twelve men around, all pure-bred Germans. I camou-flaged myself well and my heart was working well. I took out all the twelve Germans. I never hurry, if my heart is beating fast, like a propeller, I never shoot. When I hold my heart, I shoot. If I shoot badly, it would kill me. I took the binoculars from round a [German] officer's neck. I reported to the *politruk*, "I carried out your order, and I've brought you a present."'

Bulatov: 'I love hunting blackcock. I used to dream about them feverishly day and night.' (The corps commander presented Bulatov with his sniper's rifle. Bulatov began to sweat all over and cursed.)

Ivanov, Dmitry Yakovlevich, from Yaroslavl: 'I was cut off for eighteen days in an enemy encirclement. For about five days we had to live without food, and for about three days we had no water. We swam across the Don, found our people, and they sent us on a reconnais-sance mission.' (He winks at the corps commander and laughs.)

Romanov (small, with a big mouth): 'I've killed 135. Please, put our scores on the table, and I will tell you all about it.'

50th Guards Rifle Division.[11] Conversation with soldiers about defence. '[Commanders told us] "Get ready, we are going to advance!" And we had wanted to plant some tobacco here.'

Red Army soldier Ostapenko, Dmitry Yakovlevich. He had been captured in the Caucasus, then escaped and walked back to his father's village near Voroshilovgrad. He suddenly read in the newspaper that he had been made a Hero of the Soviet Union, posthumously, for fighting against German tanks. He didn't get particularly excited about the newspaper. And his father, immediately after he saw the newspaper, went to see the regiment commander. 'You know, comrades have taken my barley, by accident.' Petukhov said to him: 'Oh, shit, please don't tell anyone we've taken your barley. I'll give you ten carts of barley.'

---

11   The 50th Guards Rifle Division had been with the 5th Tank Army in Operation Uranus, the encirclement of the Sixth Army at Stalingrad. From December 1942 until April 1943, it was part of the newly formed 3rd Guards Army.

Meeting of Red Army soldiers at the regiment. Theme: 'The Red Army – an army of avengers.' When Red Army soldier Prokhin spoke about girls who were sent to Germany against their wishes from the station at Millerovo and how they had shouted from the locked wagons: 'Mama, Mama, save me!', soldiers started to cry. 'We have to wipe Hitler's men off the face of the Earth.'[12]

Grossman visited Krasnodon, a large mining town of the Donets basin in the most eastern part of the Ukraine.

Conditions of miners' work under the Germans. Those who were working underground got six hundred grams of ersatz bread, and those above ground, three hundred grams. One day of absence from work meant a concentration camp. 'Under the Germans, there was a canteen. One could see Berlin at the bottom of a plate of soup.' (There wasn't a single gleam of fat in the soup.) They were beaten with lashes while working.

One of the miners he interviewed said: 'When the Germans entered the city, we were coming out of the mine. I ran home, took a piece of bread, abandoned my family and went away.' And who would worry about their family? 'What we do worry about is the mine. If the mine is all right, we'll be all right too.'

A woman told him: 'A German was billeted in my house. He received a letter and cried. His wife and children had been killed by a bomb. Another one took a harmonica and started to play: "Volga, Volga, my own mother."

'I met eight men, soldiers. "Take off your clothes! Wash!" Each of them gave me his underwear. They said to me: "We've come to you like we would come to our mother and father."'

He carried on to Voroshilovgrad, now called Lugansk, just over one hundred kilometres to the north-west.

Platoon Commander Vasilenko has been killed. The Party commission was giving people Party membership during the approach march

12 Unfortunate girls like these were not, however, treated with any sympathy by Red Army soldiers when Soviet forces reached Germany. Many of them were raped, as Grossman himself discovered in 1945.

to the fighting. Vasilenko became a Party member at the battery during a battle in the snow near Stolskoe.

Grossman was struck by the change in morale during the course of the past few months since the victory at Stalingrad.

An artillery officer recounted his experience: 'The enemy attacked us two to three times a day with groups of ten to fifteen tanks. We took up all-round defence. We had twenty field guns. We felt calm and were in good spirits.' (Just imagine what it would have been like in 1941.)

'The batteries are in the snow all the time. There's no forest, and no time to dig bunkers. Frost, wind, we've gone through so much. There's only one thing that my men want: to advance.'

People killed. Telephone operator Tupitsin is dead. He used to run with a cable to the forward observation group which moved with the infantry. He would carry a reel in one hand and a grenade in the other hand. He used to say: 'Though I'm old, my feet are bound to take me to Voroshilovgrad.' But he never reached it.

Advance through the mud. Its advantages and shortcomings. Germans wrote: 'Russians didn't start the attack because the weather was good.'[13] It's not true! Both sides have difficulties moving in the mud.

However, Germans are not so well prepared for the physical hardships, when a 'naked' man is facing nature. A Russian man is brought up to hardship, and his victories are hard earned. Germans, on the other hand, are prepared for easy victories that would be based on technological superiority, and they give in to the hardship caused by nature. General Mud and General Cold are helping the Russian side. (But it is true that only those who are strong can make nature work for them, while the weak are at the mercy of nature.)

Grossman was frustrated by the lack of action in the Donbass and by his editor's failure to allow him time to write. He complained in a letter to his father on 20 March.

---

13 German front-line soldiers on the Eastern Front were indeed convinced that the Red Army always waited for the worst weather conditions before attacking. As mentioned above, they referred to it as 'weather for Russians'.

They keep promising to give me leave to write a novel, but so far it is only talk. That has been going on for three months. My health is fine. It is true that I have had problems with my heart, but now it is all right.

I see Mama in my dreams. She was right in front of my eyes, and so vivid, the whole night while I was travelling. After this I felt very strange all of the following day. No, I don't believe she is still alive. I travel all the time around areas that have been liberated, and I see what these accursed monsters have done to old people and children. And Mama was Jewish. A desire to exchange my pen for a rifle is getting stronger and stronger in me.

He wrote again to Ortenberg.

Comrade Editor . . . Under the circumstances, I deem my continued stay on the Bukovskoi sector useless and inexpedient. Therefore I would like to ask you to summon me back.

Grossman's request did him no good. He was sent off on another assignment in April which exasperated him, as he recounted to his father.

Just as I thought, my trip was useless. There was a complete lull [in the fighting], and with spring thaws, the river flooded the area, and because of this it was impossible to travel anywhere. I still haven't collected my wits to write for the newspaper again. It is hard for me to write about everyday matters after Stalingrad . . . Take your letter to Captain Tikhomirov at *Krasnaya Zvezda* and ask him to send it with someone who'll be travelling in my direction, or, even better, with the secret post.

TWENTY

The Battle of Kursk

On 1 May 1943, Grossman returned with great anticipation to see once more those whom he had come to know so well in Chuikov's army, now in reserve, forming part of the Steppe Front behind the Kursk salient. The reunion, however, was to prove a shock to him.

> I've arrived at the 62nd Stalingrad Army. It is now stationed among gardens that are beginning to blossom – a wonderful place with violets and bright green grass. It is peaceful. Larks are singing. I was excited on the way here, I so wanted to see the people of whom I have so many memories.
>
> Meeting and dinner with Chuikov on the terrace of a dacha. Garden. Chuikov, Krylov, Vasilyev, two colonels – members of the military council.
>
> The meeting was a cold one, but they were all boiling. Dissatisfaction, ambition, insufficient awards, hatred of anyone who had received greater awards, hatred of the press. They spoke of the film *Stalingrad* and cursed.[1] Great people producing a heavy, bad impression. Not a single word about the fallen men, about memorials, about immortalising the memory of those who never came back. Everyone is only talking about themselves and their accomplishments.
>
> Morning with Gurtyev. The same picture.
>
> There's no modesty. 'I did it, I, I, I, I, I . . .' They speak about other commanders without any respect, recounting some ridiculous gossip: 'I was told that Rodimtsev said the following . . .' The main idea is, in fact: 'All the credit belongs to us, the 62nd Army. And in the 62nd Army, there's just me. All the others are unimportant.' Vanity of vanities.

---

1   This film, based on newsreel taken of re-enactments just after the events, was eagerly watched by audiences in the Soviet Union, but few realised quite how staged it was. Film archives contain numerous examples of discarded footage of soldiers getting up after being shot and going through the motions again.

In a way, Grossman should have been prepared for this. Already in Stalingrad he had encountered senior commanders, especially Yeremenko, who were prepared to belittle their subordinates in conversations with him, a journalist. Yeremenko had made remarks such as: 'Rodimtsev's division could have fought better'; 'I used to reprimand Gurtyev'; 'I transferred Chuikov into the [Tsaritsa] tunnel'; 'Red Army soldiers have produced a good impression on me, unlike the officers. There is a lack of power of will in them that comes from ignorance.'

Presumably one of the reasons why Chuikov was so bitter and why he loathed Marshal Zhukov so much – a resentment which surged up again just before the battle of Berlin – was that he had not been told about the plans for Operation Uranus until almost the last moment. It must have appeared to him that he and his 62nd Army, instead of being the principal heroes of Stalingrad, had become little more than the tethered goat while the armies of General Rokossovsky's Don Front had been the hunters surrounding the tiger.[2]

Grossman could not have known that his unease at the lack of activity in April and May 1943 reflected an argument right at the top. Stalin wanted to push on with further offensives. He could not entirely accept the idea that the war still had to go through a number of stages and that it could not be ended with a single dramatic push. Marshal Zhukov, Marshal Vasilevsky and General A.I. Antonov, the *Stavka* chief of operations, had a very hard time convincing him that the Red Army should stay on the defensive, ready to deal with the German onslaught being prepared. While waiting, they would prepare a huge strategic reserve for their own summer offensive immediately afterwards, something which the Red Army had not yet attempted. Stalin, with great reluctance, had accepted their arguments in a crucial Kremlin meeting on 12 April.

The major German summer offensive, Operation Zitadelle, as it was called, probably achieved less surprise than any other offensive in the

---

2   Marshal Konstantin Kostantinovich Rokossovsky (1896–1968), the son of a Polish cavalry officer, was always suspect in the eyes of Stalin. He was arrested in 1937 during the purge of the Red Army and tortured by the NKVD. He was released after the Russo-Finnish war and commanded IX Mechanised Corps during the German invasion in 1941. He played an important role during the battle of Moscow when commanding the 16th Army. In 1942, he commanded the Don Front in the key phase of the Stalingrad campaign. He was the main commander for the battle of Kursk in 1943 and later commanded the 1st Belorussian Front in Operation Bagration and the advance to Warsaw. In late 1944, Stalin moved him to command of the 2nd Belorussian Front, because he did not want a Pole to have the glory of taking Berlin. That honour was given to his friend and rival, Marshal Zhukov. After the war, he was made the Defence Minister of Poland.

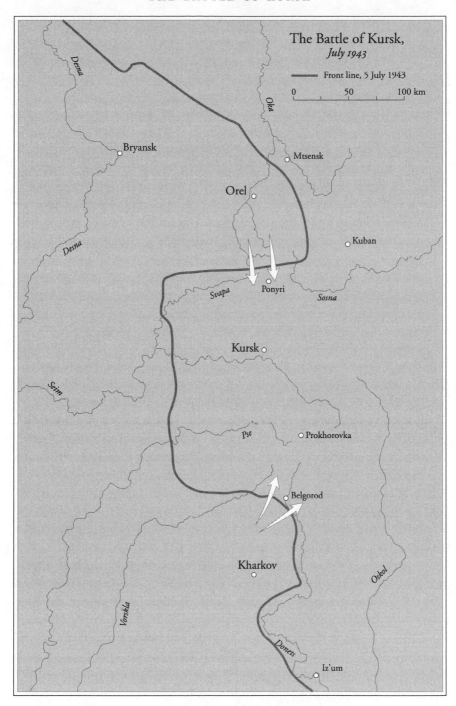

The Battle of Kursk, *July 1943*

Stalingrad citizens return to the ruined city.

whole war. The German plan of attack could, logically, take only one form, with armoured spearheads aiming for the base of the Kursk salient, one from the north and the other from the south. Hitler allocated fifty divisions, of which nineteen were armoured with 2,700 tanks and assault guns. The whole operation was supported by more than 2,600 aircraft.

Details of German preparations, and the increasing delays affecting the operation, were passed to the Soviet Union in a veiled version from Ultra intercepts. Information also came from many other sources, including air reconnaissance and partisan intelligence networks inside the occupied territory. As a result, the *Stavka* was able to concentrate over a million men to the defence of the area (giving them a superiority of more than two to one) and invest in the most effective defence lines ever undertaken on the Eastern Front. In addition, a half-million-strong reserve, to be know as the 'Steppe Front', was assembled and deployed in the rear, ready to counter-attack.

Hitler, on the other hand, was convinced that the newly improved Mark VI Tiger tanks would prove invincible. The battle of Kursk was to become famous as the greatest clash of armoured forces in the history of the world, but this tends to divert attention from the importance played by other arms. Soviet sappers laid vast minefields, the Red Army artillery, especially the hundreds of batteries of anti-tank guns, played a major role, as did the Shturmovik ground-attack aircraft, concentrating their cannon and armour-piercing bomblets on German tanks.

Grossman, who reached the front just before the start of the battle, started by interviewing intelligence officers at the headquarters of the Central Front commanded by Marshal Rokossovsky. Notes he jotted down afterwards reflected on the Germans' obstinacy at attacking such massively well-defended sectors as the north flank of the Kursk salient. This line of attack south from Orel, the lesser of the two assaults, was referred to by the Red Army as the 'Orel axis'.

A gigantic burden had fastened the Germans to the Orel axis, although pilots kept telling them how strong our defence was. (There's no freedom of will. Mass dominates over brain.)

Underestimation of the enemy, of the enemy's strength. This is typical of Germans. It's due to their successes over the past few years.

Danger of preconceived ideas, due to the controversial character of facts. Concentration of enemy Luftwaffe groups plays an important role in deciphering.[3] Reports on the arrival of generals and field marshals.

A [German] sapper was captured during the night of 4 July. He revealed that the attack was beginning and that the order had gone out to clear mines. Thanks to this we were able to lay on a two-hour artillery counter-preparation bombardment at dawn on 5 July.

Usually, operations staff are somewhat conceited and despise reconnaissance [intelligence] men.

We entered the village of Kuban[4] in dust and smoke, amid the flow of thousands of vehicles. How can one possibly find one's friends in this terrible mess? Suddenly I saw a car with luxurious new tyres standing in a shed. I said prophetically: 'This car with

3   It is not entirely clear what Grossman means by this. Considering the Red Army mania for secrecy, it seems surprising that even a correspondent from *Krasnaya Zvezda* would have been told anything about deciphering, and yet his remark appears to reflect the experience of British signals intercepts, that the Luftwaffe's slack attitude to signals security greatly helped the cracking of their codes.
4   Just under 100 kilometres south-east of Orel and about 130 kilometres north-north-east of Kursk.

Knorring and Grossman in their jeep just before
the Battle of Kursk, July 1943.

incredible tyres belongs either to the Front Commander
Rokossovsky, or to the TASS correspondent Major Lipavsky.' We
entered the house. A soldier was eating borscht at the table. 'Who's
billeted in this house?' The soldier replied: 'Major Lipavsky, TASS
correspondent.' Everyone looked at me. I had that feeling probably experienced by Newton when he discovered the law of gravity.

Grossman went to Ponyri to interview anti-tank gunners who had done
as much as anyone to break the back of the German onslaught. Ponyri
station was about a hundred kilometres north of Kursk. It was here on 6
July, the second day of the battle, that Rokossovsky launched the first
desperate counter-attack with the 2nd Tank Army. In less than a week his
Central Front had fought the German Ninth Army's thrust to a standstill.

Visit to Ponyri. Shevernozhuk's regiment. Stories about 45mm
cannons firing at [Tiger] tanks.[5] Shells hit them, but bounced off

5   Grossman, like most Red Army men, often talks of a 'T-6' tank in the Soviet style of desig-
nating armoured vehicles, when actually referring to the Mark VI Tiger. For simplicity, we have
put 'Tiger' in square brackets whenever the phrase T-6 is mentioned in the original text. Some of
his interviewees also use the name 'Tiger', and that remains unchanged.

like peas. There have been cases when artillerists went insane after seeing this.

After his visits to the northern sector, he went to the more important southern sector, where the attack also on 5 July was mounted by General Hoth's Fourth Panzer Army. This formation mustered the elite of Nazi forces, including the Panzergrenadier Division *Grossdeutschland* and the II SS Panzer Corps, with the three SS divisions: *Leibstandarte Adolf Hitler, Totenkopf* and *Das Reich*. Using the Tigers as their battering ram, Hoth's forces broke through into the third line of defence, but then were hit by the counter-attack of Katukov's 1st Tank Army. The crucial point came after a week of fighting when a large tank force of II SS Panzer broke through to the rail junction of Prokhorovka. General Vatutin, the commander of the Voronezh Front manning that sector, immediately contacted Marshal Zhukov. Zhukov agreed to an immediate counter-offensive with five armies, of whom two came from the Steppe Front reserve. The attack on 12 July was led by the 5th Guards Tank Army, which had played the chief role in the encirclement of the German Sixth Army at Stalingrad the previous November.

The Tiger's more powerful 88mm gun forced the Soviet tankists into almost suicidal charges across open country in order to close with the enemy before they themselves were knocked out. Some even ended up ramming their German adversaries. At Prokhorovka, a battle involving over 1,200 tanks, Soviet armoured forces suffered a casualty rate of over 50 per cent, but it was enough to smash the last great effort of the Wehrmacht's panzer arm. The battlefield was covered with burned-out tanks in all directions. Observers compared the sight to an elephant graveyard. Within another six days, the surviving German forces had to carry out a fighting withdrawal. The Anglo-American invasion of Sicily prompted Hitler to withdraw key formations from the battle, to bring them westwards to address the new threat to Southern Europe. Hitler may well have wanted an excuse by this stage to extricate himself from a disastrous battle, in which the Wehrmacht had been decisively outfought. The Red Army had proved once again the dramatic improvement in the professionalism of its commanders, the morale of its soldiers and the effective application of force.[6]

Grossman had been with an anti-tank gun brigade which guarded the key sector in the battle. As Ortenberg wrote later: 'The brigade had to

6 Some historians have even been tempted to cite Kursk as the turning point of the war, but as has been indicated, the defence of Moscow was the geopolitical turning point, and Stalingrad the psychological one.

confront the Germans who were trying to break through towards Belgorod along the Belgorod–Kursk highway, from south to north. Vasily Grossman saw the battlefield with his own eyes. He saw the destroyed materiel of the enemy and our damaged or burning tanks and self-propelled guns. He had watched our troops retreat and advance.'

Belgorod Axis. Anti-tank Brigade. The commander [was] Nikifor Dmitrievich Chevola. 'I don't like working at headquarters,' [he said]. 'I was praying to be spared from it. I will run away to fight if there's a battle.' Chevola's four brothers: Aleksandr, an artillerist – killed; Mikhail, commander of a heavy artillery regiment; Vasily, who was a philosophy teacher, is now carrying out political work; Pavel is commander of a machine-gun battalion. His sister Matryona was a teacher before the war. She joined the army, and was demobilised after receiving a serious wound. His niece is learning to be a pilot.

'The Luftwaffe was bombing us. We were there amid the fire and smoke, yet my men became wild. They kept firing, paying no attention to all this. I was wounded seven times myself. [German] tanks wedged in, and the infantry wavered.

'Constant thunder, the ground was trembling, there was fire all around, we were shouting. As for radio communications, the Germans tried to trick us. They howled over the radio: "I am Nekrasov, I am Nekrasov." I shouted back: "Bullshit! you aren't, get lost." They jammed our voices with howling. Messers were flying over our heads, Senior Sergeant Urbisupov shot down a Messer with his sub-machine gun as it dived at him. The Messers strafe trenches, first along them and then across them, so as to cover all the curves.

'We had no sleep for five nights. The quieter it is, the more tense it feels. We feel better when there's fighting, then one begins to feel sleepy. We ate when we could and never had much time for it. Food would become black at once from the dust, particularly fat. When we were taken out of fighting to have a rest, we went into a barn and fell asleep at once.'

Nikolai Efimovich Plysyuk, commander of the 1st Regiment: 'There isn't any infantry in front of our artillery. There's just us and Death. There was only one Willys [jeep] left on the last day of fighting. I would have awarded it a Gold Star, because on its own it saved the whole regiment. And the men dragged one cannon six kilometres with their hands. They were all wounded, all bandaged up.'

Gun-layer Trofim Karpovich Teplenko: '[It was] my first battle. [It was] twilight. We loaded tracer shells, I hit him with the first shell. A tank is no threat to artillery. It's sub-machine-gunners and infantry who interfere with our work and cause us trouble. Of course, it's fun when one hits a [Tiger]. My first shell hit the front of it, under the turret . . . and the tank stopped at once. After that I hit it with three shells, one after another. The infantry in front of me were shouting 'Ura!' and were throwing up their helmets and *pilotkas*, jumping out of their trenches.

'This was a face-to-face battle. It was like a duel, anti-tank gun against tank. Sergeant Smirnov's head and leg were torn off. We brought the head back, and also the legs, and put them all into a little ditch, and covered them over. After the battle, the corps commander was standing by the road in the dust. He shook hands with the anti-tank men and gave them cigarettes . . . An anti-tank gun after a battle is like a human being who's alive but who's suffered. The rubber is torn on the wheels, and its parts have been damaged by shell fragments.'

Teplenko's account of the 45mm anti-tank gun taking on German Tigers effortlessly appears somewhat optimistic when one reads excerpts which Grossman copied from the brigade war diary.

A gun-layer fired point-blank at a Tiger with a 45mm [anti-tank] gun. The shells bounced off it. The gun-layer lost his head and threw himself at the Tiger.

A lieutenant, wounded in the leg and with a hand torn off, was commanding the battery attacked by tanks. After the enemy attack had been halted, he shot himself, because he didn't want to live as a cripple.[7]

7 The prospect of being mutilated or becoming a cripple always represented a far greater fear for Soviet soldiers than being killed. There was of course the unshakeable belief that a woman would never want to look at them again. This may have been a misleading male nightmare, but the true awfulness of their fate did not become apparent until after the war when maimed and crippled Red Army soldiers were treated with unbelievable callousness by the Soviet authorities. Those reduced to a trunk with stumps were known as *samovars*. After the war they were rounded up and sent to towns in the Arctic circle so that the Soviet capital would not be made unsightly with limbless veterans.

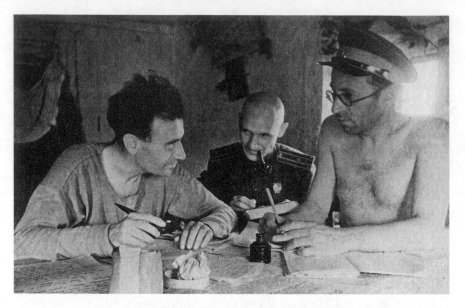

Galin, Bukovsky, and Grossman at Kursk.

Grossman was with Chevola's anti-tank brigade near Ponyri station during at least part of that epic battle.

> This battle lasted three days and three nights . . . Black smoke was hanging in the air, people's faces were completely black. Everyone's voice became hoarse, because in this rattling and clatter one could hear words only if they were shouted. People snatched moments to eat, and pieces of white pork fat immediately became black from dust and smoke. No one thought of sleep, but if someone did snatch a minute to rest, that was usually during the day, when the thunder of battle was particularly loud, and the ground trembled, as if during an earthquake. At night, the quietness was frightening, the nerves were strained and quietness scared away the sleep. And during the day one felt better in chaos, which had become habitual.

Grossman's 'ruthless truth of war' did not necessarily make things easy for his editor at *Krasnaya Zvezda*, but Ortenberg certainly respected him, as his own comments show. 'Grossman remained true to himself. In Stalingrad, Vasily Semyonovich used to spend days and nights with the main characters of his articles, in the very heat of the fighting. He did the same here at the Kursk salient. The following lines are a proof of this: "I happened to visit the units that received the hardest blow from the enemy . . ." "We were lying in a gully listening to the fire from our guns and explosions of German shells . . ." He had seen the wounded and killed Soviet soldiers. He thought it disgraceful to write nothing about them. With great difficulties, we managed to get the following truthful lines from his essay published: "The battery commander, Ketselman, was wounded. He was dying in a pool of dark blood . . .'" Soviet censorship wanted to suppress such harsh images, but in this case at least, Ortenberg managed to persuade them to leave Grossman's work untouched. This was the piece in question:

There wasn't anyone in the whole world at that moment who deserved rest more than these Red Army soldiers sleeping among puddles of rainwater. This gully, where the ground and leaves were trembling from shots and explosions, was to them like a most remote rear area, like Sverdlovsk or Alma-Ata. The sky which was filled with sparkles and white clouds from the fire of anti-aircraft guns, the sky in which twenty-six German dive-bombers banked and dropped into a dive to attack a railway station, was a cloudless, peaceful sky. Here they were, sleeping on the wet grass, among flowers and soft, furry burdock leaves . . .

An officer, whose flank the brigade was covering, had retreated, allowing the brigade to withdraw. But the brigade commander, who could clearly see the consequences of withdrawal, answered: 'We won't retreat, we'll stay here to die!' And he was permitted to do that.

At dawn, German tanks started to attack. [Enemy] aircraft attacked at the same time and set the village on fire . . .

Battery commander Ketselman was wounded. He was dying in a puddle of black blood; the first artillery piece was broken. A direct hit had torn off an arm and the head of a gun-layer. Senior Corporal Melekhin, the gun commander, the cheerful, quick virtuoso of this death struggle in which tenths of seconds sometimes determine the outcome of a duel, was lying on the ground with heavy shell-shock, looking at the cannon, his stare heavy and murky. The gun was reminiscent of a ragged, long-suffering man. Strips of rubber were hanging from the wheels, torn by the explosions . . .

Only the amunition bearer, Davydov, was still on his feet. And Germans had already come very close. They were 'seizing the barrels',

Grossman and Baklanov (centre). Celebration with the
13th Guards Rifle Division.

as artillerists say. Then the commander of the neighbouring gun, Mikhail Vasiliev, took control. These were his words: 'Men, it isn't a shame to die. Even cleverer heads than ours sometimes happen to die.' And he ordered them to open fire at the German infantry with canister. Then, having run out of anti-personnel rounds, they began to fire at the German sub-machine-gunners at point-blank range with armour-piercing shells. That was a terrible sight.

Grossman also caught up with the 13th Guards Rifle Division, which had been commanded at Stalingrad by General Rodimtsev. He took the opportunity to interview its new commander about the fighting.

A meeting with Rodimtsev's 13th Guards Division at the Kursk salient. It is now commanded by General Baklanov, a young man who started the war as a captain. He had been an athlete in Moscow.

'*Sovinformburo* has been writing ever since the war began that "German pillboxes have been destroyed", but I've never seen a single German pillbox. They've only got trenches. The men are now fighting intelligently, without frenzy. They fight as if they were working.

'Our weaknesses show up in the offensive. Reinforcement units get moved to new locations. They don't have time to get used to the situation. Some commanders don't know their calibres and the range of their artillery fire. They don't know the established quantity of mines per kilometre, the established quantity of wire per kilometre, the rate of fire to suppress enemy defences. "Some fire needed, over there!"' and he waves his hand.

'Sometimes regimental commanders give false reports during battles. I usually go out two hours before an attack to check communications, yet the regimental commander goes to his command post ten minutes before the attack and then reports to me: "Everything is ready, I know everything." The danger of arrogance, of conceit is great.

'There are many commanders who don't care about their soldiers' food and everyday life, they don't try to study the soldier's soul. Commanders are sometimes very harsh, but during breaks [in the fighting] they don't go to their men, talk to them and ask questions. Often this is because commanders are too young. It is sometimes the case that a [junior officer] has soldiers who have sons older than he is.

'[The cry of] "Forward, forward!" is either the result of stupidity, or of fear of one's seniors. That's why so much blood is being shed.'

Grossman found once again, even after all the improvements effected during the course of the previous year, that units continued to suffer from the inability of Red Army commanders and staff officers to think things through.

Colonel Vavilov, Deputy Divisional Commander on Political Work. 'We were put on alert at midnight on [8/9] July. The order was to have regiments formed up by dawn. We started moving on the 9th during the day. That day was terribly hot. Seventy men went down with sunstroke in one regiment. We were carrying machine guns, mortars, ammunition. During the night of the 9th we had three hours of rest. We arrived in the area of Oboyan, began to organise defensive positions and dug in. And then the order came at once, to carry on another twenty-five kilometres. At dawn on the 12th, we came to the start point, and at once entered the fighting, with

Grossman beside one of the German Tiger tanks destroyed at Kursk.

two regiments. And didn't General Zhukov say: "It is better not to begrudge a retreat of five to six kilometres than to send tired men, with no ammunition, into battle!"'

On the other hand, Grossman was the first to acknowledge that some things had definitely improved.

> From the point of view of artillery, the Kursk operation is more sophisticated than the Stalingrad one. In Stalingrad, the beast was beaten in its lair. In Kursk, the artillery shield resisted the enemy's attack and the artillery sword started crushing them during the [counter-attack].[8]

Grossman also interviewed some pilots from a regiment of Shturmovik fighter-bombers engaged on ground-attack operations, mainly against tanks.[9] Shturmovik regiments claimed the virtual annihilation of the 3rd,

8   Grossman in fact wrote 'the advance', but the Red Army often used this term when Western armies would refer to the attack or the offensive, or, as in this case, 'the advance' was the great counter-attack.
9   The Ilyushin-2M 'Shturmovik', a robust fighter-bomber, well armoured against ground fire, was one of the few effective Soviet aircraft of the Second World War. It was armed with two 23mm cannon and either rockets or anti-tank bombs. The crew consisted of a pilot and a rear-gunner who was also the radio operator.

9th and 17th Panzer Divisions during the battle. The Shturmoviks were often flying at less than twenty metres off the ground, as their pilots liked to boast, but their casualties were very heavy.

Shalygin, Nikolai Vladimirovich, [from] Saratov, major in a Shturmovik regiment: 'Aleksukhin was flying at very low level, attacking vehicles, in fact so low that he returned with the tips of his propeller bent. I made a dive and saw tanks in the barley. The shape of their turret gives them away.

'Pilot Yuryev came back with blood streaming down his face. "May I report?" He reported and collapsed unconscious. The gunner-signaller had climbed out first, with blood all over him.

'This excitement of a hunter, I feel as if I were a hawk, not a man. And one does not think about humanity. No, there are no such thoughts. We clear the way. It's good when the way is clear and everything is on fire.'

The way was about to be made even clearer for the Soviet general offensive. This developed out of the counter-attack at Prokhorovka on 12 July. Operation Kutuzov, launched on the same day on the northern flank, was aimed against the German occupied territory between the Kursk salient and the city of Orel. The Germans had not expected such a rapid reaction. For Grossman, this was a moment of fierce joy. He had a bitter memory of the German capture of the city in the autumn of 1941.

Ortenberg, remembering what Grossman had been through at the time, made sure that he was the correspondent who covered the liberation of Orel. 'I must say that I had never forgotten this episode. And on the July days when we had no doubts that Orel would be liberated, I said to Grossman: "Vasily Semyonovich! Orel is your trauma. I would like you to be there on the day of its liberation. So that you can remember the day when you left it." Grossman was in Orel on the day of its liberation and wrote an essay about the frightening, tragic days and hours [of its fall to the Germans in 1941] . . . When I read this essay, I understood what Grossman had gone through during those October days of 1941. I met him a year after the battle of Kursk, when I was already at the front.[10] During our conversation I reminded him of the unhappy

10 Ortenberg left *Krasnaya Zvezda* to become a 'member of the Military Council', or chief commissar, of an army. It has been suggested that Ortenberg, also a Jew, was moved from such an influential post at a time of rising anti-Semitism within the Stalinist hierarchy.

episode and let him understand that I felt guilty about it. He smiled and said with sincerity: "I was not angry with you." And he added: "There was no time for it.'"

We reached Orel on the afternoon of 5 August by the Moscow highway. We had driven through the cheerful and businesslike Tula, past Plavsk, Chern, and the further we went, the fresher appeared the wounds that the Germans had inflicted on our land.

In Mtsensk, grass was growing in the ruins of houses, the blue sky was looking through the empty eye sockets of windows and torn-off roofs. Almost all villages between Mtsensk and Orel were burned. The ruins of *izbas* were still smoking. Old people and children were rummaging in the piles of brick looking for the surviving household objects: cast-iron pots, frying pans, metal beds disfigured by fire, sewing machines. How bitter and familiar this sight was!

There was a freshly adzed white board with the word 'Orel' nailed up by the railway crossing . . . The smell of burning was hanging in the air, a light blue milky smoke was rising from the dwindling fires . . .

A loud-speaker unit was playing 'The Internationale' in the square. Posters and appeals were being glued to the walls, leaflets were being handed out to the population. Red-cheeked girls, traffic controllers, were standing at all the crossroads, smartly waving their red and green little flags. A day or two would pass, and Orel would start coming back to life, to work and to studying . . .

I remembered the Orel which I had seen exactly twenty-two months ago, on that October day of 1941 when German tanks broke into it from the Kromsk highway. I remembered my last night in Orel, the ill, terrible night, the humming of fleeing vehicles, the weeping of women running after the retreating troops, the sorrowful faces of people, and the questions that they were asking me, full of anxiety and suffering. I remembered Orel's last morning, when it seemed as if the whole city was crying and rushing about, seized with a terrible panic. The city was then still in its full beauty, without a single window broken, but it gave the impression of being doomed, of having been sentenced to death . . .

And listening to the speech of a tank colonel, who was standing on top of a dusty tank overlooking the bodies of soldiers and officers killed in the battle for Orel, hearing his simple, abrupt words of goodbye echoing in the burned-out houses, I understood. This meeting today and that bitter parting on the October morning of 1941 are inseparably linked with one another.

Grossman on the Belgorod Axis after the battle of Kursk.

Oleg Knorring, Ilya Ehrenburg, and Grossman.

A similar operation on the southern side of the Kursk salient led to the recapture of Belgorod, and eventually Kharkov on 28 August. The Germans refer to this extended engagement as the Fourth Battle of Kharkov. As might be imagined, little of the city was left standing. During this fighting on either side of the Kursk salient, Grossman wrote to his father on 28 July.

> Dear Papa, I've been driving along lots of roads for three weeks, like a Gypsy. It is much nicer to travel in summer than in winter. One does not need to worry about finding a place to spend the night, the sun is shining, rains are warm, meadows are in brighter blossom than ever. But often these meadows don't smell of flowers; they have another, frightening smell.

Grossman began to realise that there was also another frightening smell in the Soviet Union – a renascent anti-Semitism. Ilya Ehrenburg, with his acute political nose, had sensed this well before the idealistic Grossman. Early in the war Ehrenburg had noted the Kremlin reaction to Henry Shapiro, the Reuters bureau chief in Moscow. Ehrenburg had known Shapiro since before the war, talking to him for hours in the Metropol and Moskva hotels about their shared love of Paris. Shapiro commented to Ehrenburg at one point that while Stalin was prepared to talk to Henry Cassidy of Associated Press, he never received him. 'With your name,' Ehrenburg answered, 'you'll never get an answer.'

In November 1941, Ehrenburg had heard anti-Semitic remarks from Mikhail Sholokhov, the author of *And Quiet Flows the Don*.[11] 'You are fighting,' Sholokhov told him, 'but Abram is doing business in Tashkent.' Ehrenburg exploded, calling him a 'pogrom-monger'. Grossman, hearing of this, wrote to Ehrenburg about all the Jewish soldiers he had met at the front.

> I think about Sholokov's anti-Semitic slander with pain and contempt. Here on the South-Western Front, there are thousands, tens of thousands of Jews. They are walking with machine guns into the snowstorms, breaking into towns held by the Germans, falling in battle. I saw all of this. I saw the illustrious commander of the 1st Guards Division, Kogan, tank officers and reconnaissance men. If Sholokhov is in Kuibyshev, be sure to let him know that comrades at the front know what he is saying. Let him be ashamed.

But clearly Grossman regarded Sholokhov as an aberration at that stage.

By early 1943, Ehrenburg found that his references to Jewish suffering were being censored. He complained to Aleksandr Shcherbakov, the chief of the Red Army Political Department, but Shcherbakov retorted: 'The soldiers want to hear about Suvorov, but you quote Heine.'

Ehrenburg and Grossman, having furiously disagreed with each other in the past on literary matters, now became much closer. 'Vasily Semyonovich Grossman came to Moscow for a short stay,' wrote Ehrenburg, 'and we sat together till three in the morning. He told me about the front, and we made guesses about how life would go after victory. Grossman said: "I have a lot of doubts now. But I don't doubt the victory. This is probably the most important thing."'

At Ehrenburg's urging, Grossman joined the Jewish Anti-Fascist Committee. One of the leading members of it was the actor Solomon Mikhoels.[12] Towards the end of 1942, Albert Einstein and other members of the American Committee of Jewish Writers, Artists and Scientists contacted the Jewish Anti-Fascist Committee in the Soviet Union to suggest

11   Sholokhov, Mikhail Aleksandrovich (1905–1984), winner of the Stalin Prize in 1941 and the Nobel Prize in 1965. He was accused by Solzhenitsyn among others of plagiarising the work of the anti-Bolshevik cossack, Fyodor Krukov, but subsequent studies have tended to confirm that Sholokhov's prose was his own.
12   Mikhoels, Solomon (born Solomon Vovsi, 1890–1948), founder of Moscow State Jewish Theatre, chairman of Jewish Anti-Fascist Committee, murdered by the KGB in Minsk.

that they assemble a record of Nazi crimes. Mikhoels was enthusiastic and once official Soviet permission was obtained, Ehrenburg began to organise a group of writers. In the autumn of 1943 he recruited Grossman. Grossman, who saw more of the territories just liberated from the Nazis than anyone, was to prove one of the most important contributors. By the end of 1944, Ehrenburg rightly sensed that the Stalinist authorities would suppress their work and despaired. He fell out with the Jewish Anti-Fascist Committee. Grossman, who witnessed at first-hand Majdanek and Treblinka, refused to be thwarted and took over much of the work.

PART FOUR

From the Dnepr to the Vistula
1944

TWENTY-ONE

The Killing Ground of Berdichev

After the victory at Kursk, Stalin and his marshals launched a general offensive during the late summer of 1943. This was intended to push the Germans back to the line of the River Dnepr. Hitler for once recognised the need for withdrawal and agreed that the Dnepr with its high western bank offered the best line of defence. Leaving terrible destruction in their wake, German units raced back ahead of the exhausted and overextended Red Army. Smolensk was recaptured at the end of September and Kiev was retaken on 6 November. Along the way, Grossman attached himself to the headquarters of General Gorishny, whose 95th Rifle Division he had encountered in Stalingrad.[1]

> A report arrived that a girl from the medical battalion, Galya Chabannaya, had been killed. Both Gorishny and his deputy, Colonel Vlasenko, cried out.[2] 'Oh, God,' Gorishny said. 'When we left Stalingrad after the victory, we would run out of carriages at the stations and throw each other into the snow. And I remember how we rolled her in the snow, and she laughed so loudly that the whole train could hear. There wasn't another person in our division who laughed more loudly or more happily.'

> The deputy battalion commander, Lieutenant Surkov, has come to the command post. He hasn't slept for six nights. His face is over-grown with a beard. One can see no tiredness in this man, he is still seized by the terrible excitement of fighting. He will perhaps fall asleep half an hour later, field bag under his head, and then it would be useless to try to wake him up. But now his eyes are shining and his voice sounds harsh and excited. This man, who had been

---

1   The 95th Rifle Division had become the 75th Guards Rifle Division.
2   Major General (later Lieutenant General) Vasily A. Gorishny (1903–1962) and Colonel (later Major-General) Aleksei M. Vlasenko.

a history teacher before the war, seems to be carrying within him the glow of the Dnepr battle. He tells me about German counterattacks, about our attacks, about the runner whom he had to dig out of a trench three times, and who comes from the same area as he and was once his pupil at school. Surkov had taught him history. Now they both are both taking part in the events about which history teachers will be telling their pupils a hundred years from now.

When they reached the bank of the Dnepr, the soldiers didn't want to wait for the pontoons and other official river crossing transport to arrive. They crossed the wide and fast-flowing river on rafts, in fishing boats, on pontoons improvised from barrels and covered with planks of wood. They crossed under the enemy's heavy artillery and mortar fire, under attack from German bombers and fighters. There were cases when soldiers transported regimental guns on gates, and when a group of Red Army soldiers crossed the Dnepr on groundsheets stuffed with hay.

The Liberation of the Ukraine was an emotional process, especially for those like Grossman who remembered bitterly the late summer of 1941.

Old men, when they hear Russian words, run to meet the troops and weep silently, unable to utter a word. Old peasant women say with a quiet surprise: 'We thought we would sing and laugh when we saw our army, but there's so much grief in our hearts, that tears are falling.'
When our troops enter a village, and the cannonade shakes the air, geese take off and, flapping their wings, fly heavily over the roofs. People emerge from the forest, from tall weeds, from marshes overgrown with tall bullrushes.
Every soldier, every officer and every general of the Red Army who had seen the Ukraine in blood and fire, who had heard the true story of what had been happening in the Ukraine during the two years of German rule, understands to the bottom of their souls that there are only two sacred words left to us. One of them is 'love' the other one is 'revenge'.
In these villages, the Germans used to relieve themselves in the halls and on the doorsteps, in the front gardens, in front of the windows of houses. They were not ashamed of girls and old women.

While eating, they disturbed the peace, laughing loudly. They put their hands into dishes they were sharing with their comrades, and tore boiled meat with their fingers. They walked naked around the houses, unashamed in front of the peasants, and they quarrelled and fought about petty things. Their gluttony, their ability to eat twenty eggs in one go, or a kilo of honey, a huge bowl of smetana, provoked contempt in the peasants . . .

Germans who had been withdrawn to the rear villages were searching for food from morning till night. They ate, drank alcohol and played cards. According to what prisoners said and [what was written in] letters found on dead German soldiers, the Germans considered themselves the representatives of a higher race forced to live in savage villages. They thought that in the wild eastern steppes one could throw culture aside. 'Oh, that's real culture,' I heard dozens of people say. 'And they used to say that Germans were culti-vated people.'

On a windy and overcast morning, we met a boy on the edge of the village of Tarasevichi, by the Dnepr. He looked about thir-teen to fourteen years old. The boy was extremely thin, his sallow skin was tight on his cheekbones, large bumps protruded on his skull. His lips were dirty, pale, like a dead man's who had fallen face flat on the ground. His eyes were looking in a tired way, there was neither joy nor sadness in them. They are so frightening, these old, tired, lifeless eyes of children.

'Where is your father?'

'Killed,' he answered.

'And mother?'

'She died.'

'Have you got brothers or sisters?'

'A sister. They took her to Germany.'

'Have you got any relatives?'

'No, they were all burned in a partisan village.'

And he walked into a potato field, his feet bare and black from the mud, straightening the rags of his torn shirt.

But soon Grossman was to hear of far worse horrors wrought by the German occupation.

People who had come from Kiev told me that the Germans had surrounded with a ring of troops a huge mass grave in which the bodies of 50,000 Jews killed in Kiev in the autumn of 1941 were buried. They were hastily digging up the corpses, putting them on trucks and taking them to the West. They tried to burn some of the corpses on the spot.

As Grossman says, even before Kiev fell, details had already started to emerge of a great massacre of Jews – a *Gross-Aktion* by SS *Sonderkommando 4a* from *Einsatzgruppe C* and two police battalions. This had taken place at Babi Yar at the end of September 1941. The round-up of Jews in Kiev had been organised for the SS by staff officers with the headquarters of the German Sixth Army, then commanded by the Nazi, Field Marshal von Reichenau.

Planning for this *Gross-Aktion* had begun on 27 September 1941. The army town commandant issued posters ordering the Jews of Kiev to prepare for 'evacuation'. This was a deliberate attempt to conceal their fate. 'You should bring with you identity papers, money and valuables as well as warm clothing,' they were told. Soviet Jews, who had been told nothing of Nazi anti-Semitism, partly as a result of the Nazi-Soviet pact, turned up as ordered with little idea of the fate awaiting them. The SS *Sonderkommando*, which had expected between 5,000 and 6,000 to turn up, was amazed when 33,771 Jews appeared, just over half of the Jewish population of Kiev. The crowd was so enormous that more Sixth Army troops were summoned to assist in the transport of the Jews out to the ravine of Babi Yar, where the killing squads were waiting along the lip of the ravine.

The Kiev Jews were first forced to hand over their valuables, then told to strip naked before being shot. The executions took place over two days. The site was later used for more massacres of Jews, Roma Gypsies, partisans and Communist Party members. Altogether approximately 100,000 people died there. Soviet civilians, slipping through the lines in October 1943, reported that the Germans had ringed off the site in an attempt to eliminate traces of the massacres by exhuming the corpses for burning.

Grossman was attached to the headquarters of General Vatutin's 1st Ukrainian Front and heard of these reports. His fears about the fate of Jews in the Ukraine proved to be an underestimate. The scale of the slaughter was numbing. In the autumn of 1943 he had written an article entitled 'Ukraine without Jews'. This appears to have been turned down by *Krasnaya Zvezda* and it appeared in *Einikeit*, the journal of the Jewish Anti-Fascist Committee.

There are no Jews in the Ukraine. Nowhere – Poltava, Kharkov, Kremenchug, Borispol, Yagotin – in none of the cities, hundreds of towns, or thousands of villages will you see the black, tear-filled eyes of little girls; you will not hear the pained voice of an old woman; you will not see the dark face of a hungry baby. All is silence. Everything is still. A whole people has been brutally murdered.

It soon became clear to Grossman that his reports on what was to be known later as the Holocaust were unwelcome to the Soviet authorities. The Stalinist line refused to accept any special categories of suffering. All victims of Nazism on Soviet soil had to be defined as 'citizens of the Soviet Union' without qualification. Official reports on atrocities, even those describing corpses wearing the yellow star, avoided any mention of the word Jew. In late 1943, Grossman joined Ilya Ehrenburg on a commission to gather details of German crimes for the Jewish Anti-Fascist Committee, an organisation which later attracted the suspicion of the Stalinist authorities. Ehrenburg and Grossman planned that all the material collected should be published in a 'Black Book' but this would be suppressed after the war, partly because of the Stalinist position on Soviet suffering – 'Do Not Divide the Dead' – and partly because the involvement of Ukrainians in the anti-Semitic persecution

The Red Army reaches the Dnepr at Kiev.

was embarrassing for the authorities. The subject of collaboration during the Great Patriotic War was almost entirely suppressed until after the fall of Communism.

Grossman was determined to emphasise the personal tragedy as much as the vast collective crime. He sensed instinctively that horror on such a scale should never be reduced to statistics which dehumanised the victims. This is why he always searched for names or some sort of personal detail to return their individuality.

There's no one left in Kazary to complain, no one to tell, no one to cry. Silence and calm hover over the dead bodies buried under the collapsed fireplaces now overgrown by weeds. This quiet is much more frightening than tears and curses.

Old men and women are dead, as well as craftsmen and professional people: tailors, shoemakers, tinsmiths, jewellers, house painters, ironmongers, bookbinders, workers, freight handlers, carpenters, stove-makers, jokers, cabinetmakers, water carriers, millers, bakers, and cooks; also dead are physicians, prothesists, surgeons, gynaecologists, scientists – bacteriologists, biochemists, directors of university clinics – teachers of history, algebra, trigonometry. Dead are professors, lecturers and doctors of science, engineers and architects. Dead are agronomists, field workers, accountants, clerks, shop assistants, supply agents, secretaries, nightwatchmen, dead are teachers, dead are babushkas who could knit stockings and make tasty buns, cook bouillon and make strudel with apples and nuts, dead are women who had been faithful to their husbands and frivolous women are dead, too, beautiful girls, and learned students and cheerful schoolgirls, dead are ugly and silly girls, women with hunches, dead are singers, dead are blind and deaf mutes, dead are violinists and pianists, dead are two-year-olds and three-year-olds, dead are eighty-year-old men and women with cataracts on hazy eyes, with cold and transparent fingers and hair that rustled quietly like white paper, dead are newly-born babies who had sucked their mothers' breast greedily until their last minute.

This was different from the death of people in war, with weapons in their hands, the deaths of people who had left behind their houses, families, fields, songs, traditions and stories. This was the murder of a great and ancient professional experience, passed from one generation to another in thousands of families of craftsmen and members of the intelligentsia. This was the murder of everyday traditions that grandfathers had passed to their grandchildren, this was the murder of memories, of a mournful song, folk poetry, of life, happy and bitter, this was the destruction of hearths and cemetries, this was the death of the nation which had been living side by side with Ukrainians over hundreds of years . . .

Khristya Chunyak, a forty-year-old peasant woman from the village of Krasilovka, in the Brovarsky district of the Kiev oblast, told me how Germans in Brovary were escorting a Jewish doctor, Feldman, to be executed. This doctor, an old bachelor, had adopted two peasant orphans. The locals were very fond of him. A crowd of peasant women ran to the German commandant crying and pleading for Feldman's life to be saved. The commandant felt obliged to give in to the women's pleas. This was in the autumn of 1941. Feldman continued to live in Brovary and treat the local peasants. He was executed in the spring of this year. Khristya Chunyak sobbed and finally burst into tears as she described to me how the old man was forced to dig his own grave. He had to die alone. There were no other Jews alive in the spring of 1943.

General Vatutin's armies, having established bridgeheads across the Dnepr, then exploited their success south of Kiev towards Grossman's home town

Red Army soldiers talking to Soviet citizens liberated by their advance.

of Berdichev. Field Marshal von Manstein counter-attacked repeatedly during December, trying to turn Vatutin's right flank, but on Christmas Eve, he was surprised by a well-concealed Soviet offensive launched near Brusilov.

At the beginning of 1944, Wehrmacht commanders faced the painful truth that despite all the casualties they had inflicted, the Red Army had become a formidable fighting machine in the course of just over a year. German divisions were severely reduced and the new drafts of troops insufficiently trained. Their panzer divisions had not recovered from the battle of Kursk, while Soviet armoured forces were constantly replenished with tanks rolling off the vast production lines in Chelyabinsk just beyond the Urals. Red Army formations had also acquired a vastly superior mobility, thanks to the constant shipments of Dodges and Studebakers supplied by the United States. It is an irony unacknowledged by Russian historians that the Red Army managed to advance as rapidly as it did to occupy Central Europe thanks largely to American aid.

During the winter offensive which began in late December 1943, the Red Army pushed forward in the north to force the Germans back from Leningrad. In the south, the four Ukrainian Fronts launched coordinated attacks from Kiev down to the Black Sea. Vatutin's operation with the 1st Ukrainian Front, which began on 24 December from the bridgehead just south of Kiev, took Zitomir on New Year's Eve. Kazatin, seventy kilometres to the south, was also seized, and the town of Berdichev in between the two was finally cleared on 5 January 1944, after heavy fighting by the 18th Army and the 1st Tank Army.

Grossman had his own very personal reasons for wanting to be in the Ukraine. He was determined to discover what had happened in Berdichev where he feared that his mother and other relations had perished. He wrote to his wife as soon as he was close to Berdichev.

Dearest Lyusenka, I reached my destination today. Yesterday I was in Kiev. It's hard to express what I felt and what I suffered in the few hours when I visited the addresses of relatives and acquaintances. There are only graves and death. I am going to Berdichev today. My comrades have already been there. They said that the city is completely devastated, and only a few people, maybe a dozen out of many thousands, tens of thousands of Jews who lived there, have survived. I have no hope of finding Mama alive. The only thing I am hoping for is to find out about her last days and her death . . . I've understood here how dear to each other the handful of survivors must be.

He also wrote to his father, probably on the same day in January, telling him of the death of a friend in Kiev.

I am going to Berdichev today. People say that the Jewish population there has been killed, and the town is almost completely destroyed and empty. I embrace you, my dear one. I have such a heavy feeling in my soul. Your Vasya

Grossman visited the execution sites out by the airstrip and the Yatki ghetto where the Jews of Berdichev had been rounded up. Tirelessly, he interviewed witnesses, both the few Jewish survivors and local Ukrainians. For him, the greatest shock was to discover the major role which local Ukrainians had played in the horror. Many had been recruited as auxiliary police by the German authorities, who gave them rifles and peaked hats and white armbands. They encouraged them to torment the Jews, then to assist in the round-ups and executions.

Grossman, who had tended as a young man to avoid the Jewishness of Berdichev, now felt doubly burdened with guilt. Out of Berdichev's population of 60,000, just over 30,000 were Jews. Between 20,000 and 30,000 had been murdered in Berdichev in the first major massacre in the Ukraine. Grossman recognised that many Ukrainians were taking revenge for the Stalinist repression and famines in the 1920s and 30s, using the Jews as scapegoats. They were also shameless in looting the possessions of the Jewish population of the town. But Grossman noted the fact that most of the Jewish survivors he interviewed had in fact been saved or helped by ethnic Russians or Ukrainians. His notes from his interviews went towards his work for *The Black Book*.

About 30,000 Jews were killed in Berdichev. The brothers Pekilis, Mikhel and Wulf, survived. Many people in the city knew the Pekilis family. They were well-known stonemasons, the father and five sons. They built houses in Berdichev, built factories in Kiev, and even took part in building the Moscow underground. When the Germans came, Mikhel and Wulf escaped. They were building beautiful stoves for peasants and lived under the stoves. Then they dug a hole under a German establishment in Sverdlovskaya [Street], where they sat for 145 days. A Russian engineer, Evgeny Osipovich, was feeding them. Then, they fled from this coffin and found the partisans. Mikhel and Wulf Pekilis took part in the liberation of Berdichev.

A boy from Berdichev: 'They called me Mitya Ostapchuk, but my name is Khaim Roitman. I am from Berdichev. I am thirteen now. Germans killed my father, and my mama, too. I had a little brother, Borya. A German killed him with a sub-machine gun, killed him in front of me . . . It was so strange, the earth was moving! I was standing on the edge of the hole, waiting. Now they'll shoot me, [I thought]. A German came up to me, squinted. And I pointed: "Look, there's a watch!" There was a piece of glass glittering there. The German went to pick it up, and I ran as fast as I could. He was running after me, shooting, a bullet made a hole in my cap. I ran and ran, and then stumbled and fell. I don't remember what came next. An old man, Gerasim Prokofievich Ostapchuk, picked me up. He said: "Now you're Mitya, my son." He had seven children, I became the eighth.

   'Some Germans came once, all of them were drunk. They began to shout, they'd noticed I was dark. They asked Gerasim Prokofievich: "Whose boy is he?" And he answered: "Mine." They scolded him, said he was lying, because I was dark. And he answered, so calmly, you know: "He is my son by my first wife. She was a Gypsy."

   'When Berdichev was liberated, I went into town. I found my big brother, Yasha. He survived, too. Yasha is big, he is sixteen. He is fighting. When Germans were leaving, Yasha found the swine who'd killed our mama, and shot him.'

Grossman's article, 'The Killing of Jews in Berdichev', was censored by the Soviet authorities with the double purpose of reducing emphasis on the Jews as victims and camouflaging the degree of Ukrainian collaboration in the atrocities.

The seizure of Berdichev by the Germans was sudden. German tank units broke through to the city. Only a third of the population could get away in time. The Germans entered the city on Monday, 7 July, at seven in the evening. The soldiers were shouting: '*Jude kaputt!*' from their trucks and waved their arms. They knew that almost all the Jews were still in the city.

   Woodworker Girsh Giterman, who escaped from Berdichev on

the sixth day of the occupation, told me about the first crimes committed by Germans towards Jews. German soldiers had forced a group of people to leave their flats in Bolshaya Zhitomirskaya, Malaya Zhitomirskaya and Shteinovskaya Street. All these streets were close to the leather plant. The people were then brought to the tanning unit of the plant and forced to jump into huge pits filled with astringent catechu.[3] Those who resisted were shot, and their bodies were also thrown into the pits. The Germans thought this execution funny: they were tanning Jewish skin.

A similar comical execution was carried out in the old city: Germans ordered the old men to put on their *tallit* and *tefillin* and hold a service in the old synagogue, praying to God to forgive their sins against Germans.[4] The door of the synagogue was locked, and it was set on fire. A third farcical execution was carried out near a watermill. They seized several dozen women, ordered them to undress, and announced to them that they would spare the lives of those who made it to the other bank. The river was very wide by the mill, as it had been dammed up. Most women drowned before they reached the opposite bank. Those who did make it to the west bank were forced to swim back at once.

Another example of a German 'joke' is the story of the death of an old man, Aron Mazor, kosher butcher by profession. A German officer looted Mazor's flat and ordered the soldiers to carry off the belongings that he had selected. He himself stayed behind with two soldiers in order to have some fun. He had found Mazor's big knife and discovered Mazor's profession. 'I'd like to see your work,' he said, and ordered the soldiers to bring in the neighbour's three little children.

The minds of these thousands of people were unable to comprehend a simple and terrifying truth, that the state itself encouraged and approved these 'unsanctioned' executions, that Jews were outlaws who were the most natural objects for torture, violence and murder. However, not one of those who had been moved to the ghetto imagined that the move was just the first step towards the well-prepared killing of all the 20,000 Jews.[5]

---

3 Catechu is a tannin obtained from the tree *Acacia catechu*.
4 The *tallit* is a prayer shawl and *tefillin* are ritual black leather boxes containing scriptural passages attached to the head and to the hand.
5 The figure of 30,000 cited earlier was established later, when the full scope of the massacres became apparent.

An accountant from Berdichev who had visited the family of his friend, the engineer Nuzhny, in the ghetto, told me how Nuzhny's wife had cried a lot and was very worried because her ten-year-old son Garik would be unable to go back to his Russian school in the autumn.

Old doctors in Berdichev lived with the hope that the Red Army would come back. There was a moment when they comforted each other with the news, which someone had reportedly heard on the radio, that the German government had received a note demanding them to stop outrages against Jews. But by this time [Soviet] prisoners of war brought by the Germans from Lysaya Gora, had already started digging five deep trenches in the field close to the airfield, where Gorodskaya [Street] ends and a paved road leading to the village of Romanovka begins.

On 4 September, a week after the ghetto was established, 1,500 young people were ordered to prepare for agricultural work. The young people packed little bundles with food, said goodbye to their parents and set off. On the very same day all 1,500 boys were shot between Lysaya Gora and the village of Khazhina. The executioners had so cleverly misled their victims that none of the doomed people had suspected the forthcoming murder until the last minute. It had even been hinted that after the work was completed they would be allowed to take a few potatoes home to the old people in the ghetto. And during the few days remaining to them, those who had stayed in the ghetto never learned the fate of the young boys. This execution removed from the ghetto almost all the young men who were capable of resistance.

Preparations for the operations were completed. Pits were dug at the end of the Brodskaya Street. Units from an SS regiment arrived in Berdichev on 14 September and the city police was put on standby. The whole area of the ghetto was surrounded during the night of 14 September. At four in the morning [on 15 September] the signal was given, and the SS and police began driving them out and on to the market square. The way they behaved showed people that their last day had come. The executioners killed those who could not walk, old people and cripples, in the houses. The whole city was woken by the terrible screams of women and children's crying. Soon the market square was filled with many thousands of people.

Four hundred people had been selected, including the elderly doctors Tsugovar, Baraban, Liberman, female doctor Blank, electrician Epelfeld, photographer Nuzhny, shoemaker Milmeister, old stonemason Pekelis and his sons Mikhel and Wulf, and tailors, shoemakers, metal workers and several hairdressers. These professional people were allowed to take their families with them.

Many of them were unable to find their wives and children whom they had lost in the crowd. The witnesses tell about the shocking scenes that they saw there: people shouted the names of their wives and children trying to sound louder than the distraught crowd, while hundreds of doomed mothers were trying to hand them their sons and daughters, begging them to say that they were theirs and save them from death. 'You won't find yours anyway in this crowd.'

The first sub-machine-gun bursts sounded. I do not know whether the Germans did this on purpose, or whether they just did not realise that the execution site was only fifty to sixty metres from the road along which the doomed people were being brought in. The column passed the 'scaffold' and thousands of pairs of eyes saw the dead falling down . . . Then the people were taken to sheds at the airfield where they waited for their turn, and then walked back again, this time to the place where they would be killed.

This slaughter of the innocent and helpless went on all day. Their blood poured on to the yellow clay ground. The pits filled with blood, the clay soil was unable to absorb it, blood overflowed the pits and there were huge puddles of it on the ground. Rivulets of it flowed, accumulating in depressions . . . The executioners' boots were soaked with blood.

Grossman never wrote in any of his articles or for *The Black Book* about the fate of his mother. This finally came out in his novel *Life and Fate*, where she is given the identity of Anna Shtrum. His mother had been one of the thousands of victims executed out by the airfield. His sense of guilt and horror can best be estimated by the two letters which he wrote to her after the war. The first was in 1950.

Dear Mama,

I learned about your death in the winter of 1944. I came to Berdichev, entered the house where you used to live and which Aunt Anyuta, Uncle David and Natasha had left, and I felt that you had died. But as far back as September 1941 my heart already felt that you weren't here any more. One night at the front I had a dream. I entered your room. I knew for sure that it was your room, and I saw an empty armchair, and I knew you had slept in it. A shawl with which you'd covered your legs was hanging down from the armchair. I looked at it for a long time, and when I woke up I knew that you weren't any longer among the living. But I didn't know then what a terrible death you had suffered. I only learned about it when I came to Berdichev and talked to people who knew about the mass execution that took place on 15 September 1941. I have tried, dozens, or maybe hundreds of times, to imagine how you died, how you had walked to meet your death. I tried to imagine the person who killed you. He was the last person to see you. I know you were thinking about me a lot during all that time.

Now it's been more than nine years since I've stopped writing letters to you, telling you about my life and work. And I've accumulated so much in my soul in these nine years that I've decided to write to you, to tell you, and, of course, to complain to you, as no one else is particularly interested in my sorrows. You were the only one who was interested in them.

I can feel you today, as alive to me as you were on the day when I saw you last, and as alive as when you read to me when I was a little boy. And my pain is still the same as it was on that day when your neighbour in Uchilishchnaya Street told me you were dead. There was no hope of finding you among the living. And I think that my love for you and this terrible sorrow will not change until the day I die.

He wrote again in 1961 on the twentieth anniversary of her death.

My darling, twenty years have passed since the day of your death. I love you, I remember you every day of my life, and my sorrow has never left me in these twenty years.

I last wrote to you ten years ago, and in my heart you are still the same as you were twenty years ago . . . I am you, my own one. And as long as I am alive, you are alive, too. And when I die you will live in the book which I have dedicated to you and whose fate is so like yours.[5] And it seems to me now that my love for you is

5   He is of course referring to *Life and Fate*. It has been suggested that this letter is an answer to the last letter written by Anna Shtrum to her son in the novel, the letter which Grossman felt his mother had never had time to write to him herself.

becoming greater and more responsible because there are so few hearts left now in which you still live. I've been thinking of you all the time during these last ten years when I was working . . .

I've been rereading today, as I have for many years, the few letters to me which have survived out of the hundreds that you had written. I also read your letters to Papa. And I cried today once again reading your letters. I cried when I read: 'Zema, I also don't think I will live long.[6] All the time I am expecting a disease to get me. I am afraid I will be very ill for a long time. What is the poor boy going to do with me then? It would be so much trouble for him.'

I cried when you – you, so lonely, whose only dream in life would be to live under the same roof with me – wrote to Papa: 'It seems to me sensible if you'd go and live with Vasya if he's got room. I am telling you this once again, because now I am well. And you don't need to worry about my spiritual life: I know how to protect my inner world from things around me.' I cried over your letters because you are in them: with your kindness, your purity, your bitter, bitter life, your fairness, your generosity, your love for me, your care for people, your wonderful mind. I fear nothing because your love is with me and because my love is with you always.

---

6   Zema was her diminutive for Vasily Grossman's father, Semyon Osipovich Grossman (1870–1956).

TWENTY-TWO

Across the Ukraine to Odessa

At the beginning of March, Grossman was attached to the headquarters of the 3rd Ukrainian Front. The Germans had held on to the Black Sea coast despite being outflanked by the thrust of the 1st Ukrainian Front to the north.

In the first week of March, Marshal Zhukhov had taken over from Vatutin, mortally wounded on 29 February when ambushed by Ukrainian partisans of the UPA.[1] Zhukhov directed a new offensive towards Ternopol. Also in the first week of March, Marshal Konev's 2nd Ukrainian Front attacked towards Uman, which they seized along with large quantities of military stores just five days later, on 10 March. Two hundred German tanks, six hundred guns and many thousands of vehicles, immobilised in the deep mud and abandoned by their crews, were taken along the way.

Red Army soldiers cursed the spring mud of the *rasputitsa*, but the Germans suffered far more. Konev's armoured columns pushed onwards to seize bridgeheads across the southern reaches of the Bug. They were less than a hundred kilometres from the Moldovian border and the River Dnestr, which was first crossed on 17 March, twelve days after the start of the offensive. German divisions, reduced to a fraction of their usual strength, had to fight their way out of encirclements and retreat rapidly, slipping through between Soviet armies. In many cases, parachute supply drops by the Luftwaffe kept them going. But the will to escape was intense. No German wanted to suffer the fate of Paulus's Sixth Army at Stalingrad.

Meanwhile, in another coordinated offensive, Malinovsky's 3rd Ukrainian Front had swept forward from the Ingulets, crossing two more

---

1 The UPA was the *Ukrainska povstanska armiia*, or Ukrainian Insurgent Army, an extreme nationalist and anti-communist organisation which had collaborated with the Germans, but also fought them when the Ukraine was treated as ruthlessly by the Nazis as were other areas of the occupied territories.

rivers and attempting to cut off seven German divisions. The advance, however, was at the mercy of the elements.

Before the attack, the Military Council of the Front had been thinking above all of the weather. They kept looking at the barometer. A professor of meteorology had been summoned, as well as an old man, expert in the local weather, who could forecast it by looking at some indications of which no one else knew. Officers attended lectures on meteorology.

On 6 March, General Rodion I. Malinovsky's 3rd Ukrainian Front launched an offensive along the Black Sea coast to capture Odessa. The enemy consisted of the German Sixth Army, a re-creation of the original army at Stalingrad – this was on Hitler's orders, as if it would wipe out the defeat – Lieutenant General I.A. Pliev's cavalry, IV Guards Cavalry Corps and IV Mechanised Corps. Cavalry was of great use in the heavy mud.

The front HQ was in the village of Novaya Odessa, some ninety kilometres from Odessa. Terrible mud. If Rudnyi hadn't helped, I wouldn't have managed to drag my suitcase from the airfield to the headquarters.

Advancing in the mud requires an enormous physical effort. Quantities of petrol which would otherwise have been sufficient to go hundreds of kilometres are burned up over a few hundred metres. Mobile groups are cutting off German communications, supplies and liaison. Sometimes Germans retreat chaotically.

The whole steppe is filled with the howling of vehicles and tractors tearing themselves out of the mud. The 'roads' are hundreds of metres wide.

Grossman described the advance in great detail for an article in *Krasnaya Zvezda*.

Finally, the sun is getting hotter and hotter, and light clouds of dust have already appeared flying behind the trucks. A thin, swarthy captain in a greatcoat whose flaps are covered with scales of brown and red earth inhaled this dust with delight: 'Oh, imagine how dreadful the mud has been if dust – this scourge of the war – now seems nicer than all the spring flowers. For us, the dust smells good today.'

Several days ago, a shrill howling of one-and-a-half-ton trucks, three-tonners, five-ton YAZ, tractors, caterpillar transporters, Dodges and Studebakers hung constantly over this steppe.[2] They were howling in an angry effort to break out from the mud's claws to catch up with the sleepless infantry. Their fierce but powerless wheels only threw out sticky lumps of mud, spinning in the oily, slippery ruts. And thousands of sinewy, thin, sweating people were heaving at the rear ends [of bogged-down vehicles], their teeth clenched, day and night, under the eternal rain and the eternal, three times accursed, wet, melting snow . . .

In the Ukraine, spring 1944: soldiers try to manoeuvre a truck loaded with artillery shells that is stuck in the mud.

2   The YAZ 210G was the Red Army's workhorse truck, a five-ton, canopied six-wheeler. Soviet drivers preferred American Lend-Lease vehicles. Red Army tank drivers, on the other hand, hated the American Grant which, being petrol-driven, was more likely to catch fire when hit than the diesel-engined T-34.

Who will recount the great feats of our people? Who will recreate the epic of this unprecedented offensive, this sleepless advance that went on day and night? Infantrymen were marching, loaded with one and a half issues of ammunition,[3] and their greatcoats wet and as heavy as lead. A severe north wind sprang upon them, their greatcoats froze and became rigid like sheet iron. Cushions of mud, weighing a pood apiece, stuck to the boots. Sometimes, people only managed a kilometre an hour, so hard was this road. For many kilometres around, there wasn't a dry patch of land. Soldiers had to sit down in the mud to have some rest or take off their boots to rewrap their foot cloths. Mortar men were moving forward beside the riflemen, and each of them was carrying half a dozen bombs hanging on loops of rope on their backs and chests.

'That's all right,' they said. 'It's even harder for the Germans. It's death for Germans now . . .'

No work was more terrible than building a bridge over the Southern Bug. The sappers only had a tiny bridgehead on the west bank, the enemy was pressing hard, and the sappers were building the bridge not just under German fire, but right in the midst of the firing itself. The marsh seemed bottomless: a test pile went in eleven metres deep, as if into pastry.[4]

Once Malinovsky's armies had captured the city of Nikolayev at the mouth of the Bug, the way to Odessa lay open before them. Marshal Konev was ordered to swing some of his formations southwards to trap the German Sixth and Eighth Armies as well as the hapless Romanian Third Army between his forces and Malinovsky's armies.

The German military authorities have sent the commander of the 16th Motorised Division[5] for trial by court martial. His explanation: 'Without their vehicles, my men are weaker than an infantry division.'

The enemy fear being encircled. They don't believe that their defence lines are strong, because their commanders keep deceiving them the whole time.

---

3 A standard issue of ammunition was increased by 50 per cent during an advance because resupply became far more unpredictable than when stationary in defence.
4 On 11 March 1944, detachments of Bogdanov's 2nd Tank Army and Kravchenko's 6th Tank Army had seized bridgeheads across the southern Bug.
5 This was the 16th Panzergrenadier Division commanded by Major-General Günther von Manteuffel, and reconstituted as the 116th Panzer Division later.

Characteristics of our officers during this new phase: (1) Will; (2) Confidence; (3) Scorn towards the enemy; (4) Ability to fight using the force of tanks and artillery, the infantry being small in number; (5) Ability to save, to keep account of every cartridge and shell – a big war with poor reserves; (6) They have learned to hurry, but it isn't their motto, it is just in everyone's blood. They hurry to cross the rivers, because it is much quicker to use a branch than to wait for days on end for pontoons. The speed of pursuit matches the speed of the enemy's retreat.

Odessa was finally secured on 10 April. It had been garrisoned mainly by the Third Romanian Army. The Romanian occupation of the south-western Ukraine was almost gentle in comparison to the German treatment of the population. Grossman entered with the liberators and looked around Peresyp, a district in Odessa.

The day of the capture of Odessa. The port [is] empty. Puffs of smoke. Thunder of military vehicles and equipment pouring into the city. Crowds of people. Scorched corpses carried out of the Gestapo building. The charred corpse of a girl, with beautiful golden hair intact.

Signs over Romanian canteens: 'Entrance forbidden to Germans.'

The first meeting of the Odessa OBKOM. The OBKOM Secretary has invited me to participate. This is the first time that I, not a member of the Party, have attended such a meeting.

There is a lot of food – sugar, cakes, flour. The locals are cursing Romanians reluctantly, as if out of politeness.

The prospect of the end of the war hastened the optimism of many civilians as well as Red Army soldiers. With the defeat of fascism, they told themselves, Stalin could disband the NKVD secret police and the Gulag camps. Grossman had already heard such talk in the trenches of Stalingrad, and it appears that he shared their hopes. But he now seems to have sensed that Stalinism would not change its spots.

Odessa's old men in the boulevard. Their fantastic talk about a complete reorganisation of Soviet government after the war.

A poet, who had published under the Romanians a book of poetry [entitled] *I Sing Today*. Our conversation. He is an extremely unpleasant person. Suddenly I see his mother standing under the window outside. In her eyes there is a terrible fear for her son.

Aisenshtadt Simon, the son of a famous rabbi from the little town of Ostrovets.[7] A Russian girl had saved his life. She had been sheltering him in her room for more than a year. His story. Ghetto in Warsaw. The uprising. Poles had brought in the weapons. Polish Jews had to wear a white armband. Belgian and French Jews – a yellow one. Treblinka near Warsaw. The extermination camp for Jews. There was a chamber with moving knives, it was in a basement, under a *banya*. The bodies were cut into pieces and then burned. There were mountains of ashes, twenty to twenty-five metres high. In one place Jews had been chased into a pond full of acid. Their screams were so terrible that local peasants abandoned their homes. Fifty-eight thousand Odessa Jews were burned alive in Berezovka.[8] Some of them were burned to death in railway carriages. Others were taken to a clearing where Germans poured petrol over them and them set them on fire.

The account of OBKOM Secretary Ryasentsev. Domanevka was the place where Jews had been executed.[9] The executions were carried out by the Ukrainian police. The chief of police in Domanevka had killed 12,000 people himself.

In November 1942, Antonescu issued a law giving rights to Jews.[10] Mass executions, which had gone on throughout 1942, halted. The chief of police in Domanevka and eight of his closest associates were arrested by Romanians, taken to Tiraspol[11] and sent for trial. The court sentenced them to three months forced labour for their unlawful deeds towards the Jews.

Outrage was caused by the public prosecutor [from Domanevka], a Russian lawyer from Odessa, who killed eight or nine people a

---

7 A town about 270 kilometres north of Odessa.
8 Berezovka (or Berozovka) is about eighty kilometres north of Odessa on the railway line to Cherkassy and Nikolayev.
9 Domanevka is another forty kilometres north-north-east of Berezovka.
10 Marshal Ion Antonescu, the anti-communist military dictator of Romania, did not share his ally's anti-Semitism. The Romanian authorities were granted a semi-autonomous military command of the Odessa region by the Nazi government.
11 Tiraspol is a large town on the River Dnestr inside Moldovia, which the Romanians had reclaimed after losing it to Stalin in 1940. It was reintegrated into the Soviet Union as soon as the Red Army reoccupied it.

Grossman having his boots cleaned in the streets of Odessa, April 1944.
The bootblack was cut out of the shot for political reasons.

day for amusement. This was called 'going shooting'. They used to
kill people in separate lots. Children were thrown alive into dry
moats with straw burning on the bottom.

By the time Antonescu's order was published, there were about
380 Odessa Jews left in Domanevka and forty children in a nursery.
They are still alive, have no clothes or shoes. The total number of
Odessa Jews executed in Domanevka was about 90,000. Those who
survived received aid from the Jewish committee in Romania.
Romanian Jews were executed, too, along with Jews from Odessa.
They had been tricked into going to Domanevka. This was how one
of the richest Romanian millionaires was executed. He was brought
to Domanevka under the pretext of organising the excavation and
exploitation of the local ceramic clay. There were three Jews who
participated in the torture and executions. They have been arrested.

In Odessa, they had rounded up Jews and let them go home.
Then, on 10 January 1942, they herded them into a ghetto in
Slobodka. It was very cold, and when they were being driven from
the ghetto to the trains, there remained hundreds of corpses of old
people, children and women lying around in the streets.

Having discovered that so many people he had known were now dead, Grossman had a contrary experience that spring, not far from Berdichev. He visited a tank brigade of the 1st Ukrainian Front, which was refitting at Vinnitsa, where Hitler's headquarters, code-named *Wehrwolf,* had been based. He had dinner with the brigade commander, 'a short, calm and good-natured man', as Ortenberg described him in this account. 'During dinner, when talking of dates and places of battles, Grossman realised that this was the very same Babadzhanyan who had commanded the 395th Regiment, and whom he had made the hero of his novel [*The People Immortal*]. "Yes, I was there," confirmed Babadzhanyan. "But you killed me."

'"I killed you," Grossman answered, "but I can resurrect you, too."'

With the tank commander Colonel Babadzhanyan, Grossman's hero who later crushed the Hungarian rising in 1956.

TWENTY-THREE

Operation Bagration

After the complete liberation of Leningrad and the rapid reconquest of the Ukraine, Stalin consulted with his *Stavka* advisers. They consisted of Zhukov, the deputy supreme commander; Vasilevsky, the chief of the general staff; his deputy, General Antonov;[1] and General Shtemenko,[2] the chief of operations. In late April, the front commanders were allowed to consolidate their positions and go on to the defensive while the operational plan was decided. By the end of April, Stalin had chosen Belorussia for the next major blow. A success there would provide them with an intermediate position ready to strike towards Berlin early the following year.

After the defeated Germans in the south were thrown back into Romania, Grossman was transferred northwards to the eastern border of Belorussia, the last major area of Soviet territory still under Nazi occupation. He found himself close to where he had started the war less than three years before. Eastern Belorussia was now to provide the start line for the most ambitious operation in the Nazi-Soviet conflict.

The *Stavka* had just been informed by the Americans and British that Operation Overlord would take place at the end of May. Planning to attack the great Belorussian bulge went ahead under conditions of total secrecy. Apart from Stalin, only five men were privy to the plan. They knew that they had to mislead the Germans about the axis of attack. The tank armies in the south were kept there and grouped together to suggest the preparation of another massive blow south of the Pripet marshes. Radio silence was also imposed on the three Ukrainian Fronts to suggest an imminent attack and rumours were spread of a naval

---

1 General Aleksei I. Antonov (1896–1962) was regarded as the most competent staff officer produced by the Red Army during the war, and became chief of the general staff in 1945.
2 General Sergei M. Shtemenko (1907–1976) was chief of the operations directorate and took over from Antonov when he was promoted in 1945. Shtemenko did not suffer when Stalin purged, sidelined and threatened other senior Soviet generals in the immediate post-war years. He became chief of the general staff in 1948.

landing on the Black Sea coast of Romania. The Germans fell for the diversion. They reinforced the southern sectors, especially around Lvov.

The Soviet plan involving 1,250,000 men was finalised on 20 May. Meanwhile, newly reinforced tank formations were secretly moved to the eastern border of Belorussia. Stalin himself chose the operational code name of 'Bagration' in honour of the great Georgian general who had been mortally wounded at Borodino. Rokossovsky, a Pole who been arrested before the war and tortured by Beria's NKVD, had dared to stand up to Stalin in a furious argument over the first phase, which involved flanking attacks via Vitebsk and Bobruisk on the two flanks of the 'Belorussian Balcony' to encircle Minsk. Both Molotov and Malenkov tried to persuade Rokossovsky not to disagree with the *vozhd*, the boss. 'Do you know who you are arguing with?' they said. But Stalin respected Rokossovsky's courage and accepted his point.

The Western allies landed in Normandy on 6 June, while the Red Army waited impatiently for new equipment and reinforcements to arrive on a severely overtaxed railway system. Grossman noted the reaction to events in Normandy.

> On the subject of the Second Front. Great enthusiasm on the first day. Spontaneous meetings, shooting, saluting, then a sharp decrease of interest.
>
> A trait of character: one man said when he was on a train and learned about the attack by the Allies: 'Well, probably they won't even detrain us now.'

Few soldiers, or even officers, ever had a chance to discover anything about life beyond their own unit, so an outsider like Grossman was bombarded with questions.

> Those most often asked by officers and soldiers are on international matters, and they are very numerous. They include the Second Front, Japan, Turkey, Iran, and hundreds of other issues. Questions about internal affairs are less numerous. Asking their questions, people apparently want to find out about the duration and course of the war.

Grossman joined General Batov's 65th Army, part of Marshal Rokossovsky's First Belorussian Front, in time for the great offensive. After several delays, it finally began on 22 June, the third anniversary of the Nazi invasion. Two days later, three of Rokossovsky's armies – Gorbatov's 3rd Army,

Romanenko's 48th and Batov's 65th – emerged from the boggy forests on the northern edge of the Pripet marshes to attack the German Ninth Army round Bobruisk on the River Beresina. On 27 June, the German defenders – some 5,000 men from the 383rd Infantry Division – managed to fight off the first attempt to storm the town. Then they found that they were surrounded. Led by their commander, General Hamann,[3] they tried to fight their way out of the north side of the city, but were cut off by Gorbatov's 3rd Army. Grossman, describing the scenes he encountered in Bobruisk, was unlike most Soviet journalists who concentrated on extolling the collective strength of the Red Army. He was always interested in the individual, even amid the dehumanised carnage of the battlefield.

Sometimes you are so shaken by what you've seen, blood rushes from your heart, and you know that the terrible sight that your eyes have just taken in is going to haunt you and lie heavily on your soul all your life. It is strange that when you sit down to write about it, you don't find enough room for it on paper. You write about a tank corps, about heavy artillery, but suddenly remember how bees were swarming in a burning village, and a barefooted old Belorussian climbed out of a little trench where he was hiding from shells and took the swarm off a branch, how soldiers were looking at him, and, my God, one can read so much in their thoughtful, melancholy eyes. In these little things exists the soul of the people and our war with its suffering and its victories . . .

How [were we] to find our old Stalingrad acquaintances[4] amid this dust and smoke, roar of engines, clatter of tank tracks and self-propelled guns and the squeaking of long columns of carts moving west, and a flow of barefooted children and women wearing white kerchiefs, moving east, back home? Some kind people advised us to look for a well-known feature of this division in order to avoid unnecessary stops and enquiries. This was a camel called Kuznechik [Grasshopper] in the supply unit of its artillery regiment. This camel, who came from Kazakhstan, has come all the way from Stalingrad to the Beresina. Liaison officers usually look for Kuznechik

3 Lieutenant General Hamann was captured. He was later executed in 1945 for war crimes.
4 This is presumably the former 308th Rifle Division, commanded at Stalingrad by General Gurtiev, which became the 120th Guards Rifle Division in September 1943. This mainly Siberian formation had defended the Barrikady factory in Stalingrad. During Operation Bagration it formed part of the 3rd Army.

in the supply unit and do not need other enquiries to find the headquarters which is on the move day and night. We took this unusual
advice as a joke and moved on.

The first thing we see when we return to the dust and thundering
of the main road is a brown camel pulling a cart. He is almost bald,
having lost his hair. It proves to be the famous Kuznechik. A crowd
of captured Germans is moving in the opposite direction. The camel
turns his ugly head towards them, his lower lip turned down with
a look of disdain. It is probably the unusual colour of the prisoners'
unforms or their unusual smell that have caught his attention. The
driver [of the cart] says to the soldiers escorting the prisoners, in a
businesslike way: 'Give these Germans to us here. Kuznechik is going
to eat them now!' And presently we learn this camel's biography. He
hides in craters from shells and bombs if there's a bombardment.
He has already earned three wound-stripes and the medal 'For the
Defence of Stalingrad'. The commander of the artillery regiment,
Kapramanyan, has promised the driver a decoration if he reaches
Berlin with Kuznechik.[5] We followed the route indicated by
Kuznechik and found the division.

I didn't find many of my old acquaintances in Gurtiev's division, whom I remembered well from our brief encounters. Gurtiev
himself was killed in the fighting for Orel when a shell exploded
at the observation post. He protected General Gorbatov with his
body. Splashes of this soldier-general's blood were found on
Gorbatov's cap.

When we entered Bobruisk some buildings in it were ablaze and
others lay in ruins. To Bobruisk led the road of revenge! With difficulty, our car finds its way amid scorched and distorted German
tanks and self-propelled guns. Men are walking over German corpses.
Corpses, hundreds and thousands of them, pave the road, lie in
ditches, under the pines, in the green barley. In some places, vehicles have to drive over the corpses, so densely they lie upon the
ground. People are busy all the time burying them, but they are so
many that this work cannot be done in just one day. And the day
is exhaustingly hot, still, and people walk and drive pressing hand-
kerchiefs to their noses. A cauldron of death was boiling here, where
the revenge was carried out – a ruthless, terrible revenge over those

5 Kuznechik, the camel, became even more famous less than a year later when he did reach
Berlin and was led across the city by his driver to spit at the Reichstag.

who hadn't surrendered their arms and tried to break out to the west.

A German soldier wounded in the legs is sitting on a low sandy bank of the Beresina by the route into the burning and destroyed Bobruisk. He raises his head and looks up at the tank columns moving across the bridge, at the artillery. A Red Army soldier comes up to him, takes some water from the river in a tin and gives it to him to drink. I couldn't help thinking, what would this German have done in the summer of 1941, when panzer columns of their troops were moving east across this bridge, if he had seen one of our soldiers with wounded legs sitting here on the sandy bank.

Grossman was allowed to interview captured German generals. Lieutenant General von Lützov, the commander of XXXV Army Corps, was a fifty-two-year-old Prussian, who had been captured near Bobruisk in another of the encirclements.[6] According to most accounts, he had collapsed under the strain of defending an impossible postion while Hitler refused requests to retreat.

Leutnant-General [sic] Lützov does not praise our army particularly highly. The soldiers are devoid of initiative. When they have no leader on the battlefield they do not know what to do. The artillery is strong. The [Soviet] air force drops bombs with no aim whatsoever.

Lützov was complaining about his total lack of freedom of action. For example, he needed permission from army headquarters to leave a position, the army needed permission from the headquarters of the army group, and the army group needed that of the general staff headquarters.[7] Lützov received permission to retreat with XXXV Army Corps only when the ring of encirclement had already been closed.

SS [sic] General Heyne about himself: 'I'm a *Frontschwein*.'[8]

6 Generalleutnant Kurt-Jürgen Freiherr Henning von Lützov, who had been born in 1892 near Marienwerder, was sentenced in Moscow on 29 June 1950 to twenty-five years' imprisonment for war crimes (a sentence handed out to many German generals as the Cold War intensified). He was released and repatriated in January 1956.
7 OKH (*Oberkommando des Heeres*), the army general staff, had responsibility for all operations on the eastern front. The OKW (*Oberkommando der Wehrmacht*) was responsible for all operations everywhere else.
8 Lieutenant General Hans-Walter Heyne, commander of the 6th Infantry Division, was also captured in the area of Bobruisk. Heyne was not a member of the SS, a term which many Soviet accounts use with abandon. '*Frontschwein*' was presumably Heyne's heavy joke. The usual phrase was '*Fronthase*', or 'front hare'. Heyne, a fifty-year-old from Hanover, was sentenced to twenty-five years, and served most of his sentence in Vorkuta. He was released and repatriated in December 1955.

Most of the German generals, officers and soldiers captured during Operation Bagration were forced to march through Moscow in a victory parade on 17 July. Soviet propaganda had been so exaggerated that many Russian children had expected to see ravening beasts, not defeated soldiers. In any case, it underlined the importance of this massive German defeat in which the Wehrmacht lost around a third of a million men, an even greater loss than at Stalingrad.

Soviet intelligence officers evidently briefed Grossman on what they had found among the captured papers and on other interrogations of prisoners.

A German map had been captured. The data marked was absolutely identical to the map compiled by our intelligence department, not only divisions, but also the reserves, forming-up points, etc., were identical.

A captured German officer says that German officers are constantly discussing possible attacks by the Russians.

Few believed they'd manage to hold the line. More often, they speak about the gigantic 'Belorussian' mousetrap.

[Before the Soviet attack] Feldmarschall Bush went round the front units to 'inspire cheerfulness and perseverance'. Germans have already withdrawn some units from the front and are pulling them far inland, probably in connection with the invasion by the Allies.

For the advance against Minsk to the north-west, Grossman rejoined General Batov's 65th Army. In just over a week, the defence lines of Army Group Centre had been destroyed. The Germans had lost 200,000 men and 900 tanks, but Soviet casualties had also been terrifying in many sectors. Even Red Army generals hardened to the slaughter were shaken. Yet the battle had only just begun. Hitler and the German high command had still not realised that the Soviet strategy was aimed at two sets of pincers, an inner encirclement of Minsk, and an outer encirclement to trap the whole of Army Group Centre.

On 3 July, Soviet tanks entered the suburbs of Minsk. Another 100,000 German soldiers were trapped, and nearly half of them were killed. Grossman's notes at this stage are random, including past atrocities, revenge and descriptions. Italian soldiers, who had already suffered in Russia for the fascist cause which most of them did not believe in, then found themselves after the armistice as prisoners and slave labourers of the

Germans. Grossman even heard of some being killed by former Red
Army soldiers serving the Wehrmacht in some capacity.

> Italians executed by Vlasov men.[9] Mass killing of [Red Army] pris-
> oners of war on the 12/13 February 1944. In the morning the whole
> length of Sovyetskaya Street was piled with many thousands of
> bodies.
>
> Fire in the districts close to the river: hundreds of thousands of
> people who have lost all their possessions in the fire are sitting on
> their bundles. Armchairs, paintings, deer's heads with horns; girls
> holding kittens.
>
> [German] Prisoners are walking on their own; they are sulky.
> One of them straightens his uniform whenever he sees a vehicle,
> and salutes it.

Another version of this description suggests that the German prisoner in
question was probably suffering from battle-shock.

Revenge killings were unsurprising after the appalling anti-partisan
war waged in Belorussia by the Germans and their auxiliaries, whom the
Red Army often referred to generically as *Vlasovtsy*.

> A partisan, a small man, has killed two Germans with a stake. He
> had pleaded with the guards of the column to give him these
> Germans. He had convinced himself that they were the ones who
> had killed his daughter Olya and his sons, his two boys. He broke
> all their bones, and smashed their skulls, and while he was beating
> them, he was crying and shouting: 'Here you are – for Olya! Here
> you are – for Kolya!' When they were dead, he propped the bodies
> up against a tree stump and continued to beat them.
>
> *Vlasovtsy* are being killed. People are killing their compatriots, a
> man from Orel kills a man from the Orel region, an Uzbek kills
> an Uzbek.
>
> There are already next to no German airfields left on our terri-
> tory. Our fighters are already flying over their land. It won't be long
> now before their country is ablaze.

9 It is most unlikely that they would have been members of General Vlasov's Russian Liberation
Army (ROA), as he states. ROA units had been transferred to the Western Front. The term 'Vlasov
men' was inaccurately used by the Red Army for any 'former Soviet citizen' in Wehrmacht uniform,
even *Hiwis*, or *Hilfsfreiwillige*, the most reluctant form of recruit from prison camps used for heavy
labour.

Harmonicas. Everyone has got hold of a German harmonica. It is a soldier's musical instrument, because it is the only one which can be played, even quite easily, when sitting on a jolting cart or a vehicle.

There are fourteen nationalities in the division.[10]

It's so hard to find any paper to make cigarettes that there are cases of men using their wound certificates and other documents.

Signaller Skvortsov is small, plain. He has three fiancées. One of them has sent him a photo, but this wasn't her photo. The second one has made a suit for him, size 48, while he wears 46. He shouts to the girls from the political department: 'We're all in the reserve here. Why are you chasing stars and shoulder-boards? When the war ends, you'll be left with nothing.'

A gun-layer, Guards Sergeant Konkov, was the only one to survive. He forced forty captured Germans, threatening them with his sub-machine gun, to manhandle the howitzer, and fired point-blank.

Grossman had great admiration for General Batov, the commander of the 65th Army, who had been ordered by Rokossovsky to head west for Warsaw.

Batov is not prone to Russian optimism. Routine is harmful even in victorious actions.

And like the best commanders at Stalingrad, such as Gurtiev who had made his men dig trenches, then 'steamed' them with tanks, Batov believed in realistic exercises.

Training before an offensive. 'If there's a swamp with water up to one's chest, one must train in the swamp. If there's a gully – then lie down in the gully.'

Conversation with the chief of staff of artillery. Russian artillery. Russian guns. The masterpiece of Russian artillery is the 152mm howitzer. It is a cannon and howitzer at the same time.

---

10 It is not clear whether Grossman was still with the 120th Guards Rifle Division at this stage. Nationalities refer to different state identities within the Soviet Union – Russian, Ukrainian, Kazakh, etc. Even Soviet Jews were classified in many Red Army documents and tables of statistics as a separate nationality.

Artillery suits the spirit of the Russian people. An artillery spotter is an infantryman, he brings to the gun the richness and enterprise of his character. Strength of firepower. The Germans, having started with [an emphasis on] technology at the beginning of the war, are now turning to infantry, while we, having started with infantry, are finding more and more support in technology.

German reconnaissance is poor. They fire on an area. They [also] abandon guns easily. They flee [even] before the infantry does, while our infantry usually starts running away before the artillerists.

Although the German artillery's bag-charge of nitroglycerine is more powerful than our pyroxylin, German cannon is fragile and does not last long.

On 13 July, another blow was launched at the Germans. The 1st Ukrainian Front, now commanded by Marshal Konev, attacked Lvov, the operation the Germans had been expecting before Operation Bagration. It was the first stage of a charge which would take Konev's armies right through to the Vistula, where, just over two weeks after crossing the start line, they seized the Sandomierz bridgehead on the western bank less than two hundred kilometres south of Warsaw. Meanwhile, Rokossovsky's 1st Belorussian Front charged westwards towards the Vistula north and south of Warsaw.

As the 65th Army stormed on to Polish territory, Soviet troops had mixed, if not deeply confused, feelings about the local population. This must have been especially true of those who knew how the Soviet Union had behaved towards Poland in 1939, stabbing it in the back as part of the Molotov–Ribbentrop pact. The Poles were their traditional enemy, they were largely anti-communist and reactionary in Soviet eyes, yet they were ferociously anti-German and had resisted bravely. Now they suffered looting and rape at the hands of their supposed liberators. Grossman, no doubt conscious of the Poles' reputation for anti-Semitism, may have felt ambivalent himself as he scribbled a note to prompt him later. 'About Poles. Belief in God. Platoons of believers. Platoons of non-believers. Catholic priests. Hierarchy.'

He wrote an article celebrating the liberation of Poland. Grossman had no idea of how appallingly the people of eastern Poland had been treated after the Red Army invasion of 1939, when the country was divided up between Nazi Germany and the Soviet Union. Many of the poorer peasants looked forward to the land reform promised by the Polish Communist puppet government set up in Lublin. The more educated, however, had good cause to fear that the Stalinists would again continue their policy of eradicating all those who might attempt to challenge communist hegemony.

From deciduous forests, from marshes overgrown with bright and thick grass, thousands of Polish peasants are drifting, by foot and in carts, along the deep sandy surfaces of country roads. They are carrying back to their villages the belongings that they hid from the Germans. They are driving cows, calves and horses. These crowds of peasants in felt hats and jackets, walking barefoot, these peasant women in headkerchiefs and aprons, loaded with winter clothes, pillows, blankets, mirrors, home-woven carpets, walking towards our front tank, infantry and cavalry units, are, in fact, expressing inexhaustibly the friendship and trust Polish people have for the Red Army. This countermarch of the Polish peasants driving livestock from the forests and carrying their belongings back to their houses among the thunder of Soviet artillery expresses the Polish peasants' understanding of the moral and political honour of our troops.

I asked whether people had looked forward to the Red Army's arrival. Several people said the words which I had heard before:

'We waited for it like for God!'

There's only one kind of complaint and lament that I didn't hear in Poland, only one kind of tears that I didn't see: those of Jews. There are no Jews in Poland. They have all been suffocated, killed, from elders to newly-born babies. Their dead bodies have been burned in furnaces. And in Lublin, the Polish city with the biggest Jewish population, where more than 40,000 Jews had been living before the war, I haven't seen a single child, a single woman, a single old man who could speak the language that my grandparents spoke.

Yet, as Grossman would soon find out for himself when he continued to investigate the operation of the Holocaust in Central Europe, the Poles, despite their anti-communism, were quite unlike the Ukrainians. Very few had collaborated with the Nazis.

TWENTY-FOUR
Treblinka

In July 1944, Grossman, once again accompanied by Troyanovsky, rejoined General Chuikov and his Stalingrad Army, now renamed the 8th Guards Army. Troyanovsky described the approach to the city of Lublin in eastern Poland. 'The road to Lublin is literally crammed with troops. There is much air activity on both sides. Writer Vasily Grossman and I take turns to watch the sky. It had been raining. There is water in the ditches and in bomb and shell craters, yet one still often has to hide in them from the enemy's Messerschmitts.'

Troyanovsky also recorded their meeting with General Chuikov. Grossman wasted no time in questioning the general, both of whose hands were bandaged.

'What about Lublin?' Grossman asked.

'Lublin will be liberated. It's a matter of a few hours. It's something else that I am concerned about.' We said nothing. 'Look, one could almost touch Berlin with one's hand now. And it's the dream of every Soviet warrior to take part in capturing Berlin. But I'm afraid that the [*Stavka*] leadership could change their minds and move my army to another axis. It's happened a few times before. Yet it's perfect logic and common sense. Just think: *stalingradtsy* advancing on Berlin!'

While Chuikov fretted over his army's right to glory in the advance on Berlin, his soldiers were just about to discover the camp of Majdanek, on the other side of Lublin.

The Red Army's deep thrusts into Poland in the summer of 1944 produced even more ghastly revelations than those of the massacres at Babi Yar, Berdichev and Odessa. Majdanek, a prisoner-of-war camp for captured Red Army soldiers, had been turned into a concentration and extermination camp. Prisoners from Gestapo headquarters in Lublin were executed in the camp while fighting continued in the city. On 24 July,

280

the crematorium itself was set on fire, in an attempt to cover the crimes, just before Soviet troops reached the camp.

Even though Grossman was on the spot, his rival Konstantin Simonov, who had replaced him at Stalingrad, was brought in to write about Nazi crimes there for *Krasnaya Zvezda*. Simonov, a favourite of the regime, avoided any emphasis on the Jewish identity of victims in his article. The Main Political Department of the Red Army also brought in Western journalists from Moscow, and the Kremlin set up a Special Commission for the Investigation of Crimes Committed by Germans at the Extermination Camp of Majdanek. Since many non-Jewish Poles and Russian prisoners had also suffered at Majdanek, the Soviet authorities felt able to use the camp for their own propaganda.

The site of Treblinka, further north, was reached by other troops from the 1st Belorussian Front almost at the same time as Majdanek. This was the first *Aktion-Reinhard* extermination camp to be reached, but the SS, on Himmler's direct order, had attempted to destroy all traces of its existence.[1] The Red Army managed to locate about forty survivors from the camp – some were hiding in the surrounding pine forests. Grossman, who was allowed to go there, lost no time in interviewing these survivors and also local Polish peasants. His account, a careful reconstruction from these interviews of the experience undergone by the 800,000 victims, is generally regarded as his most powerful piece of writing. Grossman instinctively seems to have sensed the main theme of his piece. How did a camp staff of roughly twenty-five SS men and around a hundred Ukrainian auxiliary *Wachmänner* manage to kill so many people? He soon discovered that they achieved their goals by deceit, followed by psychological disorientation and then sheer terror. The article was published in November in *Znamya* under the title 'The Hell Called Treblinka'. It was quoted later at the Nuremberg International Military Tribunal.

Thrift, thoroughness and pedantic cleanliness – all these are good qualities typical of many Germans. They prove effective when applied in agriculture and industry. But Hitler has put these qualities of the German character to work committing crimes against humanity. In the labour camps in Poland, the SS acted as if it was all about growing cauliflowers or potatoes.

1 Treblinka is a little over twenty kilometres south-east of Ostrów Mazowiecka, a town northwest of Warsaw on the road to Bialystok. The camp lies half a dozen kilometres from the River Bug. The other two *Aktion-Reinhard* camps were Sobibor and Belzec.

Majdanek as Grossman would have seen it in July 1944.

The camp was divided into rectangles. Barracks were built in absolutely straight lines. Birch trees were planted along the sand-covered paths. Asters and dahlias grew in the fertilised soil. Concrete pools were made for the water fowl, there were pools for washing with comfortable steps, outbuildings for the German personnel, a model bakery, a barber's shop, garage, petrol station, warehouses. The camp of Lublin-Majdanek and dozens of other labour camps where the Gestapo had planned a long and serious operation were organised according to the same formula, with little gardens, drinking fountains and concrete roads.

Camp No. 1 existed from the spring of 1941 until 23 July 1944. Surviving prisoners were annihilated when they could already hear an indistinct faraway rumble from Soviet artillery. In the early morning on the 23 July, guards and SS soldiers drank some schnapps for courage and began the liquidation of the camp. By the evening, all prisoners at the camp were killed and buried.

A carpenter from Warsaw, Max Levit, survived. He was wounded and lay under the corpses of his comrades until it was dark, and then he crawled into the forest. He told us how, when he was already

Round-up of Jews in the Warsaw ghetto.

lying in the trench, he heard the team of thirty boys from the camp sing the song 'My Motherland is Vast' just before the execution. He heard how one of the boys shouted: 'Stalin will avenge us!' He heard how the leader of the boys, the camp favourite, red-haired Leib, who fell down into the trench after the salvo, lifted himself a little and asked: 'Papa guard, you've missed. Please could you do it once again, one more time?'

Now we know the whole story about German *Ordnung* at this labour camp . . . We know about the work at the sand quarry, about those who did not fulfil the norm and were thrown into the pit from the cliff. We know about the food ration: 170 grams of bread and half a litre of slops which they called soup. We know about death from starvation, about the swollen people who were taken outside the barbed wire on wheelbarrows and shot. We know about incredible orgies of the Germans, about how they raped girls and shot their forced lovers immediately afterwards, how a drunken German cut off a woman's breast with a knife, how they threw people down from a top-floor window six metres from the ground, how a drunken company would take ten to fifteen prisoners from the barracks during the night and practise different methods of killing, without haste, shooting the

doomed men in the heart, back of the head, eye, mouth, temple
. . . We know about the chief of the camp, the Dutch German Zan
Eilen,[2] a murderer, lover of good horses, a fast rider and lecher. We
know about Stumpfe, who was seized by fits of involuntary laughter
every time he killed one of the prisoners, or when an execution was
carried out in his presence. He had the nickname 'Laughing Death'
. . . We know about the one-eyed German from Odessa, Svidersky,
whose nickname was 'Master Hammer'. He was considered the unsur-
passed specialist in 'cold' death, and it was he who had killed, in the
course of several minutes, fifteen children aged from eight to thirteen,
who had been declared unfit for work. We know about the thin SS
man Preie who looked like a Gypsy, whose nickname was 'Old Man'.
He was gloomy and reticent. He worked off his boredom by sitting
by the camp's rubbish pit and waiting for prisoners who came secretly
to eat potato peelings. He made them open their mouths and shot
into their open mouths. We know the name of professional murderers
Schwarz and Ledeke. It was they who amused themselves by shooting
at prisoners walking back from work at dusk. They killed twenty,
thirty or forty people every day. All these people had nothing human
in them. Their distorted brains, hearts and souls, words and deeds,
their habits were like a frightening caricature barely reminiscent of the
features, thoughts, feelings, habits and deeds of normal Germans.

The order in the camp, and the documentation of murders, and
love of monstrous jokes that somehow reminded one of those of
drunken German soldiers, and the singing in chorus of sentimental
songs among the puddles of blood, and the speeches with which
they constantly addressed the doomed men, and their preaching,
and religious sayings printed neatly on special pieces of paper – all
these were the monstrous dragons and reptiles that developed from
the embryo of traditional German chauvinism, arrogance, egoism,
self-assurance, pedantic care for one's own little nest, and the iron-
cold indifference to the destiny of all that is living on the Earth,
from the ferocious belief that German music, poetry, language, lawns,
toilets, sky, buildings are the greatest in the Universe . . .

But those living in Camp No. 1 knew well that there was something a hundred times more terrible than their camp. In May 1942,

2   Grossman here is referring still to Treblinka I. The first camp commandant of Treblinka II was
Obersturmführer Imfried Eberl and he was replaced in August 1942 by *Obersturmführer* Franz Stangl.
Kurt Franz was the deputy commandant.

Germans began to construct another camp, an executioner's block.

The construction proceeded rapidly. More than a thousand workers were involved. According to Himmler's plan, the building of this camp had to be kept top secret, and not a single soul should be given a chance to leave it alive . . . Guards opened fire without warning if someone passed the camp by accident a kilometre away . . . The victims who were brought in trains on a special railway line did not know what their fate would be until the last moment. Even guards who accompanied the trains were forbidden to enter the area within the second fence of the camp . . .

When the carriages were fully unloaded, the *Kommandantur* of the camp would telephone for a new train, and the empty train would go further along the railway to the quarry, where the carriages were loaded with sand [for the return journey]. The advantage of Treblinka's location became clear: trains full of victims came from all directions, from the west, east, north, and south.

The trains had come over a period of thirteen months. There were sixty carriages in each train, and there was a number written on each carriage: 150, 180 or 200. This was the number of people in the carriage. People working on the railroad and peasants kept a secret count of these trains. Peasants from the village of Wulka (the closest one to the camp) . . . said to me that there were days when six trains passed on the Sedletz line alone, and there was almost not a single day when at least one train did not pass. And the Sedletz line was only one of those which supplied Treblinka.

The camp itself, with its perimeter, warehouses for the executed people's belongings, the platform and other auxiliary premises, covers a very small area, just eighty metres by six hundred. And if one would have the slightest doubt about the fate of the millions[3] of people who had been brought here, one could have reflected that if these people had not been killed by Germans straight upon arrival, then where would they have lived? These people could have been an entire population of a small country or a small European capital city. The area of

3 Grossman, basing his estimate on the numbers of trains he had heard about and their size, produced the calculation that around three million people must have been killed here. Subsequent research has shown the figure to be between 750,000 and 880,000. The reason why Grossman's estimate was excessive is probably quite simple. He was right about the sixty carriages per train, but he does not seem to have discovered that because the station platform by the extermination camp was so short, the trains used to halt some way off, and only a section at a time was shunted to the platform. Thus it was not five trains of sixty carriages per day, but generally a single train split up into five sections.

the camp is so small that if the people who were brought here would have continued to live even a few days after their arrival, there would not be enough room behind the barbed wire for the tide of people flowing in from all over Europe, from Poland and Belorussia. For thirteen months, 396 days, the trains left loaded with sand or empty, not a single man from all those who reached Camp No. 2 ever returned . . . Cain, where are they, those whom you brought here?

The summer of 1942, the period of the fascists' great military successes, was declared a good time to carry out the second part of the scheme of physical annihilation . . . In July, the first trains started coming to Treblinka from Warsaw and Chenstohova. People were told that they were being taken to the Ukraine to work in agriculture. They were allowed to take twenty kilograms of luggage and food. In many cases, Germans had forced their victims to buy railway tickets to the station of Ober-Maidan, which was the cover name the German authorities had given to Treblinka. The point of giving Treblinka this name was that rumours about the terrible place had soon started to circulate all over Poland, and the SS men stopped using the word Treblinka when putting people on trains. However, the way people were treated on the trains left no doubt about the future fate of the passengers. At least 150, but usually 180–200 people were forced into a single freight car. During the journey, which lasted sometimes two or three days, prisoners were given no water. People were suffering so much from thirst that they drank their own urine. Guards charged one hundred zloty for a mouthful of water, and usually just took the money giving people no water in return. The people were squashed against one another, and sometimes had to stand up all the way. A number of old people with heart problems would usually die before the end of the journey, particularly during the hot days of summer. As the doors were kept shut all the time until the end of the journey, the corpses would begin to decay, poisoning the air in the wagon . . . If one of the passengers lit a match during the night, guards would start shooting at the side of the freight car . . .

Trains from other European countries arrived at Treblinka in a very different manner.[4] The people in them had never heard of

4   It is estimated by the Simon Wiesenthal Centre that some 876,000 people were murdered at Treblinka II. This figure includes 738,000 Jews from the *Generalgouvernement*, beginning with the Warsaw ghetto; 107,000 from Bialystok; 29,000 Jews from elsewhere in Europe; and 2,000 Gypsies.

Treblinka, and believed until the last minute that they were going there to work . . . These trains from European countries arrived with no guards, and with the usual staff. There were sleeping cars and restaurant cars in them. Passengers had big trunks and suitcases, as well as substantial supplies of food. The passengers' children ran out at the stations they passed and asked whether it was still a long way to Ober-Maidan . . .

It is hard to tell whether it is less terrible to go towards one's own death in the state of terrible suffering, knowing that one was getting closer and closer to one's death, or to be absolutely unaware, glance from a window of a comfortable passenger car right at the moment when people from the station at Treblinka are telephoning the camp to pass on details about the train which has just arrived and the number of people in it.

Apparently, in order to achieve the final deception for people arriving from Europe, the railroad dead-end siding was made to look like a passenger station. On the plaform at which another twenty carriages would be unloaded stood a station building with a ticket office, baggage room and a restaurant hall. There were arrows everywhere, indicating 'To Bialystok', 'To Baranovichi', 'To Volokovysk', etc. By the time the train arrived, there would be a band playing in the station building, and all the musicians were dressed well. A porter in railway uniform took tickets from the passengers and let them pass on to the square.

Three or four thousand people loaded with sacks and suitcases would go out into this square supporting the old and sick. Mothers were holding babies in their arms, older children kept close to their parents looking inquisitively at the square. There was something sinister and horrible in this square whose earth had been trampled by millions of human feet. The strained eyes of the people were quick to catch alarming little things. There were some objects abandoned on the ground, which had been swept hastily, apparently a few minutes before the party emerged – a bundle of clothes, an open case, a shaving brush, enamel saucepans. How did they get here? And why, right where the platform ends, is there no more railway and only yellow grass growing behind a three-metre-high wire fence? Where is the railway leading to Bialystok, to Sedlez, Warsaw, Volokovysk? And the new guards grin in such a strange way surveying the men adjusting their ties, neat old ladies, boys wearing navy shirts, thin girls who had managed to keep their clothes tidy throughout this journey, young mothers adjusting lovingly the blankets in which their babies are wrapped, the babies who are wrinkling their faces . . . What is there, behind this huge, six-metre-high wall, which is densely covered with yellowing pine branches and with bedding? These coverlets, too, are alarming: they are all different colours, padded, silk or satin. They are reminiscent of the eiderdowns that they, the newcomers, have brought with them. How did this bedding get here? Who brought it with them? And where are their owners? Why don't they need them any longer? And who are these people with light blue armbands? One remembers all the thoughts that have come into one's head recently, all the fears, all the rumours that were told in a whisper. No, no, this can't be true. And one drives the terrible thoughts away. People have a few moments to dwell on their fears in the square, until all the newcomers are assembled in it. There are always delays. In each transport there are the crippled, the limping, and old and sick people, who can hardly move their feet. But finally everyone is in the square.

An SS *Unteroffizier* suggests in a loud and distinct voice that the newcomers leave their luggage in the square and go to the bathhouse, with just their personal documents, valuables and the smallest possible bags with what they need for washing. Dozens of questions appear immediately in the heads of people standing in the square: whether they can take fresh underwear with them, whether they can unpack their bundles, whether the luggage of different people piled in the square might get mixed up or lost? But some strange force makes them walk, hastily and silently, asking no questions, not looking back, to the gate in a six-metre-high wall of wire camouflaged with branches.

They pass anti-tank hedgehogs, the fence of barbed wire three times the height of a man, a three-metre-wide anti-tank moat, more wire, this time thin, thrown on the ground in concertina rolls, in which the feet of a runner would get stuck like a fly's legs in a spiderweb, and another wall of barbed wire, many metres high. And a terrible feeling of doom, of being completely helpless comes over them: it's impossible to run away, or turn back, or fight. The barrels of large-calibre machine guns are looking at them from the low wooden towers. Call for help? But there are SS men and guards all around, with sub-machine guns, hand grenades and pistols. They are the power. In their hands are tanks and aircraft, lands, cities, the sky, railways, the law, newpapers, radio. The whole world is silent, suppressed, enslaved by a brown gang of bandits which has seized power. London is silent and New York, too. And only some-where on a bank of the Volga, many thousands of kilometres away, the Soviet artillery is roaring.

Meanwhile, in the square, in front of the railway station, a group of workers with sky-blue armbands is silently and efficiently unpacking the bundles, opening baskets and suitcases, unfastening the straps on the bags. The belongings of the newcomers are being sorted out and evaluated. They throw on the ground someone's carefully arranged sewing kits, balls of threads, children's underwear, undershirts, sheets, jumpers, little knives, shaving sets, bundles of letters, photographs, thimbles, bottles of perfume, mirrors, caps, *valenki* made from quilts for the cold weather, women's shoes, stock-ings, lace, pyjamas, packs of butter, coffee, jars with cocoa, prayer shawls, candleholders, books, rusks, violins, children's blocks. One needs skill to be able to sort out all these thousands of objects within minutes and appraise them. Some are selected to be sent to Germany. Others – the second-rate, the old and the repaired – have to be burned. A worker who'd make a mistake, like putting an old cardboard suitcase into a heap of leather ones selected to be sent to Germany, or throwing a pair of stockings from Paris, with a factory label on them, into a heap of old mended socks, would get into serious trouble. A worker could make only one mistake.

Forty SS men and sixty *Wachmänner* were working 'on the trans-port'.[5] This was how they referred to the first stage which I have just described: receiving a train, unloading people at the 'railway station' and getting them into the square, and watching the workers who sorted and evaluated the luggage. While doing this job, the workers often secretly shovelled into their mouths pieces of bread, sugar and sweets which they found in the bags with food. This was not allowed. It was, however, permitted to wash hands and faces with eau de Cologne and perfumes after they'd finished their work, as water was in scarce supply, and only Germans and guards could use it to wash. And while the people, who were still alive, were

5   Most reports seem to suggest that Treblinka functioned on the basis of around twenty-five SS personnel and a hundred Ukrainian *Wachmänner* auxiliary guards, but some of the ones mentioned here by Grossman could have been train guards not based at Treblinka. Grossman could not reveal the fact that the *Wachmänner* were Ukrainian. That is why he speaks of 'SS men' and 'policemen'. The workers were selected Jewish prisoners who would last a few weeks before being killed themselves.

preparing for the bathhouse, their luggage would have already been sorted, valuable things taken to the warehouse, and heaps of letters, photographs of new-born babies, brothers, fiancées, yellowed wedding announcements, all these thousands of precious objects, infinitely important for their owners, but only rubbish for the owners of Treblinka, were piled in heaps and carried to huge holes, where already lay hundreds of thousands of such letters, postcards, visiting cards, photographs, pieces of paper with children's scribbles on them. The square was swept hastily and was ready to receive a new delivery of people sentenced to death.

But things did not always go as well as I have just described. Rebellions sometimes broke out in cases when people knew about their destination. A local peasant, Skrzeminski, twice saw how people broke out of trains, knocked down the guards and rushed towards the forest. They were all killed to the last man. In one of these cases, the men were carrying four children, aged from four to six. The children, too, were killed. A peasant woman, Maria Kobus, told about similar cases. Once, she saw how sixty people who had reached the forest were killed.

But the new batch of prisoners have already reached the second square, inside the camp's fences. There is a huge barrack in this square, and another three on the right. Two of them are warehouses for clothes, the third one for shoes. Further on, in the western part of the camp, there are barracks for SS men, for guards, warehouses for food and a farmyard. Cars and an armed vehicle are standing in the yard. It all looks like an ordinary camp, just like Camp No. 1. In the south-east corner of the farmyard, there's a space fenced off with tree branches, with a booth at its front, on which is written 'Sanitorium'. Here, all frail and very sick people are separated from the crowd. A doctor in a white apron with a Red Cross bandage on his left sleeve comes out to meet them. I will tell you below in more detail about what happened at the sanitorium. There, Germans used their Walther automatic pistols to spare old people from the burden of all possible diseases.

The key to the second phase of handling the newcomers was the suppression of their will by constantly giving them short and rapid orders. These commands were given in that tone of voice, of which the German Army is so proud: the tone which proved that Germans belonged to the race of lords. The 'r', at the same time guttural and hard, sounded like a whip. 'Achtung!' carried over the crowd. In the leaden silence, the *Scharführer's*[6] voice pronounced the words, which he had learned by heart, repeating them several times a day for several months: 'Men stay here! Women and children undress in the barracks on the left!'

This was when the terrible scenes usually started, according to witnesses. That great maternal, marital, filial love told people that they were seeing each other for the last time. Handshakes, kisses, blessings, tears, brief words uttered by husky voices – people put into them all their love, all the pain, all the tenderness, all the despair. The SS psychiatrists of death knew that they had to cut these feelings off immediately, extinguish them. The psychiatrists of death knew the simple laws that prove true at all slaughterhouses of the world. This moment of separating daughters and fathers, mothers and sons, grandchildren and their grandmothers, husbands and wives was one of the most crucial. And again, *'Achtung! Achtung!'* resounds above the crowd. This is just the right moment to confuse people's minds once more, to sprinkle them with hope, telling them the regulations of death that pass for those of life. The same voice trumpets word after word:

'Women and children must take their shoes off when entering the barracks. Stockings must be put into shoes. Children's stockings into their sandals, boots and shoes. Be tidy.' And immediately the next order: 'Going to the bathhouse, you must have your documents, money, a towel and soap. I repeat . . .'

Inside the women's barracks was a hairdresser's. Naked women's hair was cut with clippers. Wigs were removed from the heads of old women. A terrible psychological phenomenon: according to the hairdressers, for the women, this death haircut was the most convincing proof of being taken to the *banya*. Girls felt their hair with their hands and sometimes asked: 'Could you cut it again here? It is not even.' Women usually relaxed after their hair was cut, and almost all emerged from the barracks with a piece of soap and a folded towel. Some young women cried, mourning their beautiful long plaits. What were the haircuts for? In order to deceive them? No, Germany needed this hair. The hair was a raw material. I've asked many people, what did Germans do with these heaps of hair cut from the heads of the living dead? All the witnesses told me that the huge heaps of black, blonde hair, curls and plaits were

6   SS rank roughly equivalent to that of staff sergeant.

disinfected, pressed into sacks and sent to Germany. All the witnesses confirmed that the hair was sent in the sacks to Germany. How was it used? No one could answer this question. Only Kon stated in his written evidence that the hair was used by the navy for stuffing mattresses or making hawsers for submarines. I think that this answer requires additional clarification.

Men undressed in the yard. Usually, Germans selected 150–300 strong men from the first lot to arrive in the morning. They were used to bury corpses and were generally killed on the second day. Men had to undress very quickly and tidily, leaving their shoes and socks in order, folding their underwear, jackets and trousers. Clothes and shoes were sorted by the second team of workers, who wore red armbands that distinguished them from those working 'on the transport'.

Clothing and shoes considered suitable for dispatch to Germany were immediately taken to the warehouse. All metal and fabric labels had to be removed from them carefully. The remaining things were burned or buried in the ground. The feeling of anxiety grew every minute. There was a strange, disquieting smell, which was at times overpowered by the smell of chlorine. Huge quantities of importunate flies seemed strange, too. Where were they all coming from, here, among pines and the trampled earth? People were breathing noisily, afraid, shuddering, peering at every insignificant little object that they thought could explain, help understand, lift slightly the curtain of secret about the fate that lay ahead for them. And why are gigantic excavators rattling so loudly there, further to the south?

A new procedure would then begin. Naked people were led to the cash office and asked to submit their documents and valuables. And once again, a frightening, hypnotising voice would shout: 'Achtung! Achtung!' . . . Concealing valuables was punishable by death . . . 'Achtung! Achtung!' A Scharführer was sitting in a little booth knocked up from timber. SS men and Wachmänner were standing next to him. By the booth stood wooden boxes, into which the valuables had to be thrown: a box for banknotes, a box for coins, a box for watches, rings, earrings and brooches, for bracelets. And documents, which no one on earth any longer needed, were thrown on the ground – these were the documents of naked people who would be lying in the earth an hour later. But gold and valuables were subject to a careful sorting – dozens of jewellers determined the pureness of metal, value of jewels, water of the diamonds. And an amazing thing was that the swine utilised everything, even paper and fabric – anything which could be useful to anyone, was important and useful to these swine. Only the most precious thing in the world, a human life, was trampled by their boots.

Here, at the cash office, came the turning point. The tormenting of people with lies ended; the torture of not knowing, a fever that threw them within minutes from hope to despair, from visions of life to visions of death . . . And when the time came for the last stage of robbing the living dead, the Germans changed their style of treating their victims abruptly. They tore rings off their victims' fingers, tore earrings out of their earlobes. At this stage, the conveyor executioner's block required a new principle for functioning efficiently. This is why the word 'Achtung!' was replaced by another one, flapping, hissing: 'Schneller! Schneller! Schneller!' Quick, hurry up! Run into the non-existence!

We know from the cruel reality of recent years that a naked person immediately loses the strength to resist, to struggle against his fate. When stripped, a person immediately loses the strength of the instinct to live and one accepts one's destiny like a fate. A person who used to have an intransigent thirst for life becomes passive and indifferent. But to reassure themselves, the SS men applied additionally at this final stage of the conveyor execution work the method of monstrous stupefaction, of sending people into the state of complete psychological, spiritual shock. How did they do that? By applying a senseless, illogical cruelty, suddenly, sharply. Naked people who had lost everything, but still were a thousand times more human than the beasts in German uniform were still breathing, watching, thinking, their hearts were still beating. The guards knocked pieces of soap and towels out of their hands and lined them up in rows, five people in each. 'Hände hoch! Marsch! Schneller! Schneller! Schneller!'

They stepped into a straight alley, with flowers and fir trees planted along it. It was 120 metres long and two metres wide and led to the place of execution. There was wire on both sides of this alley, and guards in black uniforms and SS men in grey ones were standing there shoulder to shoulder. The road was sprinkled with white sand, and those who were walking in front with their hands up could see the fresh prints of bare feet in this loose sand: small women's feet, very small children's ones, those left by old people's feet. These ephemeral footprints in the sand were all that was left of thousands of people who had walked here recently, just like the four thousand that were walking now, like the other thousands who would walk here two hours later, who were now waiting for their turn at the railway branch in the forest. People who'd left their footprints had walked here just like those who walked here yesterday, and ten days ago, and a hundred days ago, like they would walk tomorrow, and fifty days later, like people did throughout the thirteen hellish months of Treblinka's existence.

The Germans called this alley 'The Road of No Return'. A little man, who was making faces all the time and whose family name was Sukhomil, shouted with grimaces, in a deliberately broken German: 'Children, children! *Schneller, schneller!* The water's getting cold in the bathhouse. *Schneller, Kinder, schneller!*' And he exploded with laughter, squatted, danced. People, their hands still raised, walked in silence between the two lines of guards, under the blows of sticks, sub-machine-gun butts, rubber truncheons. Children had to run to keep up with the adults. Speaking about this last, sorrowful passage, all witnesses mentioned the atrocities of one humanlike creature, an SS man called Zepf. He specialised in killing children. This beast, who possessed a massive physical strength, would suddenly seize a child out of the crowd, and either hit the child's head against the ground waving the child like a cudgel, or tear the child in two halves.

Zepf's work was important. It added to the psychological shock of the doomed people, and showed how the illogical cruelty was able to crush people's will and consciousness. He was a useful screw in the great machine of the fascist state.

And we should all be terrified, but not by the nature that gives birth to such degenerates. There are lots of monstrosities in the organic world – Cyclops, creatures with two heads, as well as the corresponding terrible spiritual monstrosities and perversities. It is another thing that is terrible: these creatures that had to be isolated and studied like psychiatric phenomena were living in a certain country as active and useful citizens.

The journey from the 'cash office' to the place of execution took sixty to seventy seconds. People, urged on by the blows and deafened by the shouts '*Schneller! Schneller!*', reached the third square and stopped for a moment, startled. In front of them was a beautiful stone building decorated with wood, looking like an ancient temple. Five wide stone steps led to the low, but very wide, massive, beautiful ornate door. There were flowers growing by the entrance, and flowerpots stood there. But all around there was chaos, one could see piles of freshly dug earth everyhere. A vast excavator was throwing out tons of sandy yellow soil, grinding its steel jaws, and the dust it raised was hanging between the earth and the sun. The rattling of the machine digging from morning till evening, the enormous trench graves, mixed with a mad barking of dozens of Alsatian guard dogs.

There were narrow-gauge railway lines on both sides of the death building, along which men in baggy overalls brought dumper trucks. The wide door of the death house opened slowly, and two assistants of the chief, whose name was Schmidt, appeared by the entrance. They were sadists and maniacs, one of them tall, about thirty years old, with broad shoulders, a dark-skinned excited face and black hair, the other one younger, short, with brown hair and waxy, yellow cheeks. We know the names and surnames of these traitors to mankind. The tall one was holding a massive, metre-long gas tube in his hand, the other one was armed with a sabre.

At this moment, the SS men would unleash the trained dogs, who threw themselves on the crowd and tore the naked bodies with their teeth. SS men were beating people with sub-machine-gun butts, urging on petrified women, and shouting wildly: '*Schneller! Schneller!*' Schmidt's assistants at the entrance to the building drove people through the open doors into the gas chambers.

By this time, one of Treblinka's commandants, Kurt Franz, would appear by the building with his dog, Barry, on a leash. He had specially trained his dog to jump at the doomed people and tear their private parts. Kurt Franz had made a good career at the camp. Having started as a junior SS *Unteroffizier*, he was promoted to the relatively high rank of *Untersturmführer*.[7]

Stories of the living dead of Treblinka, who had until the last minute kept not just the image of humans but the human soul as well, shake one to the bottom of one's heart and make it impossible to sleep. The stories of women trying to save their sons and committing magnificent doomed feats, of young mothers who hid their babies in heaps of blankets. I've heard the stories of ten-year-old girls,

7 *Untersturmführer* in the SS was equivalent to lieutenant in the army. Kurt Franz was in fact Stangl's deputy.

who comforted their sobbing parents with a heavenly wisdom, about a boy who shouted when entering the gas chamber: 'Russia will take revenge! Mama, don't cry!'

I was told about dozens of doomed people who began to struggle. I was told about a young man who stabbed an SS officer with a knife, about a young man who had been brought here from the rebellious Warsaw ghetto. He had miraculously managed to hide a grenade from the Germans and threw it into the crowd of executioners when he was already naked. We were told about the battle between a group of rebels and guards and the SS that lasted all night. Shots and explosions of grenades were resounding until the morning, and when the sun rose, the whole square was covered with the bodies of dead rebels . . . We were told about the tall girl who snatched a carbine from the hands of a *Wachmann* on 'The Road of No Return' and fought back. The tortures and execution she was subjected to were terrible. Her name is unknown, and nobody can pay it the respect it deserves.

Inhabitants of the village of Wulka, the one closest to Treblinka, tell that sometimes the screams of women who were being killed were so terrible that the whole village would lose their heads and rush to the forest, in order to escape from these shrill screams that carried through tree trunks, the sky and the earth. Then, the screams would suddenly stop, and there was a silence before a new series of screams, as terrible as the ones before, shrill, boring through the bones, through the skulls and the souls of those who heard them. This happened three or four times every day.

I asked one of the captured butchers, Sh., about these screams. He explained that women started to scream at the moment when the dogs were unleashed and the whole group of prisoners were urged into the house of death. 'They could see their death coming, and beside that it was very crowded there. They were beaten terribly, and dogs were tearing their bodies.'

A sudden silence came when the doors of the gas chambers were closed, and the screams started again when a new batch of prisoners was brought to the building. This happened two, three, four, sometimes five times a day. This was a special conveyor belt to the executioners' block.

It took some time for Treblinka to be developed into the industrial complex which I have described here. It grew gradually, developing new workshops. At first, three small gas chambers were built. While their construction was still going on, several trains arrived, and the prisoners they brought had to be killed with cold steel – axes, hammers and bludgeons – as the chambers were not ready yet, and the SS men didn't want to start shooting because the noise would reveal Treblinka's purpose. The first three concrete chambers were five metres by five metres and 190 centimetres high. Each of them had two doors: one to let the people in by, and the other one to pull out the corpses. This second door was very wide, about 2.5 metres. These three chambers were built side by side on the same foundation.

The three chambers, however, did not have sufficient capacity to satisfy Berlin. Immediately after they began operating, construction commenced on the building which I described above. Treblinka's leaders were very satisfied and proud to have outstripped by such a margin all of the Gestapo's death-factory capacity. Seven hundred prisoners worked for five weeks to build the new death factory. When the construction was in full swing, an expert arrived from Berlin with his crew to install the chambers. The ten new chambers were located symmetrically on both sides of a broad concrete corridor . . . Each of them had two doors . . . The doors for corpses opened on to special platforms which were constructed on both sides of the building. Lines of narrow-gauge railway led to the platforms. The corpses were heaped on to the platforms and immediately loaded on to railway cars and taken to the huge moat-graves, which colossal excavators were digging day and night. The floor in the chambers sloped from the corridor down towards the platforms. This made the work of unloading the chambers considerably quicker (corpses were unloaded from the old chambers in a primitive fashion: carried on stretchers or hauled by straps). The new chambers were each seven metres by eight metres. The total floor area of the new chambers was now 460 square metres, and the total area of all gas chambers in Treblinka reached 635 square metres.

At this stage, Grossman worked through his calculations on the number of people killed in each batch, and extrapolated his figures to estimate that three million had been killed in ten months.

Will we be able to find in ourselves enough courage to reflect on what our people were feeling, what they were going through during their last moments in those chambers? We know that they were silent . . . In the terribly crowded state, which was bone-crushing, their chests were unable to breathe, they were standing squashed against one another, with the last sticky death-sweat pouring down, they were standing there as one body.

What pictures flashed in the glazed dying eyes? Those of childhood, of the happy peaceful days, or those of the last harsh journey? The grinning face of the SS soldier in the first square in front of the railway station? 'So this is why he was laughing.' The consciousness is waning, the minute of the terrible last suffering has come . . . No, it is impossible to imagine . . . The dead bodies were standing, gradually cooling down. Witnesses said that children were able to breathe for a longer time than the grown-ups. Schmidt's assistants looked into the peepholes twenty to twenty-five minutes later. The time came to open the door of chambers leading to the platforms. Prisoners in overalls would start the unloading. As the floor sloped towards the platforms, the bodies fell out by themselves. People who were unloading the chambers told me that the faces of dead people were very yellow, and a little blood ran from the noses and mouths of about 70 per cent of them. Physiologists can explain this.

The corpses were examined by SS men. If someone was discovered to be still alive, was moaning or moved, this person was shot with a pistol. Then the crews armed with dentist's tongs would set to work wrenching platinum and gold teeth out of dead people's mouths. The teeth were then sorted according to their value, packed into boxes and sent to Germany. Apparently, it was easier to wrench out the teeth of dead people than of those still alive.

The corpses were loaded on to the cars and taken to the enormous moat-graves. There, they were laid down in rows, closely, side by side. The moat would be left unfilled with earth, waiting . . . And meanwhile, when workers would have just begun unloading the gas chamber, the 'transport' *Scharführer* would receive a short order by telephone. The *Scharführer* would then blow a whistle, a signal for the engine driver, and another twenty carriages were slowly drawn to the platform with its simulation of a railway station called 'Ober-Maidan' . . . The excavators were working, roaring, digging day and night new moats, hundreds of metres long. And the moats stood there unfilled, waiting. They did not have to wait long.

Himmler's victims.

Himmler visited Treblinka early in 1943 at the end of the winter. He inspected the camp and one of the people who saw him there said that he went up to a huge pit and looked into it for a long time without speaking. The Reichsführer SS flew away the same day in his personal plane. Just before leaving, Himmler gave the commanders of the camp an order that confused everyone: *Hauptsturmführer* Baron von Perein, and his deputy, Korol, and Captain Franz were immediately to begin burning the buried corpses, and burn them all, to the last corpse, to take ash and cinder out of the camp and disperse them in fields and roads. There were already millions of corpses in the earth by that time, and this task seemed extremely difficult and complicated. The order was also given not to bury the dead any longer, but to burn them at once. Why did Himmler fly there for this inspection and personally give this categorical order? There could only be one possible explanation for this: the Red Army's victory at Stalingrad.

At first, the burning did not go very well. The corpses did not want to burn. It was noticed, however, that women's corpses burned better than men's, and the workers tried to use them to make men's corpses burn better. Large amounts of petrol and oil were used to burn the corpses, but this was expensive, and did not work very well. It all seemed like a blind alley. But a solution was soon found. A thickset man of about fifty arrived, a specialist and expert.

Construction of furnaces began under his guidance. These were furnaces of a special type. An excavator dug a trench which was 250–300 metres long, 20–25 metres wide and 5 metres deep. Ferro-concrete columns were installed on the bottom of the moat in three rows at equal distance from one another. They provided the foundation for steel beams along the rectangular pit. Rails were placed on these beams at a distance of five to seven centimetres from one another. This was the structure of the gigantic bars of the cyclopic furnaces. A new narrow-gauge railway was built which led from the moat-graves to the moat-furnace. Another furnace was built soon, and then a third one of the same size. Onto each furnace-grill, 3,500–4,000 corpses were loaded simultaneously.[8]

People who took part in burning the corpses say that the furnaces were reminiscent of gigantic volcanoes. A terrible heat burned the faces of the workers, flames flew eight to ten metres into the air, pillars of thick and greasy smoke reached the sky and hung in the air in a heavy immobile cloud. At night, local people from surrounding villages saw these flames from anything up to forty kilometres away. They rose taller than the pine forest around the camp. The smell of burned human meat filled the whole surrounding area. When the wind blew towards the Polish camp three kilometres away, the people there were suffocated with a terrible stench. Some eight hundred prisoners were kept busy burning corpses. This

---

8 These were nicknamed the 'roasts'.

monstrous workshop operated day and night for eight months and couldn't cope with the millions of buried human corpses, as new transports kept coming all the time.

Trains arrived from Bulgaria, and the SS and *Wachmänner* were happy about them, as the tricked people, who had no idea of their fate, had brought many valuables, and lots of tasty things, including white bread. After them, trains began to arrive from Grodno and Bialystok, then, from the rebellious Warsaw ghetto. A group of Gypsies came from Bessarabia, about two hundred men and eight hundred women and children. The Gypsies came on foot, with strings of horse-driven carts following them. They too had been tricked. They arrived escorted by only two guards, who themselves had absolutely no idea that they had brought people to die. Witnesses say that Gypsy women clasped their hands when they saw the beautiful building of the gas chamber, and never suspected what their fate would be. The Germans found this particularly amusing.

Terrible torments awaited those who arrived from the Warsaw ghetto. Women and children were separated from the crowd and taken to the places where corpses were burned instead of to the gas chambers. Mothers who went mad with terror were forced to lead their children between the glowing furnace bars on which thousands of dead bodies were writhing in flames and smoke, where corpses were squirming and jerking in the heat as if they had became alive again, where stomachs of dead pregnant women cracked from the heat, and unborn babies burned on the open wombs of the mothers. This sight could render even the strongest person insane.

It is infinitely hard even to read this. The reader must believe me, it is as hard to write it. Someone might ask: 'Why write about this, why remember all that?' It is the writer's duty to tell this terrible truth, and it is the civilian duty of the reader to learn it. Everyone who would turn away, who would shut his eyes and walk past would insult the memory of the dead. Everyone who does not know the truth about this would never be able to understand with what sort of enemy, with what sort of monster, our Red Army started on its own mortal combat.

The SS men began to feel bored in Treblinka. The procession of the doomed people to gas chambers had ceased to excite them. It became routine. When the burning of corpses started, the SS men spent hours by the furnaces, the new sight amused them. The expert who had come from Germany was walking among the furnaces from morning till night, always excited and talkative. People say that no one ever saw him frowning or even serious, the smile never left his face. When corpses fell onto the furnace bars, he used to say of them: 'Innocent, innocent.' This was his favourite catchphrase.

Sometimes the SS men organised a kind of picnic by the furnaces: they would sit down on the lee side, drink wine, eat and watch the flames. The sick quarters were also re-equipped. A round trench was dug with furnace bars installed on its bottom, on which the corpses were burning. Low little benches were made that stood around the trench, as if it were a stadium. They stood so close to the edge that those who sat on them were sitting right above the trench. Sick people and frail old people were brought here, and then 'medical assistants' would make them sit on benches facing the bonfire of human bodies. When they had had enough of this sight, the cannibals shot at the grey heads and the bent backs of people sitting down. Those killed and wounded would fall into the bonfire.

We have never had a high regard for unsubtle German humour, but hardly anyone on this planet could have imagined what the SS humour in Treblinka was like, what the SS amused themselves with, and what jokes were made. They organised football matches for the doomed men, organised a chorus of the doomed, dances of the doomed . . . There was even a special hymn, 'Treblinka', written for them, which included the following words:

'*Für uns gibt heute nur Treblinka*
Die unser Schiksal ist . . .'[9]

People with blood pouring from their wounds were forced to learn idiotic German sentimental songs just a few minutes before they died:

'*Ich bruch das Blumelein*
und schenkte es dem schönste
geliebste Madelein . . .'[10]

The chief commandant of the camp selected several children from one of the transports, killed their parents, dressed the children in the best clothes, gave them lots of sweets, played with them, and

9 'For us there is now only Treblinka which is our fate . . .'
10 'I pluck the little flower / and give it to the loveliest / most adored young girl . . .'

then gave orders to kill them a few days later when he became bored with this game. One of the main amusements were the night rapes and torture of beautiful young women and girls, who were selected from each transport of prisoners. In the morning, the rapists themselves would take them to the gas chamber.

All the witnesses remember one feature which SS men in Treblinka had in common: they loved theoretical constructions, philosophising. They all indulged in making speeches in front of the prisoners. They boasted and explained the great significance for the future of what was taking place in Treblinka. They were all deeply and sincerely convinced of the importance and rightness of their work.

They did gymnastics – they passionately cared for their own health and the convenience of their everyday life. They made gardens and flower beds around their barracks. They went for holidays in Germany several times a year, because their chiefs thought that their work was very bad for their health and wanted to protect them. Back at home, they would walk around with their heads up, proudly.

The summer of 1943 was unusually hot in this place. There was no rain, no cloud, no wind for many weeks. The work on burning the corpses went on at full speed. The furnaces had been glowing for six months day and night, but only a little more than a half of the corpses had been burned. Prisoners who had to burn the corpses couldn't stand the terrible moral torment, and fifteen to twenty of them committed suicide every day. Many of them sought death, deliberately violating the regulations.

'It was a luxury to get a bullet,' said Kosezky, a doctor who escaped from the camp. People said to me that it was many times more terrible to live in Treblinka than to die there. The cinder and ash from the burned corpses were loaded on to railway cars and taken outside the camp's fencing. Peasants from the village of Wulka, whom the Germans had conscripted, put the cinder and ash on carts and dispersed them along the road going past the death camp to the Polish punishment camp. Child prisoners with spades distributed the ashes evenly on the road. Sometimes they found in it golden coins and melted gold teeth. The children were called 'children from the black road'. The road became black from the ash, like a crêpe bandage. The wheels of vehicles made a special rustling sound on it, and when I was driven on this road, I could hear this mournful rustle, soft like a shy complaint . . .

In the song 'Treblinka', which the Germans forced the eight hundred men who worked burning the corpses to sing, there were words appealing to the prisoners to be obedient, and promising them in return a 'little, little happiness, of which they would catch a glimpse for just one minute'.

There was one happy day in the hell of Treblinka . . . The prisoners planned an uprising. They had nothing to lose. They all had been sentenced to death. Every day of their present existence was a day of suffering and torture. Germans would have had no mercy for them, witnesses of terrible crimes, they would all end up in one of the gas chambers and be replaced by new men. Only a few dozen men survived in Treblinka for weeks or months, instead of days. These were qualified specialists – carpenters, stonemasons, tailors, hairdressers. They were the ones who formed a committee for the uprising. They didn't want to escape until they had destroyed Treblinka.

A suffocating heatwave settled at the end of July. When graves were opened, steam began to rise from them as if they were gigantic boilers. A monstrous stench and heat were killing people – the emaciated men carrying the corpses sometimes fell dead on the furnace bars. Billions of heavy flies who had had too much to eat were crawling on the ground and humming in the air.

A decision was made to start the uprising on 2 August. The signal was to be a revolver shot.[11] New flames soared into the sky, this time not the heavy greasy flames of the burning corpses, but the bright, hot and violent flames of a fire. The camp buildings were burning . . . A thunder of shots was heard, machine guns started to fire from captured, rebel towers. The air was shaken with rattling and cracking, the whistling of bullets became louder than the humming of carrion flies. Axes stained with red blood began to flicker in the air. On 2 August, the evil blood of SS men poured on to the soil of the hellish Treblinka . . . They were all confused, they forgot about the system of Treblinka's defence that had been

11 The revolt was mainly organised by Zelo Bloch, a Jewish lieutenant from the Czech Army. The uprising began early, because an SS guard became suspicious. He was shot but this triggered the general action before most of the weapons had been removed from the armoury, to which the rebels had managed to obtain a duplicate key.

prepared so devilishly well, forgot about the deadly fire that had been organised in advance, forgot about their weapons.

While Treblinka was ablaze and the rebels broke through the fences, saying a silent goodbye to the ashes of their people, SS and police units were rushed in from all directions to hunt them down. Hundreds of police dogs were sent after them. German aircraft were sent up. Battles went on in the forest and in the marshes. Very few of the rebels survived, but what difference does it make? They died fighting, with weapons in their hands.[12]

Treblinka ceased to exist after 2 August. The Germans finished burning the remaining corpses, destroyed stone buildings, removed wire, burned the wooden barracks that had not been burned by the rebels. The installations of the death factory were blown up or loaded onto railway wagons and taken away. Excavators were either blown up or taken away, the numberless pits were filled with earth, the railway station was destroyed to the last brick, the railway line was disassembled and the sleepers removed. Lupins were sown on the territory of the camp, and Streben, a settler, built his little house there. Now, even this house does not exist, it has been burned.[13]

What did the Germans intend to achieve by all this? To conceal the murder? But how on earth would that be possible? Himmler has no power any longer over his accomplices: they lower their heads, their trembling fingers play with the edge of their jackets, and they recount in muffled, monotonous voices the story of their crimes, which sounds insane and delirious, incredible. A Soviet officer, with the green ribbon of the Stalingrad medal is writing the murderers' evidence down, page after page. A guard is standing at the door, his lips pressed together. He, too, has the Stalingrad medal on his chest, and his dark thin face is stern.

We enter the camp and walk on the ground of Treblinka. Little pods of lupins burst open from the slightest touch, or burst open themselves with a light tinkle; millions of little seeds fall on the ground. The sound of the falling seeds, the tinkling of the opening pods, blend together into a single melody, sad and quiet. It seems

12 It is estimated that about 750 prisoners managed to escape through the wire, but only seventy of them lived to see liberation a year later.
13 The family brought in to make the place look like a farm was Ukrainian.

as if it is a funeral ringing of little bells coming to us right from the depth of the earth, barely heard, mournful, broad, calm.

The earth is throwing out crushed bones, teeth, clothes, papers. It does not want to keep secrets. And the objects are climbing out from the earth, from its unhealing wounds. Here they are, half ruined by decay, shirts of the murdered people, their trousers, shoes, cigarette cases which have grown green, little wheels from watches, penknives, shaving brushes, candleholders, a child's shoes with red pompons, towels with Ukrainian embroidery, lace underwear, scissors, thimbles, corsets, bandages. And a little further on, heaps of plates and dishes have made their way to the surface. And further on – it is as if someone's hand is pushing them up into the light, from the bottomless bulging earth – emerge the things that the Germans had tried to bury, Soviet passports, notebooks with Bulgarian writing in them, photographs of children from Warsaw and Vienna, letters scribbled by children, a book of poetry, a prayer copied on a yellowed piece of paper, food ration cards from Germany . . . And everywhere there are hundreds of little scent bottles, green, pink, blue . . . A terrible smell of putrefaction hangs over everything, the smell that neither fire, nor sun, rains, snow and winds could dispel. And hundreds of little forest flies are crawling on the half-rotted things, papers and photographs.

We walk on and on across the bottomless unsteady land of Treblinka, and then suddenly we stop. Some yellow hair, wavy, fine and light, glowing like brass, is trampled into the earth, and blonde curls next to it, and then heavy black plaits on the light-coloured sand, and then more and more. Apparently, these are the contents of one – just one sack of hair – which hadn't been taken away. Everything is true. The last, lunatic hope that everything was only a dream is ruined. And lupin pods are tinkling, tinkling, little seeds are falling, as if a ringing of countless little bells is coming from under the ground. And one feels as if one's heart could stop right now, seized with such sorrow, such grief, that a human being cannot possibly stand it.

Not surprisingly, Grossman himself found it very hard to stand. He collapsed from nervous exhaustion, stress and nausea on his return to Moscow in August. Ehrenburg invited round the French journalist Jean Cathala to give him details of what had emerged from the liberation of Majdanek and Treblinka. Grossman was apparently too ill to leave his bed and join them.

PART FIVE

Amid the Ruins of the Nazi World

1945

TWENTY-FIVE

Warsaw and Łódź

The Red Army, after the massive operations during the summer of 1944, which had forced the Wehrmacht back from the Beresina to the Vistula, needed time to recover and re-equip. Yet at the end of July, as Rokossovsky's 1st Belorussian Front reached the eastern suburbs of Warsaw, Soviet radio stations had called on the Poles to rise in revolt behind German lines. But Stalin had no intention of coming to their aid or even letting the Western Allies help them with air drops. This was because the revolt was planned and led by the Armia Krajowa – the Home Army – which owed allegiance to the émigré government in London, and not to the Committee of National Liberation, the puppet Communist organisation set up in Lublin. The tragic, doomed heroism of the Warsaw uprising lasted from 1 August until 2 October. There is no mention of it in Grossman's notebooks, which might well reflect the complete news blackout imposed by the Soviet authorities. After the Germans had crushed the rising, they systematically destroyed a large part of the city, as Grossman would see.

Preparations for the next leap forward began in October 1944. The *Stavka* plan was a series of three simultaneous assaults with four million men. In January 1945 two Soviet fronts would attack East Prussia from the south and the east, while Marshal Zhukov, who had now taken over the 1st Belorussian Front, and Marshal Konev, with his 1st Ukrainian Front, would attack western Poland and Silesia from their bridgeheads across the Vistula south of Warsaw. The difficulties of bringing up munitions and supplies for such a vast operation had been increased by the German scorched earth policy, including the deliberate destruction of Soviet railway systems as they withdrew. Grossman appears to have left Moscow in mid-January 1945 to rejoin the 1st Belorussian Front. His vehicle stopped in Kaluga, some 250 kilometres south-west of Moscow.

An old man in Kaluga, reasonable and prone to philosophising like all watchmen, said when he was shutting the gate of the petrol station behind our [Jeep]: 'There you are, heading for Warsaw. The war's now going on over there, and there had been a time one winter when I had to open the tanks and let petrol pour into ditches. That was before the Germans came to Kaluga. Ten years will pass and boys will be learning about it at school and ask me: "Is it true, Dedka, that the Germans got to Kaluga?"'

Operation Bagration the summer before had been extraordinarily successful, but the new offensive soon proved to be the most rapid advance ever launched by the Red Army. Zhukov and Konev, spurred on by Stalin, concentrated on a speed of advance, following the break-through, which would totally disorientate the German Army. They were greatly helped in this by Hitler's insistence that every order should be checked with him first, thus allowing no freedom of action for commanders on the spot. And by the time they obtained a decision from Berlin, the situation on the ground might have changed out of all recognition.

Grossman, never forgetting the terrible humiliations of 1941, gained a fierce joy from the supremacy of the Red Army. Rather as he had been fascinated by the snipers in Stalingrad, he was now drawn to new heroes, the tank troops who exploited the breakouts into the German rear and never allowed their enemy a chance to regroup.

Tank troops. Some tankists have come from the cavalry, but tankists are at the same time artillerists, and also mechanics. They've inherited cavalry daring and the culture of the artillery. Mechanics are even more skilled than artillerists. If you want to find a front commander who is an expert in both tanks and artillery, you should get a former tankist who has been promoted to an all-arms commander.

The main problem, especially in a headlong advance outrunning supply and maintenance units, was carrying out repairs to keep tanks going and finding replacement parts. Often vehicles had ruthlessly to be canni-balised.

The 1st Belorussian Front's attack began on 14 January 1945 from the Magnuszew and Pulawy bridgeheads. The German line was broken open by the 5th Shock Army and the 8th Guards Army, the old 62nd Army from Stalingrad, still commanded by General Chuikov. The main objec-tive was to cross the River Pilica, a tributary of the Vistula, to enable the 1st and 2nd Guards Tank Armies to break out and smash the German rear. Colonel Gusakovsky, a Hero of the Soviet Union twice over whom Grossman came to know well, did not wait for bridging equipment. He later told Grossman how he ordered his tanks to smash the ice with gunfire, then drive across the river bed. It was terrifying for the drivers.

> 'Crossing of the Pilica. We blew up the ice and crossed over on the river bed, thus saving two to three hours. All that ice rose in a gigantic mountain in front of the tanks and crashed down making a terrible noise. When tanks are in pursuit across rough terrain, infantry armed with the *Panzerfaust*[1] is the greatest danger of all . . . We were moving extremely fast; there were days when we advanced 115–120 kilometres in twenty-four hours. Our tanks moved faster than trains to Berlin.'

On the right, the 47th Guards Tank Brigade, reinforced with troops from other arms, raced forward to capture an airfield south of Sochaczew, a key town due west of Warsaw. Soviet fighter regiments began operating from this new base within twenty-four hours.

> New features in our advance. Our tankists capture German airfields, this gives our aviation an opportunity to support mobile groups. A new development in the interaction of infantry with self-propelled artillery. The infantry has developed a passion for self-propelled guns, [they] don't feel naked any longer.

As soon as the 1st Belorussian Front attacked from its bridgeheads, the 47th Army on its right wing advanced to encircle Warsaw, while the 1st Polish Army, under Soviet control, advanced into the suburbs. The German commander, who had only four battalions of very unfit garrison troops, decided to evacuate the Polish capital. Hitler was overcome with rage and ordered that the Gestapo should interrogate the officers involved, including General Guderian, the chief of staff of the OKH directing all Eastern Front operations.

Soviet troops entered a city that was almost entirely destroyed and depopulated. Out of a pre-war population of 1,310,000, only 162,000 inhabitants remained. One officer described it as little more than 'ruins and ashes covered by snow'. Grossman was among the first journalists

---

1 The *Panzerfaust* was a shoulder-launched rocket propelled grenade produced in huge quantities at the end of the war by the Nazi war industry as a cheap anti-tank weapon.

to enter. Not surprisingly, one of the first places he wanted to visit was the Warsaw ghetto.

On 15 October 1941, the Nazis had sealed off the ghetto and used it as a concentration camp for Polish and foreign Jews. Up to 380,000 Jews had been held there at one time, before they were sent to their deaths. The majority had been dispatched from the *Umschlagplatz* – the railroad sidings on the north-eastern edge of the ghetto – to Treblinka. On 19 April 1943, when there were just 40,000 Jews left in the ghetto, a substantial minority, with some weapons provided by the Polish underground outside, rose in revolt. They were mercilessly crushed. The most astonishing part of the story is that they managed to keep up the fight against the SS units for nearly two months.

For Grossman, entering Warsaw was clearly an emotional moment, which he recorded first in his notebook, and then worked up in an article for *Krasnaya Zvezda*.

Warsaw! The first phrase I heard in Warsaw, when I had climbed up on to a destroyed bridge, came from a soldier turning his pocket inside out: 'Here,' he said, 'I've even got a bit of dried bread.'

Ortenberg described Grossman's arrival in Warsaw slightly differently. The Vistula had not frozen completely. There were patches of ice and water. Grossman left his vehicle in Praga, a suburb of Warsaw on the east bank of the Vistula, and started making his way between two big patches of water towards two surviving piers of the Poniatowsky Bridge. At last he reached a concrete foundation. Two middle-aged soldiers lowered a light fire ladder for Grossman from the eight-metre-high pier. It was still two metres short of the ice. The soldiers then tied a rope to the ladder and lowered it. Grossman started climbing up this dangerous contraption, which was being rocked by the wind. Grossman thanked the soldiers for their help and walked into the city.

'It's the first time in my life,' he said, 'that I've used a fire ladder to enter a city.' The change in Grossman and in other correspondents, who had been civilians before the war, was commented upon by Ilya Ehrenburg. 'It is amazing how people changed at the front! In peacetime no one could have mistaken Grossman for a military man, but at the front he gave the impression of an ordinary commander of an infantry regiment.'

Along the crumpled and explosion-twisted steel lace of a blown-up bridge, we approached a tall stone pier on the left bank of the

Vistula. The sentry, an old Red Army soldier, was standing by a small fire he had made on the quay. He said good-naturedly to the sub-machine-gunner who was standing near him: 'See, brother, what a good bit of dried bread I've found in my pocket.' These were the first words that I heard in Warsaw. And later I learned that this man in a grey crumpled greatcoat was one of those who had saved Moscow in that terrible year [of 1941] and marched 12,000 kilometres as his part in that great task, the war of liberation.

When we arrived, liberated Warsaw was looking majestic and sad, even tragic. City streets were filled with heaps of broken brick. The wide squares and straight streets in the central area of the city were covered by a network of intricate, meandering little paths, which reminded me of those made by hunters in the dense forests and in the mountains. Its inhabitants, who were now returning to Warsaw, had to climb over the piles of brick; there were only a few streets where vehicles and carts could get through.

A file of old and young men in crumpled hats, berets, autumn coats or macintoshes were walking and pushing in front of them little handcarts with thick tyres, loaded with bundles, bags and suitcases. Girls and young women were walking blowing on their frozen fingers and looking at the ruins with sorrow-filled eyes. There were already hundreds and thousands of them.

Vladislava and Sofia Kobus, two Polish girls who had been living in a cellar with Jews – Jews who have emerged from under the ground, who had spent years in the Warsaw sewer system and in cellars. Yakov Menzhitsky, a worker from a Łódź stocking factory, and his brother Aron. Isai Davidovich Ragozhek, an accountant from Warsaw. Abram Klinker, ragged, with a bruise, a shoemaker from Łódź who worked the incinerator at the Warsaw Gestapo [headquarters]. I came across these people in the deserted streets. Their faces made of paper. A shocking figure – a small stocking-maker, carrying from the ghetto to his hole in the ground a child's basket filled with Jewish ashes. He had collected these ashes in the yard of the Judenrat, at the ghetto. He will leave for Łódź tomorrow on foot, with these ashes.

The Warsaw ghetto. A wall, one and a half times the height of a man, made of red bricks, two bricks thick, with broken glass cemented along the top of it. The bricks are laid so neatly. Whose hands built this wall?

The ghetto: waves of stone, crushed bricks, a sea of brick. There isn't a single wall intact – one can seldom see an unbroken brick. The beast's anger was terrible.

Our meeting. People from the cellar [of] Zhelyaznaya 95z. People who have turned into rats and monkeys. Story about the encounter of two Jews from Łódź, in the darkness of a boiler room, in a destroyed building in Warsaw, where rats and Jews came at night to drink water. Klinker shouted when he heard a noise: 'I am a Jew. If you are rebels, please take me with you.' A voice replied from the darkness: 'I am a Jew, too.' They both turned out to be from Łódź. They found each other in the dark and hugged each other sobbing.

Their hiding place was between the Gendarmerie and Gestapo, on the fourth floor of a half-destroyed building. A Polish girl, with locks and ringlets, gave them shelter. The Polish father of their rescuer had demanded one zloty to get alcohol, 'Otherwise I will denounce you.' The ragged Abram Klinker, wanted to give me his only treasure – a fountain pen.

Grossman recounted in his *Krasnaya Zvezda* article the story of the 'bunker' hiding place on the fourth floor of a ruined building.

We have visited the 'bunker' – a secret refuge where six Poles and four Jews had been hiding for many long months. The wildest imagination would be unable to picture this stone hole made in the fourth floor of a destroyed building. To get there, one has to climb the vertical walls of a sunken staircase, run over an abyss by a girder that had been part of a floor, and squeeze oneself through a narrow black slit made in a dark storeroom. We were guided by a Polish girl who had lived in the hiding place. She walked so calmly over the abyss. And I have to confess that although I'd spent three and a half years at the front, my heart sometimes froze during this trip, sweat poured down, and everything went black in my eyes. And the people from the bunker did this trip only on dark, moonless nights.

The ghetto. One can imagine how tall the buildings had once been when looking at the huge brick waves into which these buildings have been turned. Amid the brick sea, two [Polish Roman Catholic] churches are standing.[2] A woman's head [carved from] stone is lying among red pieces of brick. Streets have been hacked through this wild masonry forest. The Judenrat building, gloomy, grey. [In] its inner yards – [are] rails, red from cinder, on which the bodies of rebels had been burned from the Warsaw ghetto. A heap of ashes in the corner of the yard – Jewish ashes.[3] Jars, scraps of dresses, a woman's shoe, a torn Talmud book.

Resistance at the Warsaw ghetto began on 19 April and ended on 24 May. The chairman of the community, Chernyakov, committed suicide on 23 July 1942. Members of the Jewish Council of the Ghetto – Gustav Tselikovsky, Sherishevsky, Alfred Stegman, Maximilian Lichtenbaum – were shot early in May.

During the uprising at the Warsaw ghetto, Shmul Zigelbaum (Comrade Arthur), who was then living in London, committed suicide in order to draw the world's attention to the tragedy of the Jewish nation.[4]

From Warsaw, Grossman continued on in the wake of the victorious Red Army, to the city of Łódź where the Nazis had also used the ghetto as a holding camp. Łódź was seized by Chuikov's 8th Guards Army on 18 January, just four days after the start of the offensive. The rapidity of the Soviet advance had not given the German authorities time to destroy the city.

Łódź. Five hundred factories and plants. Directors and owners have fled. At the moment they are managed by workers. The electric power station, trams, railway are working at full power. An old man, an engine driver, said: 'I've driven trains for fifty years, I'll be the first man to drive a train to Berlin.'

Gestapo [headquarters]: the building is intact, everything is in its place. Luxurious portraits of leaders of the German National-Socialist Workers' Party are lying around on the pavement. Children in torn felt boots are dancing on the faces of Goering and Hitler.

2 Grossman may have been referring to the Church of the Virgin's Blood at 34 Leshno Street, the centre of Catholics of Jewish descent.
3 They were not all Jewish ashes. The Nazis also used the ruins of the ghetto as an execution ground for Catholic Poles.
4 He was a member of the National Council of the Polish Government in Exile.

Munitions factories: there were three of them. Two of them were destroyed by the English air force, the third we examined today in Łódź – a gigantic facility for the manufacture of torpedoes. They had been building it since 1944, but it never started on full production. There are slit trenches in the yard, stretching parallel to the workshops. Tables in the factory canteen. Signs over some tables: 'For Germans only.' A Polish worker says: 'In the time it took me to produce eight [torpedoes], a German would make forty-five.' A twelve-hour working day. Two kitchens at the canteen for workers – German and Polish. Two sorts of food ration cards – German and Polish. Huge slogans in German in the workshops: 'You are nothing, your nation is everything.'

Punishments: when a worker was late, or dropped his tool, or seemed lazy to his foreman, they slapped his face and put him in the punishment cells (in the basements of workshops).

Łódź, or Litzmannstadt, renamed to commemorate a German general.[5] We, the four Jews, represented Russia amid the family of a Russian general, Shepetovsky (deceased). The general's daughter Irena doesn't understand any Russian, she only speaks German and Polish. Gekhtman sings Volga songs to her, burring very expressively.

In the Łódź ghetto. The song of the ghetto [was]: 'One shouldn't feel sad and cry. Everything will be better tomorrow. The sun will shine for us, too.'

The ghetto was established on 1 May 1940. They had three bloody days there every week – Wednesday, Thursday and Friday. On these days, Germans (*Volksdeutsche*)[6] killed Jews in their homes.

At first, there were 165,000 Łódź Jews in the ghetto, 18,000 Jews from Luxembourg, Austria, Germany and Czechoslovakia, 15,000 Jews from Polish Jewish settlements – Kamish and others – 15,000 from Chenstohova. The biggest number of Jews at the ghetto at one time was 250,000. A famine started. One hundred and fifty

---

5 Lieutenant General Karl Litzmann was the German commander who died in 1915 while attempting to capture Łódź in the First World War. He was awarded the Pour le Mérite, the 'Blue Max'.
6 *Volksdeutsche* were ethnic Germans living outside the Reich. These were either members of the local German minority or, more likely, members of other German minorities brought in by the Nazi authorities to settle their new *Gau*, or Nazi district, the Warthegau, an area of north-west Poland, ethnically cleansed of Poles and annexed as part of the Reich. German commanders, such as General Guderian, were given large estates there by a grateful government.

people died every day. Germans weren't satisfied by such a low mortality rate.[7]

In the first *Aktion* of December 1942, 25,000 healthy men and women were taken away, allegedly to work, and were killed. The first *Kinder-Aktion* had taken place in September of the same year. All children, from babies to fourteen-year-olds, as well as all old people and ill people, were killed (a total of 17,000 people). Trucks which took the children away returned two hours later for a new lot. They would systematically take eight hundred to a thousand people away 'to work' and kill them. By 1 January 1944, there were 74,000 people left in the ghetto. A trader in tea, Hans Biebow, was the chief of the ghetto.

Before the annihilation of the ghetto,[8] *Oberbürgermeister* Bratvich and Hans Biebow gave speeches and announced that to save the Łódź Jews who had worked for the state for four years, the leadership had decided to evacuate them to the rear. Not a single Jew turned up at the railway station. Biebow called a meeting once again and arrested lots of Jews, but then let them go back, saying he relied on their consciences. After that, they started taking away, by force, 2,000–3,000 each day. Notes found in the empty wagons revealed that they had been taken to Maslovitsy[9] and Oswencim [Auschwitz].

After the final annihilation of the Łódź ghetto, 850 people had been left there. The breakthrough of our tanks saved their lives.

Organisation of the Łódź ghetto. It had its own banknotes and coins, post and postal stamps. Schools. Theatres. Printing works. Forty textile factories. A lot of little factories. Sanatoria. A library of photographs. A history bureau. Hospitals and medical emergency aid. Farms, fields, vegetable gardens. One hundred horses. Orders and medals for labour had been introduced. Chaim Rumkowsky, the director of the ghetto, an educated Jew, [was a] specialist in statistics.[10]

---

7   Out of a population of just under five million in 1939, the Warthegau contained 380,000 Jews and 325,000 ethnic Germans.

8   Himmler gave the order to liquidate the ghetto on 10 June 1944, a few days after D-Day.

9   Maslovitsy was also where Major Sharapovich discovered the German cache of valuable books which they had seized from the Turgenev Library in Paris. These were taken back to Moscow to the Lenin Library.

10   Mordechai Chaim Rumkowsky was a controversial character to say the least. A bankrupt businessman appointed *Judenälteste*, or Jewish elder, by the Germans, he obtained complete power in the ghetto, through controlling the food supply. In an autocratic fashion, he not only ran the ghetto as if it were his private fiefdom, but decided who was to die and who was to survive, by selecting those for transports to Chelmno and later Auschwitz. Grossman's account of the ghetto seems rather optimistic. Even within a year nearly 20 per cent of the population was dying from disease and starvation.

Rumkowsky had proclaimed himself the Chief Rabbi. In luxurious prayer robes, he conducted services at the synagogue, issued marriage licences and divorces, and punished those who had mistresses. He married a young lawyer[11] when he was seventy, and had mistresses who were schoolgirls.[12] Hymns had been composed in his honour. He proclaimed himself the leader and saviour of Jews. He was the Gestapo's main support.

In fits of fury, he used to beat people with sticks and slapped them. He had been an unsuccessful, ruined tradesman before the war. The story of his death: when his brother was also put on the train, he, confident of his power, declared to the Gestapo that if they didn't set his brother free, he would get on the train together with him. Rumkowsky boarded the train and was sent to [Auschwitz]. His young wife travelled to her own death together with him. Rumkowsky had been very proud about the following incident: once, a letter was sent from Berlin to Chaim Rumkowsky, the city was not indicated, and this letter reached him in Łódź.

Łódź – the Polish Manchester. Fifteen thousand tailors had been sewing clothes there for the German Army. They were given four hundred grams of bread every day and nine hundred grams of sugar per month. At that time, people in the Warsaw ghetto were given eighty grams of bread per day.

Genicksschuss – bullet in the back of the head.[13]

Religious belief at the ghetto had decreased dramatically; in fact, Jewish workers aren't religious in general. Biebow used to send a lot of vitamins to the ghetto. Rumkowsky's assistant, the Jew Gertler, was connected with the Gestapo, but did a lot of good. He was a very kind man, and people loved him a lot.

When Gertler came to power and the Germans began to show him a lot of respect, Rumkowsky began to hate him terribly.

The hospital in the ghetto produced awe in doctors from Europe. A professor once said: 'I haven't seen such a clinic even in Berlin.'

---

11   Her name was Regine Weinberger.
12   Rumkowsky's 'mistresses' were young women threatened and forced into becoming his concubines.
13   Literally 'neck-shot' in German, in practice to the base of the skull.

Heroic death of Doctor Weisskopf at the Łódź ghetto – he had tried to bite through Bibach's throat.

The uprising at the Łódź ghetto was headed by Kloppfisch, an engineer from Łódź.

Łódź and Poznań were the two major cities of the Warthegau, the Nazi annexation of western Poland named after the River Warthe. Hitler appointed Arthur Greiser as the gauleiter. More than 70,000 Poles were killed during the process of ethnic cleansing to make way for ethnic German settlers. Hundreds of thousands more went to labour and concentration camps. After the Jews, the Poles lost the highest proportion of their population during the Second World War, even more than the Soviet Union.

The Germans had forced all Polish peasants to leave their houses, took away their land, livestock, household utensils, made them live in huts and forced them to work as farm labourers. The Germans were mostly local, but some of them (160,000) had come from the Ukraine. The children of Polish peasants did not go to school. Children had to work from the age of twelve. Churches were closed. Only one was left out of twenty. The others were turned into warehouses. Farmhands were paid twenty marks per week and given food. Children were paid six marks per month. A German peasant had the right to keep for himself enough produce to feed his family.

One Polish peasant was sent to Dachau because he had said to his German neighbour even before the Germans arrived [in September 1939]: 'Why do you speak German? You aren't in Berlin.' Before the war, Nazis used to get together for [Nazi] Party meetings, under the pretext of praying.

German [settlers] came in two waves – one in 1941, the other in 1944. Germans sold bread to the Poles illicitly, five marks for a kilo, wheat flour at twenty-five marks per kilo, and a kilo of pork fat cost two hundred marks. Thousands of Polish teachers, doctors, lawyers and Catholic priests were taken to Dachau and killed.

'The Germans called our region the "Warthegau". They forbade farmhands to move anywhere. They were slaves.'

Poles were forbidden to enter shops, parks and gardens. They could not travel by tram on Sundays, and by motor vehicle all week.

Bauerführer[14] Schwandt had three male farmhands and three female. He was a huge fat man, and paid his farmhands nothing. Before the war, he had a bar and a grocer's store. He had four *Morgens* [acres] before the war, and now he has fifty.

There was a commission that checked the fulfilment of obligatory supplies of produce by German [farmers]. Poles weren't given vodka, but Germans were allowed it on holidays. Poles would be sentenced to three months in prison for using a lighter fuelled with petrol.

Some Germans didn't believe that the Russians would come, and they made fun of those who made big carts to take away their belongings. They didn't believe it until the last day.

The [Red Army] infantry is travelling in carriages, coaches, cabriolets, shining with polish and glass. The guys are smoking *makhorka*, eating and drinking, playing cards. Carts in supply trains are decorated with carpets, cart drivers are sitting on feather beds. Soldiers don't eat army food any more. There's pork, turkey, chicken. There are some rounded faces with pink cheeks in the infantry now, this has had never happened before.[15]

German civilians caught out by our tanks are now going back. They get beaten up [on the way]. People unharness their horses. Poles are robbing them. 'Where are you going?' I asked. They answered in Russian: 'To Russia.' Here, there are five kinds of Germans: those from the Black Sea, from the Balkans, from the Baltic countries, *Volksdeutsche* and *Reichsdeutsche*.[16]

Grossman soon found that the behaviour of Red Army troops changed on foreign soil. He still tried to idealise front-line troops, while putting all the blame on rear units, such as supply and transport. In fact, the tank troops whom he so idealised were often the worst looters and rapists.

The front-line soldiers advance by day and night in fire, holy and pure. The rear soldiers who follow them rape, drink, loot and rob.

14 A *Bauerführer* was the local Nazi Party leader and organiser of peasants and farmers.
15 Red Army soldiers were looting from Polish farmers just as much as from German settlers.
16 In this case, by *Volksdeutsche* he means ethnic Germans from Poland. *Reichsdeutsche* are, of course, those from pre-1939 German territory.

Two hundred and fifty of our girls were working at the Focke-Wulf plant. Germans had brought them from Voroshilovgrad, Kharkov and Kiev. According to the chief of the army political department, these girls have no clothes, are lice-infested and swollen from hunger. And according to what a man from the army newspaper said, these girls had been clean and well dressed, until our soldiers came and robbed them blind and took their watches. Liberated Soviet girls often complain about being raped by our soldiers. One girl said to me, crying: 'He was an old man, older than my father.'

TWENTY-SIX

Into the Lair of the Fascist Beast

During this part of the advance, Grossman remained attached to the headquarters of General Chuikov's 8th Guards Army. Chuikov was furious when Marshal Zhukov, whom he detested for having claimed so much of the glory over Stalingrad, ordered his army to reduce the fortress city of Poznań, while the other armies rushed on towards the River Oder. Fighting in Poznań was the toughest street-fighting battle which the Red Army had faced since Stalingrad.

> The regimental commander complains: 'Well, we broke into a street, and civilians rushed up to us shouting: "Our liberators! Our saviours!" At this moment, the Germans counter-attacked and pushed us back. Their self-propelled gun appeared. And I saw the same civilians rush out and start hugging Germans. Well, I gave the order to fire at them with canister.'
>
> Street fighting is going on. The quieter streets are filled with people. Ladies wearing fashionable hats, carrying bright handbags, are cutting pieces of meat off dead horses lying on the pavement.

> Chuikov is organising the street fighting in Poznań. After Stalingrad, he is considered the top expert in street fighting. Theory: the essence of the battle of Stalingrad is that our infantry created a wedge between the force of German mechanical power and the weakness of German infantry. And now, circumstances have driven Academician[1] Chuikov into a situation which he cannot avoid, into the same situation as at Stalingrad, but here in Poznań, it's vice versa. He is furiously attacking the Germans in the streets of Poznań, with a huge mechanised force and little infantry. And the more numerous German infantry is stubbornly fighting its hopeless battle.

1 He refers to Chuikov as 'Academician' using an old joke. It was Chuikov who claimed to have founded the academy of street fighting in Stalingrad.

Chuikov is sitting in a cold, brightly lit room on the first floor of a two-storey villa. A telephone is ringing on the table. Commanders of units report on the street fighting in Poznań. In the pauses between telephone calls and reports, Chuikov tells me about breaking the Germans defences in the area of Warsaw.

'We had been studying the Germans' daily timetable for a month. During the day, they left the first line of trenches, and returned to it at night. Before we began to advance, we kept sending messages on the radio the whole night, we were broadcasting music and dances, and made use of confusion, bringing all our forces up into front-line positions.

'At eight thirty, the time when they usually left the first line, we fired a salvo from 250 guns. On the first day, we breached the first line. We heard on the radio how the commander of the Ninth Army was calling his divisions, getting no bloody answer. At the same time, we destroyed two panzer divisions which they had pulled up from the rear. On the whole, we did it the following way: an air raid, a barrage of fire, and then we advanced. There was a milky fog on that morning. We stopped them on the anvil of the first line and hit them with the hammer of our artillery. If we were an hour late, we would have been hitting an empty spot. And the Germans thought that we had been strategically exhausted. There were *Landwehr* and *Volkssturm* there.'[2]

Chuikov listens to the telephone, reaches to look at the map and says: 'Just a minute, I'll put on my glasses.' He reads the report, laughs happily and taps his orderly on the nose with his pencil. He says: 'Marchenko's right flank can already feel Glebov's fire. There's a fire overlap, soon there will be live communications, too.' He shouts into the telephone: 'If they try to break through to the west, let them into the open, and then squash them like mites, damn them.'

Chuikov then continued his conversation with Grossman.

'Soldiers are tired of being on the defensive. They are dying to finish the war. They limbered up for two or three days, and then began to advance thirty to fifty kilometres every day.

'There's a certain amount of looting going on: a tank is moving,

---

2   There were no *Landwehr*, as they were the territorial reserves of the First World War. The *Volkssturm* was its Nazi equivalent. Regular officers referred to this force of elderly men and young boys as the 'stew', as it was a mixture of tough old meat and green vegetables.

and a piglet is sitting on its track guard. We've stopped feeding our men. Our food isn't tasty enough for them any longer. Transport drivers are driving around in carriages, playing accordions, like in Makhno's army.[3]

'The fortress in Poznań . . . Our men were walking around on top of it, and Germans were shooting up at them [from inside]. Then sappers poured in one and a half barrels of kerosene, set it on fire, and the Germans sprang out like rats. And you know, what is the most surprising thing, with all our experience of war and our wonderful reconnaissance, we overlooked one trifle. We didn't know that Poznań was a first-class fortress, one of the strongest in Europe. We thought it was just another town and wanted to take it off the march, and here we are.'

Poznań did not finally fall until Chuikov gave orders to storm the fortress on 18 February, following nine days of heavy bombardment. By this time the beleaguered garrison was over two hundred kilometres from their own lines. Holes in the walls were blasted at point-blank range with 203mm howitzers, and flame-throwers and grenades were used to clear one room after another. On the night of 22 February, Major-General Ernst Gomell, the German commander, lay down on a swastika flag in his room and shot himself. The garrison surrendered.

Grossman did not wait for the end of the siege. He appears to have followed forward units of the 8th Guards Army on their route into the German Reich. Despite his urge to idealise the ordinary Red Army soldier, he was forced to admit the horrors resulting from their compulsion to get drunk.

The absurd death of Hero of the Soviet Union Colonel Gorelov, commander of a Guards tank brigade. At the beginning of February, he was sorting out a traffic standstill on the road a few kilometres from the German border, and was killed by drunken Red Army soldiers. Katukov[4] had been very fond of Gorelov; when giving orders to him and Babadzhanyan, he called them by their first names:

3 Nestor Makhno led a large guerrilla force of anarchists in the Ukraine during the civil war, fighting both the Whites and the Reds. They moved rapidly with small horse-drawn carts, some of which had machine guns mounted on them.
4 Colonel-General M.I. Katukov, the commander of the 1st Guards Tank Army, which fought in tandem with the 8th Guards Army more or less from the Vistula all the way to the final assault on Berlin.

Volodya and Arno. This wasn't the only example of bloody, drunken outrage.

All Soviet citizens, soldiers and civilians alike, were struck by the change, the moment they crossed the German border. A number wondered at the perfect order and prosperity of the place and wondered why any of the inhabitants would have wanted to go off to invade Russia.

> Twilight. It is foggy and rainy. A smell of forest mould. Puddles on the road. Dark pine woods, fields, farmsteads, barns, houses with pointed roofs. A huge poster: 'Soldier, here it is! The Lair of the Fascist Beast.'
>
> There is great charm in this landscape. Its small but very thick woods are beautiful, as well as the bluish-grey asphalt and clinker roads leading into them. And our artillery, self-propelled guns, and shabby staff trucks full of looted things, are moving on from Poznań.

Grossman in Schwerin as it was sacked by the 8th Guards Army.

A liberated [Russian] girl, Galya, telling me about the gallant characteristics of different representatives of the captured male international: 'There are different rules for Frenchmen.'

From Poznań across the pre-1939 German border, the road to Küstrin and Berlin, took them through the town of Schwerin. When Grossman arrived, he found the 8th Guards Army, which he had so admired at Stalingrad, looting and raping. After the war, Grossman admitted to his daughter that the Red Army 'changed for the worse as soon as it crossed the [Soviet] border'.

Everything is on fire. Looting is in full swing. Gekhman and I are given a house which has survived. Everything is untouched, the stove is still warm, there's a kettle with warm water on it, the owners must have fled a very short time ago. The cupboards are full of stuff. I categorically forbid [those with me] to touch them. The [town] commandant turns up asking my permission to billet a colonel from the general staff here who has just arrived. Of course, I agree. The colonel is majestic. A good Russian face. All night, we hear noises coming from the room where the tired colonel is staying. He leaves in the morning without saying goodbye. We go to his room: chaos, the colonel has emptied the cupboards like a real looter.

An old woman has thrown herself from a window of a burning building.

We enter a house, there's a puddle of blood on the floor and in it an old man, shot by the looters. There are cages with rabbits and pigeons in the empty yards. We open their doors to save them from the fire. Two dead parrots in their cage.

Horror in the eyes of women and girls.

At the [town] commandant's office. A group of French prisoners of war complain that some Red Army soldiers have seized their watches, giving them one rouble for each watch.

A German woman dressed in black, with dead lips, is speaking in a barely audible rustling voice. She has brought with her a teenage girl with black, velvety bruises on her neck and face, a swollen eye, with terrible bruises on her hands. This girl was raped by a soldier from the signals company with army headquarters. He is also here, pink-cheeked, fat-faced, sleepy. The commandant is interrogating him without much enthusiasm.

Horrifying things are happening to German women. An educated German whose wife has received 'new visitors' – Red Army soldiers – is explaining with expressive gestures and broken Russian words, that she has already been raped by ten men today. The lady is present.

Women's screams are heard from open windows. A Jewish officer, whose whole family was killed by Germans, is billeted in the apartment of a Gestapo man who has escaped. The women and girls [left behind] are safe while he is there. When he leaves, they all cry and plead with him to stay.

Soviet girls liberated from the camps are suffering a lot now. Tonight, some of them are hiding in our correspondents' room. During the night, we are woken up by screams: one of the correspondents couldn't resist the temptation. A noisy discussion ensues, then order is re-established.

A story about a breast-feeding mother who was being raped in a barn. Her relatives came to the barn and asked her attackers to let her have a break, because the hungry baby was crying the whole time.

It is light during the night, everything is ablaze.

When Colonel Mamaev entered a German house, children of four and five stood up in silence and raised their hands.

The liberation of German territory produced dramatic reversals of fortune. The prisoners and the slave labourers now looted from their former masters. Many young women sent back to Germany from the occupied territories of the Soviet Union had worked on farms and in domestic service, as well as in factories. Red Army soldiers had suffered far more in their prison camps than even the slave labourers.

Huge crowds on the roads. Prisoners of war of all nationalities: French, Belgian, Dutch, all loaded with looted things. Only Americans are walking light, without even hats. They don't need anything except alcohol. Some of them greet us waving bottles. The Civilian International of Europe is moving on other roads. Women wearing pants, all pushing thousands of prams full of loot. It is a mad chaos, full of joy. Where's East, where's West?

> Liberated cripples – former Red Army soldiers. One of them, mournful, dying, says: 'I will never make it back to my home.' When Germans wanted to kill them, the cripples cut the wire, got hold of a sub-machine gun and one rifle, and decided to fight.
>
> A Russian girl leaving German slavery says: 'To hell with the Frau. I am sorry only to abandon her six-year-old boy.'

After Schwerin, Grossman reached Landsberg, further down the River Warthe, which flowed into the Oder at Küstrin. In a measure close to Stalin's heart, each large Soviet formation had a commission attached to confiscate German valuables to compensate for the war damage inflicted on the Soviet Union. The members were civilian accountants dressed up rather unconvincingly as Red Army colonels. Germans obediently opened the safes for them. The real problem came with Red Army soldiers who tried to open safes on their own account. They used captured *Panzerfaust* rockets, which destroyed the safe and everything in it.

> A safe-deposit box in Landsberg. Our commission is opening safes. There's gold, jewellery, and a lot of photographs of children, women and old people. A member of the removal commission says to me: 'What the fuck did they keep these photos here for?'

> The divisional commander says to his deputy who has come to get more exact instructions on signal flares: 'I shit on your flares. Sit down and have dinner with me.'

> In a stationery shop belonging to a fat Nazi man, on the day of his ruin. A tiny girl came in in the morning and asked him to show her postcards. The fat, gloomy, heavily breathing old man put a dozen postcards on the table in front of her. The girl was choosing, seriously, for a long time, and chose one of a girl in a beautiful dress standing by a broken egg, a chicken climbing out from the egg. The old man received twenty-five pfennig from her and put it into the cash register. That evening, the old man was lying dead in his bed. He had poisoned himself. The shop was closed, yet cheerful, noisy men were carrying boxes of goods and bundles of belongings out of his apartment.

As soon as Grossman caught up with old friends and acquaintances, he pumped them for their stories. Babadzhanyan, now commanding the

XI Guards Tank Corps in Katukov's 1st Guards Tank Army, was the brave commander he had thought had been killed in 1941.

Babadzhanyan's story: 'We started on the Vistula on the evening of 15 January, by entering a breach on Chuikov's sector. We reached the Oder on 28 January. One German captain was going to Poznań to get cigarettes and we captured him right on the border. There was one day when we made 120 kilometres. All the main operations were carried out during the night. Tanks are safe at night. Our tanks are a terrifying force at night. They would break through sixty kilometres, even though we didn't have local guides (who are very important), as we did in Poland. Although one night an old man, a German, took our tanks through very well.

'A German general would peacefully take off his trousers and go to bed, having marked on the map that the enemy was sixty kilometres away, and we would attack this general at midnight.'

Grossman also came across Gusakovsky again, an officer clearly not handicapped by modesty.

Gusakovsky's brigade had a stunning success. There was, among all these destroyed bridges and tank traps, an absolutely intact road, which [the Germans] had been planning to use for a powerful counter-attack. Gusakovsky rushed along this road and got round all the enemy's defences. [His brigade] was rambling around in the enemy's rear on its own for two days while other brigades advanced by a roundabout route, or attacked the enemy head-on.

Colonel Gusakovsky, twice Hero of the Soviet Union, commander of a tank brigade: 'The town [presumably Landsberg] has been captured by one colonel, but the order of the commander-in-chief [Marshal Zhukov] mentions ten generals.'

As the Red Army approached Berlin, officers and soldiers alike dreamed of capturing Hitler alive. They were certain that they would be awarded the Gold Star of Hero of the Soviet Union and would be famous until the end of their days. Intelligence officers in headquarters, meanwhile, pored over captured documents which might have come from the Reich Chancellery in the hope of discovering more about the Nazi leader. 'At the intelligence department. I was shown an order with Hitler's signature, which was signed underneath: "Identical with original, Captain Sirkis.'"

In early February, Grossman reached the Oder, the last river before Berlin. The Red Army had counted each river in its advance westwards from the Volga at Stalingrad, and so had Grossman.

We reached the Oder on a sunny morning, at the place where it ran most closely to Berlin. It seemed so bizzare that this slushy country road, these low prickly bushes, small trees, few and far between, low hills sloping towards the river, small houses scattered here and there among the fields covered with the bright greenery of winter crop – all this, so ordinary for my eyes, seen so many times, was just eighty kilometres from Berlin.

And suddenly on this spring morning by the Oder, I remembered how in that iron winter of 1942, in a severe January snowstorm, on a night which was crimson from the flames of a village which Germans had set on fire, a horse driver muffled in a sheepskin coat shouted suddenly: 'Hey, comrades, where's the road to Berlin?' Drivers of vehicles and carts answered with a roar of laughter. I wonder if this joker, who had asked the way to Berlin near Balakleya, is still alive? And what about those who laughed at his question three years ago? And I wanted to shout, to call to all our brothers, our soldiers, who are lying in the Russian, Ukrainian, Belorussian and Polish earth, who sleep for ever on the fields of our battles: 'Comrades, can you hear us? We've done it!'

On the second day after the Red Army invaded Germany, we saw eight hundred Soviet children walking eastwards on the road, the column stretching for many kilometres. Some soldiers and officers were standing by the road, peering into their faces intently and silently. They were fathers looking for their children who had been taken to Germany. One colonel had been standing there for several hours, upright, stern, with a dark, gloomy face. He went back to his car in the dusk: he hadn't found his son.

I looked through the notebooks of pupils at school. From the first form, almost all the exercises, compositions and presentations, written in unsteady children's handwriting, were on war themes and Nazi affairs. Portraits, placards, slogans on the classroom walls, all that pursued only one goal – glorifying Hitler and Nazism . . .

German civilians are trying to deny any guilt for the enormous destructions and suffering that fascist Germany and its troops brought to the Soviet Union.

TWENTY-SEVEN

The Battle for Berlin

At the beginning of February, just after Zhukov's armies reached the Oder less than a hundred kilometres from Berlin, a row broke out. Chuikov, the commander of the 8th Guards Army, criticised Zhukov for failing to push on immediately to Berlin. In fact, Stalin had forbidden a rash advance, when tank units needed to refit and rearm, and the infantry was exhausted. The *Stavka* ordered Zhukov and Rokossovsky to clear their right flank, the Baltic coast of Pomerania. This operation, and the redeployment of armies later, meant that the final Berlin operation was delayed until mid-April.

Grossman, in the meantime, had returned to Moscow, but he was determined to be in Berlin for the kill. Fortunately, his fellow correspondents, including his old companion Troyanovsky, requested that he should be there and *Krasnaya Zvezda* duly sent him. Troyanovsky then recorded: 'On 14 April, correspondents of *Krasnaya Zvezda* were summoned by General K.F. Telegin, member of the Military Council of the Front. "I would recommend you cross the Oder," he said. "You can choose any army. The only thing I would ask you, please don't all go to Chuikov." Perhaps Marshal Zhukov did not want his chief critic to get all the publicity.

The operation was launched on 16 April with Zhukov's 1st Belorussian Front attacking due westwards from the Oder opposite Berlin, while Marshal Konev's 1st Ukrainian Front attacked futher south from the line of the River Neisse. Stalin gave Konev permission to swing north towards Berlin. He wanted to create an intense rivalry between the two marshals to accelerate the encirclement and capture of Berlin. Ever since the Americans took the bridge at Remagen on 7 March, Stalin was afraid that they might reach Berlin first.

Zhukov's forces had a far tougher time than he had expected in storming the Seelow heights above the Oder flood plain, and they suffered many casualties as their commanders forced them on. Their artillery was not within range of Berlin until the evening of 20 April. But the real fight for the city did not begin until four days later. Chuikov's 8th Guards Army and Katukov's 1st Guards Tank Army fought in from the southeast, the 2nd Guards Tank Army and the 3rd Shock Army from the north, and the 5th Shock Army from the east. Konev's troops, the 3rd Guards Tank Army and the 28th Army, had also reached the south of the city and neighbouring formations began to bombard each other. Grossman, meanwhile, was making his way back to Berlin from Moscow. He left the Soviet capital for his final journey as a war correspondent on 20 April, the day of Hitler's last birthday. He later described in an article what he saw and thought on the way to Berlin.

A village that had been burned by the Germans. All that remains of it are low sandy hills of collapsed handmade brick, an abandoned well, and a few rusted metal constructions. Smoke was rising from a depression not far away, where former inhabitants of the village were living in earth bunkers dug by Red Army soldiers during the fighting. A white-haired woman, a mother whose sons had been killed in the war, brought us water in a can and said in a melancholy voice: 'Will there be ressurrection for us?' and she indicated the burned village with a movement of her head.

And further on, along all the great roads, leading to the Neva, and the Volkhov, and to the Terek, to the tall forests of Karelia, to the steppes and mountains of the Caucasus, there are hills and hillocks, burial mounds of soldiers' graves.

Our dead children, the Red Army soldiers, sergeants, lieutenants, our good boys are asleep there for ever. Everywhere along the roads of our advance there are these kurgans, hills and hillocks, graves of our killed sons marked by plywood boards on sticks, tilted to one side, with washed-off inscriptions. The rain washed off the soldiers' names when it was crying over the graves, and united them under the single name of the killed son.

The vehicle broke down close to the Polish border, and we had to spend many hours in a field. While [the Jeep] was being repaired, I visited a hamlet. It was Sunday, and the main resident of the hamlet and her children had gone to church. Only an old woman and a traveller, a soldier dismissed from the army because of his wounds, were at home. He told me he didn't have to walk very far now: he was going to the Orel area. We began to talk. The traveller, whose name was Alexei Ivanovich, was over forty. He had served at the front since the first days of the war, and had been wounded three times. He had been in a mortar unit. His greatcoat was torn by shrapnel and covered in black stains, he was wearing a *ushanka* winter hat, foot bandages and heavy boots. This soldiers' gear was something he could bring back home. He had been living at the hamlet for about two weeks, helping the woman to sow, in return for which she gave him three poods of rye. He would be given a lift to the station at dawn, with her horses. There he intended to board an empty train going back from the front and get closer to home. Alexei Ivanovich was very happy about having earned this grain. He even led me to the hall and smiled, watching me pat the fat dense sack.

He then told me how Germans had burned his village, and his family are living in an earth bunker. 'It's good that I'm not going back empty-handed,' he said. 'I'll bring them some grain from the war, because I saw how hard it'd become for them when I went back on leave after I was wounded the second time. What sort of life is it under the earth? It's dark and wet, and there are insects. It's not so bad in the summer, but in winter it's hard.'

Grossman also made notes of that last journey to the front.

In a Willys [Jeep] from Moscow. Fires. As far as Minsk, we saw people setting grass on fire, the tall weeds that have grown in the fields during the war.

The leaden sky and frightening, cold rain for three days. An iron spring after the iron years of war. A severe peace is coming after the severe war: camps are being built everywhere, wire stretched, towers erected for the guards and [German] prisoners urged on by their escorts. After the war ends they will be repairing the roads broken by the movement of troops.

The road to Brest and Warsaw is also badly damaged. But the further west [one goes], the dryer the road and the clearer the sky. The trees along the road – apple and cherry, are all in blossom. The dachas of Berliners. Everything is wallowing in flowers – tulips, lilac, decorative pink flowers, apple, cherry and apricot blossom. The birds are singing. Nature does not mourn the last days of fascism.

In the town of Landsberg near Berlin. Children are playing at war on the flat roof of a house. Our troops are finishing off German imperialism in Berlin this minute, but here the boys with wooden swords and lances, with long legs, with their hair cut short on the back of their heads, with blond fringes, are shouting in shrill voices, stabbing one another, jumping, leaping wildly. Here, birth is being given to a new war. It is eternal, undying.

The Berlin autobahn ring. Stories had of course greatly exaggerated its width.

The highway leading to Berlin. Crowds of liberated people. Hundreds of bearded Russian peasants are walking [past]. With them are women and a lot of children. Faces of uncles with light brown beards and those of proper elders express gloomy despair. They are *starostas*,[1] and the [auxiliary] police riff-raff, who had run away as far as Berlin and have now been forced to vacate their jobs. People say that Vlasov has taken part in the last battles in Berlin with his men.[2]

The closer we get to Berlin, the more the surroundings look like the area around Moscow.

An old woman traveller is walking away from Berlin, wearing a shawl on her head. She looks exactly as if she were going on a pilgrimage – a pilgrim amid the expanses of Russia. She is holding an umbrella accross her shoulder. A huge aluminium casserole is hung by its ear on the umbrella's handle.

Weissensee – a suburb of the city. I stop the car. Some city lads, daring and cheeky, beg for chocolate, [as they] peer at the map on my lap.

Contradicting the idea of Berlin as an army barracks, there are lots of gardens in blossom. The sky is filled with a grandiose thunder of artillery. In the pauses, one can hear birds.

---

1 *Starostas*, the village elders or mayors, appointed by the Germans, rightly feared the retribution of the NKVD and had fled to Germany in front of the advancing Red Army.
2 This rumour was wrong. General Vlasov and the bulk of his troops were in Czechoslovakia, where at the last minute they sided with the Czech uprising in Prague against the Germans, but this did nothing to temper their fate at the hands of a vengeful NKVD. Vlasov was captured by a Soviet tank unit and flown back to Moscow, where he is said to have been tortured to death.

28 April 1945. Talking to Germans whose houses have been destroyed.

Grossman had himself attached to the most popular of all Zhukov's commanders, Colonel-General Berzarin.[3] Marshal Zhukov, reviving the old tsarist tradition, had appointed Berzarin, the commander of the 5th Shock Army, as commandant of Berlin, because his troops had been the first into the city. In fact, it was an inspired choice. Berzarin did not even wait for the fighting to finish. He made every effort to have essential services restored as soon as possible – a huge task after the destruction – and to make sure that the population did not starve. Many Berliners worshipped him, and when he was killed a few weeks later in a motorcycle accident, rumours spread that the NKVD had assassinated him.

> The commandant [General Berzarin] is having a conversation with the *Bürgermeister*. The *Bürgermeister* asks how much they are going to pay people mobilised for work on military objects. In fact, they have a precise notion of their rights here.
>
> Colonel-General Berzarin – the commandant of Berlin – is fat, brown-eyed, arch, with white hair although he is young. He is clever, very calm and resourceful.

---

3 Colonel-General Nikolai Erastovich Berzarin (1904–1945)

Schloss Treskow. Evening. Park. Half-dark rooms. A clock is chiming. China. Colonel Petrov has a bad toothache. Fireplace. Through the windows can be heard artillery fire and the howling of Katyushas. Suddenly, there is thunder from the skies. The sky is yellow and cloudy. It is warm, rainy, there is an odour of lilac. There's an old pond in the park. The silhouettes of the statues are indistinct. I am sitting in an armchair by the fireplace. The clock is chiming, infinitely sad and melodic, like poetry itself.

I am holding an old book in my hands. Fine pages. Written in a trembling, apparently old man's, hand is 'von Treskow'. He must have been the owner.[4]

A German, sixty-one years old. His wife, thirty-five, a beautiful woman. He is a horse-trader. [They have a] bulldog [called] Dina, '*Sie ist ein Fraulein.*' A story about soldiers taking their things away. She sobs and immediately afterwards tells us calmly about her mother and three sisters killed in Hanover by American bombs. She tells, with sheer delight, gossip about the intimate life of Goering, Himmler and Goebbels.

Morning. Trip with Berzarin and his chief of staff, Lieutenant General Bokov, to the centre of Berlin. This was where that we saw the [bombing] work done by the Americans and English. Hell!

We crossed the Spree. Thousands of encounters. Thousands of Berliners in the streets. A Jewish woman with her husband. An old man, a Jew, who burst into tears when he learned about the fate of those who went to Lublin.

A [German] lady in an astrakhan coat, who likes me very much, says: 'But surely, you aren't a Jewish commissar?'

In a rifle corps [headquarters].[5] The commander [is] General Rosly. The corps is fighting in the centre of Berlin. Rosly has two

---

4 The Tresckows (with a 'c') were an old Prussian family, of whom the best-known member was Major-General Henning von Tresckow (1901–1944), who smuggled a bomb aboard Hitler's plane on 13 March 1943, but it failed to go off. Tresckow committed suicide with a grenade on 21 July 1944. The Schloß Treskow in which Grossman was billeted was most probably Schloß Friedrichsfelde on the east side of Berlin, which belonged to the illegitimate, and much richer, branch of the family, spelt without a 'c'. They had made their money by selling cavalry mounts all over Europe. Münthe von Treskow, whose book Grossman examined, was thrown out of his house by Soviet troops and is said by the family to have died of starvation.
5 This is the IX Rifle Corps commanded by Lieutenant General I.P. Rosly, which was part of the 5th Shock Army, commanded by Colonel-General Berzarin.

dachshunds (amusing fellows), a parrot, a peacock, a guinea fowl. They are all travelling with him. There's a cheerful excitement at Rosly's headquarters. He says: 'We fear our neighbours now, not the enemy.' He says laughing: 'I've given orders to place burned-out tanks on the way to the Reichstag and the Reichschancellery so as to block our neighbours. The greatest disappointment in Berlin is when you learn about your neighbour's success.'

Grossman was fascinated by the behaviour of the defeated enemy – how ready they were to obey orders from the new authority, and how little partisan resistance there had been, unlike in the Soviet Union. His vignette below of the old German Communist was repeated frequently. These Party members emerged, expecting to be greeted as comrades by the Red Army, but instead were treated with disdain, if not contempt and even outright suspicion. Soviet citizens, having had no guidance from their own political leaders, could not understand why the working class in Germany had done so little to fight the Nazis. SMERSh and NKVD officers even arrested some German Communists as spies. In the Stalinist mindset, the fact that they had not fought the Nazis as partisans provided grounds for deep suspicion.

Colonel General Berzarin, the commandant of Berlin, receives German dignitaries.

A day in Berzarin's office. The Creation of the World. Germans, Germans, Germans – *Bürgermeisters*, directors of Berlin's electricity supply, Berlin water, sewerage, underground, trams, gas, factory owners, [and other] characters. They obtain new positions in this office. Vice-directors become directors, chiefs of regional enterprises become chiefs on a national scale. Shuffling of feet, greetings, whispers.

An old man, a house painter, produces his [Communist] Party identity card. He has been a member since 1920. This does not make a strong impression. He is invited to sit down.

Oh, how weak human nature is! All these big officials brought up by Hitler, successful and sleek, how quickly and passionately they have forsaken and cursed their regime, their leaders, their Party. They are all saying the same thing: '*Sieg!*' – that's their slogan today.

2 May. The Day of Berlin's capitulation. It's difficult to describe it. A monstrous concentration of impressions. Fire and fires, smoke, smoke, smoke. Enormous crowds of [German] prisoners. Their faces are full of drama. In many faces there's sadness, not only personal suffering, but also the suffering of a citizen. This overcast, cold and rainy day is undoubtedly the day of Germany's ruin. In smoke, among the ruins, in flames, amid hundreds of corpses in the streets.

Corpses squashed by tanks, squeezed out like tubes. Almost all of them are clutching grenades and sub-machine guns in their hands. They have been killed fighting. Most of the dead men are dressed in brown shirts. They were Party activists who defended the approaches to the Reichstag and the Reichschancellery.

Prisoners – policemen, officials, old men and next to them school-boys, almost children. Many [of the prisoners] are walking with their wives, beautiful young women. Some of the women are laughing, trying to cheer up their husbands. A young soldier with two children, a boy and a girl. Another soldier falls down and can't get up again, he is crying. Civilians are kind to them, there's grief in their faces. They are giving prisoners water and shovel bread into their hands.

A dead old woman is half sitting on a mattress by a front door, leaning her head against the wall. There's an expression of calm and sorrow on her face, she has died with this grief. A child's little legs in shoes and stockings are lying in the mud. It was a shell, apparently, or else a tank has run over her. (This was a girl.)

In the streets that are already peaceful, the ruins have been tidied.

[German] women are sweeping sidewalks with brushes like those we use to sweep rooms.

The [enemy] offered to capitulate during the night over the radio. The general commanding the garrison gave the order. 'Soldiers! Hitler, to whom you have given the oath, has committed suicide.'[6]

I've witnessed the last shots in Berlin. Groups of SS sitting in a building on the banks of the Spree, not far from the Reichstag, refused to surrender. Huge guns were blasting yellow, dagger-like fire at the building, and everything was swamped in stone dust and black smoke.

Reichstag. Huge, powerful. Soldiers are making bonfires in the hall. They rattle their mess tins and open cans of condensed milk with their bayonets.

A seemingly empty conversation has remained in my memory. It was with a middle-aged horse-driver, who had a moustache and a dark brown wrinkled face. He was standing beside his ponies at the corner of Leipzigerstrasse. I asked him about Berlin, and whether he likes the city.

'Oh, you see,' he said, 'there was such a fuss yesterday in this Berlin. A battle was going on, in this very street. German shells were exploding all the time. I was standing by the horses, and my foot bandage had become loose. I bent down to redo it, and then a shell blew up! A horse got scared and ran off. This one. He's young, but a bit naughty. And I was thinking, what should I do now, retie my foot bandage or run after the horse? Well, I ran after him, the foot bandage trailing after me, shells blowing up everywhere, my horse running, and me running after him. Well, I've taken a look at this Berlin! I was running for two hours in just one street, it had no end! I was running and thinking – well, that's Berlin. It's Berlin all right, but I did catch the horse!'

---

6   General Helmuth Weidling, the commander of LVI Panzer Corps, had been appointed commander of Berlin on 23 April by Hitler just after the Führer, due to a misunderstanding, had ordered his arrest for cowardice. Weidling, after his surrender at General Chuikov's headquarters, prepared this announcement to encourage his men to lay down their arms and halt the bloodshed.

Just to the west of the Reichstag, Grossman wandered around the Tiergarten, the central park in Berlin where all the trees had been blasted to pieces in the battle and the ground was churned up by shell and bomb blast. The great victory column, the Siegessäule, was known to Soviet troops during the battle as the 'tall lady', because of the figure of winged victory on top, which Berliners called 'Golden Elsa'. The 'fortress' he refers to below is the huge Zoo bunker, or flak tower, a vast concrete construction with anti-aircraft batteries on top and shelter inside for several thousand people. It had been Goebbels's headquarters in his role as Reich's Commissioner for Defence, but he did not die there. Goebbels and his wife Magda had shot themselves in the Reichschancellery garden after Magda had killed their six children with poison.

Memorials to victory. The Siegessäule, colossal buildings and concrete fortresses, sites of Berlin's anti-aircraft defence. Here was the Defence HQ of Goebbels's residence. People say he had given orders to poison his family and killed himself. Yesterday, he shot himself. His little scorched body is lying here, too: the artificial leg, white tie.

The enormity of victory. By the huge obelisk, a spontaneous celebration is going on. The armour of tanks has disappeared under heaps of flowers and red flags. Barrels are in blossom like trunks of spring trees. Everyone is dancing, laughing, singing. Hundreds of coloured rockets are shot into the air, everyone is saluting with bursts from sub-machine guns, rifle and pistol shots. (I learned later that many of those men celebrating were living corpses, having drunk a terrible poison from barrels containing an industrial chemical in the Tiergarten. This poison started to act on the third day after they drank it, and killed people mercilessly.)

The Brandenburg Gate is blocked with a wall of tree trunks and sand, two to three metres high. In the space [of the arch], like in a frame, one can see the startling panorama of Berlin burning. Even I have never seen such a picture, although I've seen thousands of fires.

Foreigners. [Forced labourers and prisoners of war.] Their suffering, their travelling, shouting, threats towards German soldiers. Top hats, whiskers. A young Frenchman said to me: 'Monsieur, I love your army and that's why it is painful for me to see its attitude to girls and women. This is going to be very harmful for your propaganda.'

Grossman in a Berlin street on 2 May 1945, the day of the surrender.

Looting: barrels, piles of fabric, boots, leather, wine, champagne, dresses – all this is being carried on carts and vehicles, or on shoulders.

Germans: some of them are exceptionally communicative and amiable, others turn away sullenly. There are many young women crying. Apparently, they have been made to suffer by our soldiers.

It was in Germany, particularly here in Berlin, that our soldiers really started to ask themselves why did the Germans attack us so suddenly? Why did the Germans need this terrible and unfair war? Millions of our men have now seen the rich farms in East Prussia, the highly organised agriculture, the concrete sheds for livestock, spacious rooms, carpets, wardrobes full of clothes.

Millions of our soldiers have seen the well-built roads running from one village to another and German autobahns . . . Our soldiers have seen the two-storey suburban houses with electricity, gas, bathrooms and beautifully tended gardens. Our people have seen the villas of the rich bourgeoisie in Berlin, the unbelievable luxury of castles, estates and mansions. And thousands of soldiers repeat these

341

angry questions when they look around them in Germany: 'But why did they come to us? What did they want?'

Most soldiers flocked to the Reichstag on this day of victory. Only a few, mainly officers, appear to have found the Reichschancellery. They were allowed to wander around on the ground floor, but SMERSh operatives, under the command of General Vadis, had sealed the cellars and the bunker. They were searching desperately for Hitler's body. Grossman, who went with Efim Gekhman, collected souvenirs and Nazi memorabilia. According to Ortenberg, Grossman obtained the last souvenirs in his collection on 2 May 1945 in Berlin. Grossman and Gekhman entered Hitler's office in the morning. Grossman opened a drawer of a desk, inside were stamps saying 'The Führer has confirmed', 'The Führer has agreed', etc. He took several of these stamps, and they are now in the same archive as his papers.

> The new Reichschancellery. It's a monstrous crash of the regime, ideology, plans, everything, everything. Hitler *kaputt* . . .
> Hitler's office. The reception hall. A huge foyer, in which a young Kazakh, with dark skin and broad cheekbones, is learning to ride a bicycle, falling off it now and then. Hitler's armchair and table.

Grossman at the Brandenburg Gate.

A huge metal globe, crushed and crumpled, plaster, planks of wood, carpets. Everything is mixed up. It's chaos. Souvenirs, books with dedicatory inscriptions to the Führer, stamps, etc.

In the south-west corner of the Tiergarten, Grossman also visited Berlin's zoo.

> Hungry tigers and lions . . . were trying to hunt sparrows and mice that scurried in their cages.
> The Zoological Garden. There was fighting here. Broken cages. Corpses of marmosets, tropical birds, bears, the island for hamadryases, their babies are holding on to their mothers' bellies with their tiny hands.
> Conversation with an old man. He's been looking after the monkeys for thirty-seven years. There was the corpse of a dead gorrilla in a cage.
> 'Was she a fierce animal?' I asked.
> 'No. She only roared a good deal. People are angrier,' he replied.
> On a bench, a wounded German soldier is hugging a girl, a nurse. They see no one. When I pass them again an hour later, they are still sitting in the same position. The world does not exist for them, they are happy.

Grossman returned to Moscow and in early June escaped to a dacha. At first he could not write. He collapsed with nervous exhaustion, a reaction which had been postponed, like for so many who returned from the war. But then, with rest, fresh air, fishing and long walks, he felt ready to start his self-imposed task – to honour in his writing the heroism of the Red Army and the memory of the countless victims of the Nazi invasion.

The Lies of Victory

Vasily Grossman's belief in a 'ruthless truth of war' was cruelly scorned by the Soviet authorities, especially when they attempted to suppress information about the Holocaust. At first, he refused to believe that anti-Semitism could exist within the Soviet system. He had assumed that the jibes of Sholokhov which had outraged both Ehrenburg and him were an isolated example of reactionary sentiments, leftovers from the pre-revolutionary past. But he was to find soon after the war that the Stalinist system itself could be deeply anti-Semitic. Much later, when writing *Life and Fate*, he made it appear to be overt during the war, but this was premature. There were warnings, but the anti-Semitism within the regime did not emerge fully until 1948. It then became virulent in 1952, with Stalin's 'anti-cosmopolitan' campaign and the conspiracy theory that Jewish doctors were attempting to kill Soviet leaders. Yet Stalin's anti-Semitism was not quite the same as that of the Nazis. It was based more on xeno-phobic suspicion than on race hatred.

The Jewish Anti-Fascist Committee, formed in April 1942 following the appeal the year before to 'brother Jews' throughout the world to aid the struggle, was bound to be an object of distrust to Stalin. The slightest hint of contact with foreigners had been enough to condemn countless victims of the Great Terror in 1937 and 1938. Only during the early months of the war, when the country was faced with a mortal threat, could Stalin contemplate the idea of Jews in the Soviet Union making direct contact with American and British Jews. But the suggestion that a sort of International Brigade of foreign, especially American, Jews could be recruited to fight as a separate unit within the Red Army was firmly vetoed. It is perhaps significant that almost immediately after Moscow was saved in December 1941, two of the original proponents of the scheme, the Polish Jews Henryk Erlich and Viktor Alter, were arrested. Erlich later committed suicide in prison and Alter was executed.

The Soviet authorities tolerated the Jewish Anti-Fascist Committee as a propaganda front at a time when American Lend-Lease aid was so vital to the country's survival. But the committee's energy and determination to expand its remit to cover the Holocaust was bound to put it on a collision course with Stalinist policy. The fact that the idea had partly originated in the United States with Albert Einstein and prominent American Jews later made *The Black Book* even more unacceptable to the Stalinist mind, even though the Soviet Information Bureau had given its consent to the project in the summer of 1943. Grossman, the Russian patriot, and the Francophile Ehrenburg were both assimilated Jews who had never cared for Orthodox ritual. They now identified with the fate of all the Jews of Europe. Also during the summer of 1943, once the tide of war had turned decisively against the Nazis, both Ehrenburg and Grossman found that major publications rejected most of their articles on the subject. Only small Jewish journals could be counted on to accept them, so they concentrated their efforts on the project of *The Black Book*, involving over twenty writers in the Soviet Union alone.[1] Later, Grossman pointedly asked Konstantin Simonov to contribute a section on Majdanek, but he excused himself on the grounds that he was too busy. Simonov was evidently not prepared to risk antagonising the authorities.

It was towards the end of 1944 that Ehrenburg quarrelled with the other members of the JAC's literary committee and Grossman took over editorial responsibility. But in February 1945, the Sovinformburo criticised the emphasis on the activity of traitors in the occupied territory collaborating with the German annihilation of the Jews. It was a point on which Grossman had passionately disagreed with the far cannier Ehrenburg. For the authorities, the only useful purpose of *The Black Book* was as testimony for the prosecution case against fascist Germany.

After the war, the JAC found it impossible to obtain a decision on *The Black Book* from the authorities. In November 1946, Ehrenburg, Grossman and Solomon Mikhoels, the chairman of the JAC, addressed a petition to Andrei Zhdanov, the secretary of the Central Committee.[2]

1 For details on the troubled progress of *The Black Book*, see Garrard & Garrard, pp. 199–221, Rubenstein, pp. 212–17 and, in greatest depth, Rubenstein & Naumov. An English edition of *The Black Book* was published by Vad Yashem in 1981.
2 Zhdanov, Andrei Aleksandrovich (1896–1948), born Mariupol, joined the Bolsheviks in 1915 and became Stalin's loyal henchman. After the assassination of Sergei Kirov in 1934, Zhdanov was made governor of Leningrad. He played a major role in the purges and was put in charge of the city's defence in 1941. He then reverted to his role of Stalin's cultural policeman overseeing the Sovinformburo and then the Cominform in 1947. His doctrine, known as 'Zhdanovism', was based on the notion of *partiynost*, or 'party-spirit', as the guiding principle for artists and writers. It was later alleged by the Stalinist authorities that his death in 1948 was part of the 'Doctors' Plot', but Stalin, afraid of the growing power of Zhdanov's Leningrad fiefdom, might have had a hand in Zhdanov's death, if it were from unnatural causes.

With Ilya Ehrenburg, during the war

Again there was no reply. Finally, eleven months later, in October 1947, the committee was informed that the book contained 'grave political errors' and was banned. The Cold War had begun in earnest that September, and the Jewish Anti-Fascist Committee became even more suspect after its contacts with the United States. It was closed down two months later. The type of *The Black Book* was broken up. In January 1948, Solomon Mikhoels was crushed to death by a truck in Minsk. This later proved to be a KGB operation to eliminate him. Grossman, who had accompanied Mikhoels to the station on this fatal excursion, may have suspected something when he received the shocking news, but the method of assassination used was almost too crude to be believable.

In 1945 and 1946, Grossman's career had continued to prosper, despite his work on *The Black Book*. Some of his *Krasnaya Zvezda* articles were reprinted in a small volume called *Gody Voiny*, or *The Years of War*, which was then circulated in several foreign translations. A new edition of *The People Immortal* was issued and even adapted as a play. But this success did not last much longer than a year. In August 1946, a period of ideo-logical and cultural repression was launched by Andrei Zhdanov, which was to be dubbed the *zhdanovschina*, an echo of the great terror known as the *yezhovschina*. Even without his work on *The Black Book*, a writer as honest as Grossman was bound to face a difficult time in this post-war 'lesser terror'. In September, his play *If We are to Believe the Pythagoreans* was viciously attacked in *Pravda*. Then an oblique attack was made on his wartime writing, but the main target of official displeasure remained *The Black Book*.

Subsequent attacks on Grossman were also part of the Stalinist 'anti-cosmopolitan' campaign, which began in November 1948 with the disbandment of the Jewish Anti-Fascist Committee. (With the bizarre logic of Stalinism, this more or less coincided with the Soviet Union's instant recognition of the State of Israel, a démarche purely intended to discomfit Britain.) Three months later, in January 1949, the Soviet press began a full 'anti-cosmopolitan' assault on the orders of the Kremlin. Fifteen members of the committee were arrested, interrogated, tortured and eventually put on trial in May 1952. The proceedings were all in closed session. Thirteen of the defendants were executed in August. In January 1953, a group of doctors, most of whom were Jewish, were accused in the press of plotting to kill Soviet leaders. This nakedly anti-Semitic campaign halted only because of the death of Stalin in March.

Viktor Komarev, the deputy chief of the investigative unit of the MGB interrogating the members of the Jewish Anti-Fascist Committee, bragged in a letter to Stalin 'how much I hate our enemies'. He boasted of his cruelty and of the terror he inspired in his victims.

'I especially hated and was pitiless towards Jewish nationalists, whom I saw as the most dangerous and evil of enemies. Because of my hatred of them I was considered an anti-Semite not only by the defendants but by former employees of the MGB who were of Jewish nationality.' One of the defendants, Boris Shimeliovich, was tortured so badly that he had to be carried back for further sessions on a stretcher.

Vasily Grossman and Ilya Ehrenburg were extremely fortunate not to have been among those associated with the JAC who were arrested in the first wave. They were lined up for investigation in March 1952 as preparations for the trial progressed, but in the event they were left alone. Grossman's first novel about Stalingrad, *For a Just Cause*, was published

347

in instalments that year after he was forced to make many changes to render the text politically acceptable. The novel was nominated for the Stalin Prize, but soon afterwards Grossman was furiously denounced. Party hacks were appalled that he could write about the battle of Stalingrad without mentioning Stalin. The list of criticisms extended much further. He had deliberately reduced the achievements and role of the Communist Party in the victory. Grossman, forced to write a letter of repentance, was saved from the Gulag only by Stalin's death in March 1953.

Yet however much Grossman had come to loathe Stalinism, with its constant lies and forced betrayals, he never lost his faith in the simple Russian soldier and the huge sacrifices of the Great Patriotic War. His daughter described in a memoir how, at his urging, the family would sing songs from the war in private.

A large empty room. Twilight – because evening is coming, or perhaps rain. There are three of us in the room, Papa, my stepbrother Fedya and I . . . We are singing some songs from the war. Father would start in a stern, thundering voice. His unmusical ear did not prove too great a problem. The simple melody was so familiar to us:

The aircraft is spinning around,
It is roaring, it's flying down towards the Earth's breast . . .[3]

But now my father stands up. Fedka and I stand up too. Father is standing there stooping, his hands at his side as if he were on parade. His face is solemn and stern.

Arise, the huge country.
Arise for the mortal battle.
With the dark fascist force,
With the accursed horde.

My father considered this song a work of genius: he said so often and with much conviction . . . He always stood up when he sang it.

Grossman also remained interested in the whole question of courage and cowardice. His daughter noted a conversation at home with some visitors

3 Grossman wrote down this song about a heroic Soviet pilot when visiting the aviation regiment of Vasily Stalin, the dictator's son, near Stalingrad in the early autumn of 1942.

which turned to the subject of behaviour in battle. One of them said that when a person is experiencing strong emotions, such as patriotism and anger, then fear disappears. 'Grossman replied that this was not true. "Just as there are two kinds of courage, I think you should distinguish between different kinds of fear – a physical fear which is a fear of death, and moral fear which is the fear of disgracing yourself in front of others. Tvardovsky, for example, possessed moral courage to a high degree. Other people, Simonov for example, did not possess courage in their behaviour in civilian life although Kostya Simonov was extraordinarily brave during the war."'

Grossman was not entirely a political outcast, and even during the most difficult times he received support from some Stalingrad generals. Rodimtsev, whom he had always revered, had come to his defence when *For a Just Cause* had been attacked. It was an act of considerable bravery. And in 1955, following Stalin's death, when things did not look so bad for Grossman, he had a meeting with Stalin's old crony, Marshal Voroshilov, who tried to persuade him to join the Party at last. Grossman persisted in his refusal. 'Well, it's clear to me,' Voroshilov replied in a kindly fashion, 'that you are a non-Party Bolshevik.'

In 1954, *For a Just Cause* had been republished, this time in book form, and again it was praised. During the rest of the 1950s, Grossman worked on a sequel which was to be his masterpiece, *Life and Fate*. This deliberate tribute to Tolstoy's *War and Peace* has the same epic quality, but with the battle of Stalingrad at its core. One of the great differences between the two novels, however, is the way Grossman bases his story and characters on himself and those close to him. The fact that so much of the book is taken from real life does not in any way lessen its effect as a novel. On the contrary, it forms the basis of its extraordinary power.

Grossman was convinced that under Nikita Khrushchev, the chief commissar at Stalingrad and the denouncer of Stalin at the XX Party Congress in February 1956, the way was open at last for the truth to be told. But Grossman's lack of political judgement served him badly. He failed to see that the implicit parallels between Nazism and Stalinism in his novel constituted far too harsh a reality. The heroic myths of the Great Patriotic War had taken too deep a hold. He should also have realised the full significance of the fate of the Hungarian uprising in 1956, crushed brutally by General Babadzhanyan, his hero in *The People Immortal*.

Grossman completed *Life and Fate* in 1960 and submitted the manuscript. It seemed as if his novel was being sat on due to incompetence or idleness, but in fact his editors were in a state of fear and consternation. The decision was passed upwards. On 14 February 1961, three senior KGB officers arrived to seize every copy of the manuscript. They ransacked the apartments of both Grossman and his typist, taking papers and even the carbon paper and typewriter ribbons. The manuscript was passed to the Communist Party's chief ideologue, Mikhail Suslov, the immensely powerful chief of the Cultural Section of the Central Committee.[4] Suslov's verdict was that it could not be published for over two hundred years. This remark was a striking recognition of the novel's importance.

The devastation appeared complete. Grossman's previous books were withdrawn from circulation. Reduced to penury and with only a few friends prepared to risk association with him, he soon suffered from cancer of the stomach. He died in the summer of 1964, assuming that his great work had been suppressed for ever. Ehrenburg offered to chair a committee on Grossman's work, but the Writers' Union refused. In the eyes of the Soviet authorities, Vasily Grossman was virtually a non-person in political terms.

Grossman had, however, deposited a copy of the manuscript with a friend. And this friend, who had put it in a canvas satchel, had left it hanging on a hook under some coats at his dacha. Eventually the manuscript was discovered and copied on to microfilm it is said by Andrei Sakharov, the great physicist and dissident. Vladimir Voinovich, the satirical novelist and creator of Private Chonkin (a Red Army equivalent of *The Good Soldier Schwejk*), then smuggled the microfilm out of the Soviet Union to Switzerland.[5] *Life and Fate* was published there and in many other countries across the world. It appeared in Russia only as communism itself collapsed. Grossman's unspoken promise to his mother was finally fulfilled. She lived again through the novel as Anna Shtrum. Grossman himself may have been dragged down by the wolfhound century, but his humanity and his courage have survived in his writing.

---

4   Suslov, Mikhail (1902–1982), Soviet Central Committee ideologue who had supervised the 1937–8 purges in the Ukraine and the Urals, and then in 1944–5 directed a brutal campaign of execution and deportation against national minorities who had been under German occupation.
5   Voinovich, Vladimir Nikolayevich (1932–), began to write poetry when in the Soviet Army between 1950 and 1955. He turned to prose and later became a dissident. His most famous book, *The Life and Amazing Adventures of Private Ivan Chonkin,* contributed to his ejection from the Writers' Union in 1974. He emigrated in 1980 and was stripped of his citizenship by Brezhnev.

Acknowledgements

This book could never have been possible without the agreement and assistance of the author's daughter, Ekaterina Vasilievna Korotkova-Grossman, and stepson, Fyodor Guber. We are most grateful to them for their help with manuscripts and photographs.

Once again, Professor Anatoly Chernobayev has aided us enormously with excellent advice and introductions. The staff of RGALI (the Russian State Archive for Literature and the Arts) have been unfailingly helpful. Angelica von Hase has checked out further details in Germany arising from the notebooks and Olga Romanov and Simon Marks have assisted on points of detail. We would also like to thank those who have read the manuscript for us: Sir Rodric Braithwaite, Professor Geoffrey Hosking and Dr Catherine Merridale. Needless to say, any mistakes which remain are entirely our responsibility.

The editors and publishers are grateful to Ekaterina Vasilievna Korotkova-Grossman and the Russian State Archive of Film and Photo Documents for permission to reproduce the photographs.

This book also owes its very existence to the enthusiasm of our agent Andrew Nurnberg, to Geoff Mulligan and Stuart Williams at Harvill Secker, and particularly to Christopher MacLehose, Grossman's first publisher in this country, who encouraged the project from the start, and improved the book immeasurably with his impeccable editing.

Bibliography

Adair, Paul, *Hitler's Greatest Defeat – The Collapse of Army Group Centre, June 1944*, London, 1994

Addison, Paul, and Calder, Angus (eds), *Time to Kill, The Soldier's Experience of War 1939–1945*, London, 1997

Beevor, Antony, *Stalingrad*, London, 1998

Beevor, Antony, *Berlin – The Downfall, 1945*, London, 2002

Bocharov, Anatoly, *Vasily Grossman, zhizn, tvorchestvo, sudba* (*Vasily Grossman, Life, Creative Work, Fate*), Moscow, 1990

Chuikov, Vassily I., *The Beginning of the Road*, London, 1963

Chuikov, Vassily I., *The End of the Third Reich*, London, 1967

Davies, Norman, *Rising '44*, London, 2003

Ehrenburg, Ilya, *Lyudi. Gody. Zhizn.* (*People. Years. Life.*), vol. 2, Moscow, 1990

Ellis, Frank, *Vasily Grossman, The Genesis and Evolution of a Russian Heretic*, Oxford, 2004

Erickson, John, *The Road to Stalingrad*, London, 1975

Erickson, John *The Road to Berlin*, London, 1999

Garrard, John, & Garrard, Carol, *The Bones of Berdichev, The Life and Fate of Vasily Grossman*, New York, 1996

Glantz, David M., and House, Jonathan, *When Titans Clashed, How the Red Army Stopped Hitler*, Kansas, 1995

Grossman, Vasily, *V gorode Berdicheve* (*In the Town of Berdichev*), Moscow, 1934

Grossman, Vasily, *Gliukauf!* (*Gluck auf! Good Luck*), Moscow, 1934

Grossman, Vasily, *Stepan Kolchugin*, Moscow, 1937-40

Grossman, Vasily, *Narod bessmerten* (*The People Immortal*), Moscow, 1942 and 1962

Grossman, Vasily, *Esli verit' pifagoreitsam* (*If We are to Believe the Pythagoreans*), Moscow, 1946

Grossman, Vasily, *Za pravoye delo* (*For a Just Cause*), Moscow, 1952

Grossman, Vasily, *Vsyo techyot* (*Forever Flowing*), New York, 1972

Grossman, Vasily, 'Tovarishchi' (Comrades), in *Zhurnalisty na voine*, vol. ii, Moscow, 1974

Grossman, Vasily, *Zhizu I sudba* (*Life and Fate*), Geneva, 1981, 1985

Grossman, Vasily, *Gody voiny* (*The War Years*), Moscow, 1989

Guber, Fyodor (ed.), 'Pamyat i pisma', in *Daugava*, no. 11, 1990

Hilberg, Raul, *The Destruction of the European Jews*, New York, 1985

Markish, Simon, *Le cas Grossman*, Paris, 1983

Merridale, Catherine, *Night of Stone*, London, 2000

Ortenberg, D.I., *Vremya ne vlastno* (*Time has no Authority*), Moscow, 1979

Ortenberg, D.I., *God 1942* (*The Year 1942*), Moscow, 1982

Ortenberg, D.I., *Iyun–Dekabr Sorok pervogo* (*June–December 1941*), Moscow, 1984

Ortenberg, D.I., *Sorok trety* (*1943*), Moscow, 1991

Overy, Richard, *Russia's War*, London, 1998

Rayfield, Donald, *Stalin and his Hangmen*, London, 2004

Rubenstein, Joshua, *Tangled Loyalties – the Life and Times of Ilya Ehrenburg*, New York, 1996

Rubenstein, Joshua, and Naumov, Vladimir P. (eds), *Stalin's Secret Pogrom, The Postwar Inquisition of the Jewish Anti-Fascist Committee*, New Haven, 2001

Sebag Montefiore, Simon, *Stalin: the Court of the Red Tsar*, London, 2004

Simonov, Konstantin, *Days and Nights*, New York, 1945

Todorov, Tsvetan, *Mémoires du Mal, Tentations du Bien*, Paris, 2000

Troyanovsky, P.I., *Na vosmi frontakh* (*On Eight Fronts*), Moscow, 1982

Volkogonov, Dmitri, *Stalin: Triumph and Tragedy*, London, 1991

Yeremenko, A.I., *Stalingrad – Zapiski komandujuscego frontom*, Moscow, 1961

Zaitsev, V.I., *Za Volgoi Zemli dlya nas ne bylo* (*For us there was no land beyond the Volga*), Los Angeles, 1973

Zhurnalisty na voine (*Journalists at War*), Moscow, 1966

Source Notes

Abbreviations

EVK-GP Ekaterina Vasilievna Korotkova-Grossman Papers
RGALI Rossiisky Gosudarstvenny Arkhiv Literatury I Iskusstva (Russian State Archive for Literature and the Arts), Moscow
RGASPI Rossiisky Gosudarstvenny Arkhiv Sotsialno-Politeskoi Istorii (Russian State Archive for Social-Political History), Moscow
TsAMO Tsentralny Arkhiv Ministerstva Oborony (Central Archive of the Ministry of Defence), Podolsk

Introduction

p. vii   Grossman family names russified, Garrard and Garrard, p. 53
p. viii   On the 150,000 Jews murdered in civil war, S. Yelisavetsky, *Berdichevskaya tragedia*, Kiev, 1991, p. 13, quoted in Garrard and Garrard, p. 61
p. viii   'At first glance, Father . . .', interview with Ekaterina Korotkova-Grossman, 24 December 2004
p. viii   'The wolfhound century', Mandelstam, *Sobranie Sochinenii*, vol. 1 (Munich, 1967), p. 162
p. viii   For estimates of famine victims, see Donald Rayfield, p. 185
p. x   'He was an extremely kind . . .', Ehrenburg, p. 35
p. x   On the arrest of Olga Mikhailovna, for the most detailed account, see Garrard and Garrard, pp. 121–5
p. xii   'I'll tell you about myself', Guber, p. 100
p. xiii   'During the whole war . . .', RGALI 1710/3/50
p. xiii   'talks with soldiers withdrawn . . .', RGALI 1710/3/50
p. xiii   'the penetrating, sharp foreboding . . .', Grossman, 1974, p. 37
p. xiv   'I know that the fact . . .', Ortenberg, 1991, p. 27
p. xv   'the usual smell of the front line . . .', Grossman, 1985, p. 740
p. xv   'Ever since he had arrived in Stalingrad . . .', Grossman, 1985 pp. 236–7
p. xv   for Ehrenburg's telephone call from Stalin, see Rubenstein, p. 187

p. xvii   'I think that those who . . .', 'Infantryman', Grossman, 1989
p. xvii   'The ruthless truth of war', quoted in Ortenberg, 1982, p. 293

Chapter 1: Baptism of Fire

All entries are from RGALI 1710/3/43 with the following exceptions:
p. 5   'I remember how Grossman . . .', Ortenberg, 1991, pp. 358–9
p. 5   'His tunic was all wrinkled . . .', Ortenberg, quoted in Bocharov, p. 127.
p. 6   'We are leaving for the Central Front . . .', *Voprosy literatury*, no. 5, 1968, RGALI 1710/1/100
p. 12   'On the outbreak of war . . .', RGALI 1710/1/100
p. 12   'My dear [Father], I arrived at my destination . . .', 8 August 1941, EVK-GP
p. 13   'Bogaryov saw a family of boletus . . .', Grossman, 1962, p. 316
p. 15   'Ours, ours?', excerpt from Grossman's *The People Immortal* published in *Krasnaya Zvezda*, 19 July 1942

Chapter 2: Terrible Retreat

All entries are from RGALI 1710/3/43 with the following exceptions:
p. 21   'Who can describe the austerity . . .', *Krasnaya Zvezda*, 24 July 1942
p. 21   'The next day we were able . . .', Ortenberg, 1984, p. 162
p. 22   'If you remember, in *Travel to Arzrum* . . .', Grossman, 1962, p. 380.
p. 23   'We were driving and driving . . .', Troyanovsky, p. 23

Chapter 3: The Bryansk Front

All entries are from RGALI 1710/3/49 with the following exceptions:
p. 27   'Drive to the front . . .', RGALI 1710/3/43
p. 29   'I am in good health   ', 9 September 1941 (Stamp: Checked by Military Censorship), EVK-GP
p. 29   'Dear Lyusenka . . .', 16 September 1941, Guber, 1990
p. 30   'German trenches . . .', *Krasnaya Zvezda*, 14 September 1941

Chapter 4: With the 50th Army

All entries are from RGALI 1710/3/49 with the following exceptions:

p. 34   'Shlyapin is intelligent, strong . . .', Grossman, 1989, p. 263
p. 35   'My dear [Father], I've received . . .', 1 October 1941, EVK-GP

Chapter 5: Back into the Ukraine

All entries are from RGALI 1710/3/49 with the following exceptions:

p. 38   'Grossman decided to write . . .', Ortenberg, 1979 pp. 313–28
p. 39   'The first time that we, military correspondents . . .', November 1945, RGALI 1710/3/21 'A Soviet Officer'

Chapter 6: The German Capture of Orel

All entries are from RGALI 1710/3/49.

Chapter 7: The Withdrawal Before Moscow

All entries are from RGALI 1710/3/49 with the following exceptions:

p. 55   'Tula, seized with that deadly fever . . .', Grossman, 1989, p. 288
p. 56   'People say that [Ortenberg] is a good editor . . .', Grossman, 1989, p. 289
p. 57   'The morning and evening reports from the Sovinformburo . . .', Ortenberg, 1984, p. 191
p. 60   'It's a fact, Comrade Commissar,' Grossman, 1962, p. 96
p. 61   'My dear and good [Father], I was mortally upset . . .', 17 November 1941, EVK-GP
p. 61   'We were given an apartment . . .', Ehrenburg, 1990, p. 349
p. 62   'Vasily Grossman has returned . . .', Ortenberg, 1984, p. 327
p. 62   'It is still too early to be looking . . .', Grossman to M.M. Shkapskaya quoted, Guber, 1990
p. 63   'There are very nice people around me . . .', Grossman to Olga Mikhailovna, 20 December 1941, quoted, Guber, 1990
p. 63   'When marching into European capitals . . .', *Krasnaya Zvezda*, 26 December 1941

Chapter 8: In the South

All entries are from RGALI 1710/3/49 with the following exceptions:

p. 67   'Vasily Grossman persuaded me . . .', Ortenberg, 1982, p. 70

p. 68   'Division Commander Lazko . . .', RGALI 1710/3/44

p. 73   422,700 men died in punishment units, John Erickson, 'Red Army Battlefield Performance', in Addison and Calder, p. 236

Chapter 9: The Air War in the South

All entries are from RGALI 1710/3/49 with the following exceptions:

p. 79   'Dearest Lyusenka, well, we've celebrated . . .', 1 January 1942, quoted in Guber, 1990

p. 79   'My articles are published . . .', 11 January 1942, quoted in Guber, 1990

p. 80   'It is still stinging cold here . . .', 1 February 1942, EVK-GP

Chapter 10: On the Donets with the Black Division

All entries are from RGALI 1710/3/49.

Chapter 11: With the Khasin Tank Brigade

All entries are from RGALI 1710/3/49.

Chapter 12: 'The Ruthless Truth of War'

p. 110   'Sometimes it feels that I've spent . . .', 6 March 1942, EVK-GP

p. 110   'Winter has come back to where . . .', 7 March 1942, EVK-GP

p. 110   'Vasily Grossman came to see me . . .', Ortenberg, 1982, p. 263

p. 110   'I've been given leave . . .', 8 April 1942, EVK-GP

p. 111   'Action has started at the front . . .', 15 May 1942, EVK-GP

p. 112   'I am doing a great deal of work here . . .', 31 May 1942, EVK-GP

p. 113   'Things seem to be going well . . .' 12 June 1942, EVK-GP

p. 113   'I am a key person at the editorial office now . . .', quoted in Guber, 1990
p. 114   '[After] precisely two months . . .', Ortenberg, 1982, p. 263
p. 114   '*Krasnaya Zvezda* started serialising . . .', 14 July 1942, EVK-GP
p. 114   'Today we published the final . . .', Ortenberg, 1982 p. 293
p. 114   'Yesterday Kostya Budkovsky . . .', 22 July 1942, Guber, 1990
p. 115   'I am leaving for the front . . .', 19 August 1942, EVK-GP

Chapter 13: The Road to Stalingrad

All entries are from RGALI 1710/3/50 with the following exceptions:
p. 117   'When the famous order was issued . . .', interview with Ekaterina Korotkova-Grossman, 24 December 2004
p. 118   'We were retreating from the battle . . .', RGALI 1710/3/46
p. 121   for the debate over Zoya Kosmodemyanskaya, see *Pravda*, 26 November 2002
p. 123   'What's the matter with them?', quoted in Volkogonov, p. 461
p. 123   Stalingrad Defence Committee, numerous examples can be found in RGASPI 17/43/1774
p. 130   'Those were hard and dreadful days . . .', RGALI 1710/1/102

Chapter 14: The September Battles

All entries are from RGALI 1710/3/50 with the following exceptions:
p. 136   'We arrived in Stalingrad soon after an air raid, *Krasnaya Zvezda* 6 September, 1942, RGALI 1710/1/102
p. 139   'He was not a stranger . . .', Ortenberg, 1982, p. 382
p. 140   'When on the march, one's shoulder . . .' *Krasnaya Zvezda*, 20 September 1942, RGALI 1710/1/102
p. 141   'three to five well-armed . . .', 16 August 1942, TsAMO 48/486/28
p. 141   Execution in 45th Rifle Division, TsAMO 48/486/25
p. 144   '"Comrade Chuikov," said Khrushchev', Chuikov, 1963, p. 84
p. 148   'The road turned south-west . . .', 'The Stalingrad Battle', RGALI 1710/1/102
p. 151   'My own one, my good one . . .', Guber, 1990
p. 152   'You already know about . . .', 5 October 1942, Guber, 1990

Chapter 15: The Stalingrad Academy

All entries are from RGALI 1710/3/50 with the following exceptions:

p. 154   'Sometimes, the trenches dug . . .', 'Stalingrad Army', RGALI 618/2/107

p. 158   'Sometimes it is very quiet . . .', 'With Chekhov's Eyes', RGALI 1710/1/101

p. 158   'It was probably because Grossman . . .', 14 November 1942, Ortenberg, 1982, p. 415

p. 159   Zaitsev as a sniper, Zaitsev, p. 59

p. 160   'for days', Grossman, 1985, p. 236

p. 168   'The earth around the landing point . . .', *Krasnaya Zvezda*, 4 November 1942

Chapter 16: The October Battles

All entries are from RGALI 1710/3/50 with the following exceptions:

p. 174   'You know, I am a superstitious man . . .', Ortenberg, 1979, pp. 313–28

p. 180   'All the correspondents . . .', 12 January 1943, Ortenberg, 1991, p. 25

p. 180   'When he wrote . . .', 'I remember how he would . . .', Ortenberg, 1982 p. 392

p. 180   'I've written an angry letter to the editor . . .', Guber, 1990

p. 181   'It is only here that people know . . .', *Krasnaya Zvezda*, 26 November 1942, RGALI 1710/1/101

p. 187   'In the light of rockets . . .', 'The Stalingrad Battle', RGALI 1710/1/102

p. 188   'Once, in mid-October, he told officers . . .', Ortenberg, 1979, pp. 313–28

Chapter 17: The Tide Turned

All entries are from RGALI 1710/3/50 with the following exceptions:

p. 190   'I work a lot, the work is stressful . . .', 13 November 1942, EVK-GP

p. 192   'watched the beginning of . . .', 1 December 1942, Ortenberg, 1982, p. 429

p. 193   'We wandered into an empty house . . .', interview with
          Ekaterina Vasilievna Korotkova-Grossman, 24 December
          2004
p. 193   'Old women's kerchiefs and earrings . . .', RGALI 1710/1/101
p. 193   'A babushka told us how . . .' RGALI 1710/3/50
p. 194   'Ice is moving down the Volga . . .' 'On the Roads of the
          Advance', RGALI 618/2/107
p. 197   'When one enters a bunker . . .', 'Military Council', *Krasnaya
          Zvezda*, 29 December 1942, RGALI 618/2/107
p. 198   'I work a lot . . .', Guber, 1990
p. 199   'All those who, for a hundred days . . . ,' 'The New Day',
          RGALI 618/2/107
p. 199   'We are walking on a waste land . . .', 'Stalingrad Army', RGALI
          618/2/107
p. 200   'I think I will be in Moscow in January . . .', 11 December 1942,
          EVK-GP
p. 200   'Red Army soldiers wound the gramophone up . . .', RGALI
          618/2/107

Chapter 18: After the Battle

All entries are from RGALI 1710/3/50 with the following exceptions:
p. 203   'My dearest Lyusenka, I've just come back . . .', Guber, 1990
p. 204   'There is no one to cry for him . . .', 31 December 1942, EVK-GP
p. 204   'The winter sun is shining over mass graves . . .', 'Today in
          Stalingrad', *Krasnaya Zvezda*, 1 January 1943
p. 205   'Why did General Ortenberg order Grossman . . .', Ehrenburg,
          1990, p. 350
p. 205   'Well, my [dear Father] . . .', 2 January 1943, EVK-GP
p. 209   'The old teacher . . .', RGALI 618/2/107
p. 211   'I am waiting for the plane . . .', Grossman to Olga Mikhailovna,
          17 February 1943, Guber, 1990
p. 211   'I was very disturbed and offended . . .', Guber, 1990
p. 211   'People say that some are born . . .', Ehrenburg, 1990, p. 350
p. 212   'we received a note . . .', 25 May 1943, Ortenberg, 1991, p. 246

Chapter 19: Winning Back the Motherland

All entries are from RGALI 1710/3/51 with the following exceptions:

p. 213   'Months of war passed one another . . .', Ortenberg, 1982, p. 459

p. 219   'absolutely incorrect attitude . . .', TsAMO 48/486/25

pp. 219–20 'Soviet brotherhood' and 'To indoctrinate soldiers and officers . . .', TsAMO 48/486/24

p. 224   'They keep promising to give me leave . . .', 20 March 1943, EVK-GP

p. 224   'Just as I thought, my trip was useless . . .', 4 April 1943, EVK-GP

Chapter 20: The Battle of Kursk

All entries are from RGALI 1710/3/51 with the following exceptions:

p. 225   'I've arrived at the 62nd Stalingrad Army . . .', RGALI 1710/3/50

p. 226   'Rodimtsev's division could have fought better . . .', RGALI 1710/3/50

pp. 231–2 'The brigade had to confront . . .', Ortenberg, 1991, pp. 355–6

p. 234   'This battle lasted three days and three nights . . .', typescript for editorial board of the journal *Oktyabr*, RGALI 619/1/953

p. 234   'Grossman remained true . . .', Ortenberg, 1991, pp. 355–6

p. 235   'There wasn't anyone in the whole world . . .', *Krasnaya Zvezda*, July 1943, RGALI 1710/1/101

p. 238   'From the point of view of artillery . . .', RGALI 1710/3/50

p. 239   'I must say that I had never forgotten . . .', Ortenberg, 1991, pp. 379–80

p. 240   'We reached Orel on the afternoon . . .', 'Return', *Krasnaya Zvezda*, August 1943, RGALI 1710/1/101

p. 242   'Dear Papa, I've been driving . . .', 28 June 1943, EVK-GP

p. 243   'With your name . . .', quoted Rubenstein, p. 198

p. 243   'You are fighting . . .', quoted Rubenstein, p. 205

p. 243   'The soldiers want to hear . . .', quoted Rubenstein, p. 207

p. 243   'Vasily Semyonovich Grossman came to Moscow . . .', Ehrenburg, 1990, p. 347

p. 243   On the Jewish Anti-Fascist Committee, see Rubenstein pp. 214–16, and Rubenstein and Naumov

Chapter 21: The Killing Ground of Berdichev

All entries are from RGALI 619/1/953 with the following exceptions:

p. 247 'A report arrived that a girl . . .', 'In the Advance', 15 October 1943, RGALI 1710/1/101

p. 251 'There are no Jews in the Ukraine . . .', quoted in Garrard and Garrard, p. 170

p. 252 'There's no one left in Kazary . . .', 'Murder of the People', September 1943, typescript, RGALI 1710/1/101

p. 254 'Dearest Lyusenka, I reached my destination today . . .', Guber, 1990

p. 255 'I am going to Berdichev today . . .', n.d., EVK-GP

p. 255 'About 30,000 Jews were killed in Berdichev . . .', RGALI 1710/1/104

p. 256 'They called me Mitya Ostapchuk . . .', RGALI 1710/1/123

p. 256 'The seizure of Berdichev by the Germans . . .', RGALI 1710/1/123

p. 260 'My darling, twenty years . . .', Guber, 1990

Chapter 22: Across the Ukraine to Odessa

All entries are from RGALI 1710/1/100 with the following exceptions:

p. 263 'Finally, the sun is getting hotter and hotter . . .', 'Thoughts about the Advance', RGALI 1710/1/101

p. 269 'a short, calm and good-natured . . .', Ortenberg, 1979, pp. 313–28

Chapter 23: Operation Bagration

All entries are from RGALI 1710/3/50 with the following exceptions:

p. 272 'Sometimes you are so shaken by what you've seen . . .', Grossman, 1989

p. 274 'Leutnant-General [sic] Lützov does not praise . . .', RGALI 1710/1/100

p. 275 'A German map had been captured . . .', RGALI 1710/1/100

p. 276 'Italians executed by Vlasov men . . .', RGALI 1710/3/47

p. 276 'A partisan, a small man . . .', RGALI 1710/3/47

p. 277 'Signaller Skvortsov is small . . .', RGALI 1710/3/47

p. 277   'Training before an offensive.', RGALI 1710/3/47
p. 279   'From deciduous forests, from marshes . . .', 'In the Towns and
          Villages of Poland', RGALI 1710/3/21

Chapter 24: Treblinka

All entries are from RGALI 1710/1/123 with the following exceptions:
p. 280   'The road to Lublin . . .', Troyanovsky, p. 182
p. 280   'What about Lublin? . . .', Troyanovsky, p. 183
p. 306   On Grossman's nervous exhaustion, see Rubenstein p. 425,
          n. 64, and Jean Cathala, *Sans Fleur ni Fusil* (Paris, 1981)

Chapter 25: Warsaw and Łódź

All entries are from RGALI 1710/3/51 with the following exceptions:
p. 309   'An old man in Kaluga, reasonable and prone . . .', 'The Road
          to Berlin', *Krasnaya Zvezda*, 9 February 1945, RGALI 1710/3/21
p. 312   'It's the first time in my life . . .', Ortenberg, 1991, p. 359
p. 312   'Along the crumpled and explosion-twisted . . .', 'The Road to
          Berlin', *Krasnaya Zvezda*, 9 February 1945, RGALI 1710/3/21
p. 313   'When we arrived, liberated Warsaw . . .', 'The Road to Berlin',
          Krasnaya Zvezda, 9 February 1945, RGALI 1710/3/21
p. 314   'We have visited the "bunker" . . .', 'The Road to Berlin',
          Krasnaya Zvezda, 9 February 1945, RGALI 1710/3/21

Chapter 26: Into the Lair of the Fascist Beast

All entries are from RGALI 1710/3/51 with the following exceptions:
p. 326   'changed for the worse . . .', interview with Ekaterina Korotkova-
          Grossman, 24 December 2004.
p. 330   'We reached the Oder on a sunny morning . . .' 'The Road
          to Berlin', *Krasnaya Zvezda*, 28 February 1945, RGALI 1710/3/21

Chapter 27: The Battle for Berlin

All entries are from RGALI 1710/3/51 with the following exceptions:
p. 331   'On 14 April, correspondents . . .', Troyanovsky, 'While Taking
         Berlin', *Zhurnalisty na voine*, p. 180
p. 332   'A village that had been burned by the Germans . . .', 'On the
         Borderline between War and Peace', RGALI 618/11/52
p. 341   'It was in Germany, particularly here in Berlin . . .', 'On the
         Borderline between War and Peace', RGALI 618/11/52

Afterword: The Lies of Victory

p. 346   'grave political errors', Rubenstein, p. 217
p. 347   'how much I hate our enemies', Rubenstein and Naumov, pp.
         xii–xiii
p. 348   'A large empty room . . .', *Songs from the War*, memoir by
         Ekaterina Korotkova-Grossman
p. 349   'Grossman replied that this . . .', interview with Ekaterina
         Korotkova-Grossman, 24 December 2004
p. 349   'Well, it's clear to me . . .', interview with Ekaterina Korotkova-
         Grossman, 24 December 2004

Index

FINLAND

Gulf of Finland

SWEDEN

Leningra

Tallinn

ESTONIA

Novgorod

Tartu

Pskov

Baltic Sea

Riga

LATVIA

W Dvina

Veliklìye Luk

Siaulai

Daugavpils

LITHUANIA

Viteb

Danzig

Konigsberg

Kaunas

Borisov

Orsha

Oder

Landsberg

E. PRUSSIA

Vilnius

Niemen

Minsk

Mogilev

BERLIN

Kustrin

Schwerin

Grodno

Bobruysk

Neisse

Poznań

Vistula

Brenanovia

GERMANY

Oder

WARSAW

Treblinka

Pripet Marshes

Dresden

Breslau

Brest

Elbe

PRAGUE

POLAND

Pulawy

Mozyr

Pilsen

Lublin

Cracow

Sandomierz

Lutsk

Vistula

Lwów (L'vov)

Zhitomir

Kiev

Brno

Ternopol

Berdichev

SLOVAKIA

Vinnitsa

VIENNA

Stanislav

Bratislava

Chernovtsy

Danube

AUSTRIA

Dnestr

S Bug

BUDAPEST

HUNGARY

Cluj

Domanevka

Jassy

Kishinev (Kisinau)

Odes

YUGOSLAVIA

BELGRADE

Galati

ROMANIA

Sarajevo

BUCHAREST

Constanza

Danube

BULGARIA

Elbe